W9-BOL-864

THE BAD & THE BEAUTIFUL

THE BAD & THE BEAUTIFUL

HOLLYWOOD IN THE FIFTIES

SAM KASHNER

AND JENNIFER MACNAIR

W. W. NORTON & COMPANY

NEW YORK / LONDON

Printed in the United States of America
First Edition

The text of this book is composed in Electra with the display set in Futura Light
Composition by Tom Ernst
Manufacturing by Quebecor Fairfield
Book design by JAM Design
Production manager: Julia Druskin

Library of Congress Cataloging-in-Publication Data

Kashner, Sam.
The bad & the beautiful : Hollywood in the fifties / Sam Kashner and Jennifer MacNair.— 1st ed.
p. cm.
Includes bibliographical references and index.
ISBN 0-393-04321-5
1. Motion pictures—California—Los Angeles—History. I. Title: Bad and the beautiful. II. MacNair, Jennifer. III. Title.
PN1993.5.U65 K34 2002
791.43'09794'9409045—dc21 1884226 2002000317

W. W. Norton & Company, Inc., 500 Fifth Avenue, New York, N.Y. 10110
www.wwnorton.com

W. W. Norton & Company Ltd., Castle House, 75/76 Wells Street, London W1T 3QT

1 2 3 4 5 6 7 8 9 0

To our sisters,

Gella Pearl and Meghan Susan

CONTENTS

Introduction 11

CHAPTER 1 Wink, Titter, and Flirt: *Confidential* Magazine 17

CHAPTER 2 The Lavender Closet: Bill Tilden, Lizabeth Scott, Tab Hunter, and Noël Coward 47

CHAPTER 3 Alvah Bessie's Dream 64

CHAPTER 4 High School Confidential: Manny Robinson, Sydney Chaplin, Charlie Chaplin Jr., and John Barrymore Jr. 81

CHAPTER 5 Requiem for a Rebel: Nicholas Ray and the Doomed Trinity 99

CHAPTER 6 Sacred and Profane: Hollywood's Religious Revival, *The Robe*, and Richard Burton 123

CHAPTER 7 The Artist and "Charlie Movie Star": Douglas Sirk and the Making of Rock Hudson 139

CHAPTER 8 Legal Aliens: Expats, Artists, and Oscar Levant 156

CHAPTER 9 Love and Hate: *A Place in the Sun* and *The Night of the Hunter* 176

CHAPTER 10 Bell, Book, and Scandal: Kim Novak and Sammy Davis Jr. 196

CHAPTER 11 A Cookie Full of Arsenic: *Sweet Smell of Success* 217

CHAPTER 12 The Housewife and the Sweater Girl: How *Peyton Place* Saved Lana Turner 244

CHAPTER 13 Lana, the Sequel: *Imitation of Life* 264
CHAPTER 14 Sheer Bitchery: Louella Parsons, Hedda Hopper, and Sheilah Graham 275
CHAPTER 15 The Dark at the Top of the Stairs: William Inge's American Dreams 308
CHAPTER 16 The Waxworks: Mae West, Gloria Swanson, and *Sunset Boulevard* 327

Coda 349
Acknowledgments 355
Bibliography 357
Index 365

THE BAD & THE BEAUTIFUL

INTRODUCTION

FOR HOLLYWOOD, the 1950s began ominously with *Sunset Boulevard*, a story told by a corpse. Perhaps the greatest movie Hollywood ever made about its own decline, *Sunset Boulevard* was very much about the city's power and imagery, about its worship of youth and its own past. Only director Billy Wilder could imagine Hollywood as a place where the dead go on speaking, talking about their lives as if nothing has changed. A Viennese Jew who immigrated to Hollywood to escape the Nazis, he savored the macabre and saw the city at the beginning of the 1950s as a macabre place. And if Wilder had had his way, *Sunset Boulevard* would have opened on a tableau of talking corpses.

In the film's original opening sequence, newly arrived bodies at the Los Angeles morgue talk about how they got there:

> The corpse lying next to me asks how I died and I say I drowned. And he asks me how can a young guy like you drown and I say, "Well, first I was shot in the back," and then he says, yeah, he was shot also. He was a Chicago gangster killed in Los Angeles. Then a little kid on a slab across from me says, "I drowned too—swimming with my friends off the Santa Monica pier. I bet him I could hold my breath two minutes." Some dame is over by the kid and she says he shouldn't be

> unhappy as his parents will come and take him to a nice place. Then from way down there's this great big Negro corpse and he says, "Hey man, did you get the final score on the Dodger game before you got it?" And I say, no, I died before the morning papers came out. . . .

Charles Brackett, Wilder's writing partner, hated the opening scene; he thought it was "morbid and disgusting." He wasn't alone. When Paramount previewed *Sunset Boulevard* in Evanston, Illinois, headquarters of the Women's Christian Temperance Union, the audience jeered and filled out preview cards deriding Wilder's masterpiece. When Wilder complained to Paramount that Evanston, Illinois, was simply too unsophisticated for his movie, the studio demographers sent Wilder's Gothic take on Hollywood to a town they insisted was the most sophisticated in America: Great Neck, Long Island. But they hated *Sunset Boulevard* there, too. "The most sophisticated town in America" walked out on it.

Paramount reacted to the preview audiences' disdain by refusing all showings for the next six months, and Wilder was sent back to rewrite the opening scene. The final version that made it into the film was no less bizarre, opening with the corpse of Joe Gillis, the young screenwriter, telling the story of how he wound up floating facedown in Norma Desmond's swimming pool.

The dead speak here in *The Bad and the Beautiful*, too—the Red-hunting, keyhole-peeping editor of *Confidential* magazine; the bitter, striving queens of Hollywood gossip; and the forgotten, tortured artist William Inge, whose plays were made into some of the biggest films of the 1950s. Our book is a snapshot of Hollywood during the era of Joe McCarthy and the blacklist, a chronicle of its film stars and bottom-feeders, its icons and illusions. This is not a comprehensive history of Hollywood in the 1950s, but a kind of archaeological dig by two writers too young to have experienced the decade firsthand.

To younger generations, the 1950s are as far off in time as the Civil War was to someone writing in the Jazz Age. We have unearthed these stories to entertain, to offer a prismatic—rather than an academic—view of 1950s Hollywood. Some stories are familiar, such as the gruesome death of Lana Turner's boyfriend Johnny Stompanato, but less is known about Grace Metalious, the author whose novel *Peyton Place* led to Turner's only Oscar nomination. And while many may remember Kim Novak from *Vertigo* and *Pal Joey*, they may not know about her dangerous relationship with Sammy Davis Jr.

Like Norma Desmond herself, in deep denial that her days as a star were gone, Hollywood in the 1950s also wanted to cling to the past. It was in trouble—besieged by television, which was growing ever more popular, and weakened by the court-ordered breakup of studio-owned movie theater chains and the erosion of the studio system. But while the industry refused to adapt, the movies themselves reveal the profound changes transforming Hollywood and postwar American life.

The nation was just beginning its battles over civil rights in the 1950s and films like *The Defiant Ones* and *Imitation of Life* explored the meaning of race in America. *Sweet Smell of Success* illustrated the corrosive effect of gossip and the burgeoning tabloid culture, fed by the success of *Confidential* magazine and the enduring power of columnists like Walter Winchell and Hedda Hopper. Melodramas such as *All That Heaven Allows* and *A Summer Place* meanwhile focused on the biggest challenges facing a woman in the 1950s: how to have love and sex without losing her good reputation.

Of all the seismic shifts under way in America, though, the widening influence of television was the most hated by Hollywood. When Joe Gillis first recognizes Norma Desmond in *Sunset Boulevard* and delivers the unintentional insult, "You used to be big," it provokes one of the film's most famous lines: "I *am* big. It's the pictures that got small." The line encapsulated all the fears of the dinosaur studio moguls who watched in disbelief as their empires began to crumble.

By 1950 the struggle against television had escalated into a war. Weekly moviegoing had dropped from about sixty million to forty million ticket-buying customers. At the end of World War II, the number of television sets in the entire country stood at about 6,500, mostly in barrooms. By 1948 that figure had jumped to well beyond one million, and by 1950 TV was in eleven million homes. Milton Berle was "Mr. Television" on Tuesday nights in *Texaco Star Theater*. His show, along with *Philco Playhouse* and *General Electric Theater* (a second act for Ronald Reagan after he was washed up in the movies), turned in tidy little dramas, free of charge, to families who could eat their dinners on TV trays and use the commercials to get second helpings from the kitchen or make quick runs to the bathroom. Comfort and convenience replaced the glamour of going out to the movies.

Television was making stars out of character actors whose movie careers had stalled: Lucille Ball, Chuck Connors, Walter Brennan, Robert Young, and Raymond Burr. Conversely, if you were a star on television, they didn't want you in the movies. The studios developed an ironclad policy against hiring television actors. They had tried to make a movie with Uncle Miltie at the end of the 1940s. It flopped. They tried to do one with Liberace—it didn't succeed either. George Reeves, who played Superman on television, also found himself shut out of film roles. Studios thought he was too recognizable as the Man of Steel, that moviegoers would never accept him as any other character. He finally got a role in 1956's *Westward Ho, the Wagons!*, playing an Amish man in a beard and broad-brimmed hat surrounded by Disney Mouseketeers. It was the last movie he'd ever make.

Inspired by this fear of the "Lilliputian television screen" and almost as if to emphasize the difference and impress audiences, Hollywood began the 1950s hell-bent on sprawling dramas and wide-screen technology. It took on the biggest projects conceivable, especially the pious epic. Perhaps in an effort to compensate for the brutality of the blacklist, it created a new genre of budget-busting, star-studded films. *David and Bathsheba* begat *The Robe*; *The Egyptian* begat *Land of the Pharaohs* and *The Ten Commandments*. As film historian Michael Wood has observed, "Hollywood was Egypt, and Rome, and Jerusalem, the ancient world of the epics was a huge, many-faceted metaphor for Hollywood itself because these movies are always about the creation of such a world. . . . [D]oom and apocalypse lurk around these optimistic values."

The budgets for these epics were enormous, the studios would often hire thousands of extras for a single scene, and the potential for chaos was unlimited. On a particularly bad day during the filming of *The Ten Commandments* when everything that could go wrong did, one disgruntled actress was heard to say, "Who do you have to fuck to get out of this picture?"

In 1952 Fred Waller and his two partners (popular broadcaster Lowell Thomas and Merian C. Cooper, *King Kong*'s producer) captured New Yorkers' imaginations with *This Is Cinerama*, a technological development using three cameras that made the movies even bigger. Other versions of the wide-screen technique appeared in Paramount's VistaVision, Warnerscope, Todd-AO, Vistarama, Naturama, and Emergo (in which Vincent Price famously summons an avenging skeleton that leaps from the screen in *House on Haunted Hill*). The search for new ways to lure people into the theater soon led to 3-D movies, which required viewers to don special glasses to see the scissors-wielding hand of Grace Kelly plunging toward them in *Dial M for Murder*, or the oozing face of Vincent Price jumping out at them in *House of Wax*, or the eerily realistic marine sorrow of *Creature from the Black Lagoon*. By the end of the decade, the movie industry would outdo itself with Smell-O-Vision, in which scents piped into the theater, rigged up under each seat, provided clues for a movie called *Scent of Mystery* (a dubious achievement resurrected by director John Waters for his 1981 film *Polyester*).

The poet Frank O'Hara, who visited Los Angeles in 1956 and was an inveterate moviegoer, wrote a poem entitled "To the Film Industry in Crisis." In the poem, O'Hara sings a swan song to Hollywood, recognizing its desperate ploy to lure audiences away from television with its technical novelties—

> To you,
> glorious Silver Screen, tragic Technicolor, amorous
> Cinemascope,
> stretching VistaVision and startling Stereophonic Sound,
> with all
> your heavenly dimensions and reverberations and
> iconoclasms!

But Hollywood's growing sense of insecurity and fear of irrelevance had yet to take a firm hold when *Sunset Boulevard* was released in the summer of 1950. It did well at the box office and got outstanding reviews. One audience, however, hated the film: a pod of aging movie moguls. Louis B. Mayer, still holding onto his fiefdom as the head of MGM, roared his denunciation of *Sunset Boulevard* and its creator.

"You bastard," shouted Mayer. "You have disgraced the industry that made you and fed you. You should be tarred and feathered and run out of Hollywood!"

Wilder was momentarily stunned. He tried to think of the perfect comeback but his feelings were too complicated for a ready retort. Then his instincts took over:

"Fuck you," Wilder said.

A decade earlier, even five years earlier, Wilder's remark would have been career suicide. But L. B. Mayer's reign as the alleged "king of Hollywood" was drawing to a close. He no longer had the power to ruin a rebellious director like Wilder. A year after *Sunset Boulevard*'s 1950 release, Mayer would retire from his post as chief of MGM.

If *Sunset Boulevard* was Wilder's creepily magnificent ode to Hollywood, as well as a bill of divorcement from his European past, then there is even more reason to regard it as the overture to this book. *Sunset Boulevard* made a star out of William Holden, it briefly resurrected Gloria Swanson from the fate of the other waxworks seen playing bridge in that ineffable scene, and told us all we needed to know about Hollywood both then and now—it is a weird place and ultimately unknowable. William Carlos Williams was right, the pure products of America do go crazy. These are some of their stories, and some of their secrets. The beauty secrets of the dead.

CHAPTER 1

WINK, TITTER, AND FLIRT: *CONFIDENTIAL* MAGAZINE

IN BOLD, brash typefaces, *Confidential* magazine sang out its top stories: "The Truth About Tab Hunter's Pajama Party," "Sinatra and DiMaggio's Wrong Door Raid," "Nude Body Found in the Apartment of Will Rogers' Daughter!," and "Picasso Is an Opium Addict!" Tom Wolfe called it "the most scandalous scandal magazine in the history of the world." But beyond its screeching headlines and provocative photo montages of surprised and outraged actresses, *Confidential* can be read as a guidebook to 1950s America, a keyhole look at the nation's secret fears, unspoken desires, and paranoid nightmares.

Two favorite obsessions of *Confidential* were race and sex. In issue after issue, articles such as "They Passed for White," "Pearl Bailey and the Drummer Boy," and "White Women Are Ruining My Marriage" preyed on the average white American reader's fears of "the other" just as the civil rights movement was stirring and gathering force in the Deep South. A particular target was Sammy Davis Jr., whose flirtations with white actresses like Ava Gardner were turned by *Confidential* into full-blown Hollywood scandals.

And in stories like "The Lavender Skeletons in TV's Closet," "Call Boys of Manhattan," "Is It True What They Say About Johnnie Ray?," and "Hollywood—Where Men Are Men, and

The first issue of *Confidential* magazine hit newsstands in December 1952 and sold 250,000 copies. Circulation eventually ballooned to five million. "Everyone reads *Confidential*, but they deny it," said Humphrey Bogart. "They say the cook brought it into the house." *Courtesy of the authors.*

Women, Too," *Confidential* tapped into a whole world of pervasive homophobia and prurient fascination with homosexuality.

Confidential also fixated on the more obvious attributes of female beauty, registering the social shift toward a new kind of femme fatale: the Kewpie-doll blonde with cartoon measurements. Anita Ekberg, Jayne Mansfield, Marilyn Monroe, and unknown chorines with gigantic breasts were blazoned across the pulp pages of *Confidential*.

Even the advertisements in *Confidential* reflected America's postwar gender anxieties. The offerings generally fell into four categories. The first category could be called the "Samson" ads, featuring a "he-man" voice, hairstyle, and physique:

I GAINED 60 LBS. of Handsome, Hard-Hitting MUSCLES!
(Which of These 2 MEN Is YOU?)

DEVELOP YOUR VOICE TO COMMAND . . .
People Always React to a Convincing, Masterful Voice!

Check the Kind of Body You Want! Right in the Coupon Below

Three Weeks and I Made This "Sad Sack" Hep

You, Too, May Quickly and Easily Train for a New, Success-Winning, HE-MAN VOICE

A second category promised feminine (white) beauty:

Skinny Girls Don't Have OOMPH!

Make Your Skin Look Whiter, Sexier

Spot Reducer (featuring a zaftig brunette in a striped bathing suit)

A third category advertised general life, finance, and health-improving gimmicks:

MEAT CUTTING OFFERS YOU SUCCESS AND SECURITY . . . PEOPLE MUST EAT

Rupture-easer

Men Past 40 Getting Up Nights?
The Cause May Be Glandular Inflammation

It's Easy to Hypnotize

Throw Away That Truss!

Play Real Music Almost Overnight

But Robert Harrison, the visionary, bottom-feeding founder of *Confidential*, always insisted that the magazine did its share of public-service exposés, mixed in with "saucy tales of celebrity misconduct."

"That's one thing everybody forgets about *Confidential*," Harrison said. "We ran a lot of stories exposing the rackets, the jukebox rackets, the garment rackets, gambling, this deal where they had a regular casino going in an airplane. We drove that operation out of New York. . . . We ran stories exposing how children were dying from eating candy-flavored aspirin, and how boric acid was poison. . . ."

They also ran a story about how the big tobacco companies were lying to the public about the safety of their product—this was in 1953—and horror stories about how hospitals routinely padded bills and sometimes gave patients the wrong medications or amputated the wrong limbs. An inside look at a backwater Georgia prison and its use of sweatboxes and chain gangs published in the December 1952 issue made *I Was a Fugitive from a Chain Gang* look like *A Day at the Races*. "Devil's Island for Boys" in the April 1953 issue of *Confidential* described an Arizona state penal institution for boys from eight to eighteen who were routinely made to walk barefoot through the scorching desert outside Phoenix, their heads shaved, until their scalps turned red and blistered. The exposés roused public outrage and led to an investigation.

No other newspaper or magazine was doing those kinds of gut-wrenching stories then, but that's not where Harrison's heart was. He'd discovered his calling—his true, *sin*sational, Now-It-Can-Be-Told calling—as a sixteen-year-old office boy at the gossip-mongering *New York Daily Graphic*, where Walter Winchell, coincidentally, purveyed an early version of his column called "Broadway Hearsay." Crossing paths with Winchell would be the beginning of a beautiful friendship for the dapper Harrison, one he would later cash in on as *Confidential* adopted Winchell as a kind of official mascot, publishing a gushing paean to the staccato-voiced gossip maven in practically every issue (*Winchell Was Right About Josephine Baker! Are Their Faces Red! Winchell Was Right!*).

Back when New York City had a dozen big newspapers, the *Daily Graphic* made its reputation for "gutter journalism" with stories about eloping heiresses, unmarried mothers, poisoning pastors, and absconding brokers. Some people called it "the *Daily Pornographic*." Wolfe called it "one of those xanadus of inspired buncombe in the twenties. . . . [It] blew up scandal and crime stories like pork bladders." Its greatest contribution to the tabloid genre, however, was probably its composite, pasteup, airbrushed photographs that told the whole sordid story in cleverly collaged images with lots of décolletage. Young Harrison—sweeping the floor, running errands—paid close attention.

Harrison graduated from the *Daily Graphic* to *Motion Picture Daily* and *Motion Picture Herald*, both published by Martin Quigley. No slacker he, Harrison used his off hours and the boss's office to put out his own rag, a girlie mag called *Beauty Parade*, an offense for which he was promptly fired. "Quigley fired me and it was on Christmas Eve, I want you to know!" he'd recall some two decades after the event, for Harrison was something of a grudge collector. But he was launched in his new trade: *Beauty Parade* caught on, and it was soon followed by five other girlie magazines, including the naughtily named *Wink*, *Titter*, and *Flirt*.

By 1952 all six girlie mags had gone belly-up. So what did the by now inveterate creator of magazines do? In one week's time he dreamed up *Confidential*. It would go beyond the reigning kings and queens of gossip like Walter Winchell, Louella Parsons, and Hedda Hopper. The savvy publisher had noticed that Senator Estes Kefauver's publicized hearings on organized crime, begun in 1950, had galvanized the nation and created a thirst for sensational gossip. The hearings had run like a long-term televised film noir, bringing together gangsters both high and low, and making them squirm on the hot seat under Kefauver's relentless questioning. Harrison realized that the American public was mesmerized; men stayed home from work and families planned their meals around the hearings just to see crime figures ratting on their friends. If you could watch that kind of thing on television, why not read about scandalous misdeeds in the privacy of your own home?

Harrison was a genius. In December 1952 the first issue hit the stands and sold 250,000 copies.

Confidential favored layouts with big bands of red, lots of pictures, and headlines exploding on top: "The Real Reason for Marilyn Monroe's Divorce," "Why Sinatra Is the Tarzan of the Boudoir," "Eddie Fisher and the Three Chippies," and "Pssst! Heard About the Latest Hollywood Kick? Call Fernando Lamas, GRanite 2-5563."

Harrison once asked the gossip columnist Earl Wilson what he thought of the magazine.

"I think it's a disgrace," Wilson answered.

"You think it stinks now," Harrison said proudly, "but wait till you see the next issue!"

"The first issue of *Confidential* was lousy," remembered Harrison. "I must have ripped that thing apart three times before I published it, and it still wasn't right."

To ensure the continued success of his brand-new brainchild, Harrison did a piece on Winchell in the magazine's April 1953 issue. Winchell's own career as the most powerful gossip columnist of the 1930s and 1940s was in trouble in the new decade, and he felt a kind of kinship with this newer, bolder purveyor of schlock. But he was also a touchy paranoid, so Harrison had to make the tone of the story just right—slavishly sycophantic. It was a gamble that paid off big-time:

> I took the magazine over to Winchell and showed it to him. We had this story called "Winchell Was Right About Josephine Baker." Josephine Baker had made a scene in some club, I forget which one, she said she was being discriminated against because she was a Negro or something like that, and Winchell said she was exploiting the race thing, and there was a lot of criticism of Winchell over what he wrote. So we ran this story . . . and he loved it.

In fact, he loved it so much that he held it up on an episode of his television broadcast *The Winchell File*, sealing its fate for the scandal-loving decade to come. *Confidential* had arrived, blessed by the pope of gossip:

> I'm telling you, from then on, this thing flew. . . . [W]e started running a Winchell piece in every issue. We tried to figure out who Winchell didn't like and run a piece about them. One of them was "Broadway's Biggest Double Cross." It was about all the ingrates who Winchell had helped to start their careers who turned their backs on him. . . . And he kept on plugging *Confidential.* It got to the point where we would sit down and rack our brains trying to think of somebody also Winchell didn't like. We were running out of people, for Christ's sake!

Assistant editor and writer Jay Breen would come to the magazine's headquarters at 1697 Broadway and sit in an adjacent room while a fellow they called "the Reader" recited the stories slated for the next issue. The Reader, whoever he was, had a truly great voice: perfect diction, resonance. It was "like Sir Ralph Richardson reading Lear's soliloquies under a spotlight." Harrison had a theory that if you read the magazine out loud, "every weak spot in a story would stand out." So there would be the Reader, with his plummy English diction, reciting such works as "Errol Flynn and His Two-Way Mirror" and "How Mike Todd Made a Chump of a Movie Mogul."

"He was a fabulous writer," Harrison said of Jay Breen. "We were asked by many schools of journalism to come and lecture. They wanted to know how we did it. . . . But you know what ruined Breen? He was making too much money, and that started him drinking. He must have been making forty or fifty thousand a year, and he never had money like that before. The trouble was, I guess, he had it too good! After a while he was drunk all the time." Once, when Breen's kidneys went into shock, one whole issue of *Confidential* was put together in Memorial Hospital. Breen was in one room for treatment and Harrison in the next, and the two worked around the clock to put out the issue.

Outrage against the magazine grew throughout much of the 1950s. Soon the entire movie industry would be after Harrison, its creator. Some L.A. gangsters would hang him upside down by his heels out of his office windows. Congressmen were excoriating him, and half the newspapers in the country were denouncing him. He became "too hot to be seen with," so he used to meet at least one of his Hollywood informants in a phone booth. The two of them would get right in there in the same booth and talk.

But Robert Harrison was unfazed, and as far as he was concerned, *Confidential* magazine was a thing of beauty. The sales were exceeding four million at the newsstands each issue—a record for newsstand sales. People were puzzling over "what kind of creature could publish *Confidential*," and even how such a phenomenon could crop up in the middle of the twentieth century, especially so soon after the war, which was supposed to have ennobled everyone.

Harrison was a born promoter. Somebody once described him as a "weird-looking bird with eyes like a hooded falcon" that kept "darting from left to right so you can't eyeball him." Harrison often sported a silk cravat, a white polo coat, and a white fedora. He drove a custom-made Cadillac and was usually adorned with a buxom woman. Tom Wolfe, who met the publisher in 1964 for a profile he was writing, perhaps described him best. "The man is an aesthete," he wrote. "The original *aesthete du schlock*."

Celebrities, Communists, homosexuals, millionaires, intellectuals, and society dames were all grist for the *Confidential* mill. But they weren't the only ones made to suffer by Harrison's muckraking. Howard Rushmore, *Confidential*'s own editor and its main writer, would become the magazine's most spectacular victim.

HOWARD RUSHMORE was a zealot, a Red-hunting reporter who would do anything—even stage his own kidnapping—to make the world safe for democracy. He was the godfather of our tabloid age, using his inflammatory articles for the *Journal American* and later his reporting for *Confidential* to carry out his own personal witch-hunts. He made Senator Joseph McCarthy look soft on Communism. His stunts were so extreme that FBI chief J. Edgar Hoover branded him a "nut." He became a professional Commie-hunter, a fink, a patriot with a persecution complex, a movie fan who had all of Hollywood on the run, a morose-faced farm boy who flipped allegiances so many times nobody—not even Rushmore himself—finally knew where he stood. By the end of his life, the "ex-newspaper man, ex-editor, ex-Commie, ex-star of two sensational trials" was a man without a country.

Rushmore embodied contradiction. He was proud of being a tenth-generation American whose father's family dated back to Colonial New England. "My mother's people were also farmers," he once said, "who came to the dark and bloody ground with Daniel Boone from the East." But he spent six years as a Communist Party member and movie critic for the *Daily Worker*.

Rushmore had grown up in a poverty-stricken farm community in his mother's hometown of Mexico, Missouri. He was reserved, almost shy, in his personal manner. He was also obsessed with guns. An only child, he devoured books, and at the age of sixteen wrote for the school paper, the *Yellow Yap*. A precocious journalist, he also went to work for the local newspaper, the *Mexico Missouri Ledger*. James Sterner was a classmate at Mexico High School and later became the editor of the *Ledger*. He remembered that Rushmore was expelled in

Howard Rushmore, editor in chief of *Confidential,* loathed sleazy celebrity gossip and would later appear as the star witness against the magazine in a 1957 series of trials for libel and slander. *Bettmann/Corbis.*

his junior year for writing "a series of inflammatory articles in the school paper in which he criticized the administration and faculty. Howard was a born journalist," Sterner added. "He didn't want to study. He wasn't interested in sports. He just wanted to write." After being expelled, Rushmore was then enrolled in a private Catholic school where he was the only Methodist. And he was the butt of jokes for another reason: at sixteen he stood a gaunt six foot five, towering over his classmates.

Rushmore became interested in radical causes after witnessing a lynching just outside his hometown. He also read Jack Conroy's proletarian novel *The Disinherited*. Conroy would later say that "Howard Rushmore had the kind of old-line American background that the Communists have always tried to exploit. They quickly made their use of him." His family had been hard hit by the Depression. His mother was devout and ambitious, but his father was a defeated man. Sterner remembered that "Howard's father never expressed much interest in politics, but his mother was a staunch Democrat who loved Roosevelt." Rushmore would later vilify Roosevelt in the pages of *Confidential*, offering proof that Roosevelt was a Trotskyite whose real name was Rosenfeld. He would also try to "out" Eleanor Roosevelt as a lesbian, but that story was too hot even for *Confidential*.

George Sokolsky worked alongside Rushmore on the *Journal American*, using his column as judge, jury, and executioner against alleged Communists. "Howard Rushmore never really knew why he joined the Communist Party," Sokolsky believed, "except that, as a product of the Depression, he sought social justice. He was a southerner who hated racial discrimination, a son of the Bible Belt who was violently antireligious. So he found a berth at the *Daily Worker* . . . as a movie critic. It was a lousy job."

He quit the party on Christmas Day, 1939, after refusing to pan *Gone With the Wind*. When the only black member of the *Daily Worker*'s editorial board insisted that Rushmore call on viewers to boycott the $4 million movie, Rushmore refused to comply. He said, "I'm not anti-Negro, neither do I weep tears for the fallen southern aristocracy." But Rushmore's grandfather had been a water boy in the Confederate army, and his memories of his grandfather's tales of the Confederacy had been stirred by the Civil War epic. He thought it was a wonderful picture.

After he left the Communist newspaper, he nursed an epic grudge against his old comrades and quickly became the leading Red-hunter for the Hearst newspaper chain. He made news as often as he wrote it, as a professional government witness and as an informer for Senator McCarthy. For fifteen years he was the chief anti-Red sharpshooter for the *Journal American*, praised by McCarthy as "one of the outstanding Americans of our time." He even introduced McCarthy to Roy Cohn. A few years later, however, he would lose his job on the newspaper when he turned around and attacked Cohn and another McCarthy aide-de-camp, G. David Schine.

Ex-Communists are never trusted, though, which is why the FBI opened a file on Howard Clifford Rushmore in December of 1939, after he was fired by the *Daily Worker*.

Using his experience as a former party member, Rushmore peddled himself to the *Journal American* as an expert on subversive activities. One of his first stories for the newspaper, "Reds Revealed on Warships in Navy Yard" (November 27, 1949), alarmed the FBI. He seemed to know too much about the bureau's ongoing investigations.

J. Edgar Hoover responded to this article with a request to the attorney general to place a technical surveillance on Rushmore's home telephone. Within hours the New York office sent Hoover an FBI teletype marked SECRET: HOWARD RUSHMORE TECHNICAL SURVEILLANCE INSTALLED AS OF 11:30 AM THIS DATE COVERING RESIDENCE 3217 83 STREET JACKSON HEIGHTS TELEPHONE HAVERMEYER 9–5268.

At the same time the FBI was tapping his phone, Rushmore was appearing as a government witness in the second deportation trial of West Coast labor leader Harry Bridges in San Francisco. He also appeared in Seattle to testify before the state legislature's committee investigating "alleged subversive activities at the University of Washington." At one point in his testimony, Rushmore went through a litany of high government officials who were Communists, charging that 150 employees of the government in Washington were operating a Soviet spy ring, with Communist cell units set up in the State Department and other government buildings. He waved a typewritten document that he described as an FBI report—a gesture that prefigured Joe McCarthy's waving of unexamined texts at Senate hearings ("I have here in my hand . . ."). The FBI was alarmed. Was that really a bureau document, and if so, how had it come into Rushmore's hands? They found the answer when they approached him in the lobby of his hotel and asked him to produce the document in question. He took out a four-page letter he had typed himself.

In an office memorandum marked "SECRET," an FBI agent named A. H. Belmont concluded that Rushmore's "Washington State testimony was found either intentionally or unwittingly to misrepresent specific details in Bureau espionage cases." Rushmore had engaged in "patriotic lying" with his more fanciful stories: spy rings operating out of a violin store in Dupont Circle and a jeweler's shop on Madison Avenue.

Before long, Hoover's handwritten notes began appearing on the bottom of FBI memoranda pertaining to Rushmore: "I told Wall to shy away from him and not become involved. . . ." While the FBI declined Rushmore's eager offers to find Communists for them, Rushmore became more and more enamored of the agency and its august director. He began writing articles in the *New York Journal American* that were mash notes to Hoover—"the F.B.I. is the greatest and most efficient organization this country has ever known." When he asked the bureau for permission to write a human-interest feature on Hoover for the *American Mercury* magazine, the bureau declined. In June of 1953, Rushmore wrote to the FBI asking for a chance to meet his hero face-to-face. Hoover politely demurred. Nobody at the FBI would return his phone calls, and Hoover had refused to meet with him—he had pretended to be out of town when Rushmore showed up one day at the Justice Department.

In the spring of 1953, Senator McCarthy wrote to Hoover to ask if the Bureau had information on "Howard Clifford Rushmore" of 6 East Ninety-sixth Street. Rushmore had applied for a position on McCarthy's Subcommittee on Investigations—he wanted nothing more than to sit at the senator's right hand. McCarthy asked the FBI to furnish them "with any information reflecting upon his character, loyalty, and integrity."

The bureau responded by advising McCarthy that the FBI considered Rushmore an unreliable reporter, a "so-called specialist on Communist matters" who was in the habit of embellishing rumors and "drawing heavily on his own past experiences and imagination." Hoover's agent believed that "everything written by Rushmore on Communist matters should be heavily discounted as to veracity. . . . [His] writings have proved unreliable, due to his tendency to sensationalize and blow up fragments of information." The FBI considered him more interested in publicity than in routing out Communists in high places.

McCarthy hired Rushmore anyway—he was just the kind of man the committee was looking for. But that, too, would be a short-lived relationship. While working for McCarthy as "director of research," Rushmore made arrangements with all of McCarthy's investigators to bring their information directly to him. It became a common occurrence to pick up the *Journal American* before the hearings were held and discover that Rushmore had prominently published the names of suspects and future witnesses—not unlike the leaks in Kenneth Starr's grand jury investigation of the Clinton White House. His fondness for public innuendo—often based on erroneous information—would have its full flowering in the Starr-Clinton era. Rushmore's tactic was to create an atmosphere of fear and suspicion. He also stumbled upon a number of secondary gains: his Red-baiting articles sold newspapers and brought him national recognition; he also discovered that if you said something was true often enough, people believed you. Rushmore helped usher in the tabloid age by seeing the world as a madhouse, and by outing everyone's sins but his own.

Roy Cohn was furious; he issued instructions that none of the staff were to furnish information to the new research director without first clearing it with him. Feeling betrayed, Rushmore broke with Cohn and left the committee; he felt that McCarthy had failed to appreciate his "competence and knowledge." The FBI reported in another secret memo that Rushmore "couldn't work with others."

Rushmore was becoming a bitter man. He excoriated Cohn from the pages of the *Journal American*. He also took to criticizing the two boyish Torquemadas of McCarthy's committee—Cohn and David Schine—on a radio show called *Out of the Red*, which he shared briefly in the mid-fifties with a former Communist turned informer named Harry Matusow. (Matusow had made his reputation informing on folk singers—especially Burl "RED Rock Candy Mountain" Ives—and denouncing the Boy Scouts as a nest of subversive activity.)

Former Communist Party members turned informers were a hot ticket in the mid-1950s. Rushmore's *Out of the Red* broadcasts and his Communist exposés in the pages of the *Journal American* brought him more and more publicity. In March of 1953, Rushmore was invited to take part in a panel made up of "ex-party members" discussing the topic "Why a Million American Communists?" at Fordham University. Rushmore proudly described himself in the program notes as "the first reporter to expose Russian espionage and the Atomic Bomb conspiracy of December 1945. . . . [Westbrook] Pegler tabbed him as one of the nation's 'foremost enemies of treason in American journalism.' Mr. Rushmore is listed for 'liquidation' by the Russian Secret Police on their 'Purge Lists' of 60 American newspapermen."

The panel of four ex-party members took their show on the road, appearing "on radio, television, and in person in New York City, Forest Hills, Englewood, Mineola, Far Rockaway, etc."—better known as the Babylon line of the Long Island Rail Road.

But Rushmore's attacks on Roy Cohn didn't sit well with the *Journal American*. The newspaper fired him, in part for his increasingly paranoid behavior, but also for the big tabs he ran up at the Stork Club and El Morocco. It was there, among the zebra-striped banquettes, that Rushmore, out of a job and beginning to drink a little too much, met Robert Harrison.

Harrison and Rushmore couldn't have been more different. Rushmore was tall and lanky with one of those raw-boned, Depression-era faces; Harrison was a dapper man with longish hair given to wearing silk cravats and alligator shoes. Rushmore came out of the American heartland. Harrison had grown up in Manhattan, where he had launched his series of girlie magazines. On his off hours he had begun putting out his "fetish series," which featured heavy-ankled brunettes in photomontages, with punning titles such as "Trunk and Disorderly" (a model in a black brassiere and panties attempts to fold herself into a steamer trunk while holding a riding crop). But his fetish series eventually bottomed out. When Harrison's accountant gave him the bad news over lunch at Longchamps that his magazines were losing money, the idea for *Confidential* was born. The Kefauver hearings convinced Harrison that America was developing a taste for sensational stories on murder, extortion, sex, and intrigue. In Rushmore, Harrison had found the man who would write most of those articles.

Even before Harrison hired Rushmore as his editor, *Confidential* was a hit.

When Walter Winchell held up an early issue on his television show, *The Winchell File*, he sealed its fate for the scandal-loving decade to come. *Time* magazine's Hollywood writer Ezra Goodman noticed that "for a while, *Confidential* replaced even television as the favorite subject of conversation at Hollywood bars, cocktail parties, and Schwab's Drugstore." Even Humphrey Bogart weighed in on the subject: "Everyone reads *Confidential*, but they deny it. They say the cook brought it into the house."

Rushmore took the job because he was desperate, but he convinced himself that he had accepted Harrison's offer to write for *Confidential* in order to continue his Communist exposés. He had blown up his bridge to the McCarthy contingent by criticizing Roy Cohn. *The Journal American* had fired him. His former comrades at the *Daily Worker* had long ago denounced him on their editorial pages.

He wrote "How Walter Winchell Saved a Man from the Commie Kiss of Death" and a valentine to Hoover extolling the pugnacious FBI director in "They Couldn't Get J. Edgar Hoover Bounced!":

> The great majority of American taxpayers who regard J. Edgar Hoover as the nation's greatest public servant don't know that for years a weird clique of Communists, Fair Dealers, and even a president issued orders to get the FBI chief's job. . . . [H]e has been the target of smears, gutter accusations, dealing with his personal life, and always the favorite whine of the phony American—the "FBI is a police state."

The FBI was still paying attention to Rushmore, but now they had to read *Confidential* to do so. Rushmore anonymously sent a copy of the magazine to the Department of Justice, with a scribbled note:

> These pages from March issue of "Confidential"—none of its writers have been denounced or sued to this date. This article on our dear Mr. J. Edgar Hoover!! If we lose him & Sen. McCarthy—the Commies have the world—for with McCarthy out—not one soul in Washington would dare to lift a finger—lest they antagonize a pinko or someone else.

Rushmore was on a junket to the West Coast to hire informers for the magazine when Robert Harrison realized that dirt on movie celebrities was paying off in increased circulation. That's when the marriage between Rushmore and Harrison began to sour: Rushmore hated writing Hollywood exposés. He loved the movies; he had wept watching Atlanta burn. He hated relying on the prostitutes, rogue cops, and "matrimonial investigators" the magazine hired to dredge up the dirt. Some of the stories were cruelly damaging, as in the revelation of actor Rory Calhoun's prison record. Others were just silly, as in

Rushmore's article—written under the pseudonym Brooks Martin—"Don't Be Fooled by the Glamour Pusses":

> That shapely Hungarian blonde, Zsa Zsa Gabor, got in a tiff with the Parisian [Corinne Calvet] and allegedly remarked that Corinne wasn't much of an actress, and wore falsies besides.
>
> The anguished wail from Miss Calvet's camp completely ignored what might have been considered the main issue—whether she could act. She started hurling challenges like a count from Louis XIV's court, and it all settled down to this: what she had under her sweater was all hers. And she'd love to meet Zsa Zsa in a bosom battle with all bras down. Her frontal attack went beyond the tape measure stage when she actually filed suit, saying she wanted $1,000,000 for the titters provoked internationally by Zsa Zsa's belittling crack.

Rushmore used pseudonyms for his Hollywood scandal stories, but used his own name on "Red" exposés.

Under Rushmore, adultery was *Confidential*'s favorite vice. Besides exposing the adulterous affairs of the stars, occasional "featurettes" offered a kind of how-to guide, such as "Married Today—Free Tomorrow" and "You Can Have Eight Wives at One Time."

> Let's say you're a man living in New York with a wife who no longer tickles your imagination. If you know the ropes, you can zip down to Florida, get yourself unhitched over the weekend, and be back in Manhattan in time for Monday cocktails with your new girl. Now New York doesn't recognize that Florida split, but don't let that bother you. Just take your new sweetie to Connecticut and tie your second knot.

Rushmore wrote the piece as a supposed indictment of America's strict divorce laws, but what no one knew was that Rushmore's outlandish scheme was forged from experience. In 1943 Rushmore had separated from his first wife, Ruth Garvin, and two years later married a petite strawberry blonde, an ex-model named Frances McCoy who had worked at the *Journal American* for eleven years, becoming the women's page editor. But their Bridgeport, Connecticut, ceremony may not have been legal after all. Rushmore's first wife tried to have him arrested for bigamy in 1945. She said that she and Rushmore had never actually been divorced.

Howard Rushmore's troubles were just beginning.

ON JULY 8, 1955, Rushmore flew to Chicago to appear on *The Tom Duggan Show*, a popular local program on WBKB that featured the pugilistic comic's right-wing commentary, in the tradition of Joe Pyne and Allan Burke. Before going on the program, Rushmore had dinner with Robert Harrison's brother Stephen and his wife Katharine in the Pump Room of the Ambassador Hotel. Stephen Harrison was a copy editor for the *Chicago Tribune*.

While on the air, Rushmore "confided" to the audience that he was on a secret mission to uncover the "murder" of the late Secretary of the Navy, James Forrestal, whose recent death was ruled a suicide by authorities. Forrestal had plunged to his death from the sixteenth floor of the Naval Hospital in Bethesda, Maryland, in May of 1949. Like Dan Burton, the Republican congressman from Indiana who in the mid-1990s derived so much weird pleasure from his campaign to prove that Clinton presidential counsel Vince Foster had been murdered and dumped in a public park, Rushmore insisted that Forrestal had been defenestrated by Communists. Rushmore claimed he had come to Chicago in search of a man named William Lazarovich, a Communist Party leader out of New York who went by the name of Bill Lawrence. He asked the TV audience for information as to Lawrence's whereabouts.

When Rushmore returned to his hotel after the broadcast, he received a message from the desk clerk that a man calling himself "Larry" wanted to meet Rushmore at the corner of Roosevelt and Halsted at one-fifteen in the morning. Stephen Harrison warned Rushmore that the neighborhood was not safe and offered to accompany him to the rendezvous, but Rushmore declined, saying that he'd "been in tougher spots before." He also explained that "Larry" might be scared off if Rushmore didn't show up alone.

Four days later, the *Chicago Tribune* announced that Rushmore had vanished. Back in New York, Robert Harrison had become alarmed when he failed to hear from his chief writer and editor. He called Tom Duggan in Chicago, who in turn notified Chicago police. "Editor on Red Hunt Reported Missing" ran the *Chicago Tribune* headline; the Chicago police began scouring the city, and newspapers around the country picked up the story.

The police canvassed cabdrivers lined up outside the Ambassador and questioned doormen but were unable to find anyone who remembered seeing Rushmore leaving the hotel. The detectives then broke into Rushmore's room. They found two suits hanging in the closet, his shaving kit and toiletries arranged in the bathroom cabinet, and his gray straw hat lying on one of the twin beds. Curiously, in the top dresser drawer, detectives found Rushmore's wallet, his keys, and his return ticket to New York for Flight 38, scheduled to leave at 6:25 A.M. Friday morning. Rushmore neither canceled nor made that flight.

In Rushmore's wallet was the text of a telegram he had sent to Harrison the previous day: OBTAIN PHOTOGRAF TOMORROW. PLAN IT FOR LAYOUT RED STORY —HOWARD.

Hotel officials told the police that Rushmore had slept in his room on Tuesday but was listed as a "sleep-out" on Wednesday. Like the fictional secret agent in Hitchcock's 1959 film *North by Northwest* who leaves empty suits and toiletries in hotel rooms across America, Rushmore was the man who wasn't there.

The police reached Rushmore's wife by phone. All she knew was that her husband "was on a real hot story," and she had no idea about the identity of the "Larry" who had asked to meet with him.

When Rushmore's disappearance became national news, sales of *Confidential* doubled. Extra copies of the scandal sheet were unloaded on newsstands. Press and radio built on the "Red hunt" theme surrounding Rushmore's disappearance; one reporter noted that "the atmosphere was created for a dangerous hysteria."

At first the Chicago police had been a little suspicious about Rushmore's disappearance, suspecting a publicity stunt. But when they found his suits and wallet in his hotel room, even they were convinced that something had happened to the *Confidential* editor. The FBI, also skeptical about Rushmore's activities, got involved. The police came up with three theories: that Rushmore may have met foul play from someone who sought revenge for *Confidential*'s damaging articles; that he met foul play from someone from the Communist

Party; or that he intentionally went into hiding in order to search for Bill Lawrence. Both Harrison and Rushmore had often received death threats over articles published in *Confidential*. There was also the possibility that the forty-three-year-old Rushmore, who suffered from bleeding ulcers, may have been hospitalized. But he was nowhere to be found.

And then an anonymous telephone call ruined Howard Rushmore's scheme. Somebody tipped off William Touhy, Chicago's deputy chief of detectives, that a man registered under the name "H. Roberts" in the Finland Hotel in Butte, Montana, was actually Howard Rushmore. He had been hiding in the Montana hotel while the whole country was looking for him.

The mining town of Butte, Montana, would be a logical place to look for Communists—and Communist-hunters—because of its own bloody labor history. The town itself is unique in America in that each year it loses several inches of sidewalk to the Berkeley Pit, the country's largest open mine. The town is literally disappearing.

Emmett Sullivan, the police chief of Butte, went to the hotel and asked "Roberts" if he was indeed Howard Rushmore. The man replied, "Yes, my name is Rushmore. I registered under the name of Howard Roberts because I didn't want people to know where I was. I'm here on legitimate business, on the trail of a big, big, big story. I'm doing a little dodging, and not using my own name. I often do that—exclusive stuff, you know. That's the way I operate." By the time newsmen reached Rushmore in Montana, it was too late to tell the story he had planned to unleash on the country: that he had been kidnapped by the same men who had "murdered" Secretary of the Navy James Forrestal.

Rushmore's disappearance was, in fact, a grand publicity hoax. The mystery could have been solved easily. To begin with, the phony story had been given to the press by Robert Harrison's brother Stephen, who worked for the *Chicago Tribune*. Secondly, the Lazarovich-Lawrence search was an obvious ruse, since Lawrence had lived in New York with his family at the same address for years and was listed in the phone book.

Anyone familiar with Rushmore's habits could have found the newspaperman; he was holed up in his favorite Chicago tavern before leaving for Butte, while the police were out canvassing the city for him.

At 8 P.M. on July 9, 1955, before the anonymous tip that brought police chief Sullivan to the Finland Hotel, Rushmore telephoned the FBI office in Butte and asked for the special agent in charge. Special agent Hosteny was at home, having dinner, when he received Rushmore's call. Rushmore told Hosteny that he needed to see him right away "to discuss an important matter." So the two men met at the FBI field office in the Thornton Building in downtown Butte.

Rushmore told Hosteny he had come to Butte to investigate the International Union of Mine, Mill, and Smelter Workers (IUMMSW) and to expose two Communists he described as "strong-arm men" who were to take part in a strike referendum planned for that Sunday. He had wanted to flush out the mining union's Communists and hand them over to the FBI, in an attempt to get back into the bureau's good graces and prove himself, once and for all, to his hero, J. Edgar Hoover. He had hoped to pin Forrestal's "murder" on known Communist Bill Lawrence, and to "out" two more Commies for Hoover.

The plan backfired. When news of Rushmore's hoax reached the FBI, Hoover scribbled on the bottom of the memorandum, "Rushmore must be a 'nut.' We should have nothing to do with him." When Hosteny informed Washington of Rushmore's presence in Butte, the bureau told Hosteny to alert the Chicago police as to Rushmore's whereabouts. It was Hosteny, and Rushmore's beloved FBI, who had called in the anonymous tip.

On July 11, Rushmore complained to a *Washington Star* reporter that all the publicity surrounding his disappearance had made his sources "clam up. It's like working in a goldfish bowl," he said, denying that his disappearance had been a publicity stunt. But the damage had been done. The FBI had refused to embrace him with open arms, and his veracity had been publicly called into question.

Two months later, Frances Rushmore was pulled by police from New York's East River, shivering but alive. She told them, "I didn't fall and I wasn't pushed. I jumped." She had left her position as women's page editor of the *Journal American* after eleven years for reasons of "ill health," but in truth Frances was an alcoholic who had had enough of

Howard Rushmore. Fished out of the East River, she would try to run from him one more time.

EVEN THOUGH Howard Rushmore was earning more money than he had ever made in his life and *Confidential*'s circulation of five million readers brought him his widest audience, Rushmore grew to hate the job. The plush New York office at 1697 Broadway and generous bonuses did little to allay his distaste for the dapper Harrison, whom he considered nothing more than a pornographer. And he found the tipsters and informers the magazine employed truly contemptible.

As the success of *Confidential* increased with every issue, few film stars of the 1950s escaped its scrutiny. Some were victims of an entire series of stories, their first names alone enough to titillate Harrison's readers: MARILYN, ORSON, KIM, SAMMY, LANA, AVA, FRANK, JAYNE, and ZSA ZSA. To get the lowdown on these stars, Harrison set up an agency in Hollywood run by his niece, Marjorie Mead, and her husband Fred, with the respectable-sounding moniker "Hollywood Research, Inc." The Meads lived conspicuously in a lavish, Beverly Hills home but were persona non grata at most Hollywood functions. Whenever the research team of Mead & Mead came up dry, Rushmore would pay his tipsters as much as $1,000 for an item of gossip, guaranteeing an endless stream of informers and spies, including a beautiful, dark-haired ex-actress named Francesca De Scaffa, the former wife of actor Bruce Cabot, who would sleep with various movie stars and record their conversations on a miniature tape recorder hidden inside her wristwatch.

Francesca De Scaffa was rumored to have been the mistress of the Shah of Iran. As Bruce Cabot's former wife, she knew many Hollywood personalities and had access to their homes. For the two years that Rushmore was the editor of *Confidential*, she had supplied much of the magazine's material on Hollywood. She reported directly to Rushmore, who paid her between $30,000 and $40,000 for informing on her friends. She would end up supplying the magazine with thirty stories.

Hollywood Research, Inc. unearthed compromising photographs and films, and when they couldn't find them, they took them, making use of the latest technical refinements such as infrared and ultrarapid film and high-powered telephoto lenses. That's how they caught Anita Ekberg on film "in the southern half of a bikini!"

Rushmore and Harrison made sure that each article was based on a piece of film or a tape recording, evidence that was checked by Harrison's attorneys before publication. During this period, *Time*'s Ezra Goodman observed that Hollywood had become a beehive of private eyes, tapped telephones, and recording machines. It sometimes seemed as if every telephone had a tape recorder attached to it—you never knew whether your conversation was being recorded or not. Miniature recording machines that could be concealed on one's person were big sellers appealing to everyone from members of the vice squad to vice presidents in charge of production. Rushmore's expertise in the Communist-hunting business was now being put to use in the sex scandal trade, and Rushmore increasingly resented it.

Part of *Confidential*'s impact in the 1950s was due to its rogue status. The Hollywood press corps then was about as autonomous as Tass (the Soviet news agency), because all the stories published about the stars were dictated by studio bosses and hired press agents. If you printed something about, say, Rock Hudson, that wasn't approved by Universal Pictures, you didn't get invited to press conferences anymore. You were blackballed from the Hollywood beat. *Confidential* changed all that. Who needed a press conference when you could bug a movie star's telephone? Or hire a prostitute to inform on her clients? So Harrison's little magazine, published in New York City without any help or hindrance from the studios—was mightily feared in Hollywood. For all of *Confidential*'s sleazy style and downright bad taste, the magazine proved that most mainstream reporting was like a thrown fight, with too many pulled punches. Harrison had found a way to bypass the Hollywood PR machine, and at long last tell the whole truth about its stars. And that's what the American public really wanted, wasn't it? The truth about the most beautiful and glamorous people in America. For every fawning celebrity profile, there's always the antidote to be found in the pages of the *Star*, the *National Enquirer*, the *Globe*—*Confidential*'s heirs. Rushmore knew that people wanted, *needed*, to see the other side of the klieg lights: stars without makeup, without glamour, without studio protection, without the cloaks of beauty, wealth, and power.

Rushmore and Harrison were becoming two of the most hated men in Hollywood, and it wasn't just Hollywood stars and producers who hated them. Harrison's exposés of the gambling and garment industry rackets tipped off organized crime figures as well. Harrison was kidnapped by one gang of thugs, but managed to talk his way out of a concrete overcoat. On another occasion, he was dangled out of a high-rise apartment window by a couple of guys with cauliflower ears. During a hunting trip to Santo Domingo (Harrison thought of himself as a Hemingway figure, a big-game hunter with a gift for short sentences), someone took a few shots at the scandal-pusher.

Yet it didn't take the movie studios long to start playing both sides of the fence. Officially, they were outraged, but secretly they found a way to play *Confidential*'s game and use the magazine for their own purposes. Ezra Goodman wrote, "There was a great deal of hypocrisy about *Confidential.* Hollywood itself," Goodman claimed, "was far from blameless. Some of *Confidential*'s most scandalous stories were leaked by the studios themselves in order to discipline or punish recalcitrant performers." Or to buy off another story that hit too close to home. For example, *Confidential* was fed the information about Rory Calhoun's prison record by his own studio, Universal, in exchange for *Confidential*'s killing a piece on Rock Hudson and Tony Perkins, stars far more important to them. Kim Novak was "sold down the river" by Columbia Pictures to get *Confidential* to kill a story about its thuggish studio head, Harry Cohn, which producer Mike Todd had peddled to the magazine. *Confidential* was always happy to oblige. Some Hollywood press agents, noting that any publicity is good publicity, even planted stories about their clients in the pages of *Confidential.* After a story appeared linking Sammy Davis Jr. with Ava Gardner, the entertainer himself sent Harrison a pair of solid gold cuff links.

Confidential's reign of terror would last five years.

When it dawned on Rushmore that the public cared more about "Errol Flynn and His Two-Way Mirrors" than they did about Communists in the State Department, Rushmore finally broke with Harrison. He said he found it "increasingly repulsive" to work there, but he was also incensed by Harrison's plans to hire *New York Post* columnist Murray Kempton and sportswriter Jimmy Cannon—writers Rushmore considered too left-leaning (Kempton had once been associated with the Young Communist League). Rushmore's two-year tenure as the magazine's chief writer and editor had come to a close. But it wasn't enough to just walk away: Rushmore would switch sides one more time, becoming the star witness in two sensational libel and obscenity trials against *Confidential* magazine.

Hollywood, too, had had enough. In May 1955, the year Rushmore left *Confidential*, Robert Mitchum surprised Hollywood by asking the powerful Los Angeles attorney Jerry Giesler to file a lawsuit against *Confidential* in Santa Monica Superior Court for $1 million in damages. His suit claimed that Harrison's story, "Robert Mitchum—The Nude Who Came to Dinner" was "completely and entirely false and untrue." *Confidential* won the suit on a technicality, based on the grounds that the magazine couldn't be liable in California because "it was not doing and never had done business in the state and had no assets there." But Mitchum's pursuit of Harrison and Rushmore gave courage to other film stars. In February of 1957, the beautiful but troubled black actress Dorothy Dandridge, who starred in *Carmen Jones*, filed suit against *Confidential* after an article appeared describing her alleged exploits at a nudist camp ("What Dorothy Dandridge Did in the Woods"). She asked for $2 million in damages.

The lawsuits had begun.

Dozens of stars who had been slandered joined in a criminal libel and conspiracy trial against the magazine. But the lawsuit instantly created another problem for Hollywood and an even more dangerous one for the movie industry itself. Now it was only a matter of time before Hollywood's biggest personalities would be cross-examined in public about their private lives: a schlockmeister's dream come true. The press began calling it "the Trial of 100 Stars."

After quitting the magazine, Rushmore went straight to Jerry Giesler and offered himself as a witness in lawsuits against *Confidential* in exchange for a job in the movies. (This was after making a "gentleman's agreement" with Harrison not to do anything damaging to the magazine.) Giesler turned him down.

The People of the State of California v. Robert Harrison et al. started in Los Angeles on August 2, 1957, filed by Attorney General Edmund G. "Pat" Brown (the future governor of California and father of Jerry). The plaintiffs in the case were the subjects of several articles cited as libelous and/or obscene:

Maureen O'Hara Cuddled in Row 35

How Long Can Dick Powell Take It?

Robert Mitchum—The Nude Who Came To Dinner

Have You Heard About Corinne Calvet?

Mae West's Open Door Policy?

Howard Rushmore, now the state's star witness, gave the most damaging testimony against *Confidential*. He spent two days in front of Judge Herbert V. Walker, spicing up his testimony with names such as Clark Gable, Marilyn Monroe, Deanna Durbin, Doris Duke, and even Fulgencio Batista, the president of Cuba. Rushmore hurled accusations and made scandalous charges, revealing for the first time the "highly confidential secrets of how *Confidential* magazine got the purple stuff that made it a multimillion-dollar publication."

Rushmore found himself, yet again, in the position of a man who was suspected by everybody. He was finished in Hollywood, where he had angered everyone—including the prosecution—by dropping names no one had wanted mentioned, such as Clark Gable, Tyrone Power, Desi Arnaz, and those of several U.S. senators.

The case came to a close in Los Angeles in October 1957 after two months of headlines, more than two thousand pages of lurid testimony, and a record fourteen days of jury deadlock. The outcome was essentially a stalemate: the major charges against *Confidential* were dropped, but Harrison announced that the magazine would "cease and desist publishing stories about the private lives of celebrities."

Confidential won its libel and obscenity case, but it really lost: without scandal, the magazine became a shadow of its former self. Circulation dropped and the floodgates opened. Many out-of-court settlements would follow. The magazine would have to pay $40,000 to Liberace, and almost as much to a dozen other celebrities. Bankrupt from defending his "*aesthetique du schlock*" in court, Harrison was forced to sell the magazine. But he refused to disband Hollywood Research, Inc. or abandon the idea that one day *Confidential* would make a comeback.

Clarence A. Linn, the deputy attorney general of California who was given the job of prosecuting *Confidential,* said "I saw Rushmore in New York. . . . He seemed to be laboring under the impression that he and even his wife were being boycotted everywhere. . . . Rushmore thought he was going to be a great man by testifying, but he knew he was slipping. He was a man with a super ego. He was an unstable man."

Rushmore was finished in the journalism business. Back in New York, Rushmore had become a nonperson. He began drinking heavily. After leaving *Confidential,* Rushmore drifted from one scandal magazine to another, from one girlie magazine to the next. "I hate this sort of thing," he told Martin Richmond, one of his few remaining friends. Richmond remembered that Rushmore "was in debt, he was mentally disturbed, he had developed a persecution complex. I don't think he knew what he was doing those last years, yet once upon a time he was a gentleman. And he was always a pretty good writer." The jobs were running thin, and so was his money. He was still paying a weekly sum to his first wife, Ruth. They had separated twenty years earlier when he had publicly threatened her life.

Rushmore still thought of himself as a Commie-hunter, but no legitimate magazine or newspaper would go near him. He was reduced to freelancing articles like "The Secret Love John Garfield Carried to the Grave" and "The Bachelor Senator and the Toni He Could Not Hide" for magazines like *Tipoff* and *Scamp,* the dregs of the business he and Harrison had brought into the world. Like the Berkeley Pit eating up the city streets of Butte, Montana, Rushmore's livelihood as a purveyor of sleaze was devouring him. The only job he was able to get after leaving *Confidential* was the "outdoor editor" of *True War* magazine, headquartered in a dive on Forty-second Street.

A few days before Christmas of 1957, Frances Rushmore left their East Ninety-sixth Street apartment to stay with a daughter from a previous marriage on Jane Street in the West Village. She had finally had enough. Rushmore was now completely alone. He was drinking more than he was eating, and he walked the streets of New York a gaunt, haunted man. Tom Wolfe described Rushmore, formerly robust, as beginning to look like "a couple of eye sockets" mounted on a piece of modern sculpture, "a man drowning in his own turbulent juices." While working at his last job for *True War*, he took to carrying a seven-inch Commando army knife tucked into his waistband.

All he had ever wanted to be was an American patriot. Like his idol J. Edgar Hoover, this prairie-born bookworm believed that the truth was out there, if you just dug deep enough. "It's hard to believe now," Martin Richmond observed, "but Howard Rushmore went through life seeking truth and justice. His disappointments were constant, almost daily."

RUSHMORE, THE would-be patriot, in the end became the kind of tabloid story he had always hated.

Edward Pearlman was a taxi driver living on Morris Avenue in the Bronx with his wife and young daughter. He was on the night shift on January 3, 1958, looking for fares uptown. A little after 7 P.M., he picked up a couple on Madison Avenue, a tall man and a light-haired woman. The woman entered the cab, and the man pushed his way in behind her. She shouted, "I don't want that man with me!"

"I'm her husband, driver. Don't worry about it."

Pearlman looked at the woman, who insisted, "I want no part of him. We're separated."

Pearlman said, "Why don't you be a good fellow and get out?" But the man refused, folding his big frame into the back of the cab.

"They gave me an address," Pearlman recalled almost forty-one years later from his home in Fort Lauderdale. "They seemed normal until they started arguing. I heard the man say, 'Wait, I'll give you your money,' and the woman replied, 'I don't want your money.' Then she screamed, 'Oh my god!' I heard the shots—boom boom and flashes! I stopped the cab and turned around. She was on the seat and he had the gun to his temple. He shot himself. I drove to the nearest police station, the one on Third Avenue at 104th Street, and ran inside."

The woman slumped in the seat with blood oozing out of her head.

Howard Rushmore became the kind of lurid tabloid story he had always hated when he shot his wife, Frances, and then himself in a New York City taxicab on January 3, 1958. *Bettmann/Corbis.*

Patrolman Ralph Schantz ran to the curb, opened the door of the taxi, and removed the .32 caliber revolver, still gripped in the dead man's hand. At first, only a tentative identification was made from papers found in his suit jacket. But the reporters who soon gathered around the station house recognized him as Howard Rushmore. They pressed forward to capture a flashlit grainy image of the tangled bodies for the next day's newspapers.

Dr. Benjamin Vance, the assistant medical examiner, said that Frances Rushmore was shot in the right side of the neck and in the head. Rushmore had one bullet in his temple. Another had been fired through the roof of Pearlman's cab. Police said that Frances Rushmore had hailed the cab in a vain effort to escape from her husband.

The police told Pearlman that he was lucky he wasn't killed. The newspapers contacted him; one gave him twenty-five dollars for an interview. Another came to his house in the Bronx and took pictures of him and his family. At the Yellow Cab headquarters on Eleventh Avenue, they had to clean up all the blood and repair the hole in the taxi's roof. Pearlman became a big shot in the cab company.

In the days that followed, detectives learned that a few hours before the murder-suicide, Rushmore had called a friend to tell him "how very low he was, and how he had felt an enormous lack of dignity because of what he called the 'repulsive material' he had spent so much of his time with."

ROBERT HARRISON had just jumped into a taxi at Idlewild Airport when the cabdriver said, "Hey, did you hear that? The publisher of *Confidential* just shot himself!"

"The publisher of *Confidential*? Where did he shoot himself?" Harrison asked.

"In the head. In a cab. He shot himself through the head right in back of a cab."

But the publisher of *Confidential* was sitting in the back of a cab. He knew they had to be talking about Rushmore.

Howard Rushmore's body lay unclaimed in the Bellevue Hospital morgue. Five days later, his first wife, Ruth, arranged for a short private service and for Rushmore's body to be cremated. His ashes were then taken back to Mexico, Missouri, back to the "dark and bloody ground."

Robert Harrison would outlive Howard Rushmore by twenty years. His last days were spent living under an assumed name in a Manhattan hotel, hiding out from a world that had long forgotten him. Harrison continued to meet his sources in sleazy hotel lobbies and phone booths. Before his death, he would start yet another publication, a tabloid newspaper called *Inside News*. It, too, went out of business, but not before Harrison dreamed up his last big cover story, set in a burst of red and worthy of *Confidential*: "Who Really Killed Howard Rushmore?"

CHAPTER 2

THE LAVENDER CLOSET: BILL TILDEN, LIZABETH SCOTT, TAB HUNTER, AND NOËL COWARD

AS FAR as the editorial staff of *Confidential* was concerned, homosexuality was a kind of sexual equivalent of Communism, a dirty little secret that it was the magazine's duty to expose. Even the vocabulary was often interchangeable, except that the code word "Red" was replaced by "lavender." In *Confidential*'s July 1953 story "The Lavender Skeletons in TV's Closet," we're treated to the alliterative style; in key positions as directors, producers, and leading men, "video's vivid violets are giving the television industry a black eye—and the hottest scandal around today!"

The very same issue featured an exposé of the country's biggest tennis stars. "Bum Check Raps, White Slavery Charges, Immorality Convictions and Embezzlement Arrests Help Keep These Racquet Boys IN SHAPE FOR COURT APPEARANCES—AND WE DON'T MEAN TENNIS COURTS!" tattled *Confidential*. The worst offenders on the list were tennis pros John Howard, who married John Barrymore's daughter Diana, and "Big Bill" Tilden—Charlie Chaplin's private tennis coach.

The article first chronicles the exploits of Johnny Howard, the handsome, all-American tennis star who suddenly left town and turned up married to Diana Barrymore. "After six months on the pro tournament circuit," *Confidential* enthused, "Diana was barred from escorting her new husband to several tournaments.

Why? Because after returning from a party one night at the swank Louisville Boat Club, they beat the hell out of a cop who had the misfortune of trying to arrest them for drunken driving and disturbing the peace."

Johnny dropped out of tennis for a year, "during which the following occurred," wrote Jay Breen in *Confidential's* breezy house style:

> 1. Diana and John were divorced;
> 2. John was arrested, charged with transporting attractive girls across the U.S.-Mexican border. 3. John was arrested again, on suspicion of being a "business agent" for three beautiful babes in a Chicago apartment house. Howard has shrugged off the incident by explaining to intimates that the three women were fighting over his affections.
>
> "I've been in many a tight spot, but I've never been convicted yet," he boasts. "It's the convictions that count, not the arrests."

But the lowdown on Johnny Howard was just an appetizer for what was to come when *Confidential* caught on to the Bill Tilden story. It began innocuously enough: "Nobody would dare question the greatness of Big Bill, the last to retire from the Golden Age of Sport, the era that included Babe Ruth, Jack Dempsey, Bobby Jones, Paavo Nurmi, Johnny Weissmuller and Earl Sande."

"But," he continued, "there was an abnormal contributory factor to Tilden's amazing longevity in competition, 35 years of championship or near-championship form."

The secret of Tilden's longevity? *Confidential* tells us:

> While champs in other fields occasionally broke training to dally with chorus chicks till the wee hours, Big Bill was always fast asleep by 10:30. For Tilden's dissipation was always with juveniles who had to go to school the next day and consequently had to be in bed early. . . . This practice earned Tilden two jail sentences, one of three months duration, one for a year. Swishy characters from Greenwich Village to Montmartre to Sunset Boulevard bled Big Bill for the half million dollars he earned over the years with his cannonball serve and blazing forehand and backhand drives.

Tennis star Bill Tilden won the U.S. national singles championship seven times in the 1920s. He later gave tennis lessons to Greta Garbo, Errol Flynn, Farley Granger, and Shelley Winters. *Bettmann/Corbis.*

It was the televised pro championships held in Cleveland in 1951 that gave *Confidential* its chance to pounce on Tilden.

He had arrived in Cleveland to broadcast the play-by-play of the tournament. *Confidential*'s story described the "strange look" in Tilden's eyes when he surveyed the tournament players: "A look which prompted one irate matron to write in saying she didn't mind the greatest player of all time when he played tennis, but that she resented this 'lecherous-looking' man ogling the ball boys as he described a tennis match on TV."

"BIG BILL" TILDEN was the preeminent tennis player of the Jazz Age, the U.S. national singles champion seven times in the 1920s and the U.S. clay court champion. He was a smart, articulate player whose methods influenced later tennis greats such as Billie Jean King and Rod Laver. He was also an ardent fan of the movies and movie stars. Tilden met Douglas Fairbanks in 1920, in the lobby of London's Savoy Hotel on his first trip to Wimbledon. A few years later, on a visit to Los Angeles, he met Charlie Chaplin and played tennis on Cecil B. DeMille's court. "It was through Douglas Fairbanks that I became acquainted with the man I consider the greatest genius of the screen and the most brilliant comedy brain in the world—Charles Spencer Chaplin," Tilden wrote in his autobiography.

Chaplin was mad for tennis. Tilden thought he played "remarkably well" and that his forehand was "especially good." Tilden soon was a perpetual guest at the Chaplin estate on Summit Drive, in the hills overlooking Sunset Boulevard. Every Sunday afternoon in the 1940s, Chaplin hosted a tennis party that he called the Big Tea. Chaplin's children, his wife, and for a time his teenage mistress, Joan Barry, all took part in the festivities. Chaplin once told Tilden that these matches, "played for our own amusement, could draw $100,000 gates." Tilden's protégés would be there, including some of his better students such as Greta Garbo, Errol Flynn—considered by some the best tennis player in Hollywood—Olivia de Havilland, and Farley Granger accompanied by Shelley Winters. Of Garbo, Tilden said, "Her tennis is somewhat awkward and unorthodox, but not ineffective; she hits a wicked Western forehand that really moves along."

Although he had found fame as a tennis player, Tilden would have given anything to be a movie star. He often put an article in front of the names of his favorite celebrities, referring to them as "the Bankhead" or "la Pickford." The other players on the tour found Tilden's affectations pretentious and annoying. But Tilden did know both actresses and had given them tennis lessons. He had appeared in two Broadway plays, *The Kid Himself* and *They All Want Something*. He had even toured the country in *Dracula*, playing the title role for sixteen weeks. He joked that he had also "tarnished the screen" in two silent films, *Haunting Hands* and *The Music Master*, and in a few tennis films for MGM and Warner Brothers.

Tilden's obsession with celebrity began in childhood. His family had a summer home in an artistic colony in the Catskill Mountains, called the Onteora Club. Artists from New York—actors, opera singers, and society painters—gathered around the tennis court to watch the young prodigy. "It was at a tender age that I began collecting famous friends," Tilden said. He grew accustomed to being the center of attention.

Clifton Webb rented Constance Bennett's estate one summer and asked Tilden to visit and offer instruction to the famous houseguests, including Garbo and Katharine Hepburn. But after his first arrest for corrupting the morals of a minor, Tilden was banned by most of the tennis and country clubs in Los Angeles. A tatty, old luxury hotel offered him a job. The Chateau Elysees, high up in the Hollywood Hills, gave him a place to stay, and every morning he would eat breakfast from a box of cereal he kept in the bathroom. He'd then head out to the hotel's tennis court, trying to ignore its distinct slope, the result of being built over a garage.

Tilden also found work giving private tennis lessons on David Selznick's court and at Joseph and Lenore Cotten's, whose house in Brentwood Tilden thought had "the warmth and atmosphere of a home—not the usual showplace." The jobs allowed Tilden to remain close to his idols and hold fast to his unrealistic dreams of becoming a film star or a serious writer. After an early breakfast, he'd drive through the hills in his '42 Packard Clipper, the backseat full of his sweaty clothes. He'd visit the estates of movie stars he knew, coaching a little or playing for his own amusement on the tennis courts of the famous. At night he would visit the Little Club on Sunset or another club near the Farmers Market to play cards. He met Carole Lombard playing bridge at the Palm Springs Tennis Club, and Betty Grable, then at the peak of her career, often accompanied Tilden. George Raft and Buster Keaton were also regular bridge partners.

By the late 1940s, Bill Tilden knew he was no longer at the top of his game, no longer a great champion, but he never stopped playing or believing in tennis. Even in his most desperate financial straits Tilden would refuse to take money from someone who didn't treat tennis as serious business. He could be cruel to women and young students, barking out criticism. "You silly bitch!" he would yell if one of his female students didn't push herself or made a mistake. He would complain about how Americans ran only from their knees and not from their hips.

After coming into an inheritance of about $25,000, Tilden spent most of it investing in plays that he would star in, like Lillian Hellman's *The Children's Hour* and something by Booth Tarkington called *The Fighting Littles*.

In the late 1940s, Tilden and a friend were driving from Arizona to Palm Springs in his roadster when Tilden lost control of the car. He injured his neck and back, although not seriously. Still, it left him shaken. "My nerves were still shot from the accident. I couldn't seem to quite get hold of myself," Tilden said. "For the first time in my life, I found myself slipping badly and with a queer, compelling restlessness I had never known." He developed a phobia that someone might see him naked and stopped showering. He would wear the same thing for days—a threadbare sweater and dirty, wrinkled pants. Unable to play serious tennis, Tilden began instructing young boys, which ultimately led to another arrest.

On November 23, 1946, just before ten o'clock in the evening, two officers on patrol in Beverly Hills watched a '42 Packard Clipper careen down Sunset Boulevard. The driver looked young. Suspicious, the police turned on their siren and signaled for the car to pull over.

The Packard was stopped at the intersection of Rexford and Sunset. Tilden, already seen in the passenger seat, switched places with the young man. The officers approached the car. Tilden held out his driver's license. But the policeman quickly ordered the boy out of the car. As he stood up, the officers noticed that the boy's fly was open, four buttons undone.

In his autobiography, Tilden characterized the incident with his young student as "fooling around, indulging in horseplay." But when police took Tilden into custody, he signed a full statement. Foolishly, he refused counsel, and because of his vanity didn't carry his reading glasses with him, so he was reduced to having the station-house ser-

Bill Tilden talks to reporters at the L.A. county jail. On a five-year probation after an earlier incident with a young male student, Tilden was arrested again in 1949 for making improper advances to a teenage boy. *Bettmann/Corbis.*

geant tell him what was in the statement. He signed it without having read it himself.

Sometime later, Bill Tilden tried to reach Jerry Giesler, the attorney who had so brilliantly defended Errol Flynn on statutory rape charges. But Giesler refused to have anything to do with the case. Tilden hoped Charlie Chaplin could somehow rescue him, but Chaplin had his own troubles and couldn't afford to associate with his friend. Chaplin's brilliant solution was for Tilden to jump bail and leave the country as quickly as possible. Yet Bill Tilden still believed all of his legal problems would be alleviated with the help of his powerful friends. And he felt sure that a jury would never send the greatest tennis player in the world to prison.

The court moved swiftly. Judge A. A. Scott sentenced Bill Tilden to one year in the county jail. A week later, the tennis star was prisoner number 9413, cleaning and polishing kitchen utensils at the Castaic Honor Farm, a minimum-security prison forty miles north of Los Angeles. His fifty-fourth birthday passed there without celebration. But Tilden adapted well to life at Castaic, bizarrely describing the place as if it were a spa. "The beds are excellent, the food adequate in every way . . . and the climate close to perfect," Tilden said. "If a man must pay for an error, there is no better place at which to do it than Honor Farm." Tilden performed his jobs at the facility so well that Judge Scott granted an early release to Tilden after he served seven and a half months of his one-year sentence.

But the major condition of Tilden's release prevented him from associating with juveniles, either as a coach or as a friend. His lawyer even had to have the court approve his apartment's location, lest it be too close to a school. Without young students to teach, Tilden was virtually unemployed. Charlie Chaplin welcomed Tilden back into his circle, but many of Tilden's old Hollywood friends shunned him. He moved from one shabby apartment to another in Hollywood and West Los Angeles, quickly squandering his savings. He took solace in writing, finishing a play called *New Shoes* that was staged at the El Patio Theater. The play told the story of a mentally ill mother and a kidnapped son, and featured some incidents of sibling incest. The *Los Angeles Times* described *New Shoes* as "well written" but "malodorous."

He was also writing his autobiography, filling it with celebrity names and chapter titles such as "I Let Down My Hair" and "Coaching the Stars." Offering a strange, cracked-mirror view of Tilden's sexuality, *My Story* detailed how Tilden was attracted to women, but also tried to explain, vaguely, how same-sex relationships sometimes developed in the world of sports. He wrote that "twice in my life I even considered marrying. Both women were famous and both of the stage." In the same book, though, he wrote that "in all branches of athletics, which throw the same sex together constantly and intimately, with strong, close friendships growing up often based at least in part on admiration for physical perfection, an attraction may arise almost like that of love."

The court had treated Tilden strictly like a criminal and the conditions of his release proved too onerous for him. He soon violated his parole in spectacular fashion. On January 28, 1949, police issued another warrant for Tilden's arrest after a sixteen-year-old hitchhiker had identified Tilden as "the tall man" who kept trying to open his fly. His hands were cold, Tilden had said, and he just wanted to warm them up. When the police came for him, Tilden insisted there had been some mix-up, but the hitchhiker had noticed that the hand that kept trying to touch him was missing the top of the middle finger (the tennis pro had had part of his middle finger removed after he developed a gangrenous infection twenty-seven years earlier). The boy had also observed in great detail Tilden's face and clothes. He could recall the things in the backseat of the car and the numbers on the license plate. The state had an airtight case and even Tilden's probation officer lost patience with him, recommending that he be sent back to prison.

This time Chaplin did try to save his friend by calling on Judge Scott personally. He offered to assume responsibility for Tilden and allow him to live in Chaplin's home in the south of France. "Bill can start a tennis club there," Chaplin said. "I'd be happy to let him live there rent free until he's earning a living again." But the judge could never consider such a deal since it was illegal. Tilden himself pleaded with the judge, saying he'd rather serve his sentence on the honor farm than under the difficult terms of his probation, which left him unable to teach his young students.

Judge Scott ordered Tilden to serve one year in prison for his probation violation, but let the sentence for the new molesting charge run concurrently. There was no one to meet Bill Tilden when he was released just before Christmas after serving ten months of his sentence. The second arrest had further alienated his Hollywood friends. The sporting goods manufacturer Dunlop sent out an urgent order to all its salesmen to remove from the shelves any equipment marked with Tilden's name. Yet just a few days before his release from prison, the Associated Press "poll of the half-century" was announced: Bill Tilden was voted the greatest athlete in his sport.

By the early 1950s, Tilden was teaching on a public, "pay-as-you-play" court near Grauman's Chinese Theatre. He was barred from the Los Angeles Tennis Club. Occasionally he would drop over to the Beverly Wilshire Hotel to ask if there was anybody around looking for a fourth for doubles. He was letting himself go again, though, and the tennis pro at the Wilshire sometimes had to give him a clean shirt or a new pair of shorts because his own had become so rank.

Tilden went back up Summit Drive to Chaplin's house, haunting it like a ghost. Chaplin had left the country, never to return, but had given Tilden the use of his court for his dwindling number of students. When there was no money, Tilden had to pawn his trophies, but he had too much dignity and could not bear to bring them to the pawnshop himself. His three silver cups fetched forty-five dollars. Tilden had always exercised daily, but after the inactivity of two jail terms, his health was suffering. He developed a nagging cough and would often have to put his racquet down and lean against the net for support.

But "Big Bill" Tilden, nearing sixty, could still compete with the world's best players and decided to return to the U.S. pro championships. On Friday night, June 5, 1953, his protégé Arthur Anderson had invited Tilden to a family dinner to celebrate his departure the next day for the championships back east. When he failed to arrive, Anderson drove to Tilden's apartment on North Argyle and asked Tilden's landlady to let him in.

Anderson found Bill Tilden dead on his bed, dressed to go out, wearing a coat and tie. He even had his shoes on. Beside the bed were his bags, already packed for the trip to the championship in Cleveland.

The cause of death was coronary thrombosis.

Tilden left behind a few trophies that had not been pawned and $140 worth of American Express traveler's checks. In June of 1953, just days before his death, Tilden's humiliation was complete, thanks to Robert Harrison and *Confidential* magazine when they published "Bad Boys of Tennis" and referred to Tilden as one of "the most arrested players of this so-called gentlemanly game of tennis."

Few attended the memorial service that took place at the Pierce Mortuary the following Wednesday. The professional tennis association had not even bothered to send a wreath. Hollywood, too, stayed away. The studios that Tilden had hoped would invest in his plays and ideas for films showed no interest. Bill Tilden had become box office poison. He lay in his casket in a brown suede jacket and an immaculate tennis sweater with red deer running across the chest, a gift from Joseph Cotten. His body was then cremated, because it was the cheapest method, and shipped back to Pennsylvania for burial.

At the end of his autobiography, the ever optimistic Tilden had written, "I trust that whatever of good I have done in this world will be set against my mistake and found to outweigh it in the final balance."

"DON'T SELL the twisted twerps short! Once they met in secret. Today, they've organized as the 'Mattachines' . . . with a goal of a million members and a $6,000,000 bankroll!" The unfolding saga of Bill Tilden emboldened publisher Robert Harrison and his homophobic editor in chief Howard Rushmore to further exploit the subject in the pages of *Confidential*.

"The Lavender Skeletons in TV's Closet" details how "a limp wrist is necessary and often possesses surprising talents." *Confidential* trots out every stereotype as it unfolds "the lavender and lace-shirt situation" for its five million readers:

> They revel in the warmth of the spotlight and just love showing what they can do with one wave of their scented hands.
>
> The way they have jam-packed television confirms a prediction made by the eminent Dr. Kinsey that homosexuality is increasing vastly.
>
> *Confidential* then invites its readers to guess the "gay identities" of
>
> (a) a "rough and ready" TV detective who's really so delicate that writers of his scripts have strict orders never to include women's undergarments as "prop clues" in his weekly dramas. He can't control his compulsion to don the stuff.
>
> (b) a co-hero of a "space drama" for kids. They'd probably toss up the breakfast food he coaxes down their gullets if they knew his favorite

diversion is going to Greenwich Village parties "in drag," with taffeta skirts swishing at his ankles.

As if these innuendoes were not enough, *Confidential* introduces a paranoid note:

> No one wants to point the finger at one of these hands-on-hips boys because it's such a nasty business to get mixed up in. Hell hath no fury like a swish scorned, and these queeries have been known to exact vicious revenge by accusing completely virile and normal men of being abnormal themselves!

With stories such as "Hollywood—Where Men Are Men, and Women, Too!" Juan Morales (a pseudonym for Rushmore) takes his readers on a one-night romp "through this never-never land of lads who like to be lassies." We go along with *Confidential* and one "vice-squadder" to Jack's on Sunset Boulevard:

> a favorite eating place for the queen bees, who generally hit it only for sustenance, not sex. Down the street, at 8795 Sunset, we found the Cafe Gala, the swankiest queer-upholstered saloon on the Coast . . . a "very chic" bar with a "startling view of the city lights twinkling below." . . . It has the obvious touch of a decor called "early homo-sexual." . . . Incidentally, three of the Hollywood columnists are not the marrying kind.

Hollywood's secret world of gay men was not Harrison's only target; lesbians fascinated the magazine as well—even more so, as they had the added attraction of offering titillation to their male readers.

In September 1955, *Confidential* asked, "Why Was Lizabeth Scott's Name in the Call Girls' Call Book?" The busting of a house on Laurel View Drive for prostitution allegedly turned up a "little black book" containing the names and phone numbers of "cinema greats which would have made banner headlines coast to coast—had the whole story come out! . . . But what stopped men from the vice squad cold was an entry on the 'S' pages: Scott, Lizabeth (4) Ho 2-0064, Br-2-6111."

> The astounded cops at first refused to believe their eyes. Could that name be that of the honey-blonde star they'd seen in a dozen top movies? If so, what was it doing rubbing elbows with a zesty collection of customers for a trio of cuddle-for-cast cuties?
>
> To all questions about what Miss Scott's name was doing in their classy directory of customers, the older girls would only mumble, "We don't want to get anyone in trouble." . . . The juvenile [*Confidential* reported that one of the three women arrested was just seventeen] cracked enough to convince the cops that their first suspicions were right.

Scott was a box office concoction of blonde hair, defiant expression, and an immobile upper lip. She worried that the *Confidential* article, despite the fact that there was no truth to it, would have a chilling effect on her career. In fact, she wouldn't work for two years after the story's publication. It was Elvis Presley, of all people—or at least an Elvis Presley movie—that gave Lizabeth Scott the chance to revive her career. (She appeared as Elvis's smitten but hard-nosed manager in Presley's second movie, *Loving You*, the story of Deke Rivers, a country boy turned, not surprisingly, teenage singing sensation.) *Confidential* wrote that "Liz was a strange girl, even for Hollywood, and from the moment she arrived in the cinema city. She never married, never even got close to the altar."

"Her movie career," reported *Confidential*, "went off like a rocket" with such hits as *You Came Along*, *The Strange Love of Martha Ivers*, and *Dead Reckoning*, but faded just as quickly. Liz "had few friends and never went out of her way to make new ones," the magazine told its readers, but now "was taking up almost exclusively with Hollywood's weird society of baritone babes."

Typical of every "lesbian" story Harrison would run throughout the magazine's life span, *Confidential* then links Lizabeth Scott to a Parisian lesbian named "Frede,"

> Paris's most notorious Lesbian queen and the operator of a nightclub devoted exclusively to entertaining deviates like herself. . . . A woman with dark, bushy hair who hasn't been seen out of mannish attire in the last 15 years, Frede has gotten on intimate terms with

more than one famed American actress who visited her strange nitery. Liz was welcomed into the inner circle as though she'd spoken a magic password.

Confidential wanted its readers to feel like insiders—to share a certain vicarious frisson. Like Edward R. Murrow's show *You Are There*, *Confidential* put its readers in the front seat, riding along with the vice squad as it pounds on the back door of those "swanky" houses and learns their secrets. "The insiders don't have to ask what . . . such seductive females are doing . . . [T]hey've known for years . . . Now you do, too."

Tab Hunter and Dan Dailey were frequent targets of *Confidential* for their "problem." The song-and-dance man Dan Dailey's was that he couldn't seem to have a lasting relationship with a woman. *Confidential* explains:

> A friend suggested the Meninger clinic in Topeka, "an outstanding hospital for the mentally ill. [Another actor had made the trip there—Robert Walker.] Dailey's studio told him not to go. He said sorry, and went anyway. . . .
>
> When the actor began the program, he was a bundle of nerves. As the days passed, he learned to relax. He chopped wood and painted pictures of horses—good ones too. He talked to psychiatrists. He tooled copper and made enamel ashtrays and walnut wooden bowls. He took piano lessons, started a novel and learned how to play tennis. He transplanted trees, raked leaves, shoveled snow and played baseball.
>
> After seven months, Dailey was relaxed and happier. Was he cured? The doctors said no.
>
> They told Dailey he had a choice . . . either solve his problem permanently through psychoanalysis, a painful treatment involving two or three years [!] and a lot of money. Or he could simply avoid marriage.

"He never could marry again," *Confidential* concludes, with crocodile tears.

ROBERT HARRISON also couldn't wait to tear down Tab Hunter, poised for stardom after having just appeared in *Battle Cry*, a war picture directed by Raoul Walsh and based on the best-seller by Leon Uris. The former Arthur Gelien, rechristened Tab by his agent Henry Willson, supposedly was part of a "gay pajama party."

A police detective at a gay bar had struck up a conversation with "a couple of lispers," wrote *Confidential* in September of 1955, "who happily prattled that they were set for a big binge that very evening, at 2501 Hope Street in Walnut Park, a suburb of Los Angeles." One drink led to another and the pair finally invited "the snooper" to come along. There was only one "dashing requirement," wrote *Confidential*—"bring pajamas." The story continued:

"The detectives and his pals arrived around 10:30 P.M. and one of the couples at the wingding had already changed into his pajamas. Thirty minutes of watching the strange goings-on was enough for the cop. Walking to a window, he quietly signaled outside and a few minutes later the whole party was under arrest. Off they went to the Firestone Park sheriff's station, where they were booked before being hustled off to the Los Angeles County jail."

There were no big names in the catch, so far as the cops could tell. Mostly students, a few bit actors, even a traveling Bible salesman. But "one handsome hunk of a man in the crowd seemed to stand out," wrote *Confidential* in the fall of 1955. "Arthur Andrew Gelien" was the name he gave the booking sergeant, age nineteen, social security number 562-32-1946, born in New York City."

In the space reserved for occupation, he told the desk sergeant to write "None." *Confidential* reported: "Artie and his playmates were first charged with violation of California's Penal Code, Section 647.5 which calls for the arrest of idle, lewd or dissolute persons or associates of known thieves. . . ."

Neither the judge, who heard Art's plea of guilty, nor the attorney who defended "the Pajama Playboy," as *Confidential* was fond of calling him, knew they'd "just brushed with a future movie star. But they had, for "Arthur Andrew Gelien—the good-looking kid with the bad boy friends—was the Tab Hunter the bobby-soxers rave about today."

Confidential's revelations about Tab Hunter broke at the same time that the lanky actor's most important film, *Battle Cry*, was about to be released. The public relations machinery at Universal Pictures, in *Confidential*'s pun-intended prose style, "erected a stout screen" around Hunter which asserted his masculinity: "He's pictured taking horses over hurdles, water skiing, swimming and the like."

Gossip columnists were fed a constant stream of items about Tab Hunter's yen for this or that starlet: "First, there was a mysterious doll named Joy, then another by the name of Lori Nelson." He was also linked with Debbie Reynolds. In half a dozen interviews, he even "panted for Lana Turner."

Confidential concluded the story with, "Tab seldom, if ever, goes to pajama parties anymore, but who can blame him? After all, he learned the hard way that you can't tell who is wearing that nightshirt next to you. It could be an understanding chap. It could also be a cop!"

IN NOVEMBER of 1955, during one of his frequent trips to America, Noël Coward took note of the phenomenon of *Confidential*'s tremendous popularity and its dangerous modus operandi. He was on his way to perform in Las Vegas—these were the whimsical English playwright and lyricist's "Elvis" years—when he wrote in his diary that

> success also must be routinely attacked. In America today, there has emerged *Confidential.* Anyone successful and in the public eye is fair game and, libel laws in the USA being curious to say the least, these magazines are permitted to assert freely that so-and-so is a dope addict, so-and-so likes little girls, and so-and-so's private life is one long homosexual orgy, etc. The so-and-so's in question are public figures and usually very popular ones. The circulation is apparently enormous and rising steadily. It seems nothing can be done to stop them. Marlene, the Windsors, Elsa Maxwell, Van Johnson, Valentina, Garbo, Tab Hunter, Bob Mitchum, etc., already have been vulgarly pilloried.

Coward, in New York for a television appearance, visited with Cole Porter in his apartment in the Waldorf Towers. "Wait and see," the author of *Private Lives* told his old friend. "Wait and see how soon it is before I get it."

But Coward needn't have worried. In fact, he found a way to go after *Confidential.* It was even a part of his 1955 cabaret act, with his ad-libbed parodies of popular songs which mentioned *Confidential*'s "silly scandals."

After a series of theatrical flops in the late 1940s, Coward was desperate for cash in 1955. In an attempt to solve his financial difficulties, Coward agreed to appear at the Desert Inn in Las Vegas. He was nervous about how the Americans would respond to his British style of humor, particularly an audience of noisy and impatient gamblers. His salary would be $40,000 a week, making Noël Coward the highest-paid entertainer in Las Vegas, with the exception of Liberace.

Coward's debut at the Desert Inn on June 7, 1955, according to one witness, was "somewhat strained on account of his ferocious nerves." He had a lot to lose. Coward, then fifty-five, had suffered more than ten years of bad critical notices for his plays, although he had never stopped writing them. His songs, in the early rock-and-roll era, were quickly aging if not considered passé. It seemed like a very long time since drama critic Alexander Woollcott had described Coward as "destiny's tot."

But by the midnight performance that first night, Coward began what one of his acquaintances called "one of the greatest personal successes of his life." "Mr. Coward socked across his act to a glittering first night audience of theatrical luminaries (Humphrey Bogart, Lauren Bacall, Judy Garland, Frank Sinatra, David Niven, Joan Fontaine, Zsa Zsa Gabor) the likes of which have never appeared under one roof here simultaneously," *Variety* crowed the next day. "He proved, snugly and commercially, that in his premiere American appearance, he is socko café fare." Coward soon grew weary of the twice-nightly performances, alone onstage except for an accompanist. He began referring to his audiences of slot-machine-playing Americans as "Nescafé society." By midsummer 1955, Coward's voice was suffering from overuse. He closed his show, after making a killing, and left Las Vegas, the town he described as "endlessly enthralling, like a vast cruise ship."

Privately, Coward was worried about *Confidential* magazine and the potential damage it could do him. But publicly he battled it with his strongest weapons, his charm and wit. And the celebrities who flocked to see him in Las Vegas—Frank Sinatra even chartered a private jet to get there—cheered him on as much for that as for his performance.

CHAPTER 3

ALVAH BESSIE'S DREAM

IN 1952 Hollywood made a movie, *The Atomic City*, about a leading American scientist whose "weak-kneed wife" attempts to persuade her husband to cast his lot with the Commies in order to rescue their kidnapped son. There was widespread speculation that the scientist was modeled on J. Robert Oppenheimer, the developer of the atomic bomb who would end his career racked with regret over his role in unleashing the devil's own power. Of course, Oppenheimer was excellent grist for *Confidential*'s mill. As far as the magazine was concerned, the father of the atomic bomb was just another egghead with a suspiciously Jewish-sounding name. Oppenheimer's trials allowed Rushmore to bring together two magnificent obsessions—adultery and world Communism—with two exposés, "The Love Story Oppenheimer's Wife Never Knew About" and "The Strange Death of J. Robert Oppenheimer's Red Sweetheart." *Confidential* reported in November 1954:

> The father of the atomic bomb has been making the headlines for more than a year with his "on again, off again" flirtations with the Commies. But what you didn't read is even more shocking—the inside details . . . as told by nationally known Communist hunter Howard Rushmore.

Rushmore, in his first piece for the scandal magazine, described the 1944 suicide of Dr. Jean Tatlock, a psychiatrist who was the daughter of John Tatlock, an English professor at the University of California at Berkeley. Rushmore used the loss of Oppenheimer's security clearance by the Atomic Energy Commission based on "fundamental defects in his character" as the occasion for reviving the sad story of Jean Tatlock's suicide and the postmortem investigation into Oppenheimer's romantic involvement with her.

Rushmore described Tatlock's

> Ophelia-like death in the pillow-lined bathtub . . . in the same apartment where she had entertained for the entire night a married man whose name has been on Page One of the nation's newspapers for the past year. . . .
>
> What made this sad-eyed scientist with the crew haircut and the almost posed look of a wistful Ivy Leaguer leave at a critical stage in the development of the world's most dangerous weapon to keep a tryst at Jean's apartment at 1405 Montgomery Street in San Francisco?
>
> . . . American security officers could stop his trysts with his Communist girlfriend; but if they did, Oppenheimer might refuse to finish the atom bomb.

Rushmore warned *Confidential* readers in the fall of 1954 that they should be concerned about what "the world's outstanding scientist and a dreamy eyed young psychiatrist discussed that June night in 1943 in the darkness of her Telegraph Hill apartment, with intelligence officers lurking outside. . . . The world," he concludes, "will never know."

Rushmore had plenty of company in his Red-baiting. An entire directory called *Red Channels*, distributed in New York and Los Angeles, was devoted to naming actors, directors, and screenwriters whose possible connections to Communist-backed organizations made them too hot to touch.

Screenwriter Alvah Bessie, for instance, was the underpaid drama critic for the *New Masses* and had an on-air radio broadcast for fifteen minutes every Sunday morning over New York's WQXR. Bessie had fought for the republicans in the Spanish Civil War and had written a

Edward Dmytryk, Alvah Bessie, and Ring Lardner Jr. just before departing for Washington, D.C., where they pleaded guilty to charges of contempt of Congress. They had refused to testify about their Communist affiliations. *Bettmann/Corbis.*

good book about it called *Men in Battle*, which became a modest bestseller. He even received a Guggenheim Fellowship for creative writing.

Bessie was an active, even dogmatic member of the Communist Party. He first crossed paths with *Confidential*'s Howard Rushmore during a visit to the *Daily Worker*, the Communist newspaper Rushmore wrote for. In the 1940s, Warner Brothers offered Bessie $150 a week to go to Hollywood to write scripts. Bessie packed his bags. He worked on a number of successful films, such as *The Very Thought of You*, *Hotel Berlin*, and the Errol Flynn war film *Objective, Burma!*, until he was called before the House Committee on Un-

American Activities and refused to name names. As a former critic for a Communist weekly, Bessie was an easy target who would go to prison as one of "the Unfriendly Ten," the ten writers held in contempt of Congress for not answering questions about their political affiliations.

After he had been cited for contempt, before he went to prison, Alvah Bessie had a dream. He was in a New York City hotel room with his wife, Clare. The room was full of people he had never seen before. He soon discovered that everyone there was a member of the Central Committee of the Communist Party. Later in the dream, two men took Alvah Bessie aside. The meeting had mysteriously changed into a cocktail party and the men whispered to him that his wife was having a clandestine love affair with an FBI agent.

When she heard about his dream, Bessie's wife suggested that he go see a psychiatrist. The psychiatrist wanted Bessie to write his autobiography. "Writers work better that way," he told him. The psychiatrist told Alvah Bessie he needed deep analysis that would take many years to complete. But then the psychiatrist said he would have to refer him to another doctor because he was simply too busy to take on new patients. The next day Bessie began his autobiography, working furiously for five days, then giving up in disgust.

It turned out that the psychiatrist recommended to Bessie had worked with many writers in Hollywood, and that at least six of his patients had turned up at subsequent investigations—as informers. In fact, the man was not a psychiatrist at all. Years later, Bessie learned the man was an FBI agent. Since he was already in contempt, however, it's doubtful that the "psychiatrist" supplied the committee or the agent with any useful information about him. And if he intended to turn Bessie into an informer, he failed miserably.

Bessie and Clare did not have enough money to leave Hollywood, like so many other screenwriters and actors under investigation. At least not until the case had been resolved. They survived on food donated by friends, but eventually, in late 1949, even that ran out. Bills began to pile up and Bessie had no way to pay them. He could not find work, of course. Other blacklisted writers had managed to save some money and now helped their wives establish small dress or cosmetic shops. Bessie remembered one writer who sold wallpaper and another who opened a bar. Still others moved to New York in hopes of launching television careers.

Bessie turned next to Charlie Chaplin, whom he had met several times before, once at the home of Clifford Odets, where they all listened to some of the first long-playing records, and then to a strange diminutive man named Lewis Browne who had just written a book called *How Odd of God (To Choose the Jews)*.

Bessie was now determined to sell Chaplin on the idea of making a modern version of *Don Quixote* with Walter Huston playing the Knight of La Mancha and Chaplin as Sancho Panza. He would set the play in Spain under Franco's reign of terror, and what would drive Quixote mad, in Bessie's version, was not the romances of chivalry but his belief in the American homilies that Bessie had always heard as a boy, such as "A man is judged by the appearance he makes," "A woman's place is in the home," and "Work hard and you will succeed."

Chaplin listened intently. He watched Bessie as the writer explained his story, one that he knew Chaplin would turn into a "great film." Chaplin thought Bessie had a good idea but was reluctant to get involved with the project. Because Chaplin had been criticized for his own behavior for so long—for his repeated dalliances with teenage girls and not a few skirmishes with the Internal Revenue Service—he feared the press would "crucify" him for taking on a great classic. And besides, Chaplin said, "I like the things I do to be my own." "By the time you're through with it, it will be your own," Bessie told Chaplin. But Chaplin only shook his head. When Bessie climbed into his car and shook hands with Chaplin, he felt something in his hand; it was a folded-up hundred-dollar bill.

Chaplin's gift would not last long, so Bessie next approached his old friend the actor Lee J. Cobb, whose gravelly voice and blustery manner made Bessie think of him as a character straight out of Dostoyevski. If so, he was a Dostoyevski character with a movie contract, one that brought him $1,500 a week. On weekends Cobb would fly in his personal airplane to Las Vegas, where, like Dostoyevski himself, he would drop great sums at the gaming tables.

Cobb and Bessie were friends, although they could never seem to agree on anything, not even how they first met. According to Cobb, it was back in 1940: a review Cobb wrote of one of his own performances—

calling it "pure, stunning, dignified and heartbreaking"—appeared under Alvah Bessie's byline in the *New Masses*. According to Bessie, however, that review of Cobb's performance was written by Bessie himself. Cobb wrote Bessie a fan letter saying that he was "the only critic who had ever properly evaluated what [Cobb] was trying to do."

During the House Un-American Activities Committee hearings, Cobb became seriously depressed. He refused to say a word to anyone, including his wife and child. As he watched his friends being humiliated, their careers destroyed, his depression seemed bottomless. In the midst of the hearings, Cobb sent a telegram to Alvah Bessie. It was full of love for his old friend: Cobb told Bessie how proud he was that he was standing up "for the preservation of our freedom."

But when Bessie asked his friend for $500—just a loan—Cobb's face grew even more solemn. He looked like the juror he would play in 1957's *Twelve Angry Men*. Cobb, in that booming voice of his, told Bessie that he wasn't solvent enough to loan him the money.

Bessie was stunned, knowing that Cobb could pick up the phone and get him the money "in less than five minutes." But Cobb said he couldn't give it to his friend, and that even if he could, it wouldn't solve Bessie's problem. Alvah Bessie didn't recognize his own voice when he called his old friend a "cocksucker." Cobb's long, Dostoyevskian face filled with sadness.

In *Twelve Angry Men*, Cobb was always the first one to take his jacket off in the heat. This time he just reached for the doorknob. The whole terrible farce would have made a great movie. But it would never be made.

Meanwhile, a court had already convicted John Howard Lawson and Dalton Trumbo, two of the Unfriendly Ten. Adrian Scott remained in the hospital recuperating from surgery. Seven still faced trial. They left from Los Angeles International Airport, where three thousand people had gathered to show their support for them. Bessie spotted the solemn face of his former friend Lee J. Cobb in the crowd. Cobb stood directly behind the police lines in the front row, watching as Bessie kissed his inconsolable wife and two of his children good-bye.

Three separate judges tried the seven defendants, all in one morning. Five received the maximum sentence—one year in prison and a $1,000 fine.

A class picture of the Hollywood Ten, minus one, on the steps of the U.S. Marshal's Building, where they awaited fingerprinting after their surrender. They are (left to right) Robert Scott, Edward Dmytryk, Samuel Ornitz, Lester Cole, Herbert Biberman, Albert Maltz, Alvah Bessie, John Lawson, and Ring Lardner Jr. Only Dalton Trumbo is missing. *Bettmann/Corbis.*

Then it was Alvah Bessie's turn to stand before Judge David A. Pine.

Pine looked like central casting's idea of a judge with his dignified manner and white hair. He seemed to listen carefully. He offered an occasional smile, too, when he heard a cogent argument from one of the attorneys. Judge Pine retired to his chambers to read a supplementary brief and to browse through some of the hundreds of letters urging leniency, if not probation, for these writers who had never committed any kind of offense before.

Just ten minutes later, Judge Pine returned. He found Alvah Bessie and his two codefendants guilty as charged, and just as the judges in the Lawson and Trumbo cases had done, he ruled as "irrelevant" every constitutional issue that Bessie's attorneys had presented to the court. Bessie received a one-year sentence and was fined $1,000.

Bessie's wife did not have the money to make the trip from Los Angeles to Washington. She wasn't there to see the bailiff put handcuffs on her husband or to watch a U.S. marshal walk him out of the courtroom and into a holding pen.

It was not a set. James Cagney wasn't there to go crazy in the mess hall. It was a filthy bull pen, the paint peeling off the walls. The smell of urine hung in the hot June air, wafting from an open latrine in the corner. The men, "mostly Negroes," sat on scarred wooden benches, too dejected to even ask each other ask how they had gotten there.

On the other side of the wire, Bessie saw writers Herb Biberman and Edward Dmytryk being brought in to be booked. They held up their hands—six fingers, meaning they had drawn six months, instead of the twelve Bessie had pulled.

For Bessie, the strangest moment of all came when he was sent to his individual cell. The metal doors closed behind him with a clang. In the cell were two cots, a toilet without a seat, a washbasin. Bessie's cell mate joined him later and they tried to talk, but the man didn't speak any English, so Bessie just stood at the entrance to the cell and grasped the bars. He didn't know why he did it except out of some instinctive urge, the by-product of watching countless prison films.

Two packs of cigarettes slid through the bars, handed to Bessie by a passing guard. "Lawson and Trumbo bought these for you," the man said. Bessie asked where his friends had gone.

"Shipped out—a couple days ago."

Bessie tore open the pack and lit one of the cigarettes with shaking hands, wondering if he could survive his sentence for one night, let alone one year.

In prison, he thought of the past and the present. He saw the world as he saw it years before. Bessie remembered the moment in *The Life of Emile Zola* (made by Warner Brothers) in which the prisoner Alfred Dreyfus, played by Joseph Schildkraut, is released from his cell on Devil's Island. The door opens, the warm afternoon beckons. Did he do it? Did he actually walk through the open door? Alvah Bessie couldn't remember.

ANOTHER VICTIM of the anti-Communist fervor *Confidential* helped to fuel was the great Yiddish-speaking actor who specialized in gangsters—Edward G. Robinson. Sadly, another subsequent victim was one of the greatest private art collections in Hollywood.

Eddie Robinson and his wife had been collecting art since the 1920s. Art was a religion to them. Not only was their collection the most remarkable in the movie colony, it was one of the best private collections of Impressionist paintings in the country.

Corot's *L'Italienne* hung on the wall in the living room, Daumier's *Second Class Coach* over the sofa on the opposite wall. There was Cézanne's *Black Clock*, and a girl by Renoir. Just steps away were a Seurat, a Géricault, a Pissarro, more Renoirs, and van Gogh's *Country Road*. Underneath the trees of Arles stood a group of 1,200-year-old Tang figures. In the dining room, the Robinsons ate breakfast surrounded by four Degas pastels and one of his rare sculpted ballerinas. (Another one was at the Metropolitan Museum in New York.)

Across from the Degas hung a painting of flowers that seemed to burst into flame. And in the library hung Grant Wood's famous *Daughters of the American Revolution*. The Robinsons had also collected the lace collar, brooch, and blue cup Wood used in the painting, and they sat in a shadow box beside it. A Hopper, a Bonnard, even a Vuillard portrait of Eddie's son, Edward Jr. (nicknamed Manny)—executed when the Robinsons visited Paris in 1937—hung in the Robinson home on Rexford Drive. But that was just downstairs. The Robinsons displayed still more art on the upper floors of the house. Over the stairs hung an early Matisse, in the dressing room was a Dufy. A Monet graced the bedroom along with a portrait by Frida Kahlo of a woman and child.

For Robinson, however, there were no more films. The money he had loaned Dalton Trumbo, whose name was in *Red Channels*, was enough to make Robinson's phone stop ringing. He was accused of having contributed to eleven different committees that had now been labeled Communist front organizations. At the Hillcrest Country Club, someone got up and walked out when Eddie came in to play cards.

By 1955 the Robinson marriage was also disintegrating. Gladys had suffered a series of mental breakdowns, and now the two started divorce proceedings. Eddie was worried about the fate of his art collection during a protracted and bitter divorce, so he arranged to send the paintings to the Los Angeles County Museum, where they would be safe and beyond the reach of his wife. When Gladys Robinson returned from one of her European trips, she found the walls of the house completely empty. Stunned, she ordered the museum to return the collection immediately.

But the museum's exhibition was incredibly popular, with record crowds lining up to see it. So when Gladys learned that she alone could not get the paintings back, she persuaded the museum at least to change the catalog copy from "The Edward G. Robinson Collection" to "The Gladys Lloyd Robinson and Edward G. Robinson Collection."

In the end, the only way out was for Eddie to sell the paintings and divide the money with Gladys. She was getting anxious to have her share of the proceeds, threatening to sell her half of the collection at a reduced rate. The exhibit had generated interest from potential buyers. Eddie called them "ghouls" and "vampires," but if forced to part with his paintings, he wanted them to sell for what they were worth. He learned that an interested buyer was building a new house in Paris and was thinking of installing the paintings there. And the beauty of the deal was that the gentleman in question would even let Eddie buy back many of the paintings for an agreed-upon price, after a suitable amount of time had elapsed. But that agreement was not put in writing. The same offer to buy some of the paintings back eventually was made to Gladys, but she refused it. She wasn't interested in the paintings; she just wanted the money.

Stavros Niarchos and his wife, the sister of Aristotle Onassis, would soon own all seventy-four paintings in the Robinson collection. After the exhibit had traveled to the San Francisco County Museum and finished its run there, Gladys Robinson insisted that the pictures be returned to the house. She rehung them in their proper places and invited everyone over to bid them farewell before their ultimate sale to Niarchos.

Eddie Robinson felt doomed by his own political sympathies and even his generosity. He first appeared before the House Un-American Activities Committee in 1947, then heard nothing from the panel for three years. In the fall of 1950, Robinson again flew to Washington with his files, offering to explain his financial contributions to certain left-wing causes. But Robinson was trying to defend himself against ghosts, against phantoms that spoke in whispers behind his back. He had sent a $2,500 check to Dalton Trumbo and his wife, had taken pity on a family in need—and now no one in Hollywood would touch him.

Gladys was in Europe during most of the trouble. But Eddie's son Manny soon began to feel sorry for him. He didn't act like a tough father anymore. "He just sounded like the lonesomest guy in the world," Manny said. Manny decided to leave New York and return to California to be near his father during those difficult days in the winter of 1951. He was shocked to see the physical change in his father brought on by his ordeal. He seemed to have aged ten years. With Gladys away in Europe, Eddie couldn't even stand to be alone in the big house on Rexford Drive. He preferred to stay with friends, returning to the house only to pick up the mail.

Manny and Eddie commiserated, wandering around Beverly Hills like a couple of condemned men. Manny was waiting to hear from the local draft board as to whether he was going to wind up in Korea, while his father was waiting for the call to testify again before the House Committee in hopes of beating the allegations. "Either snap my neck or set me free," Robinson told the committee. "If you snap my neck, I will still say 'I believe in America.' "

Gladys wrote letters from Europe filled with plans for a new life abroad. She was convinced that Eddie should start all over again making pictures in Europe. Hollywood might be through with him, but they still had plenty of friends abroad who would be happy to have him in their movies. But that wasn't what he wanted. He wanted the chance to clear his name.

After Robinson's third appearance in Washington in the spring of 1952, the chairman of the committee declared: "Well, actually this Committee has never had any evidence presented to indicate that you were anything more than a very choice sucker. I think you are number one on the sucker list in the country." A moment or two later the committee adjourned, declining to indict Edward G. Robinson.

It had been three years in hell.

BECAUSE THERE was no written understanding between Stavros Niarchos and Eddie Robinson, it's hard to say if Niarchos ever really intended to sell any of the paintings back to Eddie. Soon after the sale of his pictures, Eddie Robinson tried in vain to contact Niarchos by mail and by cable; one time he even traveled to Europe in an attempt to reach the new owner of the Gladys Lloyd Robinson and Edward G. Robinson Collection. But Niarchos evaded all of the old actor's efforts to get in touch with him. One of the things that angered Robinson was the report that Niarchos had moved some of the pictures onto his yacht, where the salty air was no doubt ruining them.

Finally, a letter came from Niarchos's secretary giving Eddie permission to come to the Niarchos house. It was being remodeled, the secretary wrote, and the family thought it would be a good time for him to come and see the collection that once belonged to him.

Eventually, Robinson was given the opportunity to buy back a few of the paintings at greatly inflated prices. But having entered the B-picture phase of his career (floating around in films like *A Bullet for Joey,* starring George Raft), Robinson couldn't afford to buy back the most expensive and important pictures. So Renoir's *After the Bath* and van Gogh's portrait of Père Tanguy, and those Tahitian flowers of Gauguin's that used to make the dining room look like it was about to burst into flame—not to mention Cézanne, Degas, Lautrec—they would all be lost to him.

Of all the paintings in his collection, Henri Matisse's *La Desserte* held special meaning for Eddie Robinson, reminding him of his mother and the traditional dinner on the Jewish Sabbath. But it was never returned to him. His other great love from the collection was Georges Rouault's *Head of a Tragic Clown.* For this actor who had suffered so much, seeing the painting was an emotional experience. When Robinson stumbled across *Head of a Tragic Clown* on exhibit in a European museum years later, he burst into tears.

Before the roof fell in, Robinson had made a movie for Joe Mankiewicz called *House of Strangers*—that was his life now. He didn't recognize anyone. Not Hollywood. Not himself. Not even his own son, who was in deep trouble with the law and clearly in need of a psychiatrist.

It was Cecil B. DeMille who put Eddie Robinson back to work in Hollywood. DeMille was one of the most conservative men in the country and as close as Hollywood came to a patriarchal figure. When the part of Nathan was discussed for DeMille's epic *The Ten*

Commandments, someone suggested that Robinson would be ideal for the part—adding, however, that under the circumstances, he was of course unacceptable.

But DeMille felt the actor had been done an injustice, and decided to offer him the part: Eddie Robinson, haranguing the idolaters in front of the Golden Calf. So it was DeMille who made it safe to hire Eddie Robinson again. Three years later, Robinson would close out the decade as a man doing battle with his kid brother, played by Frank Sinatra, in a movie for Frank Capra called *A Hole in the Head* (1959).

For Eddie Robinson at least, the blacklist was over.

LEE J. COBB'S treatment of Alvah Bessie came back to haunt him. Less than two years after refusing to help his old friend with a $500 loan, Cobb was named as a Communist before the House Un-American Activities Committee by fellow actor Larry Parks, who had portrayed Al Jolson in the wildly popular *Al Jolson Story* but whose career subsequently foundered. Like Cobb, Parks had flirted with a number of Communist-leaning organizations that sprang up in America's postwar years. And as Cobb would do after him, Parks named names before the committee.

Cobb had resisted HUAC for over two years, refusing to testify, then meeting with the FBI, then finally agreeing to appear before the committee in executive session. Like Alvah Bessie, he too ran out of work and money. But unlike Bessie's wife, who took up her husband's cause by writing articles and angry letters to editors, Cobb's wife was institutionalized as an alcoholic. On June 2, 1953, in Room 1117 of the Hollywood Roosevelt Hotel, Cobb became an informer.

At that point he probably wished he had stayed away from Hollywood when he had had the chance. Cobb, who was born Leo Jacoby on the Lower East Side of New York in 1911, had studied to be a violinist until a broken wrist ended his career. When he was seventeen years old, he ran away to Hollywood, but returned to New York for two unhappy months to study accounting at New York University. At the age of twenty-three, Cobb joined the Group Theatre, where he appeared in such productions as Clifford Odets's *Waiting for Lefty* and *Golden Boy*. There he met some of the same party members who would later cause him grief with the House Un-American Activities Committee. The

Group was also where he would meet "the boys"—Elia Kazan, Harold Clurman, John Garfield, and Lee Strasberg.

Elia Kazan sent Cobb the script of Arthur Miller's *Death of a Salesman*, asking him to consider the part of Willy Loman, the play's angry central figure. As Willy Loman, Cobb would be acclaimed as "the next Barrymore," one of the major talents of the American theater. Back then, his talent seemed boundless—the kind of gift that would keep you safe and successful forever.

Yet Cobb would go on to name twenty people as Communists before the executive session. He would also "out" two character actors, Phil Loeb and Sam Jaffe, saying they controlled a left-wing caucus within Actors' Equity called the Forum, although, he would add, "I never knew them to be Communists."

In the course of his testimony, Cobb described an attempt by one of the "Unfriendlies," John Howard Lawson, to "rewrite the precepts of Stanislavski's method of acting." Asked by the committee why Lawson would want to do this, Cobb replied, "The excuse was . . . however good Stanislavski was, he would be so much better if he were a Communist."

At the close of his testimony, Cobb endorsed not only HUAC's right but its "duty" to investigate Communists "within any environment of the United States." Though he had evaded them for two years, Cobb called his testifying before HUAC "a privilege. . . . I can only say that I am sorry for those who haven't [testified] and that more haven't done so."

By 1953 Lee Cobb had no money and no one to borrow it from. With two young children to worry about, he was worn down. "I didn't act out of principle," Cobb would later say about testifying, "I wallowed in unprincipledness. . . . You start out by wanting to keep your friends. In a totalitarian country they want you to betray your friends—and you persuade yourself finally that it is your duty." On the tortuous road to that conclusion lie "many bleached bones. . . . "

Not long after his testimony, Lee J. Cobb suffered a massive coronary. Shunned by most of his old friends and without work in Hollywood, Cobb was certain that his career had come to an end. When he entered the hospital, he was on the verge of bankruptcy.

IT WAS more than ironic that Cobb had a role in Elia Kazan's *On the Waterfront,* which has been described as a glorification of a stool pigeon, made in 1954 after Kazan himself had named names for HUAC. In *Waterfront,* the dockworker played by Marlon Brando is redeemed when he informs on the corrupt labor bosses of the longshoremen's union. Kazan's film created a context in which the naming of names is the only honorable thing to do: "Squealing may be relative, but in *Waterfront* it is mandatory." Screenwriter Budd Schulberg, producer Elia Kazan, and actor Lee J. Cobb had all informed; *Waterfront,* for all its greatness, is seen by many critics as a not-so-veiled defense of their conduct before HUAC.

Frank Sinatra had campaigned to play the role of Hoboken-born Terry in *On the Waterfront,* the role in which Brando would break hearts. When Kazan told him that *Waterfront* would actually be filmed in Hoboken, Sinatra envisioned returning to his hometown as a conquering hero, and he went so far as to meet with the director about his costumes in the film. But as an actor, Sinatra was not yet a star. After his role in Kazan's film version of Tennessee Williams's *A Streetcar Named Desire,* Brando was already hot. Producer Sam Spiegel could only raise $500,000 on Sinatra's name; with Brando in the lead role of Terry Malloy, he could raise twice that amount.

Brando had first refused to work for Kazan because of the director's testimony before the Senate House Committee. He overcame his scruples by telling Kazan—and himself—that he was only taking the role because Kazan gave him Friday afternoons off so he could drive across the river into New York to see his psychiatrist. Kazan later wrote: "If there is a better performance by a man in the history of film in America, I don't know what it is."

When Kazan sent Sinatra a letter of apology informing him that the role had gone to Brando, Sinatra was devastated. It would be months before he could even respond. "For me to tell you that I was not deeply hurt would not be telling you my true feelings," he wrote.

Sinatra hated Brando, whom he called "Mumbles." Heartbroken over losing the role, Sinatra took Sam Spiegel to court, suing him for $500,000 over breach of contract; the two men settled amicably out of court; no money exchanged hands.

FRANK SINATRA had always admired Lee J. Cobb's acting. They had met a few years earlier when they both appeared in *The Miracle of the Bells* in 1948. He liked to say that Cobb was robbed when he didn't win the Academy Award for his performance as the corrupt, cigar-chomping labor boss Johnny Friendly in *On the Waterfront*. After Cobb's heart attack in June 1955, Sinatra called him in the hospital. In what Cobb described as Sinatra's "unsentimental fashion," he moved into Cobb's life, sending the actor dozens of books and flower arrangements. He brought special Italian delicacies into Cobb's hospital room, hiding them from the watchful eyes of the nurses. He kept reminding the forty-four-year-old actor of all the great roles he still had ahead of him. Sinatra told Cobb that he wanted him to direct one of his own future film projects.

When Cobb was about to be discharged, he learned that Sinatra had paid all of his hospital bills. He then arranged for the broken actor to recuperate at a convalescent home in the Hollywood Hills for six weeks, again paying all of Cobb's expenses. Sinatra called him every day.

Cobb was grateful, but perplexed. Sure, the two men had acted together in *The Miracle of the Bells*, but that was it. Sinatra and Cobb had never been close friends. After Cobb recovered, Sinatra moved him into his own home in Palm Springs, and then arranged for him to move into a beautiful apartment in Los Angeles. "It was one of those places that very rich people live in—clean and beautiful," Cobb's wife remembered.

Lee Cobb couldn't figure out Frank Sinatra. He was generous but elusive during those months. He never stayed or visited long enough to be thanked or embraced, or shown any gratitude. He reminded Cobb of the Lone Ranger. Occasionally, however, the two men had long talks. They talked about life and death. Cobb's future wife was often present when the two men met in the living room of the new apartment. She recalled that Sinatra seemed to understand how hard it was to keep going, "how elusive the will to live can be." She thought that Sinatra admired Cobb because he himself had just emerged from the depths, his own career having suffered a painful drought.

Sinatra's generosity helped save Cobb's life, but could not save his career. After *On the Waterfront*, Cobb played the father in *The*

Brothers Karamazov, and he even got to play King Lear in Lincoln Center. He reprised the role of Willy Loman onstage, as if returning to an old friend he seemed to know more intimately now. But at the end he would wander through television, guest-starring in forgettable second-rate dramatic series, a ghost shambling among the black-and-white images.

Alvah Bessie was released in 1951 from the federal penitentiary in Texarkana, Texas, after serving ten months of his one-year sentence. Immediately he was blacklisted by the major studios and refused to write under a pseudonym. "I was thrown out of Hollywood on my ass, and I've been involved in a struggle to stay alive ever since," Bessie told one interviewer in 1977. "People say it's now pretty fashionable to say you were blacklisted, but if that's fashionable, I haven't gotten any offers from Hollywood yet."

He said life after prison was "a form of nonexistence." He took a series of odd jobs and eventually found work at the Hungry i nightclub in San Francisco as a stage manager and soundman for seventy dollars a week. He sought solace in great literature, especially in translating the works of French writers such as Théophile Gautier, Pierre Louys, and Octave Mirbeau. He also wrote novels, including a kind of roman à clef about Marilyn Monroe called *The Symbol*, which was made into a television movie in the 1970s.

He never got over his resentment of "friendly witnesses," such as the director Elia Kazan, who named names before HUAC. Until his death in 1985, he called Kazan "an ineffable fink." Eighteen years later, Bessie's son, Dan, protested the Motion Picture Academy's decision to honor Kazan with a lifetime achievement award. "I think Kazan should be given an Oscar," said Alvah Bessie's son, "but with the names of the Hollywood Ten engraved on the back of it."

CHAPTER 4

HIGH SCHOOL CONFIDENTIAL: MANNY ROBINSON, SYDNEY CHAPLIN, CHARLIE CHAPLIN JR., AND JOHN BARRYMORE JR.

IF COMMUNISM was America's great threat from without in the 1950s, then juvenile delinquency was the great threat from within. Adults began looking upon their own children as aliens. A judge in Boston complained in 1953 about "the spectacle of an entire city terrorized by one-half of one percent of its residents. And the terrorists are children."

In 1954 the Senate Subcommittee on Juvenile Delinquency chaired by Estes Kefauver began holding hearings on "the social problem of juvenile delinquency." Benjamin Fine published an influential book in 1955 called *1,000,000 Delinquents*, and the following year the *Saturday Evening Post* called delinquency "the shame of America."

The Second World War, which sent fathers off to fight and mothers off to factory jobs, allowed a whole generation of kids to grow up relatively unsupervised. America's postwar affluence provided more leisure time. Teenagers didn't have to work after school in family businesses or on farms. The erosion of the authority of the father (think of Jim Backus in an apron in *Rebel Without a Cause* and James Dean's rage) was another factor.

Danger did lurk in school yards and youth hangouts, but that threat really came from gangs, not mobs of middle-class teenagers. Yet the fear of juvenile delinquency became a national obsession in the 1950s, blown all out of proportion. It was something new in America, and Americans didn't know how to react.

Hollywood itself was in something of a quandary. Having found a new market, the film industry didn't want to alienate teenagers who had money and leisure time. It didn't want to squelch the burgeoning youth culture that for the first time treated teenagers as a specific segment of the population with their own fads and enthusiasms, their own specialized consumer goods. As one critic has observed, "Hollywood was understandably loath to bite the little hands that fed it." But Hollywood didn't want to alienate parents, either, by catering to what were perceived as hordes of rebellious teenagers.

Hollywood soon resolved its dilemma, exploiting the national problem in a blizzard of films: *The Wild One* (1954), *Rebel Without a Cause* (1955), *Blackboard Jungle* (1955), *Crime in the Streets* (1956), *Hot Rod Girl* (1956), *I Was a Teenage Werewolf* (1957), *The Delinquents* (1957), *Jailhouse Rock* (1957), *Juvenile Jungle* (1958), *High School Hellcats* (1958), and finally *High School Confidential!* (1958), its title inspired by *Confidential* magazine.

As America relished its postwar affluence, it became more difficult to blame teen crime on poverty. The specter of "bad" kids from good neighborhoods terrified a whole generation of parents, and was explained away in part by the "sickness" model of behavior: delinquents weren't criminals, they were disturbed, sick, troubled. In the 1956 film *The Unguarded Moment*, John Saxon plays a "sex maniac" stalking Esther Williams, his teacher. "Experts" and families clashed repeatedly in films about juvenile delinquency. In *High School Confidential!*, the teachers have to be lectured by drug experts from the police department on how to recognize drug paraphernalia, and "mollycoddling parents" are blamed for allowing their kids to smoke marijuana.

No one understood the new generation gap and the rise in "delinquency" better than the sons and daughters of movie stars—the tragic offspring who knew even as children that they were supposed to pick up the flaming torch and run with it without having anywhere to go or any idea of how to get there. They were second-generation royalty in Hollywood, accorded all the rights thereof except the right of succession. They called themselves "the Juniors"—Edward G. Robinson Jr., Sydney and Charlie Chaplin Jr., John Barrymore Jr. They grew up in absolute terror, afraid of their parents and terrified of their nurses and nannies. They soon discovered it was much easier to make news by being bad than by being good.

OF ALL these unhappy children, none were as miserable as Eddie Robinson Jr. It was trouble that made the Robinsons a family. Maybe it started back when Eddie Jr.—known as Manny—turned thirteen. Harry Warner was so impressed by Manny Robinson's bar mitzvah cer-

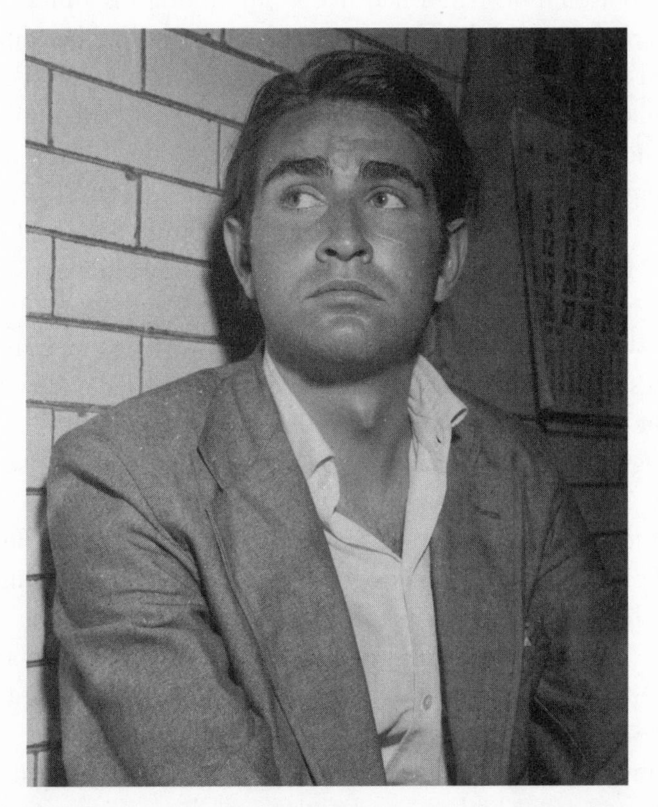

The son of tough-guy actor Edward G. Robinson, "Manny" ran afoul of the law more than once. Here he sits in a Hollywood jail in the summer of 1954. Two cabdrivers identified him as having held them up, but the case was later dismissed. *Bettmann/Corbis.*

emony that he decided to make a film out of it for release as a short subject for National Brotherhood Week. Warner promised the thirteen-year-old that he would be back to film the ceremony, "starring *you*, Manny." Manny wanted to be an actor like his famous dad, so what could be better than starring in a Harry Warner production? He had already memorized his lines.

Crews from Warner Brothers swarmed Temple Emanu-El on Wilshire Boulevard, setting up cameras, lights, and cables. Warner Brothers' director of short subjects would preside over the bar mitzvah documentary. The rabbi sent out an all-points bulletin for the congregation to appear in the picture, scheduled to be shot over three days.

Manny Robinson performed like a pro, hitting his "lines" so well that the shoot wrapped up in just one day. He joked that he could have finished before lunch if the cantor hadn't flubbed his part. People at the studio were talking about "a certain quality that came through on film" and Manny's wonderful "technique."

Manny was the star, and his father had only a bit part.

But a few weeks later, Eddie Sr. suddenly announced that he had asked Mr. Warner to withhold the picture from general release. Manny was devastated and confused. He couldn't understand why his father would hold him back from his dream of becoming an actor. Warner's bar mitzvah film would have its only showing in New York, at a private screening for Manny's grandmother and uncle.

Things got worse over the years. Eddie Sr. sent Manny to New York to study acting, but Manny began drinking too much. Eddie accused Manny of squandering every opportunity he had created for him, abusing the freedom he had been given to become a serious actor. Seeing his own opportunities shrivel under the glare of the HUAC hearings, Eddie felt that his son's life had become unmanageable. Above all, he couldn't stand by while Manny drank himself into a stupor—he was thinking of having his son committed.

Manny eloped to Mexico. When he returned, he borrowed money from a press agent he knew and settled with his wife in a tiny apartment on Doheny for ninety-five dollars a month and started work in an airplane parts factory in Beverly Hills. Manny had confided his woes to a press agent, only to see his confidences turn into the March

1956 *Confidential* headline: "What Edward G. Robinson Doesn't Know About His Own Son":

> It's doubtful even Eddie's father knows the entire story of his ne'er do well son. Some of the facts he couldn't miss . . . bad check charges, drunkenness, disturbing the peace, attempted armed robbery and so on.
>
> Thus, it's been no secret to Robinson that, so far, his boy has been one prize bad egg. . . .

The *Confidential* story cautioned "it is a wise father that knows his own child," quoting from *The Merchant of Venice*, act 2, scene 2, in a long red banner that streaked across a photograph of Eddie Robinson's chest. The article continued on various pages of the magazine, with tiny photographs of Eddie Robinson and Manny, face-to-face like cameos in a locket. *Confidential* was quick to paint Manny as a deadbeat, as a leech afraid of work, and Eddie Robinson as "the famed tough guy with a soft spot for his wayward son."

The Robinson story had all the great themes of *Confidential*'s explosive first year—abortion, abandonment, the disappointments of a great house, the dissolution of a lineage ("Little Caesar's son"), drunkenness, disturbing the peace, and of course what Frank Sinatra called "splitsville"—divorce. *Confidential* even quoted Judge Wolfson handing down the divorce decree to Manny's bride: "You should be grateful you have such a great father-in-law. He's a great man."

Confidential was nothing if not a magazine of bad manners. Addresses were given out if at all possible. Nancy Robinson could be found after the divorce "in her shabby, down-at-the-heels apartment at 405 South Barrington Street." She came to "plead for money to feed the baby" at the Robinsons' "million dollar mansion" at 910 Rexford Drive. Howard Rushmore, the ex-Communist, still liked to write about the poor having to go begging at the decadent palaces of the rich.

Confidential claimed to be doing the Robinson family a public service, asking "impertinent questions" of an "old man" in order to spare him embarrassment and real heartache. In fact, Eddie Robinson knew all there was to know about his son, even before the March 1956 issue of *Confidential*. Now, thanks to Robert Harrison, everyone in America also knew.

It all seemed so hopeless. *Little Caesar* was just a movie, released before Manny was even born. Eddie Robinson played a tough, omnipotent gangster. With his fedora, a cigar screwed into the side of his mouth, and a gat in his hand, his portrayal of "Rico" Bandello was an iconic image in Depression-era America, an image that haunted Manny Robinson all his life. Every time he got into trouble, the myth of Little Caesar was trotted out to explain it. It didn't matter that it wasn't real. Did anyone suspect Raymond Massey's son of acting like Abe Lincoln?

ONE OF the first producers to come around before Manny's divorce offered the couple a contract with an advance of $250 a week. They signed the contract and paid their rent. Now they were committed to star in something called *Bride of the Gorilla*. When Eddie Robinson Sr. read the contract several weeks later, he told Manny that it was one of the worst he had ever seen.

But Manny found an ingenious way of breaking his contract. Not long after signing to appear in *Bride of the Gorilla*, Manny was arrested for writing a bad check for $138 to a Laguna Beach garage. It was a tough deal. If Manny's father had owned a shoe store or tended bar at the Knickerbocker Hotel, the check would've been covered, nobody would've heard about it again. But the owner of the Laguna Beach garage was trying to teach Manny Robinson a lesson. So instead of going to Eddie Sr., the garage owner went directly to the district attorney.

Bail was set at $10,000 for Manny Robinson. He got out of jail in time to read the *Mirror* headline—it didn't name Manny, but his picture was there, with his head in his hands, his eyebrows grown together, looking woebegone in a glen plaid suit and a striped tie with a huge knot. Manny hated those pictures, hated the way his eyebrows grew together in front. After his first arrest he even went to a salon to have his eyebrows plucked.

Manny often felt exploited by the newspapers. He hated the way they delighted in his troubles, reporting his problems with the same glee as *Confidential*. The story of Manny's acquittal was just a small, one-column story, tucked away inside the city's newspapers. *Confidential* didn't cover it at all. But Manny learned to use the press to his own advantage. Through columnist Paul Coates, Manny shamed his father into releasing money Manny explained had been left to him by his uncle, but which in reality amounted to just a few war bonds. Manny told Coates about the fight in Little Caesar's bedroom, how Eddie threw his son out, even called the police.

"We need the dough," Manny told the columnist. "I can't get a job. The baby's due in April. There'll be doctor bills. We have no place to live. . . . I was drunk. I admit it. But how much can a guy stand? . . . I ran up to his room and grabbed him. I shook him and said, 'For God's sake talk to me, I'm your son.'"

It had been like this all his life.

Little Caesar had tried to be a good father. He tried taking his son to baseball games and to prizefights downtown. But Manny was always afraid of his father. Even as a little kid he was scared of Little Caesar. Manny would plead with him, "Pop, please take the cigar out of your mouth." Manny thought his father always looked so tough with a cigar; without it he was just like any other guy.

After his arrest, the Army didn't want Manny. Even the producers of *Bride of the Gorilla* didn't want him. At least Manny had managed to get out of a bad contract. He tried becoming a salesman for his father's tobacco company, pushing "the Edward G. Robinson blend" on the West Coast. He hated the job of a salesman. He hated going out like Lee J. Cobb as Willy Loman, weighed down with his satchels of tobacco, introducing himself as "Edward G. Robinson Jr."

Eventually, he fell into a job on the radio. Five nights a week for six weeks. Then he had a brainstorm: he would interview his father on the air. The two acted out a scene from Arthur Miller's play *All My Sons*. It was the big scene when the son discovers that the father's been turning out faulty military parts, making him responsible for the death of the second son. The first son confronts the father, finally venting all his hurt and rage. Eddie Sr. had played the father in the movie version, so he knew the part well.

Manny would always say that reading the climactic scene with his father over the airwaves had been the high point of his life. Manny was so moved by the experience, he wanted to persuade his father to try to find a movie they could do together, if only just something for television. Maybe after that Manny would be able to get work on his own. But he couldn't bring himself to say the words. When the program ended, he just stood there and watched his father walk out of the studio.

ALL THE cabdrivers knew Manny Robinson. He had been busted at least four times for driving under the influence and another time for writing that bad check. He was on probation and couldn't risk driving, so he had to rely on taxis for getting around. He ran up enormous bills and charged them to his father. Cabdrivers often roused Eddie Sr. in the middle of the night, standing at his front door with their hands out, waiting to be paid for Manny's nighttime rides.

Manny Robinson was in police custody again in the summer of 1954. The line of questioning soon became clear. They were after him for suspicion of armed robbery. The cops brought in two cabdrivers. Both identified Manny. One of the drivers swore that it was Manny Robinson who had hit him on the head with a flashlight and fled with twenty-seven dollars. Another driver testified that in a separate incident Manny had pointed a gun at him and stole eleven dollars. But Manny claimed he had never seen either man before in his life.

The next day's headline in the paper was "Jail Stars Son as Taxi Bandit." There were three huge pictures of Manny on the front page.

Robinson's own lawyers, Jerry Giesler and Rex Egan, both felt that Manny was too much of a wimp to pull off a robbery. They suspected someone was trying to set him up, knowing that even with a few bottles of Scotch in him, Manny wouldn't do anything so brazen.

Manny's parents entered the court with him every day of the trial. The image wasn't lost on *Confidential*. Eddie, Manny, and Gladys walking down the courthouse steps arm in arm. "Eddie has been trying to play in real life the glory-gone 'Little Caesar' role his father created on celluloid. . . . Young Goldenburg . . . ooops, we mean Robinson, also believes in the Stanislavski (Live your Part) method—only he relives his dad's old crime roles. . . ." They were tightening the screws. They were letting both of the Robinsons know their place. Eddie's father wasn't even really an American—not with a name like Emmanuel Goldenburg. After all, his patriotism was a matter for Congress to decide.

The 1950s were unkind to Edward G. Robinson, shown here with son Manny during a court appearance. In addition to being unjustly tainted by the blacklist, he also endured a messy divorce and had to sell his art collection to pay alimony and creditors. *Bettmann/Corbis.*

The trial began in October 1954 but ended with a hung jury. The D.A.'s office, however, decided against a second trial, and the charges against Manny Robinson were dismissed. Things started looking up for Manny Robinson. In the summer of 1956, he finished a bit part in Josh Logan's *Bus Stop*, the film version of the William Inge play. Manny had also raised some money to mount his own film production of a story called *Cargo of Fear*. Manny was working every day at a real office, attending to the film's casting and every other detail. He had a part in mind for his friend Charlie Chaplin Jr., and they decided to discuss it over dinner.

Later that night, Manny drove Chaplin's friend Marty Barth home. They were just two blocks from Manny's apartment when he steered the car down a steep incline and treacherous curve called Slaughter Hill. His Thunderbird slid out of control and hit a parked car. When he helped Barth from the car, he noticed blood trickling down his face. Barth would lose an eye because of the collision.

Manny earned a sentence of three years' probation and sixty days on an honor farm for his role in the accident. Manny also had to pay Barth's medical bills, and was warned that he'd land back in jail if he violated his probation by drinking.

A deputy led Manny away. He was told to remove his watch, the gold ring that was a present for his bar mitzvah. The deputy held out a manila envelope to catch them. Manny hesitated. He had worn that ring since he was thirteen. "You'd better take off those things," the deputy advised. "Guys have had a finger cut off when another prisoner tried to steal a ring." Manny relinquished his few belongings.

Edward G. Robinson visited Manny at the honor farm. The authorities had to give him a private room to meet with his son, since they thought a celebrity might stir up the other inmates. "I had learned my lesson in jail. But I wasn't the only one," Manny recalled. "I think Mom and Dad had also learned a thing or two. Dad was eager now to do everything to help me with my career."

But the bitter memories would linger. No matter how much progress they made toward reconciliation, Manny and Eddie would always have a troubled relationship. It would always be like that one night Manny invited three of his friends into the Robinson mansion on Rexford Drive. It was late and the house was dark. Manny had brought his friends over to listen to the tape of the radio show he had done with his father. He wanted his friends to hear the scene from *All My Sons* that had closed out the program, maybe the only thing in his life he was proud of.

Manny offered his guests a drink; he always needed one to help him get through the scene, especially the part where the son rages against his father. Manny started to cry a little. He turned his head away so no one would notice.

And then Edward G. Robinson came into the room. He was standing there in his robe and slippers, he was shouting at Manny to stop playing "that damn thing in the middle of the night."

Manny was too embarrassed to speak. Eddie started to hit him across the face. The room was filled with the sound of Manny's voice on the tape recorder, shouting at his father. In between you could hear Eddie's voice shouting at Manny. Manny just stood there with his head down as his father kept hitting him. One of Manny's friends tried pulling Eddie Robinson away from his son. As the tape played on, Manny's voice echoed in the background as he thanked his father for coming on his show.

Edward G. Robinson wrote a memoir that was published just after he died in 1973. In it, he revealed another of the Robinson family's troubles. In addition to being blacklisted by Hollywood and having to deal with Manny's problems, Eddie in the 1950s had to cope with an increasingly ill wife. He confessed in his book that his wife's "episodes" and high-strung manner were in fact symptoms of manic depression and that her "visits" to "spas" were extended stays in mental hospitals. "I lied about Gladys' illness as long as she was alive: I was worried, fearful. . . . I was also, in my heart, ashamed," Robinson wrote. "I tell the truth now, since Gladys sadly died last year and cannot be hurt by my words; because Manny, I think, has always known the truth."

Even after his death, though, Eddie did not relent in his punishment of Manny. In his will, he established a trust fund for Manny from the estate, which included $5 million in Impressionist art Eddie had managed to buy back from the old collection that had been sold and scattered. But Manny would only see his inheritance, Eddie wrote in his will, "on condition that he comport himself in a manner that the trustees believe reasonable." Gladys Robinson, who died in 1972, had bequeathed to her son only a tea set, a baby chair, and a painted portrait of Manny, for what she described in her will as his "unbearable misconduct toward me."

Manny himself would die a year after his father, in February of 1974. Just forty years old, he was found unconscious in the West Hollywood home he shared with his third wife. The death was attributed to natural causes. The second paragraph of his *New York Times* obituary mentioned his "several brushes with the law" and detailed his unsuccessful attempts at an acting career. Sadly, the brief story was the longest notice he'd ever gotten.

CHARLIE CHAPLIN JR. and Sydney Chaplin had been placed by their father in a military academy on Melrose Avenue in Hollywood, which they would describe as run by a sadistic ex-army major who routinely brutalized the two boys. For most of their childhood, Charlie and Sydney rarely came home, even for brief visits with their father. Years after he had left it, Sydney Chaplin would spit and shudder whenever he drove past the school.

Charlie Jr. and Sydney were the offspring of Chaplin's disastrous, short-lived marriage to sixteen-year-old Lolita McMurray, whom the great actor renamed Lita Grey. Chaplin was already famous when Lolita was first introduced to him at the age of six. Her mother had taken her to a Hollywood restaurant to celebrate her birthday when she spotted the famous silent film star and brought her child over to meet Chaplin. She was twelve when one of her mother's friends reintroduced her. Chaplin was impressed enough to cast her as the angel in *The Kid*. Four years later, she appeared as the dance hall girl in *The Gold Rush*. By then she was pregnant with Charles Chaplin Jr., and Lolita's—now Lita's—uncle threatened to ruin the actor if he didn't marry his niece. So Chaplin, Lita, and her mother trundled off to Mexico for a hasty wedding. Charlie Chaplin Jr. arrived in June 1925. Sydney was born less than a year later in March 1926. Their parents divorced soon afterward.

As an adult, Sydney held court at the Beverly Hills Tennis Club and liked going to nightclubs like Ciro's or the Trocadero and eateries like Romanoff's, Perino's, and Chasen's. He wanted to enjoy himself and the Hollywood he had been isolated from during his childhood.

Sydney understood what a mixed blessing it was to have a famous name. He often would tell people he was related to Saul Chaplin, the composer who worked for MGM, but he accepted a $300 allowance from his father every month. Some of his friends thought that Sydney would have been better off without the money—it killed his ambition. Sydney never studied or tried very hard to find work. He would turn down films if they interrupted a tennis tournament.

But live theater was something else. The Circle was Hollywood's leading noncommercial theater, the first theater-in-the-round in the United States—a small room in a musty, crumbling building with 150 seats arranged in tiers around a tiny stage about the size of a big backseat in a station wagon. George Boroff, Shelley Winters's brother-in-law, owned it. Everyone associated with the Circle was serious about acting and about the theater. Winters's sister Blanche helped run it. The Circle never had much money, but movie people volunteered to work without pay. Sydney Chaplin, who was also on the Circle's board of directors, lived in an apartment behind the theater. He had never before acted on a stage, but it seemed like a pretty safe way to start. His friends talked him into appearing at the Circle in the James Barrie play *What Every Woman Knows*. Sydney's costar was Ruth Conte, a talented actress from New York who was married to the actor Richard Conte. Sydney asked Jerry Epstein to produce. It would be like Sunday brunch at the Chaplin estate on Summit Drive.

Charlie Chaplin Sr. was restless, especially when he wasn't working on a movie, and there were often long stretches, even years, between movies. That's probably why, all of a sudden, Chaplin decided to direct his son in the play. Hollywood was astonished.

Sydney was in despair. His anger and frustration came out on the court at the Beverly Hills Tennis Club. Shelley Winters watched him playing "as if he wanted to kill." He told her that he wanted to quit the play, that he'd rather pursue some other profession than acting. But, Sydney said, he didn't have any other skills, no special training for any other kind of job. For him, it was either become an actor or reenlist in the Army.

Winters tried to reassure Sydney, telling him everyone understood how difficult live theater could be. She told him how proud the community of actors was that Sydney had accepted the challenge of his first part, the lead in a serious British play.

The New Yorker writer Lillian Ross had befriended Charlie Chaplin and his wife Oona years earlier and he invited her to watch one of the play's rehearsals. Ross, with her well-tuned ear for dialogue, recalled the scene in her book *Moments with Chaplin*.

"Hello, Papa," Sydney said.

"Where's the cast?" Chaplin asked.

Epstein and Sydney told the actors to take their places. Chaplin Sr. started talking the moment the rehearsal got under way. He frowned at his cast from the front row. "All right, let's go, let's go," he said, already cracking the whip. "Keep it going, keep it going."

Ruth Conte was playing the part of the spinster daughter of a Scottish quarry owner. "Don't let it get doleful!" Chaplin cautioned. "Make it very warm. It's cold outside, but you get a glow, a warm glow."

After the actors had spoken a few more lines, he said, "Get the feeling of embarrassment rather than self-pity. I like that. I like that. It's more noble. Get all the murkiness out of it now."

Shelley Winters, her friend Marilyn Monroe, and Monroe's acting coach, Natasha Lytess, snuck into the Circle to watch their friend Sydney being directed by his father. They sat hushed in the back of the tiny theater. Charlie Sr. remained in his seat, biting his thumbnail. He watched quietly—until his son walked onstage. Sydney was playing the ambitious young man who breaks into the home of the quarry owner to study his books.

Sydney's first action onstage was to pull a book from the shelf and sit down to read it. Chaplin immediately leapt up and pushed his son out of the chair, performing the scene himself. He wanted to show his son how a stranger would assert himself in someone else's house. "Get the drama in this, Sydney," Chaplin said, and stepped off the tiny stage.

The actor hunched his shoulders and watched his son intently. But he jumped to his feet again a moment later. "Sydney, for Christ's sake, get rid of that singsong! Get rid of those inflections. Just say the thing. You're not cheeky. You're never cheeky. You're indignant. They think you're a burglar, and goddammit, you're not. You're a student."

Suddenly Natasha Lytess spoke up from the back of the theater. "Mr. Chaplin, you mustn't do that to your actors."

Marilyn Monroe and Shelley Winters slumped in their chairs. Chaplin stopped the rehearsal and thundered at the four figures in the dark, "Who invited you people to this rehearsal?"

Sydney spoke first. "Dad, I invited them. Ruth and I have the blocking now, and I would like Shelley and her friends to watch a run-through of the first scene." Sydney was ashamed to admit to his father that he had invited a drama coach to his first rehearsal.

The problem, Shelley Winters recalled, was that Chaplin was acting out all the roles himself—none of his actors could do them as well as he. It squelched any creativity on the part of his cast, and it made Sydney feel that there was no point in even trying. He might as well just go back to the tennis courts, where occasionally he could still beat his father.

Later, Sydney and his brother Charlie Jr. appeared in their father's movie *Limelight* (1952). "Now at last, it was Syd's and my turn to be targets of that drive for perfection," Charlie Jr. recalled. "After that experience, I was more than ever convinced that my father's towering reputation and his seething intensity make it almost impossible for those working under him to assert their own personality."

JOHN BARRYMORE JR. had always felt like an alien. He had his father's handsome profile and jet black hair. If anything, he was even better looking—sweeter, somehow. As a young man, photographers always got him to pose in profile, just like his famous father. He was a good actor, too, but—like Manny and both of the Chaplin boys—if it weren't for bad luck he wouldn't have had any luck at all. Like the other "Juniors," he set out at an early age to guarantee that bad luck, beginning by running away from his family at the age of sixteen. But the airport cops at La Guardia recognized the runaway because of his striking resemblance to John Barrymore Sr., and sent the unhappy teenager home.

John Jr. avoided acting in high school, afraid to compete with the oppressive fame of his theatrical family, but by the age of seventeen he had his first film contract as an actor appearing in the 1950 film *The Sundowners*. He also agreed to appear with his cousin Ethel Miglietta in the Salt Creek, Illinois, Summer Theater production of *The Hasty Heart*. But he quit abruptly after just two weeks of rehearsal. "It isn't time yet," he said. "I'm upholding the family name by staying off the stage." It was an excuse he would give time and again, and he gained a reputation for panicking, breaking contracts, and failing to show up at rehearsals. "John let the family down," his aunt Ethel told the press when her seventeen-year-old nephew walked out on *The Hasty Heart*.

He wasn't bad in a number of films—particularly as the mother-ridden "lipstick murderer" in *While the City Sleeps* in 1956, another example of the "sick" model of teenage criminal behavior. John had clashed with Fritz Lang, the film's director, but Lang managed to coax a first-rate performance from the anxious young actor, arguably the best of John's checkered career.

John's turmoil led to wrecked marriages, drunk and disorderly charges, lawsuits, arrests for drunken driving—even a hit-and-run acci-

"That name just brought me nothing but trouble," said John Barrymore Jr., son of "the great profile" John Barrymore. Drew Barrymore, John Jr.'s daughter, would find greater success with the family name. *Bettmann/Corbis.*

dent. It was an impossible situation for him—his family's expectations had forced him to flower before his time. Like Manny Robinson, John Barrymore Jr. discovered that it was easier making news for being bad than for being good.

The 1958 film *High School Confidential!* would bring two of the "Juniors" together: John Barrymore and Charlie Chaplin. Made the year after *Confidential* magazine's collapse, this unexpectedly compelling film about juvenile delinquency and the evils of marijuana also starred Michael Landon as a "good" teenager, Mamie Van Doren as a sex-starved seductress, Russ Tamblyn as an undercover agent posing as a teenager, and Jackie Coogan in a small but important role as a drug kingpin. Coogan had made his film debut in 1920, in Chaplin's silent film *The Kid*, so his very presence in *High School Confidential!* provided a connection for Charlie Jr. to his old man.

Barrymore plays a predatory high school delinquent with pomaded hair bent on supplying his teenage cronies with both soft and hard drugs for an underworld dope pusher. (By now Barrymore had dropped the "Jr." from his name and, at his agent's suggestion, used the name John Drew Barrymore. "That name just brought me nothing but trouble," he said.)

Sadly, Barrymore's role was prophetic, as the actor would spend most of the sixties making a career out of drugs, turning himself into the darling of a circle of drugged-out hippies. "St. John," they called him, taking his words as gospel. He received three years' probation after a 1966 drug raid, and after a car accident, officers who arrived on the scene found marijuana and he served sixty days in jail in Indio, California. He would be reduced to selling his father's gun collection for drugs and trading his parents' love letters for a place to sleep.

The critics thought *High School Confidential!* a piece of low-life exploitation, especially with its over-the-top performance by Mamie Van Doren as Russ Tamblyn's seductive aunt. "I did my part to corrupt [Tamblyn]," Van Doren later said. "In fact, my seduction of Russ barely made it past the censors. It was considered too sexy in the 1950s, though it contributed to the unexpected success of the movie."

High School Confidential! made money for its producer, Albert Zugsmith, as did his other trashy films—*The Private Lives of Adam and Eve*, *Teacher Was a Sexpot*, *Confessions of an Opium Eater*, and the bizarrely titled *Movie Star American Style*, or *LSD, I Hate You*. Zugsmith, however, also produced fine movies such as Doug Sirk's glossy film *Written on the Wind* in 1956 and Orson Welles's great *Touch of Evil* in 1958—the same year Zugsmith produced *High School Confidential!*

Charlie Jr. has few lines in the film, playing a narcotics officer working undercover as a waiter in the local teenage hangout. It was an easy role for Chaplin's eldest son—he had spent his life undercover, seldom heard from. He was not only under his father's massive shadow but under his younger brother's as well, ever since he complained that Sydney was given the larger role in his father's famous film *Limelight*.

Chaplin Sr. could never admit to himself that his first son was emotionally frail, requiring special attention. He never even mentioned Charlie Jr.; in fact, he hardly ever mentioned Sydney, or anything else about his first family.

While appearing in *High School Confidential!*, Charlie Jr. was making his own bid for fame by secretly writing his memoirs, with help from a married couple he had befriended in Los Angeles:

> For the longest time Syd and I didn't see our father at all. We were too young to be impressed by the fact that he was the great Charlie Chaplin. And certainly we didn't remember the bitterness of his brief marriage to our mother that ended in separation and divorce. It was a story I was to hear in later years under unhappy circumstances.

"I am proud of my name," he wrote in his book, "but it is hard to live with."

In the late 1960s, long after Chaplin Sr., his wife Oona, and their new family had left America and were living in Vevey, Switzerland, word reached them that Charlie Chaplin Jr. had died suddenly.

He had named his own memoir *My Father, Charlie Chaplin*.

CHAPTER 5

REQUIEM FOR A REBEL: NICHOLAS RAY AND THE DOOMED TRINITY

IN THE FALL of 1954, director Nicholas Ray decided he wanted to make a movie about "kids growing up and their problems." Warner Brothers wanted to make a movie about kids growing up that would be a box office hit. The rise in juvenile delinquency was America's newest fear and even the comic book was a subject for congressional investigation. While Hollywood saw an opportunity, Nick Ray saw a real crisis—the suburban *tristesse* of America's youth afflicted with a "terrifying, morose aimlessness."

What began as a studio's exploitation of a social trend became a sophisticated, subtle exploration of the nature of delinquency in Ray's *Rebel Without a Cause*. He turned the very making of the film into an act of rebellion, flouting convention as he cast and directed his actors. Ray was the anti-dictator, giving his young stars, especially James Dean, free rein in the creation of their characters. The result was a profound and complicated fable, a sort of teenage *Hamlet*.

Nicholas Ray was the perfect person to foment this creative revolution. He had a dramatic life even before he was born. His grandfather dropped dead on a Wisconsin street while carrying the first deer of the hunting season slung over his shoulders. While still in school, Ray received a Taliesin Fellowship to study architecture with Frank Lloyd Wright. After falling out with

Wright, he became involved with the WPA Federal Theater of Action, where he first met producer John Houseman and cut his teeth as an actor. He later traveled through Depression-era America researching and recording ballads with folklorist Alan Lomax.

Ray was a complicated and tragic man—a Romantic figure, a *poet maudit* of film. He was an alcoholic and a gambler who once lost $30,000 in one sitting at a Las Vegas craps table, the night before he was to marry actress Gloria Grahame. He went ahead with the marriage because Grahame was pregnant but admitted that he didn't love her, that "there was something vindictive about me. . . . I wanted to be absolutely broke." John Houseman, a lifelong friend and producer of two of Ray's best early features, described him as "inarticulate and garrulous, ingenuous and pretentious; his mind was filled with original ideas which he found difficult to express in an understandable form. . . . He left a trail of damaged lives behind him—not as a seducer, but as a husband, lover and father."

By 1954, when Ray began work on the story that would become *Rebel Without a Cause*, he had already made a series of dark, critically acclaimed films, including *They Live by Night* (1949), *In a Lonely Place* (1950), and *Johnny Guitar* (1954). Ray's best films earned him the adulation of French cinema's nouvelle vague, especially auteur Jean Luc Godard, who wrote, "There was theater (Griffith), poetry (Murnau), painting (Rossellini), dance (Eisenstein), and music (Renoir). Henceforth, there is cinema. And the cinema is Nicholas Ray." The independent filmmaker Jim Jarmusch called Nick Ray "my idol—a legend, the outcast Hollywood rebel, white hair, black eyepatch, and a head full of subversion and controlled substances. . . ." To film critic David Thomson, Ray was "the very talented, very self-destructive hero director of the late 1950s."

Rebel Without a Cause is arguably Nicholas Ray's most psychologically revealing film. Ray, who grew up with an absent, alcoholic father in Wisconsin and was raised by women, would create a kind of family from his actors, playing father to Sal Mineo, James Dean, and Natalie Wood. The family he gathered around him, though, would be more troubled than any onscreen, giving rise to the popular fiction that a "curse" hung over the film. Its principal actors—the doomed

Sal Mineo (left), Natalie Wood, and James Dean in a scene from *Rebel Without a Cause,* a story about dysfunctional families. When hundreds of kids auditioned for the film, director Nicholas Ray asked each of them, "How do you get along with your mother?" *Courtesy of the Academy of Motion Picture Arts and Sciences.*

trinity of Dean, Wood, and Mineo—would die violent, premature deaths. The "family" was unhealthy in other ways: there were rumors that forty-four-year-old Nick Ray was having sex with all three of his young actors, two of them just sixteen, during the making of *Rebel Without a Cause.*

John Houseman described Nick Ray in his 1979 memoir as "a potential homosexual with a deep, passionate and constant need for female love. . . ." One of the reasons given by the homophobic and authoritarian Frank Lloyd Wright for banishing Nick Ray from his enclave was that he thought Ray was a homosexual. More recently, the novelist and screenwriter Gavin Lambert disclosed in a memoir about the English director Lindsay Anderson that he and Nicholas Ray had had an affair while Lambert served as Ray's apprentice on his 1956 film *Bigger Than Life.* This revelation helps to explain Ray's onscreen adoration of a number of his male leads, including Farley Granger, John Derek, and James Dean—and it underlines the erotic tension between Sal Mineo's and James Dean's characters in *Rebel.*

Ray apparently recognized Sal Mineo's homosexuality even before the young actor realized it. According to Gore Vidal, Ray initiated Mineo at the Chateau Marmont, the castellated, Norman-style hotel just off Sunset Boulevard, as he prepared him for the role of Plato. "There were several bungalows around the pool," Vidal wrote in *Palimpsest: A Memoir.* "Nick Ray lived in one, preparing *Rebel Without a Cause* and rather openly having an affair with the adolescent Sal Mineo, while the sallow James Dean skulked in and out. . . ."

Though *Rebel* has been described as "the first film to catch the revolutionary unease of the young generation," it is also among the first mainstream American films to present a veiled, homoerotic relationship between its two male leads. Stewart Stern, who eventually cowrote the script with Nicholas Ray, described Plato as "the kid in school who would have been tagged a faggot. He hadn't shaved yet, and he had a picture of Alan Ladd in his locker. . . ." Plato's crush on Jim Stark is evident from the first scene, reflected in Plato's soulful, adoring gaze, and rising to his invitation to Stark to spend the night with him: "We could talk and in the morning we could have breakfast like my dad used to." In a film test of the scene in which Plato (Sal Mineo), Jim Stark (James Dean), and Judy (Natalie Wood) are hiding out in a derelict mansion—the very mansion in which *Sunset Boulevard* was filmed four years earlier—the spirited horseplay between the two young male actors suggests a love scene in which Natalie Wood is merely a bystander. Sal Mineo later claimed that "in Plato he had created the first gay teenager in films."

Indeed, Mineo portrays Plato as noticeably feminine, sometimes more girlish than the tough young women of "the gang." While Judy thrills to the danger of the "chickie run," her eyes gleaming as she drops her arms and signals the start of the race, Plato crosses his fingers and trembles, visibly disturbed by the spectacle. When he sees that Jim has survived the reckless trial, Plato fairly pants with relief and smiles nervously to himself. Later, when Jim offers his red jacket to his shivering friend, Plato takes it willingly. He clutches it to his body for a moment and smells it, breathing in Jim's scent the way a lovestruck girlfriend might.

But in 1954, when *Confidential* was busy outing "the lavender closet," the censors at the Hays Office, which enforced the Production Code, forced Nick Ray to tone down the script's erotic element between Plato and Jim Stark. That meant nixing a screen kiss Ray had scripted between the two young men. Geoffrey Shurlock, a Production Code officer, wrote a memo to Jack L. Warner, dated March 22, 1955: "It is of course vital that there be no inference of a questionable or homosexual relationship between Plato and Jim." And yet that inference remains as one of the key elements that makes *Rebel Without a Cause* truly revolutionary and perennially fresh.

In Freudian terms, *Rebel*'s thinly disguised, homoerotic content was the return of the repressed: the troubling, ambiguous sexual content that had been leeched out of American film by the conformity, paranoia, and optimism of the decade. Through James Dean—who, some claim, patterned his very persona on Nicholas Ray—the director introduced a new model of American masculinity: the "sensitive" male whose expression of manhood requires not only courage but compassion and love, even love for another male. The stoicism of John Wayne is answered by the emotionalism of James Dean, who demonstrates the courage to *feel* as well as the courage to *act*. When Dean as Jim Stark breaks down weeping at the end of the film, wrapping his arms around the legs of his emasculated father—only *then* does Stark's father discover his backbone and reclaim his masculinity.

That Ray recognized James Dean's bisexuality could only have helped flesh out the character of Jim Stark. But first had to come the story. In 1946, Warner Brothers producer Jerry Wald bought the rights to the book—and to the title—*Rebel Without a Cause*. Written by Dr. Robert M. Lindner, the nonfiction book told the story of a murderous teen whose behavior is blamed on his childhood traumas. Warner Brothers commissioned a script for *Rebel*, and its chief talent scout, William Orr, traveled to New York to cast the lead. Orr kept hearing about an actor named Marlon Brando and thought he might be the brooding young man the part required. "When he came for his screen test, he didn't say a word. He just sat there tearing up an envelope into little pieces," Orr remembered. "So I figured he must be a genius and signed him." But the film would never be made with Brando. The script sat gathering dust at Warner Brothers until the fall of 1954, when Ray wanted to make an important film that he "believed in," a film about troubled teenagers.

His decision was well timed. The American press had made juvenile delinquency the new, hot topic and Brando's *The Wild One* had been a low-budget hit. Ray was coming off the unexpected success of *Johnny Guitar,* and Warner Brothers was thrilled that he wanted to make a film about delinquency, hoping to cash in on the trend. But Ray didn't want to tell another story of alienated teens from poor neighborhoods. He wanted instead to explore the idea of delinquency among middle-class teenagers, kids who would steal a car just for "kicks" when there were two cars already parked in the garage. Thus when the studio suggested that Ray adapt the already completed script based on Dr. Lindner's case study, he rejected the idea. The psychotic protagonist of Lindner's book did not appeal to Ray. He imagined his delinquents differently. They would act out because they felt unloved, their wounds caused by affluent but ineffectual parents—especially by the absence of a strong father, just as Ray himself had felt the loss of his own unreliable father. Ray had been raised by his mother and grandmother, his father dying drunk and alone in a shabby apartment by the time Ray was sixteen.

In September 1954, Ray wrote a slightly bizarre, almost sadomasochistic original treatment entitled *The Blind Run*. The first page of the story laid out three scenes:

> A Park—Night. A man aflame is running directly toward the camera. An officer and a bench sitter run toward him, taking off their coats, then begin smothering the flames. As they do, we cut to: A wide-eyed youth of fourteen or fifteen who has been staring at the scene and who now runs behind the trees and disappears.
>
> Waterfront—Night. A girl, sixteen, stripped to the waist, is surrounded by and being whipped by three teenagers. There is a scream and a police whistle, and the boys disappear.
>
> Int. car—Sepulveda Boulevard—night. Two boys, two girls—half way up the hill going away from the valley. The lights are out on the car and they are moving very rapidly.
>
> Interior second car. Three boys, one girl—half way down the Sepulveda incline, going toward the valley. The lights are out on

their car. Both cars approach the tunnel and the faces of both groups of kids are tense with anticipation. They crash head-on.

While none of these scenes actually made it into the final version of *Rebel Without a Cause*, the essential themes of alienation and teenage angst are there. Even the "chickie-run" scene is prefigured. Ray's dark vignettes also lay the foundations for the three main characters of Jim, Judy, and Plato. Yet he wanted the story to have a classic theme and to follow the arc of great drama. In a script note to himself Ray wrote, "A boy wants to be a man—quick." He also wanted the romance between Jim and Judy to borrow some of its frisson from Shakespeare's *Romeo and Juliet*, which Ray said "has always struck me as the best play written about juvenile delinquency." He had already explored the theme of doomed, young lovers in *They Live by Night*.

Ray's initial seventeen-page treatment could not have been filmed in the 1950s. It was too lurid to pass the Production Code censors, so Ray set about finding a screenwriter. His first choice was Clifford Odets, who had written about the angry young men of an earlier generation—Ray's generation—who came of age during the Depression. Odets had written dialogue for rebels *with* causes, so Ray thought he'd be the perfect choice for a story about rebels of the atomic age. But Jack L. Warner didn't care; he vetoed Ray's suggestion. While Odets didn't write the screenplay, though, he still influenced it. Ray consulted Odets like an oracle, heeding his advice about how to write a hero. "Try to find the keg of dynamite he's sitting on," Odets told Ray. "That one single concept helped me tremendously in building the character," Ray remembered. And it was Odets who supplied Jim's wail of injustice—"I got the bullets!"—just as Plato is gunned down by a trigger-happy cop at the film's climactic finale.

Instead of Odets, Warner Brothers assigned Leon Uris, who had just written a war picture called *Battle Cry*, an adaptation of his best-selling novel and a big hit for the studio. But Ray took an almost instant dislike to Uris and his solitary way of working. Perhaps because he felt proprietary about the story, Ray even told his producer to exclude Uris from the crew's meetings with local police and social workers. Although Uris established key plot points such as the deadly game of "chicken" instead of a "blind run" and the fact that the main characters all go to the same school, he and Ray could not work together. In a swipe at the director, Uris had named the "normal" suburban town of the film's setting "Rayfield." Ray could not forgive the condescension. "It made me vomit," he said nearly twenty years later. "I didn't read the rest of it."

Ray next hired Irving Shulman to write the screenplay. Shulman wrote one of the first novels about juvenile delinquency, *The Amboy Dukes*. Published in 1947, the book took its compelling details from Shulman's experiences as a schoolteacher. He'd later grow rich off sensational celebrity biographies such as *Harlow* and *Valentino*. Shulman worked for about three months, dictating a 164-page script. Although Shulman was credited with the film's "adaptation," Ray was unsatisfied with his version. The director and the screenwriter clashed over a key scene, Ray insisting that Plato should seek shelter at the Griffith Park Planetarium instead of his own home. Shulman thought working with

Director Nick Ray (left) was rumored to have had affairs with both James Dean and Natalie Wood. The "deserted mansion" where he filmed them in this scene from *Rebel* was used by Billy Wilder in *Sunset Boulevard. Courtesy of the Academy of Motion Pictures Arts and Sciences.*

Ray began to take on a "nightmarish quality" and was anxious to publish his adapted screenplay as a novel. By then, James Dean had tentatively agreed to star in *Rebel*, and when he and Shulman failed to establish any real rapport, the screenwriter wanted to quit the project.

Nick Ray cast James Dean in the role of Jim Stark long before he had a finished script. Just after Ray completed his seventeen-page original treatment of *Rebel* in the fall of 1954, director Elia Kazan invited him to screen a rough-cut version of *East of Eden*, in which Dean debuted as the troubled Cal Trask. (Ray would name Dean's character in Rebel "Stark" as an anagram of Trask, a tribute to Dean's dazzling performance in Kazan's film.) "Leonard Rosenman was there, improvising at the piano, and Jimmy was there, aloof and solitary; we hardly exchanged a word," Ray remembered. But the two men would talk about Ray's new project when Dean visited the Warner's lot. Ray sensed that Dean was warily curious about *Rebel* and recognized that the two were "like a couple of Siamese cats sniffing each other out." With *East of Eden* about to be released, and Dean's performance in it already the talk of Hollywood, Warner Brothers knew he was on the cusp of stardom and steered him away from rogue directors like Ray. "It would be foolish, they told him, to appear in any film not based on a best-seller . . . not directed by Elia Kazan, George Stevens, John Huston or William Wyler," Ray said, but Dean wasn't "the kind of person to take such advice very seriously. . . ."

And Ray ignored the advice he received from Kazan about working with James Dean. Kazan had complained that the novice actor began "throwing his weight around" at the end of *East of Eden*, that he was abusive and sulked if he didn't get his way. But Dean and Ray seemed to enjoy the air of defiance about their unexpected, unendorsed partnership. Despite their affinity for each other, though, Dean remained reluctant and left for New York in December of 1954, without accepting the leading role in *Rebel*.

Ray, too, would travel to New York. He visited Dean just before Christmas, climbing the stairs to his fifth-floor walk-up on West Sixty-eighth Street. Ray remembered the bohemian atmosphere of the apartment, with its two small porthole windows, its piles of books, its capes and bullfighting posters. "The only light came from the scrap-wood and fruit boxes burning in the fireplace," Ray said. Dean played one record after another on the phonograph: African tribal music, Dave Brubeck, Haydn.

Ray and Dean dined together almost every night, sometimes joined by Ray's young son Tony. Ray saw his son as similar to the character of Plato in *Rebel*, and he wanted Tony's observations of Dean. Ray's son admired the young actor and noticed how comfortable Dean was around his fellow actors in the city and how intensely they discussed philosophy and the theater. Tony also saw Dean at larger gatherings with people he barely knew, how he would sit in the corner like a "healing wound." They spent a sad, rainy New York afternoon watching the French comedian Jacques Tati in *The Big Day* and playing with umbrellas at an umbrella store. (Nick Ray would later develop an aversion to umbrellas and their pointy tips, after he lost the vision in one eye.) Dean was unshaven and wrapped in a dark trench coat, wearing glasses on the end of his nose. Ray once joined Dean at a restaurant where the young actor wondered aloud, "Where are my friends?" Four of Dean's closest friends were with him at the table, but before any of them could answer, Dean got up and walked out. "Every day he threw himself upon the world, like a starved animal after a scrap of food," Ray remembered.

The rumor of an affair between Nick Ray and James Dean stems from those days—and one night—that Nick spent with Dean in his cramped New York apartment. It would become clear to observers that Dean admired Ray and in some ways patterned himself after the rebel director, down to the blue jeans and T-shirt, and even the hesitant, inarticulate speech for which Ray was known. Leonard Rosenman, *Rebel*'s modernist composer, thought the two men shared "a pathological desire for tension." Donald Spoto, one of James Dean's many biographers, noted that "Jimmy learned much from Ray—about food and wine, about architecture and film direction, and about the hazards of casual sex." When Dean confided to the director that he had a case of crabs, Ray took him to the drugstore and introduced him to a delousing solution called Cuprex. Later, against Elia Kazan's advice, Ray encouraged James Dean's passion for racing his Porsche Speedster. Ray clearly relished his own persona as a risk-taking outsider, and that posture was not lost on James Dean. ". . . [W]hat was all this fuss about Dean," asked Susan Schwartz Ray, the director's fourth and last wife, "when Dean was so clearly—to me anyway—aping Nick?"

The last night before Ray returned to Hollywood, the two men dined at Minetta Tavern on Macdougal Street in Greenwich Village. Ray sensed that Dean was close to accepting the role in *Rebel Without a Cause*, but the young actor seemed to be toying with him. The two had actually parted and Ray had begun to walk away when Dean called out after him, "I want to do your film, but don't tell those bastards at Warner's."

The ostensible reason for Ray's trip hadn't been to woo Dean but to interview other young actors for parts in *Rebel*. He talked to many pupils of Lee Strasberg, who led the Actor's Studio. He considered Method actors such as John Cassavetes, Lee Remick, and Carroll Baker, among others, but the director did not cast any of them in his film. Dean himself had never been a formal student of the Method. Strasberg had kicked him out after only three sessions.

Back in Hollywood, Ray was obsessed by his singular vision for the film, but seemed unable to articulate for a screenwriter how that vision should take shape. Each screenwriter had advanced the story, but Ray still had no script—until a young writer almost intuitively sussed out what the director had in mind. Stewart Stern, a New Yorker in his early thirties, had written a Fred Zinnemann movie starring Paul Newman called *Teresa*, which Nick Ray admired. He also came recommended by Leonard Rosenman, who had also written the score for *East of Eden*. Signed in January of 1955, Stern devoted himself to the project, posing as a social worker to spend ten days observing cases at juvenile court. He and Ray worked together in marathon writing sessions that went all night, in agreement that the "delinquency" should be relegated to the background.

Stern understood that Ray, like many artists, was childlike himself. The writer saw *Rebel* as a contemporary version of *Peter Pan*—a circle of lost boys trying to live in a world without adults. Stern also connected with the mercurial James Dean. The two liked to imitate animal calls, a bit of business that found its way into the movie when Jim "moos" as the lecturer points to the constellation Taurus on the planetarium's domed ceiling. (Ian Wolfe, who played the lecturer in *Rebel*, also played the stern, disapproving doctor who refuses to help Shelley Winters in *A Place in the Sun*).

By March of 1955, Stern had shaped Ray's inchoate imaginings into a complete story. The film would take place over the course of one day, beginning in the early morning hours as Jim, Judy, and Plato wait at the police station, guilty of various acts of "delinquency" and anxious over family problems. An outsider at a new school, Jim soon finds himself the target of a bully named Buzz. Their rivalry culminates in a nighttime "chickie run," in which they race stolen cars toward the edge of a cliff. Buzz accidentally plunges to his death. Sickened, Jim wants to go to the police and tell the truth. But—discouraged by his parents and by a sergeant too busy to listen to him—he ends up hiding out with Judy and Plato in a deserted mansion. The other guys in the gang come after Jim, thinking he's ratted them out. They terrorize Plato, who shoots at them with a pistol stolen from his mother and then breaks into the planetarium for shelter. Jim goes to his friend, surreptitiously removes the bullets from the gun, and coaxes Plato into leaving the building. A cop sees the gun and shoots Plato, who dies at Jim's feet just before dawn. The story has all the elements Ray wanted—the trajectory of a classic tragedy, the ersatz family of Jim, Judy, and Plato replacing the troubled families they had run from, and the erotic tension between Plato and Jim. Now the director would find the actors to bring it to life.

Ray announced an open casting call for the supporting roles in "the gang." Hundreds of young actors showed up. The kids had heard that the director needed believable juvenile delinquents. But this wasn't the usual audition. The would-be hoods were called in one by one and interviewed personally by Ray and his producer, David Weisbart, whom Ray had chosen because he was the youngest producer at Warner Brothers. Before they read a line, he asked them strange questions, such as "How do you get along with your mother?" and—more important—"How do you feel about your father?"

Ray rejected actress Margaret O'Brien because her answers to his probing questions were too pat. Jayne Mansfield showed up to audition, but Ray didn't even bother to put film in the camera for her screen test, considering her "an hallucination" from the Warner's casting department. The studio wanted a star for the female lead and considered borrowing Debbie Reynolds from MGM. Ray wanted Natalie Wood, but hesitated about signing her. Although she had already appeared in twenty-one movies by the time she was fifteen, her long résumé hurt, rather than helped, her chances at landing the part of

Judy. "I wasn't going to cast Natalie Wood because she was a child actress, and the only child actress whoever made it, as far as I'm concerned, was Helen Hayes," Ray said. But he soon rethought the idea of casting doe-eyed Natalie.

"The big problem," Wood said in a documentary about the making of *Rebel Without a Cause*, "was that up to that point I had really only played children, I was finding it difficult—and Nick was finding it difficult—to convince the studio that I was out of pigtails." Wood remembered:

> One day I came on an interview with a boyfriend who had cuts on his face and Nick said, "Where did he get that?" Then shortly after that I actually was in a bad car accident with Dennis Hopper. I was in hospital, sort of semi-conscious, the police were asking me my parents phone number, and I kept saying, "Nick Ray, call Nick Ray, the number is . . ." I just kept repeating the number of the Chateau Marmont. So that's who they did call. Nick sent his doctor to the hospital, then he came down and I said, "Nick, they called me a goddamn juvenile delinquent, now do I get the part?" And I got it.

Ray was impressed with Wood's "j.d." credentials. But while visiting her at the hospital, he noticed something else that made him think the young actress could play Judy convincingly. First, she had asked to see the director, not her parents, after the accident. When Natalie Wood's parents did show up, Ray was struck by their reaction. Wood's Russian mother, Maria Gurdin, expressed no interest in her daughter's condition, wailing instead that the accident was terrible because it might upset her husband, Nicholai, who had just suffered a heart attack.

Ray next cast Frank Mazzola as "Crunch." The only member of a real L.A. gang called the Athenians, Mazzola became Ray's official tough guy. He was even given an office at the studio and turned into something of a technical adviser on the film, offering his expertise on the language and rituals of gangs. Ray used Mazzola to lead another Greco-Roman game with the fifty or so boys that survived Ray's initial "audition." "Frank was to come and steal the ball; that was to cause a fight, then everybody would pile in and try to get [it]," Corey Allen remembered. Allen, a handsome young law student at UCLA who had appeared with a local acting company and played bit parts in several films, was cast as Buzz Gunderson, Jim Stark's nemesis at Dawson High and the young man who would eventually befriend Jim moments before crashing his car over the cliff in the "chickie run." But Allen and other members of the gang would be cast by Ray only after enduring a gladiatorial contest in a big amphitheater at Warner's back lot. Ray had about three hundred hopeful young men running up and down the bleachers and then playing a version of King of the Mountain on a platform that had been set up. The actor, who described himself as "not a physical young man at all," got the part of Buzz by not fighting, by walking up the bleachers and by not holding on to the ball. "That's how (Nick) cast that role," recalled Allen twenty years later. "By attitude. From that moment on, Nick and I related to each other. It didn't have to do with getting along, being one of the boys, it had to do with our psychology."

Among the big, roughhousing boys Ray had gathered on the Warner's back lot was a shy, sixteen-year-old named Sal Mineo who had just played the young Tony Curtis in *Six Bridges to Cross*. Raised in the Bronx, the son of an Italian casketmaker, Mineo had been a child actor on Broadway. Nick Ray, "saw this kid in the back who looked like my son except he was prettier." The director invited Mineo to his bungalow at the Chateau Marmont to meet James Dean, to see what kind of chemistry they had together.

"I thought I was dressed pretty sharp for those days—pegged pants, skinny tie, jacket—until Jimmy walked in with his T-shirt and blue jeans," Mineo recalled about the Sunday afternoon meeting. At first, Dean and Mineo didn't hit it off. Ray encouraged them to just talk casually to each other and as they did—about cars, about New York—a camaraderie began to develop.

They read a scene from the script and it flowed naturally. Then Ray asked Mineo if he could do improvisations with Dean. "I had no idea what he was talking about," Mineo remembered. "But I wanted that role very badly. I picked it up from Jimmy, realized that he was doing the scene but making up his own dialogue, and that that's what improvisations are." Ray had found his Plato.

With the three main characters and "the gang" chosen, Nick invited his young cast to the Chateau Marmont to prepare for shooting

Rebel Without a Cause. Ray lived beside the swimming pool in a cozy, two-story bungalow. He loved the dark shingles on the roof and the dark wood accents inside, the big fireplace. He could have privacy there, even cook his own meals. Ray would gather his actors and screenwriter around him in a loose circle in the bungalow's living room. Natalie Wood might disagree with a line for her character, Judy, and suggest an alternative. The atmosphere was creative, collaborative. Ray listened to his young actors. Most of them were still teenagers, thrilled to have their ideas and opinions taken seriously.

But they were vulnerable, too. All of them had come from troubled, if not broken, families. James Dean's mother had died when he was nine, and his cold, rejecting father sent him to live with relatives on a farm in Indiana. Natalie Wood's father was cowed by his Russian wife, a stage mother who pushed Natalie and her sister, Lana, into show business. Ray had his own demons.

It was a confluence of volatile elements, which made for great art and great melodrama offscreen. The young actors adored Ray for his belief in them, for his trust in their abilities, the way he'd sacrifice an idea of his for one of theirs. They admired his own rebelliousness, his boss-hating attitude, even the way he wore blue jeans and went barefoot. Ray, in turn, worshiped their beauty and passion, their very youth. He broke down the barriers between them, encouraging the actors to spend a lot of time together, so that they would act "as one."

"Nick's whole thing was to make us a family, to make the movie come from us rather than from his direction," remembered Steffi Sidney, who played one of the girls in the gang. But the "family" had a darker side of sexual jealousy and exploitation. James Dean told reporter Joe Hyams that he and Natalie Wood had a brief affair, Dean bragging about how they made love in his tiny Porsche, perched high over the lights of Hollywood on Mulholland Drive. The actress also had a relationship with the very young Dennis Hopper, cast as a gang member named Goon, who didn't know that Nicholas Ray had become more than a father figure to her. Leonard Rosenman's wife, Adele, was shocked to see Ray and the sixteen-year-old Wood showering together in a poolside cabana at the Chateau Marmont.

Hopper showed up at a cast party in tears when he learned of their affair. "I got into terrible problems with Nick, because we were both fucking Natalie Wood," Hopper later said. "Her parents were starting to figure it out and Nick snitched on me. I was furious with him: the studio came down on me, and he came out of it as pure as snow."

Ray's affairs with Natalie Wood and Sal Mineo (and possibly with James Dean), and his intense, personal direction of his three principal actors, led to feelings of jealousy and resentment on the set. Dean at one point felt that Ray was devoting too much attention to advising Wood on her portrayal of Judy, and he showed his resentment by sulking. It was as if Ray had become their surrogate father, and each vied for his approval and attention. After all, the role of fathers—their inadequacy, absence, and casual cruelty—is one of the themes of *Rebel Without a Cause.*

The role of Judy's father, played effectively by William Hopper (the son of Hedda Hopper, incidentally), is particularly harsh: a preoccupied man who dotes on his young son but cruelly and repeatedly rebuffs his daughter's need for affection. Then there is Jim Stark's henpecked father, cowering before his wife like a James Thurber cartoon come to life. Ray rather courageously cast Jim Backus in the dramatic role, as the actor was already well known as the voice of the myopic cartoon character Mr. Magoo (a character that James Dean imitates in a late scene). Backus portrays Frank Stark as ineffectual but warm and well meaning. "He always wants to be my pal," Jim cries. Frank watches his son carefully, genuine concern registering on his face. He prophetically warns Jim before he goes off to school, "Watch out about choosing your pals. Don't let them choose you." But Frank always fails his son at key moments, telling Jim not to make a "snap decision" and to "make a list" as Jim ponders how to meet Buzz's challenge of a chickie run. He can't answer Jim's question of what to do "when you have to be a man." One scene even has Jim mistake his father for his mother. "Mom?" Jim asks as he discovers Backus, wearing an apron, down on his hands and knees as he cleans up a tray of food he dropped. Jim later flees the house and his father gives chase, the ruffles of the swirling yellow apron fluttering behind him. As Jim leaves, he flings open the door as if unable to breathe within the confines of the house, and he kicks his foot through a portrait leaning against the wall, a grim-faced image of his tyrannical grandmother.

As Backus's portrayal veers toward caricature, Ray rather too conveniently falls into the "Momism" critique of the American family, which saw strong wives and mothers as battle-axes and emasculators. It was an influential theory throughout the 1950s that came out of Philip Wylie's popular book, *Generation of Vipers*, a shallow analysis of the American family as the cause of teen rebellion. Wylie blamed homosexuality on weak fathers and domineering mothers. Elia "Gadg" Kazan, with whom Ray had worked as an actor onstage and as an assistant on Kazan's *A Tree Grows in Brooklyn*, felt that Ray had taken the easy way out in his portrayal of middle-class parents. "I didn't like the way Nick Ray showed the parents in *Rebel Without a Cause*," Kazan later wrote about his friend's film, "but I'd contributed by the way Ray Massey was shown in [*East of Eden*]. In contrast to these parent figures, all youngsters were supposed to be sensitive and full of 'soul.' This didn't seem true to me. I thought them—Dean, 'Cal' [Trask] and the kid he played in Nick Ray's film—self-pitying, self-dramatizing, and good-for-nothing. I became very impatient with the Dean legend. . . ." But Kazan, of course, had played the seminal role in creating that legend in *East of Eden*.

Kazan was right, though, in realizing that Ray glorifies children and adolescents in *Rebel*. The parents remain two-dimensional, bankrupt both emotionally and ethically. The children, meanwhile, are more fully realized, showing maturity and bravery both in their relationships and in their moral choices. Judy's father's coldness, for instance, is highlighted by her brother's affection. When Judy returns home, shell-shocked after the chickie run, the little boy, Beau, greets her with "Hello, Darling, Baby Pie, Glamourpuss, Sweetie," the pet names her father used to call her. He wraps his arms around Judy and kisses her, offering her the warmth and love her father withheld. The pliable, pitiable Frank Stark is contrasted with Jim, of course, who has the moral courage to confront his role in Buzz's accidental death even as his parents discourage him. Jim and Judy's friendship with Plato also has a fearless quality about it. Jim is new at the high school and doesn't need an obvious loser like Plato hanging around, yet he accepts him. Judy feels unloved by her father, but she doesn't hesitate to comfort Plato at the mansion, patting his head and humming Brahms's lullaby until he falls asleep.

The one adult in *Rebel* who seems to "get" Jim, to understand why Judy might run away from home, is a sympathetic detective named

"Ray." Given Nicholas Ray's interest in understanding middle-class teen angst, and his need to be adored by his young cast, it seems more than coincidental that Jim Stark should seek out a cop named "Ray" when he wants to come clean about the chickie run.

Dean and Ray did seem to understand each other innately, whatever the real nature of their relationship. James Dean was Ray's ideal actor. Ray was impressed by the Romantic Dean, who kept a Colt .45 in his dressing room, where he also slept. "He swerved easily from morbidity to elation," Ray observed. "The depression could lift as completely and unexpectedly as it had settled in. . . . He was intensely determined not to love or be loved. He would never surrender himself." And Dean was so enamored of Ray that the two men planned to set up their own production company—plans that were derailed by Dean's shocking death in a car crash on September 30, 1955, before *Rebel Without a Cause* was even released.

Ray often isolated Dean from the other actors, preferring to work on Jim's scenes alone in his bungalow at the Chateau Marmont, particularly the scenes between Stark and his father. The key scene between Dean and Backus, when Stark returns home from the deadly chickie run, was choreographed completely from improvisations Ray and Dean did in the privacy of the bungalow. Ray felt they had captured the scene so perfectly that Ray had the art director re-create the living room on the set, down to the placement of the furniture and the director's red couch. The moment when Dean cools his fevered brow with a bottle of cold milk came from the unexpected run-through at Ray's house, too, as well as the unusual upside-down shot, meant to show Dean's perspective from the couch as his mother comes down the stairs. Ray thought the shot "was as significant and prominent as a sword in Shakespeare," symbolizing how the family itself was in danger of tipping over, the mother having usurped the father's position.

Though Ray's critique of the American family may have been shallow—even dangerous, as Kazan suggested—the power of *Rebel* is unmistakable. It's greatest strength lay in his brilliant use of his cast, the indelible performances he wrung from the three main actors. Sal Mineo makes Plato's desperation palpable as he fights off the gang members at the bottom of the mansion's empty pool, the same pool where William Holden floated in the opening scene of *Sunset*

Boulevard. Mineo conveys both fragility and fear with his longing looks at Dean, his hands that tremble even as he fires the stolen gun. Natalie Wood triumphs, too, effectively burying her "little girl" image in Judy. Her performance is punctuated by small but telling details, such as when she perches on Jim's car outside the planetarium. She's trying so hard to be a delinquent, to be accepted by the gang, but when she opens her compact, a kind of emotional shadow passes over her face, as if for a moment she doesn't like what she sees. Wood even makes the obligatory screen kiss with James Dean interesting. Her lips slowly, shyly meet his, the slight awkwardness lending the moment its authenticity.

But it was James Dean's performance in *Rebel Without a Cause* that would seal his status as an American icon. Beyond the blue jeans and bravado—which would be enough, really, to endear him to moviegoers forever—the power of Dean was both his subtlety and his great storms of emotion. He could fill with animal rage and hurt, pounding the desk in the police station scene so forcefully that he badly injured his hand. But there was sweetness in Jim's saying "I'm sorry" for stepping on the school insignia, "I'm sorry" to the teacher when he's late to the planetarium. Dean's Jim is gentle, reassuring Plato before the chickie run. He's playful, winking at Judy when he gives her the daisy compact she lost at the police station. Moments later, though, Dean shows us frustration bordering on violence, yanking Jim Backus up by the collar of his felt robe. And while Dean utters some of the film's best lines, including, "If I had one day when I didn't have to be all confused and didn't have to feel ashamed of everything . . . ," the things he doesn't say are equally resonant. When Jim finds his father in an apron, for instance, he stutters, "Dad, don't—I mean, you shouldn't—what're you?" His halting delivery underscores Jim's sense of shame and confusion. Dean, who studied Ray's every mannerism, also may have been imitating Nick Ray's halting speech. John Houseman, in his autobiography *Front & Center*, noted how Ray's speech couldn't seem to keep up with his thoughts and that he often stammered.

In addition to the deft direction of his actors, Ray also added visually compelling elements to *Rebel Without a Cause*. He began the film in black-and-white, but Jack L. Warner, hoping to capitalize on

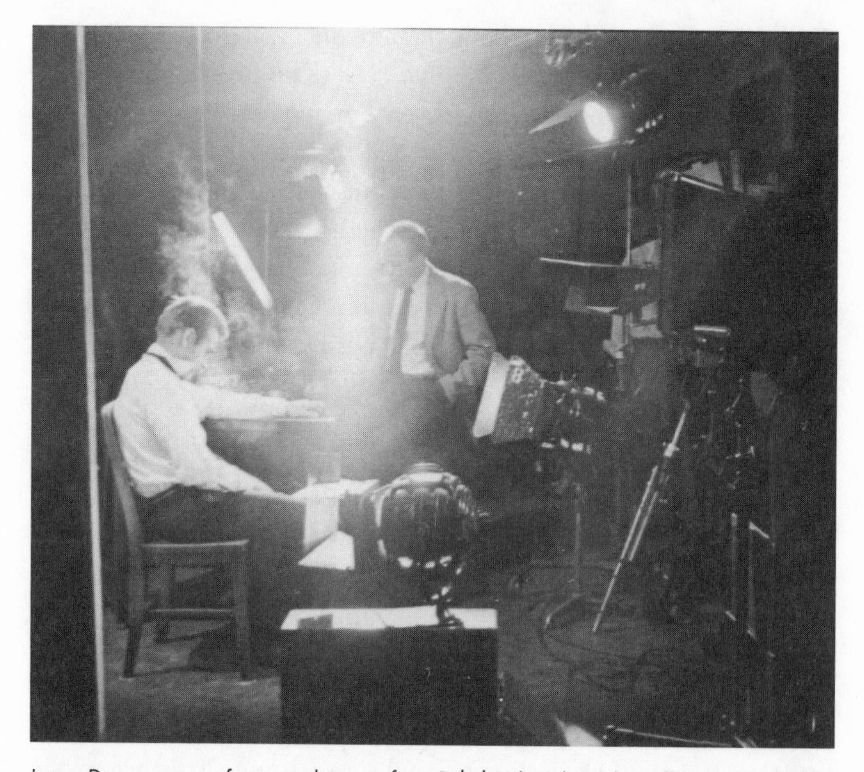

James Dean prepares for an early scene from *Rebel.* When the police officer, played by Ed Platt, summons Jim into his office, he tells Stark to take out his anger on the desk. Dean completed the scene in a single take, pounding the desk so hard he injured his hand. *Courtesy of the Academy of Motion Picture Arts and Sciences.*

Dean's burgeoning stardom, ordered that the film be reshot in Cinemascope. Ray became somewhat of a virtuoso of the wide-screen technique. He had to scrap the black-and-white footage, though, because a contractual condition of Cinemascope required that the film had to be shot in color. It was a good decision: what was lost in terms of noir quality would be made up for in Ray's brilliant use of color. Dean's black leather jacket was traded in for a red windbreaker, and in fact the color red runs through the film like a leitmotif, from Judy's scarlet overcoat and lipstick to Plato's lone red sock and the red sofa in Jim's living room.

Ray's genius shows in more than his vivid use of color and the famous upside-down shot, however. One early scene gives us the fish-eye perspective of Jim, who watches his bickering parents through a peephole at the police station. Ray seemed particularly inspired by the Griffith Park Planetarium and its resonances of eternity and nature. At the end of the lecture, when the astronomy professor illustrates how the world will end "in a burst of gas and fire," Ray—who wrote the professor's speech—focuses not on the explosion but on the reactions of the kids in the audience, recording the fear that flickers on their faces in the red and yellow light. The imagined holocaust lasts a long minute, long enough for Jim, Judy, Plato, and all of us to ponder the problem of "man existing alone." Outside of the planetarium, in the sunny California afternoon, high over Hollywood, Ray captures the parallel shots of an unfolding drama. As Buzz punctures the tire of Jim's car, Ray cuts to Jim, who deflates with the tire, sliding down the wall he leans against until his lungs empty in a sigh of resignation. Jim and Buzz then circle each other with switchblades in a fight as beautifully choreographed as any pas de deux. Ray gives us taut close-ups of the embattled Jim, and then he pulls back to show the telescope spinning on the ledge, spinning as dumbly, as relentlessly, as the Earth on its axis, immune to all human suffering.

Nicholas Ray would receive his only nomination for an Academy Award as the author of the story that became *Rebel Without a Cause*. But he would never again achieve those heights. His Hollywood career would last three more years after *Rebel*, culminating in *Bigger Than Life*, the 1956 Cinemascope film in which James Mason plays a drug-addicted schoolteacher, and the 1957 war picture *Bitter Victory*, starring Richard Burton.

Sal Mineo would also garner an Oscar nomination for his role in *Rebel* and another for playing an Israeli freedom fighter in *Exodus* (1960). Like Ray, however, his career foundered. He appeared in 1971's *Escape From Planet of the Apes*—as an ape—and then in a series of flops, in need of money after making some bad investments. By the 1970s, Mineo had the courage to "come out" about his homosexuality and even took on gay and bisexual roles in Los Angeles theater productions. He was coming home from a rehearsal of *P.S. Your Cat Is Dead* one night in 1976 when a man stabbed him to death in the garage of his apartment building. Because Mineo lived just south of the Sunset Strip, a neighborhood popular with gay men, and because he had taken on gay roles, police at first believed that his death had been some kind of homosexual crime of passion; but in reality it was a random, botched robbery. It would be two years before his killer was found.

Natalie Wood would earn her first Academy Award nomination for her portrayal of Judy. *Rebel* launched her as a successful "grown-up" actress and she worked consistently through the 1960s, landing Oscar nominations for her roles in *Splendor in the Grass* (1961) and *Love With the Proper Stranger* (1963). She saw her star dimming in the 1970s, taking on more roles in television movies than big-screen films. She was trying for a comeback of sorts in November 1981, when she slipped from her yacht and drowned off Catalina Island.

FROM 1959 through 1969, Ray lived in Europe as a self-imposed exile, where he was adored by the nouvelle vague. "In Europe," a producer friend of Ray's once said, "there's somehow more generosity towards the freaky artist, the drunken artist, the crazy artist." He continued to identify with youth culture, and was even seen in Paris during the student uprising of May 1968. One story had him in the Latin Quarter, picking up a bunch of Sorbonne radicals in his car. He opened up his glove compartment and took out a gun, telling the students, "James Dean gave this to me. I'm passing it on to you, because you'll know what to do with it." Just as Dean had once aped the rebel director, the aging Nick Ray now drew power from his association with James Dean.

When he returned to America in 1969, he spent several years as a kind of vagabond, like those hobo-poets he chronicled as a young man. For awhile, he lived in the editing room in Francis Ford Coppola's Zoetrope Studios in the warehouse district in San Francisco. He was editing a film he had made with students, but eventually he was asked to leave. Zoetrope producer Tom Luddy told film critic Jonathan Rosenbaum, "They allowed him to have a couch there and an editing table. . . . It didn't work out too well: disorderliness, chaos, drinking. I used to go back to see him and he'd be zonked out with a gallon of White Almaden Moutain Rhine. Things would break. He'd get into funny situations with things like keys and doors."

There were many abandoned projects, such as making a film about the 1968 Chicago Seven conspiracy trial (Jerry Rubin, Abbie

Hoffman, and Tom Hayden, Jane Fonda's future husband, were among the defendants). Ray had wanted Groucho Marx to portray the trial judge, Julius Hoffman. While the film was never completed, Ray did meet his fourth and last wife, Susan Schwartz, in Chicago. In 1971, he was invited to teach at Harpur College in Binghamton, New York. He shot an experimental movie with his students, called *You Can't Go Home Again*, which the critic and screenwriter Jay Cocks remembered as "strained, scrambled, desperate." Jonathan Rosenbaum, who knew Ray toward the end of his life, described the film as "cinema at the end of its tether; like the fatal test of courage in *Rebel Without a Cause*, a 'blind run' up to and maybe even over the edge of a cliff."

In his last decade of life, Susan Ray helped her husband keep body and soul together, and in 1976 he entered Alcoholics Anonymous. But by then it was too late. He had alienated too many people who could have helped put his career back on track. Occasionally he was still called upon as an actor. Europeans like the German director Wim Wenders had not forgotten him. Wenders cast him with Dennis Hopper (who had resented his affair with Natalie Wood twenty years earlier) in *The American Friend*, and the Polish film director Milos Forman put him in *Hair*, playing a rigid U.S. army general.

In 1977, László Benedek, who had directed Marlon Brando in *The Wild One* (the 1954 movie that made the world safe for *Rebel Without a Cause)*, invited Ray to teach a summer workshop in the Graduate Film Department at New York University School of the Arts, which Benedek headed. The chaotic, outlaw director became an inspiring and much-loved teacher, and the summer workshop turned into an extended appointment. "He was absolutely brilliant," Benedek said. "His students were inspired by him. I don't want to be highfalutin, but it was a spiritual teaching."

But by then—1979—Ray was succumbing to cancer. At the age of sixty-six, he was a recovering alcoholic who had lost an eye to an embolism and who had worn himself out with drugs, overwork, and abuse. Ray hadn't worked in Hollywood in twenty years, and his last, inchoate films were left unfinished and abandoned. Susan Ray described the chaos toward the end of his life: "He drank wine for breakfast, 'a source of vitamin C,' he told me. And then there were the medicaments, a briefcase full that went with him everywhere: needles, ampules of methedrine and B-complex, mysterious pills, bags of grass, blocks of hash, and fresh patches for the right eye. . . . When the moment was right, no matter where he was or with whom, he would drop his trousers to shoot himself in the hip with a mixture extracted from the little glass bottles." Elia Kazan described it as a cancer that had invaded his entire body, including his brain. Knowing he was about to die, Ray agreed to collaborate with Wim Wenders on a final film, called *Lightning Over Water*, part fiction, part documentary. Kazan wrote that Ray, "in desperate straits, knowing he was soon to die, proud to a degree that made it impossible for him to back off . . . he'd participated in a film about his own death, which was the ultimate defiance of death. Since that was the only drama left in his life, he put it on film. There he died as himself."

In the final frames of *Rebel Without a Cause*—after the death of Sal Mineo as Plato, after James Dean and Natalie Wood drive away into the milky dawn—a solitary figure appears, his back to the camera, and walks up the steps to the planetarium. It is Nicholas Ray. While the cameo adds a signature to the film he predicted would become his epitaph, it also asserts that Ray, the creator of the universe we've just seen, is the ultimate rebel outsider among the lost children whose images are still burned on our retinas.

CHAPTER 6

SACRED AND PROFANE: HOLLYWOOD'S RELIGIOUS REVIVAL, *THE ROBE*, AND RICHARD BURTON

TWENTY-FIVE SEARCHLIGHTS swept the dark sky over the Hollywood Bowl one warm night in 1951. The twenty-five thousand seats of the amphitheater were full and five thousand more people crowded onto the hillside. Famed director Cecil B. DeMille, along with studio executives Frank Freeman and Walter Wanger, also turned out for the world premiere of the film *Mr. Texas*. But this wasn't a musical or a romantic comedy made by one of their colleagues at MGM or Twentieth Century Fox. *Mr. Texas* was a production of Billy Graham Films.

Reverend Billy Graham was drawing massive crowds to his tent revivals all across America in the late 1940s and early 1950s. He recognized, though, that he could reach thousands more by harnessing the power of film, by making that flickering image in the darkened theater reflect Christian doctrine. He began in 1950 with a documentary-style movie about his "Crusade" in Portland, Oregon. Directed by Dick Ross, *The Portland Story* was shot on 16-millimeter film and shown mostly in churches. Soon after, Graham had a brainstorm. "Why don't we do a fictional story that would be a dramatic picture, totally Christian and evangelical and evangelistic, appealing to young people?" he asked Ross.

The result was *Mr. Texas,* shot in Fort Worth in early 1951.

Reverend Graham had targeted Fort Worth for his next series of revivals and the story focused on a rodeo rider who is converted to Christianity during Graham's "Crusade." It was a low-budget film, but Graham and his team of evangelicals promoted it like professionals. In what Graham described as "a fit of brashness," they rented the Hollywood Bowl for the film's premiere and invited top directors and studio executives.

But *Mr. Texas* was not quite the film fare that Hollywood's elite were accustomed to viewing. "As I look back, I blush at our brazenness . . . and at the extent to which our youthful zeal sometimes outraced our knowledge," Graham recalled later. The loudspeakers were positioned incorrectly, leaving parts of the audience without any sound at all. And when they could hear the dialogue, people quickly realized that it was not synchronized exactly with the film. The film's script suffered from a lack of sophistication as well. The climax of the movie had the converted cowboy speaking in utter clichés. "All my life I've been riding the wrong trail," he says. "I'm turning back. I'm going God's way. I think it's going to be a wonderful ride. . . ."

And then, in the middle of the premiere screening, the film projector broke. "I wanted the earth to open up and swallow me, I was so embarrassed!" Graham said. He called his "team" together for a brief but intense prayer asking God to help the technicians fix the projector. Five minutes later, it was humming again and the rest of the movie unfurled.

The reviews were terrible, but Graham was so enthusiastic about this new phase in his ministry that he showed *Mr. Texas* to British filmmaker J. Arthur Rank on his next visit to London. "Well," Rank said. ". . . It's not a technically good film but the message comes across." It bothered Graham that his first "fictional" narrative was not smoothly produced, although as late as 1997 he claimed it was still being shown around the world, and that many people had found their Christian faith because of it.

Reverend Graham approached his next cinematic endeavor, *Oiltown U.S.A.* (1954), with more savvy. He treated the press corps to "an authentic chuck wagon luncheon" complete with barbecue beef, corn, and baked beans during the filming. His hospitality earned him many a positive mention in Hollywood gossip columns. Graham also offered free showings of the film at the Shrine Auditorium in Los Angeles. Advertisements for *Oiltown U.S.A.* featured a cross towering over Houston, a cyclone in one corner. "The gripping story of one man's experience with his God!" it read. "In breath-taking NATURAL COLOR." Above it all was the clean, handsome face of the young Reverend Graham.

Oiltown U.S.A. told the story of a greedy oil man who accepts Christ into his life after seeing the world through the eyes of his daughter, played by Colleen Townsend Evans, a real movie star who had left Hollywood to pursue a more faith-based existence. Produced at a cost of $100,000, *Oiltown U.S.A.* featured religious songs and sequences of Graham preaching to sixty thousand people at a stadium revival in Houston. Dramatic footage of the Texas City cyclone disaster of 1945 also was included.

Amateurish as they were, *Mr. Texas* and *Oiltown* helped launch Graham's "film ministry." They proved so popular among churchgoers that over the years he would make about two hundred documentary-style and narrative films. Together with his television show *Hour of Decision*, which drew 6.4 million viewers during its first broadcast in June 1957, the films made Graham a celebrity. Fame has always attracted fame, and movie stars and professional athletes found the charismatic Graham hard to resist. When he brought his "Crusades" to Madison Square Garden in New York in the late summer of 1957, Graham kept the "celebrity gallery" full. Stars in the audience at his sermons included John Wayne, Edward G. Robinson, Greer Garson, Gene Tierney, ice-skater Sonja Henie, boxer Jack Dempsey, and columnists Walter Winchell, Ed Sullivan, and Dorothy Kilgallen.

Reverend Graham seemed to understand the symbiotic nature of his relationship to Hollywood. He realized that the film industry was "anathema to many of the supporters of the Crusade," yet he knew that the stars brought attention to his cause. Perhaps that's why, when he met Gloria Swanson on the Dave Garroway *Today* show in 1957, Graham gushed that "America would be a wonderful place if more of our film stars were like [her]." Swanson, by then, had been married five times. She had had a long affair with the very married and very

Catholic Joseph P. Kennedy. And she had become famous playing femme fatales in silent pictures, a whore in *Sadie Thompson*, and a lunatic obsessed with her much younger lover in *Sunset Boulevard*.

The stars themselves seemed to sense the new trend toward a kind of public spirituality. Movie magazines and gossip columns reported not only on the stars' new homes and hairdos but on their religious feelings as well. *Silver Screen* magazine detailed in December 1952 that Danny Thomas had attached an ivory St. Jude image to his leather script-binder. Gossip columnist Sheilah Graham later shared a story of a "doomed" cancer patient who asked Thomas to pray for him. The man recovered fully and became a priest, prompting Thomas to tell Graham he believed "in miracles."

Religious figures sometimes appeared in Sheilah Graham's column, too, as when she purred in October 1953 that "the handsomest man in Hollywood isn't a movie star—but Father Kelly." Kelly was the force behind a kind of spiritual trend called the "Christopher Movement." "Father is hep," Graham enthused after Kelly characterized a religious film on television with Bob Hope and Bing Crosby as "real crazy."

One of the biggest stories in the columns and fan magazines in 1950 was the decision of young actress Colleen Townsend's decision to leave Hollywood for a life more focused on her Christian beliefs. Louella Parsons in her column praised Townsend's decision to attend a Presbyterian Theological Seminary, where she would train for missionary and educational work. *Modern Screen* devoted a long article to "Colleen's Flight from Hollywood" in May 1950, featuring a photo of the twenty-year-old brunette looking suitably demure and beatific.

The article detailed how, after just three years in pictures, Townsend decided "to devote herself fully, and for always, to spreading the teachings of Christ." She explained that after the filming of *When Willie Comes Marching Home*, a John Ford film released in 1950, she began to "discuss my problem with Him Whom I reach through prayer." She told the magazine it was God's will that she leave movies. Townsend said she wanted more religious training so that she could be more effective in her visits to missions and prisons, so that she could have the answer when a potential convert asked her a question. The money she earned from her movies, Townsend said, would pay for her college courses.

Townsend also shared with readers another moment when she felt the Lord's presence. She had left a prayer meeting in Westwood and was hurrying home along Sunset Boulevard. She had an early call at the studio the next morning and was driving faster than usual when she had a sudden, unexplained urge to slow down. As soon as she did, Townsend's tire blew out. A cab driver helped her with the flat. But as she drove away she felt this "Presence" again, pushing her to turn around, to go back and "witness" to the cabdriver about Christ, how he had warned her to stop speeding. "Oh, no!" she told *Modern Screen* she answered the persistent Presence. "I'm late and I have to get up early. And besides, I hate to go up to strangers and talk like that. . . ." But she did return to the spot on Sunset, only to see the other driver pulling away in his taxi. God was just testing her faith, Colleen concluded, as he had with Abraham and Isaac. Risking embarrassment by proselytizing is not quite the same thing as sacrificing a son to God by one's own hand, but *Modern Screen* let Townsend's rather overstated observation pass without comment.

Despite her earnest intentions, Townsend did not completely retire from films. After marrying Louis Evans Jr., whose father was pastor of Hollywood's First Presbyterian Church, she chose instead to take roles only in movies made by the Protestant Film Commission or Billy Graham. Reverend Graham, in fact, described Townsend as "one of the most dedicated Christians I had met" and cast her as the daughter in *Oiltown*.

While Graham ultimately wanted to save souls, Hollywood's mainstream moviemakers wanted to save their own livelihoods. By 1950 weekly sales of movie tickets had dropped from sixty million to forty million. At the same time, the number of television sets had jumped from about a million in 1948 to eleven million by 1950. The studios needed to shore up profits; they needed something to lure people into theaters and away from the glowing cathode tubes in their living rooms. After *David and Bathsheba* grossed $6 million for Twentieth Century Fox in 1951, Hollywood embraced the moviegoing public's renewed interest in religion. And Fox's studio chief Darryl Zanuck soon imagined pairing an epic religious subject with Cinemascope, a new technique designed to demonstrate the sheer superiority of the movies over television.

Ingenious but desperate, Cinemascope spread out the projected image to nearly twice the size of the average film's. A French professor named Henri Chrétien invented the technology, which was supposed to add a three-dimensional quality to the film without requiring the spectator to wear special glasses. The first film made using this process was the very successful religious tale *The Robe.*

Based on the novel by Lloyd C. Douglas, *The Robe* takes its story from a few lines of the Bible that describe Roman soldiers casting lots at the foot of Jesus' cross to determine who will get his humble garment. From this, Douglas extrapolated a 508-page book about the fictional Marcellus, who wins the robe. The moment it touches his shoulders, the robe feels like a hair shirt to the soldier and he throws it off. Racked by guilt for his role in Jesus' crucifixion, Marcellus later tries to find the robe and destroy it, believing the garment has put a

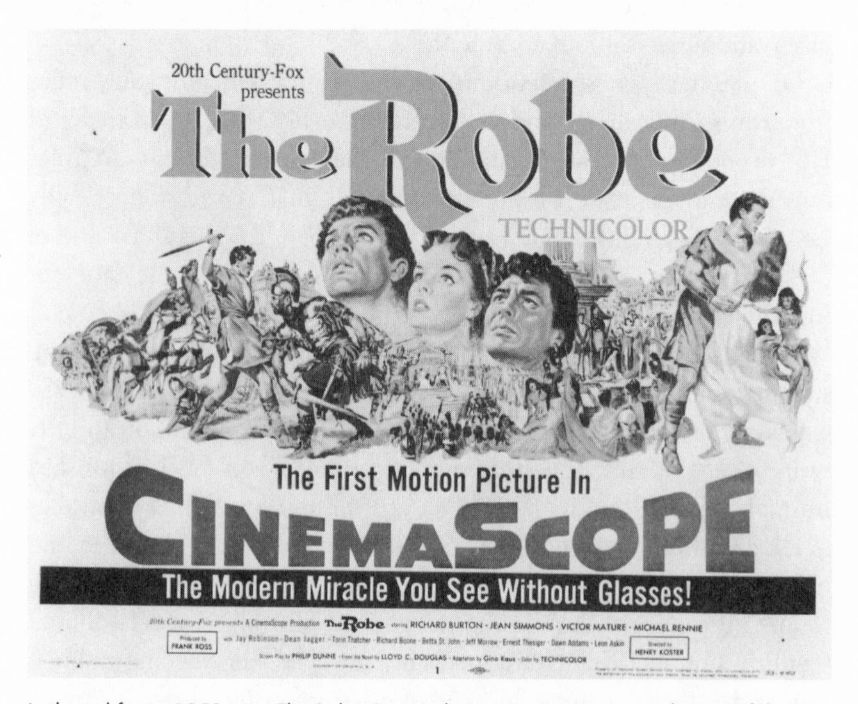

In this ad for its 1953 epic *The Robe,* Twentieth Century Fox promotes the use of the gimmicky wide-screen technique Cinemascope almost more than the film itself. When *The Robe* was a hit, though, it fueled Hollywood's hunger for religious subjects. *Courtesy of the authors.*

curse on him. As he travels through Galilee, though, he learns of the miracles Jesus performed and eventually embraces Christianity. He's later willing to die for his beliefs at the hands of the Roman emperor Caligula.

Frank Ross, a producer at RKO, had bought the rights to *The Robe* in 1942, before the book had even been released in stores. But the breadth of the story, the estimated $5.5 million budget, and the fact that it called for the casting of fifty-one significant roles slowed its production. Ross even began legal proceedings against RKO to force the project to fruition. The *Los Angeles Times* reported that by the time *The Robe* actually did begin production, five hundred actors who had tested for the film had grown too old for their assigned roles.

Ross would never make *The Robe*. Darryl Zanuck bought the rights from RKO in August of 1952, exactly ten years after Ross's original purchase. With *The Robe*, Zanuck was determined to reclaim the religious epic from Cecil B. DeMille. He also hoped the startling new Cinemascope technique would make it a colossal hit, not only luring audiences away from their televisions but generating fat profits for the studio while winning awards for its piety. But with Tyrone Power cast in the lead, the prefilming budget had ballooned to $16 million. The studio pared the budget down to $6 million, passing over Laurence Olivier to hire Richard Burton as the hero—clearly a budget-cutting decision.

The Robe was Burton's third film in a three-picture deal with Twentieth Century Fox. He certainly wanted the role—a great deal was riding on it; some said the Fox studio itself was at stake. Zanuck even told *Variety* that "Hollywood will rise or fall on the success of *The Robe*." It was to be a spiritual *Ben Hur*, Christianity in Cinemascope. It would also bring the young Burton "more money than he thought there was in the world."

Burton plays the part of Marcellus, the noble Roman converted to Christianity. Jean Simmons plays his love interest, who is wary of him at first but slowly grows to adore him and accept his conversion. And Victor Mature plays the man who shows Burton the path to his newfound faith. He had to have his hair curled for the role, prompting him to quip that he had a "temporary permanent." He also wore a gold earring in one ear and a tunic open at the chest, emphasizing his broad shoulders and making him look a little like Mr. Clean in a dark wig. Mature didn't want the role initially because he thought it was too small. He was about to be put on suspension by the studio but relented when it promised him a starring role in a "sequel" to the movie, which would be called *Demetrius and the Gladiators*.

Expectations were so high for *The Robe* that the Vatican sent emissaries to bless the set. Burton treated them to such idiotic statements as "Playing Marcellus is like playing Hamlet." He was told not to smoke in public because it besmirched the wholesome image of his character; but no one could tell Burton what to do, so he smoked. Onscreen, though, Burton seemed to drift aimlessly, wearing a metal breastplate over his starched toga.

Burton is not completely to blame for his strangely tepid performance. Good dialogue is rare in Dunne's screenplay. Douglas, who wrote the novel, purposely used plain modern dialect because he wanted *The Robe* to be accessible to as many readers as possible. Indeed, the book had been a phenomenal mainstream hit, selling two million copies in the first three years after its 1942 publication, in spite of wartime restrictions that limited its translation and distribution. But the folksy language that may have worked for the book seems inappropriate onscreen. In reference to Jesus Christ, someone says: "We gotta find out where he holes up at night. It's like finding one particular ant in an anthill." A brutal soldier hollers at Marcellus like a longshoreman, shouting "Make me obey" and "What are you waiting for?" Caligula is played to creepy perfection by Jay Robinson, with a mincing tone and manner. Yet he, too, is saddled with awkward dialogue, at one point bemoaning the fact that Christians are recruiting the "riff-raff" of the plebeian class to their new religion.

The blunt phrasing seems especially inappropriate with Burton's diction, which he had refined on the London stage. When he travels to Galilee in search of Jesus' followers, Marcellus comments to a villager, "I've heard some new ideas have sprung up." And later, at the emotional moment when he decides to sacrifice himself so his former slave Demetrius can reach safety, Marcellus says only, "For all you've been to me, thanks."

The Robe does portray Jesus subtly, in that his face is never shown. This is partly because the producers wanted to avoid having to recut the film for release in England, which forbade movies and television programs from showing likenesses of Jesus Christ. But it does lend a sense of mystery to Jesus' character and it allows viewers to maintain their own personal ideas about what he may have looked like. When Jesus' name is spoken, the camera focuses on the reactions of people around him, or on a vague figure in the distance. As he walks toward Golgotha with the cross on his back, we see only the top of the heavy beams over the crowd. When he stumbles and falls, we see only his legs. As he is crucified, we see his feet from behind the cross and hear his voice: "Forgive them, for they know not what they do."

But *The Robe* is essentially stagy and trite, with a heavy-handed use of symbolism and sound. Demetrius, when he learns of Jesus' impending execution, tries to warn him. He runs into a stranger in the street. As the man reveals himself to be Judas, thunder crashes loudly. During the crucifixion, Marcellus leans casually against Jesus' cross, and garish red drops of blood fall onto his hands. When he boards a ship for the return to Capri, he's tormented by guilt. His sleep is plagued by nightmares and the viewer literally sees a misty image over Marcellus's head: a nail being driven into Jesus' hand. The sword fight later between Marcellus and one of Caligula's captains adds some needed visual excitement and allows Burton to display a kind of dancer's agility. The swords clash and clang terrifically, though, as if the soldiers were staging a battle with pots and pans.

The final scene is the most egregiously corny, however. After Marcellus refuses to renounce Christ, Caligula sentences him and Diana to death. They smile at each other. Wearing a white gown, Diana looks like a bride ready to follow her groom "into his Kingdom." It is as if they are walking down the aisle after a wedding ceremony, but they are not. They are walking to their executions. The audience is never shown their deaths, though; the couple literally walks into the clouds, the soundtrack swelling with choruses of "Alleluiah! Alleluiah!"

Despite its questionable script, *The Robe* was a success from the beginning. The night of its premiere in September 1953 at the Roxy Theatre in New York, *The Robe* grossed $35,500, then a premiere-day and one-day record for the theater. While the *Hollywood Reporter* said that audience reaction to the film was "tremendous" and that applause erupted spontaneously throughout the film, published reviews were less enthusiastic. One film critic said that Cinemascope was "more of a new kind of crutch than a fresh kind of wing," and that while people may have been moved by the spectacle of the film, the new technique occasionally blurred the images and "couldn't make *The Robe* into a great movie."

John McCarten, *The New Yorker*'s film critic, said that Cinemascope failed to lend any three-dimensionality to the image but only enlarged already spectacular scenes. "This works out fine horizontally, but the peculiar shape of the screen occasionally gives you the impression that you're viewing the action through a mail slot," he said. "Another disadvantage is that the actors in close-ups look as if they belonged on Mount Rushmore." He went on to say that "there is nothing very profound about *The Robe*" but that it took "an unconscionable length of time to get through some of its scenes."

Columnist Sheilah Graham had another, less intellectual quibble with the film. "The picture is colossal and overwhelming—and so is the soundtrack," she wrote. "We wished it didn't blast so! For the first half of the picture it nearly knocked us out of our seats!"

The Robe was such a hit, though, that it sparked a succession of religious films, including its own sequel in *Demetrius and the Gladiators*, starring Victor Mature as a man whose faith is tested. Fox began production on *Demetrius* before *Robe* had even wrapped, billing it as the story of "Christianity's first back-slider . . . [who] becomes disillusioned with the inheritance of the meek and gives himself to excesses."

Critics panned *Demetrius*. But the film's writer, Philip Dunne, who had also penned the screenplays of *David and Bathsheba* and *The Robe*, thought it was more interesting. Dunne believed telling "the reverse half of *The Robe* story"—how a man's faith is tested, not just acquired—was more powerful. But like its predecessor, *Demetrius* featured dialogue bordering on the idiotic. One scene has Mature saying that "to be a Christian these days is anything but dull."

Newsweek magazine recognized the movie industry's spiritual trend in July 1954, writing that "Hollywood has once more become aware of the box-office magic of the Christian tradition and is exploiting it to an unprecedented degree." It reported that other biblical pictures were in the works for the next year, including Columbia's *The Big Fisherman* (1959) and *Joseph and His Brethren* (which would never be finished), Warner's *Land of the Pharaohs* (1955), and *Daniel and the Women of Babylon*. Cecil B. DeMille was set to remake *The Ten Commandments* in 1956, and MGM was about to remake *Ben Hur* in 1959. Twentieth Century Fox meanwhile readied production of *The Greatest Story Ever Told*, which it wouldn't complete until the 1960s.

But *Newsweek* also noted the rather unholy demise of accuracy in the pictures, along with their penchant for dwelling on the more sensational moments of ancient history in "gaudy" color. "The stories have dealt with Christian situations and emotions but have positively gloated over the spectacular fleshpots and cruelties in the Roman background of early Christianity," it wrote. *The Robe* may have started this trend as well. The opening scene is a slave market, where men are invited to look at women for sale. On the auction block is "a jewel from the East" who would make a good companion, and dark-haired Macedonian twins who hold each other suggestively, wearing little more than carefully draped, nude-colored veils. The scenes in Jerusalem, before Jesus' crucifixion, are full of scantily clad girls dancing on tables and half-naked men drinking wine and cavorting at the baths.

At the beginning of *The Robe*, Marcellus is a cad and a lush. In the first scenes, one woman says he was "drunk as a pig last night," while another says, "All your enemies seem to be women." Marcellus is also somehow isolated from the other citizens of ancient, decadent Rome. In other words, Burton was playing himself newly arrived in Los Angeles.

HOLLYWOOD HAS always loved a British accent. A colony of British actors—"expats"—had already settled in Hollywood: Basil Rathbone, Nigel Bruce, David Niven, James Mason, Ronald Colman, Ray Milland. For the most part, the 1950s would not be kind to them. Burton liked to stay with other London stage actors in a rather shabby residential hotel on Sunset Boulevard. "It was the thing to do if you were a . . . stage actor," Burton recalled, "to show your contempt for the contract stars to stay there in that stucco monstrosity, making it quite clear that you were your own man and not owned by some studio, and the minute the fucking lousy film you were in was over, you were going back to the great . . . THEATRE where you re-found your soul as an artist and the Real Work was done." Marlon Brando and Monty Clift were also habitués of the Sunset Towers when Burton first

An acclaimed stage actor, the Welsh-born Richard Burton at first was full of contempt for Hollywood and its movies. But after making his debut in *The Robe* (he is shown here with Jean Simmons), he went on to sign a $1 million contract. *Courtesy of the authors.*

arrived in Hollywood. (Brando gradually moved farther and farther away until he eventually bought his own house in Los Angeles—a defector from the ranks of stage actors. He in fact would never return to the theater and was greatly resented for it by the denizens of Sunset Towers.)

Burton explained to his biographer Melvyn Bragg that when he first arrived in Los Angeles, he and Paul Scofield were held up as the natural heirs to Gielgud and Olivier. But Scofield had little success. It was the decade of pretty boys like Paul Newman, Rock Hudson, and James Dean, and while Scofield's face was soulful and expressive, he was not conventionally handsome. Burton saw the great actor dismissed by the studios because he didn't "photograph well." The superficial judgment deepened Burton's contempt for Hollywood, and when he arrived he was determined to keep his integrity and return to the stage.

It was unfortunate, in a way, for the Welsh actor that he was even able to hold a film like *The Robe* together. Burton's performance showed that he could carry an expensive piece of schlock, and it set the tone for the rest of his career: his brilliant, stage-honed talents, his extraordinary voice, would be thrown away on one bloated mediocrity after another. He tried to preserve the illusion of independence by working in the theater, doing a few films in England, and spending the rest of his time watching rugby matches, but the film roles he chose were inevitably disappointing. He never established an identifiable screen persona—"there are only glimpses of what might have been." Sadly, Elizabeth Taylor thought she was paying Burton a compliment when, on the set of *Cleopatra*, she commented that, "Richard Burton is the Frank Sinatra of Shakespeare."

Burton, however, did one thing that first year in Hollywood which is hardly remembered today. He turned down Darryl Zanuck, the head of Twentieth Century Fox. Around the time of *The Robe*, Zanuck offered Burton a seven-year, seven-picture deal with Fox. Zanuck's contract even would have given the young Welsh actor time to appear on the stage in London. He would be paid $1 million if he signed, with the possibility of percentages. It was an extraordinary offer in 1953, especially for a young unknown actor with only some success on the classical stage to his credit. He had not appeared in any film worth mentioning and had no box office pull whatsoever. Yet Zanuck was prepared to give him the equivalent of almost $20 million in today's figures, just for appearing on the lot whenever a script came up. It was a brave act to turn down such an offer, but Burton didn't want to be one of those gifted stage actors—a "real" actor—who sold out to Hollywood.

Zanuck, an emperor in his own right, was not used to hearing the word "no" in response to his offers. When Burton refused the deal, Zanuck tried to force him to accept it. Burton was known for unleashing his terrific temper at moments like these, sometimes destroying a room just to show his displeasure. Eventually he was made to face Zanuck's lawyers in court. At one point one of Zanuck's attorneys jumped up, raised his fist at Burton, and said, "You shook hands with Mr. Zanuck on this agreement. You shook hands with Mr. Zanuck in his own office." Burton, who did not have a lawyer of his own, responded, "I don't believe Mr. Zanuck said that because he's an honorable man. But if he did say it, then he's a fucking liar." "The place broke up in complete confusion," Burton later wrote in his diary. "Strong men fainted and were carried off by weak men. . . ."

THE LEGEND of Burton's ballsy response to Zanuck's bullying quickly circulated through Hollywood, eclipsing the other rumors of his first year there. The tales of women visiting him in his dressing room, of his drinking prodigious amounts of alcohol and smashing his head against a wall in anger, all paled in comparison.

Richard Burton would return to London. He had defied Zanuck, which would have been unthinkable for an actor to do in the 1940s, when the studio system was at its peak and Zanuck was the powerful producer of *The Grapes of Wrath* and *Twelve O'Clock High*. Yet Burton returned to Hollywood the following year to sign a contract that gave him $1 million—and tied him to some terrible films. Try as he might, he couldn't avoid making a Faustian bargain with Hollywood. Burton didn't need the resentment of powerful studio bosses to undermine his career: he was capable of doing it all by himself, through his drinking and brawling, and through his fateful collision with the Most Beautiful Woman in the World.

Before the war with Zanuck, before he was the most famous husband in America, Burton paid his first visit to "a swank house" in Beverly Hills. Burton recalled people lounging around the pool, "all suntanned and all drinking the 'Sunday liveners'—Bloody Marys, boilermakers, highballs, iced beer." Burton remembered a lot of "wet brown arms" reaching out of the pool to shake his hand. The people were friendly and Burton considered his debut in Hollywood society "a small triumph." But when a dark-haired girl sitting on the other side of the pool, "so extraordinarily beautiful that I nearly laughed out loud," took off her sunglasses to briefly look at him and then went back to reading her book, Burton became "frustrated almost to the point of screaming." While playing "the part of the poor miner's son who was puzzled" by the attention he was getting from such glittering people, he continued to be vexed by the young woman's lack of interest.

"She was unquestionably gorgeous," Burton wrote in his diary. ". . . She was lavish. She was a dark unyielding largesse. . . ." Burton's frustration became almost unmanageable when he finished telling a "well-received and humorous story" about the death of his grandfather, only to discover that the woman in question had turned away and was now in deep conversation with her companion.

Elizabeth Taylor, nine long years before *Cleopatra*, and in 1952 barely twenty years old, had just given Richard Burton the "cold fish eye."

Regardless of Liz Taylor's initial indifference, the Welsh wonder from Stratford-upon-Avon cut a swath through Hollywood: performing Shakespeare soliloquies at dinner, imbibing astonishing amounts of liquor, reciting Dylan Thomas poetry, singing, and telling stories. He was a tangle of animal energy and genuine talent. "My liver is to be buried separately from the rest of me, with full honors," Burton was to say in a later film, in what could have been his own epitaph. The actor was alleged to have broken up nine marriages in the course of his twelve months in Hollywood. When Oscar Levant caught Burton's stage performance of *Hamlet*, "he was so vigorous and healthy that I can say positively it is the only version in which the audience feels sorry for Claudius."

Lauren Bacall and Humphrey Bogart welcomed Burton to Los Angeles. He met Sammy Davis Jr. at Ciro's and invited him to visit the set of *The Robe*. Another household that welcomed him was Jean Howard's, one of Hollywood's most celebrated hostesses and the wife of the powerful agent Charles Feldman. Jean Howard photographed Burton, his hair curled for the part of Marcellus, declaiming Dylan Thomas "to the western winds of the Pacific" in his "robust voice."

Burton came to believe that he had destroyed his film career by insisting on going back to the theater, but it was his own terrible choices in films that destroyed him—choices made to get out of bind-ing studio contracts, or to keep Elizabeth Taylor in jewels. He was excoriated in the British press for being "a bloated millionaire" and "a traitor to his country" for deserting "a sinking British empire on which the sun was at last setting."

In 1977 Burton was nominated for an Academy Award for his performance as the psychiatrist in *Equus*. After all he had been through, he was certainly the sentimental favorite to win the Oscar. When the winner was announced as "Richard . . . Dreyfuss!" Burton had to act the part of a man whose heart was not broken.

CHAPTER 7

THE ARTIST AND "CHARLIE MOVIE STAR": DOUGLAS SIRK AND THE MAKING OF ROCK HUDSON

TOGETHER WITH producer Ross Hunter, European émigré director Douglas Sirk made some of the most memorable films of the 1950s, at once conventional and subversive. Sirk would help transform the mostly B-movie studio Universal into a formidable commercial player. Along the way he would also create one of the biggest stars of the decade—Rock Hudson.

While Hunter was an actor turned producer known for his slickness and savvy in Hollywood, director Sirk was an intellectual artiste. Born Detlef Sierck to Danish parents in Hamburg, Germany, Sirk gained a reputation as an avant-garde director, staging plays by Bertolt Brecht and August Strindberg. Directing for the theater became increasingly difficult, though, after Adolf Hitler came to power in 1933. Many modern plays were *verboten*. Oscar Wilde was a homosexual, after all, and George Bernard Shaw was rumored to be a Jew.

Actors he had helped in their careers suddenly turned on Sirk, hoping to ingratiate themselves with the Nazis. One old friend informed the Gestapo of a laughably minor offense meant to illustrate Sirk's moral turpitude. Seven years before, Sirk had said his idea of paradise would be somewhere in the South Seas, relaxing in a hammock with a drink in one hand and a beautiful girl by his side. The police chastised him for preferring, presumably, a woman who was not Aryan and for endorsing a decadent lifestyle.

Sirk shifted his efforts to film, which for a short time remained less politically charged than the theater. He directed films for the prominent German company UFA and made a star of actress Zarah Leander.

The situation in Germany soon worsened, though, and became personally intolerable for Sirk. He had a son from his first marriage to actress Lydia Brinken. After their divorce, Brinken became a Nazi and obtained a court order to prevent Sirk from seeing the boy. Sirk's crime was that his new wife, Hilde Jary, was Jewish. To add insult to injury, Brinken enrolled her son in Hitler Youth and helped him land acting roles. Claus Detlef Sierck became one of the most prominent child actors in Nazi Germany. It was a bitter irony to the director that he could see his son only on the screen, watching the state-approved movies in a darkened theater.

Hoping to hasten the divorce of Sirk and his Jewish wife, the Nazis revoked his passport while granting one to her. She left for Rome in 1936 and he joined her there a year later, after creatively tricking the bureaucracy into issuing him his travel papers. From Rome they moved on to Zurich and then Paris, where Joseph Goebbels himself sent Sirk a telegram urging him to return to Germany. Goebbels told the director how important he was, how nothing would happen if he came home. Sirk remained wary and unconvinced. He and his wife sailed for America, sure "the Hitler business" would all blow over. They moved to California and grew avocados and alfalfa on a farm, biding their time until Sirk could return to Germany and the intellectual theater circle he loved so much.

Columbia studios signed Sirk, who had changed his name from Sierck, to a contract, and the first film he directed in America was *Hitler's Madman*. It told the story of Nazi official Reinhard Heydrich, whose assassination sparked a revenge massacre at Lidice, Czechoslovakia. Sirk shot the film as if it were a documentary in only a week in 1942, but Columbia chief Harry Cohn didn't want to distribute it. MGM then bought the film, the first outside property it ever purchased. The studio asked Sirk to reshoot some scenes, though, and Sirk was never satisfied with it. *Hitler's Madman* wasn't released until 1943—

to little notice from the public, although fellow directors in Hollywood such as King Vidor admired it. Sirk drifted through the war years, working on his farm more than his films.

Claus Detlef Sierck, the son he could not see for years, died on the Russian front in 1944. Sirk returned to Germany briefly, between 1949 and 1950, surviving a bizarre accident to get there. When Sirk's plane was taking off from New York, it was hit by another small plane that crashed through the roof of the passenger compartment. Sirk suffered head and neck injuries but didn't seek treatment, instead accepting the airline's offer of an immediate new flight to Germany. He was desperate to find some trace of his son. He found none. He went back to Hollywood, plagued by headaches and backaches from the accident. He was out of luck and out of money, already soured on the "American dream" that was so central to the culture of the alien country he was forced to call home.

Sirk knew that in Hollywood, if you looked poor, "you'd had it." He wore the few smart suits he had salvaged from before the war around to interviews, never letting on about the dire straits he found himself in. He hated the phoniness, especially "having to say 'sensational' to every lousy idea some guy like Harry Cohn ever had."

Sirk signed a seven-year contract with Universal and began making movies he knew weren't meaningful. If he complained about a script, the executives would tell him to find a star. Only then would they give him more money and a better story. He found many of his scripts "impossible" and resented the requisite happy endings. Universal did let him restructure the stories a bit, however, and allowed him his greatest element of control—complete freedom over his camera work and editing.

When Sirk teamed up with Ross Hunter in 1952, the collaboration proved fruitful for both. Sirk could make the films look as glossy and glittering as Hunter wanted them. And Hunter had the clout at the studio and around Hollywood to make the films successful. Sirk started to get the better stories, and even when they were melodramatic, he developed techniques that would make what at first seemed soap operas into slightly subversive commentaries on the American bourgeoisie.

Hunter could draw the big talent, usually by courting an actress whose career was faltering. He had brought Barbara Stanwyck on board for the first Hunter-Sirk collaboration in 1953, *All I Desire*. That same year, he was credited with renewing Ann Sheridan's career by starring her in *Take Me to Town*, a western/musical comedy that Sirk directed and that became a surprise hit.

In 1954 Hunter came to Sirk and said, "I have Jane Wyman." The announcement immediately piqued Sirk's interest because Wyman still had star power. She even had a story already in mind for the film. She wanted to remake an old Universal picture based on Lloyd C. Douglas's unreadable novel *Magnificent Obsession*, a nearly preposterous story about a reckless playboy named Bob Merrick who causes the death of the town's selfless doctor. Stunned by the town's reaction to him and ashamed of his behavior, Merrick repents. He becomes a doctor himself and falls in love with the dead man's wife, Helen. The climax of the film has Merrick performing a dangerous operation to restore Helen's sight, which she lost in an accident after trying to get away from him. The reformed cad cures the woman's blindness and everyone gets a happy ending.

Sirk winced when he heard Wyman's idea. Actresses always loved this movie, hoping to star in the remake. But he had reservations about the twisting plot lines, telling Ross Hunter, "Look, we'll be buried under this thing." But after wandering around his house for a few days despondent and depressed, he relented, believing it could be a successful production.

He thought that even the most clichéd story could be saved. "The stories that I got, without exception, were very trite, without any element of life to them," Sirk said. "But still the content of the trite novel could be vivified—you could wake it up—you could put something into it."

For the later *Imitation of Life*, that "it" would be the secondary theme of racial rifts in America. For *Magnificent Obsession*, "it" was more about embracing the very sudsiness of the story. Sirk called the film "a combination of kitsch, and craziness, and trashiness."

In his visual images and dialogue, Sirk calls attention to the clichés of moviemaking. The scenes make sense interpreted literally, but when one is conscious of their irony, the images become playful and campy. The opening sequence of *Magnificent Obsession*, for instance, has Bob Merrick tearing across the lake in a cherry-red speedboat

This impossible story of a widow who falls for the man that causes—and then cures—her blindness proved to be a much needed hit for Universal in 1954, and solidified the successful partnership of German émigré director Douglas Sirk and producer Ross Hunter. *Courtesy of the authors.*

named *Hurricane* as the violin-drenched musical score swells. His female companion urges him to take it easy. "Easy? Where's that get ya?" Bob replies. Later, Bob crashes his car into a highway barrier marked "DANGER." He picks up the sign and carries it into a nearby house, literally branding himself as trouble.

"Trashiness is very important, and it saves trashy stuff like *Magnificent Obsession*," Sirk later told writer Jon Halliday. ". . . There is a very short distance between high art and trash, and trash that contains the element of craziness is by this very quality nearer to art."

Sirk needed a strong male lead for the role of Bob Merrick, someone who could hold his own against Wyman. The director felt that Universal, although home to heartthrob Tony Curtis, didn't have a male star, so he set about creating a leading man from a young actor named Rock Hudson. The actor who started life as Roy Scherer Jr. had appeared in twenty-four films, mostly in supporting roles in forgettable flops such as *I Was a Shoplifter*, *The Fat Man*, and *Here Come the Nelsons*.

Sirk had directed Hudson in a small role in *Has Anybody Seen My Gal?* (1952) and thought he saw something more than good looks in Hudson's performance in *Iron Man* (1951). He also directed Hudson as an Indian in a western entitled *Taza, Son of Cochise* (1954). Sirk trusted his camera to reveal things the human eye could not. "It's the only thing in Hollywood which never let me down," he said.

The director insisted on two days of extensive testing for *Magnificent Obsession*. He asked Hudson to perform eight different scenes and finally, after consulting with Ross Hunter, decided Hudson was ready for a leading role. The film would make him a star and Hudson would go on to appear in six other Sirk films.

Casting Rock Hudson in the weepie *Obsession* was an apt choice. Although Hudson is remembered more for the way he died—of AIDS in 1985—than for his gifts as an actor, he did have a singular quality that made him perfect for melodrama, and later for the light Doris Day sex comedies.

As film scholar Barbara Klinger has written, despite his later revelations of homosexuality, Hudson in the 1950s represented a kind of "sexual normalcy." With his tall frame, broad shoulders, and chiseled chin, he exuded a nonthreatening and uncomplicated virility that was an antidote to the brooding "psycho-stars" of the day such as Marlon Brando, James Dean, and Montgomery Clift. In the same movie magazines that detailed the car crashes and other exploits of Hollywood's "bad boys," lengthy stories extolled Hudson's seemingly square existence. Photo after photo in a "Hollywood Exposé" spread in *Filmland* magazine shows athletic Rock smiling as he plays charades with

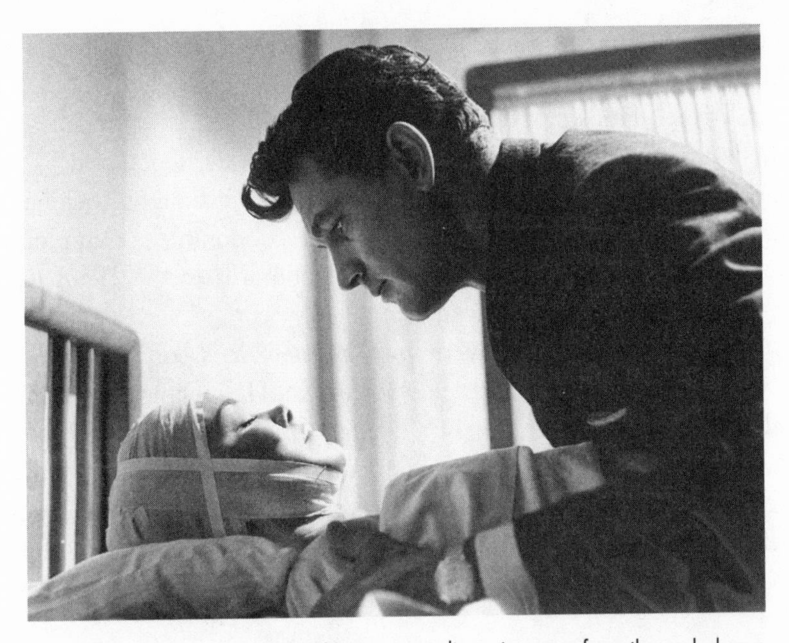

Rock Hudson hovers over Jane Wyman in a climactic scene from the melodrama *Magnificent Obsession.* Although he had appeared in twenty-four other films, the part of Dr. Bob Merrick was Hudson's first starring role. *Courtesy of the Academy of Motion Picture Arts and Sciences.*

friends or grills steaks for a backyard barbecue. Other favorite activities listed: singing around the piano and playing with his dog. His masculine appearance was also celebrated. An item in a January 1953 *Silver Screen* detailed how he had to have "man-size furniture" custom built to contain "all six feet four inches of him."

Sirk noticed the powerful effect Rock Hudson had on women. More than once, a leading lady would fall for him. One actress begged her director to instruct Rock to kiss her. "Doug, can't you get Rock to kiss me properly?" she begged. Sirk declined, knowing why Hudson's kisses seemed awkward.

But Hudson reinforced his "normal" image by consistently taking on roles in which he played a clean-cut, sensitive, morally upstanding character. So while Brando and Clift displayed a tortured and volatile masculinity in films like *On the Waterfront* (1954) and *From Here to Eternity* (1953), the gay Rock Hudson ironically would serve as a model for America's Everyman, free of angst and navel-gazing self-analysis. As one fan magazine put it, audiences needed some relief from "spooky" James Dean. "The public got tired of decay. So now there's Rock Hudson. He's wholesome. He doesn't perspire. . . . He smells of milk. His whole appeal is cleanliness and respectability—this boy is pure." (In fact, Rock's agent Henry Willson thought Rock had a definite body odor. "For God's sake, wear deodorant," he implored. Rock refused, saying it was "sissy," as deodorants in the 1950s were generally marketed toward women.)

Yet Rock's repentant playboy in *Obsession* does convey a kind of wholesomeness and innocence. He follows Helen into her waiting cab, trying to convince her he's changed his ways after causing her husband's death. She opens the door and steps into traffic. She's hit by a car while trying to escape him. Rock's mouth hangs agape in disbelief, a reaction so expected it seems weirdly genuine. Later, Helen accepts her blindness bravely, and eventually finds her way to the lake-

Director Douglas Sirk, with Rock Hudson, Jane Wyman, and Agnes Moorehead on the set of 1955's *All That Heaven Allows*. Sirk was obsessed with blindness, both literal and figurative, in his films. Ironically, he would lose his sight later in life. *Courtesy of the Academy of Motion Picture Arts and Sciences.*

side alone. She doesn't recognize the deep-voiced stranger who befriends her as Bob Merrick, the man who blinded her. Rock shows surprising restraint in these scenes, tenderness reflected in his gentle face. Wyman, meanwhile, looks absurd as a blind woman in cat's-eye, rhinestone-studded sunglasses.

The mirror images that would become Douglas Sirk's trademark also appear in *Magnificent Obsession*, as when Merrick pauses just before operating on the woman he loves. He hesitates, saying he's not qualified to perform the difficult surgery his friend Randolph has urged him to do. But then he sees an image of his friend reflected off the mirrorlike window over his head. Throughout the film, Randolph encourages Merrick with his religious philosophy, telling him anything can be accomplished by getting in touch with "the source of infinite power."

His own reflection melds with that of his friend, and the false image, the ghostly picture of the men in the window, spurs Merrick to operate. The woman not only lives but regains her sight.

Sirk saw mirrors and blindness as symbols of the human condition. He dreamed of making a film that would take place entirely in an asylum for the blind. "It would only have people constantly groping, trying to grasp things they can't see," he said. Mirrors, for Sirk, represented the distance between what we feel and what we know from our senses. "If you try to grasp happiness itself, your fingers only meet a surface of glass, because happiness has no existence of its own, and probably exists only inside yourself," he said.

Sirk also thought mirrors had a strange psychological effect on people. He believed mirrors could reveal a man's true self and therefore inspired fear. One scene from *Written on the Wind*, another melodrama Sirk later made with producer Albert Zugsmith, illustrates Sirk's point. The drunken Kyle, played by a young, intense Robert Stack, stares into a mirror. He's brooding over what he thinks is an affair between his wife and his best friend (again, Rock Hudson). He stares at himself for a moment and then throws his drink at his reflection, golden rivulets of whiskey splash everywhere, streaming down the silvered surface. It is the reverse of the stereotypical movie scene of someone throwing a drink into another man's face. In Sirk's world, men hate themselves the most.

It remains unclear whether audiences grasped all of Sirk's subtle commentaries on America and its skewed values. But it didn't seem to matter. *Magnificent Obsession* grossed $8 million in 1954, topping the receipts from the original version by more than ten times. It earned Jane Wyman her fourth Academy Award nomination and bolstered the careers of both Hunter and Sirk.

Obsession also changed Rock Hudson. One night Rock slipped into a sneak preview of the movie with his boyfriend, Jack Navaar. He ran out just before the lights in the theater came up. Navaar found him in the car in the parking lot, slumped over the steering wheel and sobbing. Rock knew he was a star.

After the release of *Obsession*, Rock Hudson got three thousand fan letters a week. *Modern Screen* magazine voted him the most popular male movie star in 1954; *Look* followed in 1955 and *Photoplay* did the same in 1957. More importantly, from 1957 to 1964, the Film Buyers of the Motion Picture Industry named him the number one box office draw. Theater owners had determined that audiences bought more tickets to his movies than to anyone else's.

But Rock Hudson's success meant increased scrutiny of his personal life. He was careful not to allow anyone to photograph him with another man. He maintained two telephone lines whenever he lived with someone, forbidding his "roommate" from answering his phone lest the caller become suspicious. Living as a gay man in the 1950s required extreme discretion. Friend and fellow actor George Nader remembered the code words used to determine if other men were gay: Is he musical? The men would never go out in groups of four, fearing it might look like a double date. If someone suggested a group go to the perennial Hollywood hangout and pie shop Du-Par's, Nader would look around the room. "Too many boys," he'd say. "Let's order in."

Sirk knew of Hudson's homosexuality and believed that flamboyant producer Ross Hunter had nudged him in that direction. When he first met Hudson, Sirk thought the actor was "near the middle of the sexual spectrum," but that after Hudson met Hunter, "that was it." According to Sirk, the studio soon had a hard time keeping Hudson's secret.

Confidential magazine meanwhile was salivating over an exposé of Rock's "alternative lifestyle." They bribed Jack Navaar with $10,000, a huge sum in 1954. Navaar proved loyal, though, warning Hudson's agent Henry Willson of the potential story instead of cashing in. The rumor at the time was that a studio head at Universal had traded information about Rory Calhoun in exchange for squelching the story. Calhoun had allegedly done time in jail for burglary and auto theft.

"Every month when *Confidential* came out, our stomachs began to turn. Which of us would be in it?" George Nader said. "The amazing thing is that Rock, as big as he became, was never nailed. It made me speculate that Rock had an angel on his shoulder or that he'd made a pact with the devil."

What Rock did have was a shark of an agent in Henry Willson. A former talent scout for David O. Selznick, Willson represented Natalie Wood, Jeanette MacDonald, and Ann Sothern. He had changed the destinies of many an actor just by changing his name. He christened Art Gelien as Tab Hunter, Merle Johnson as Troy Donahue, and Elmore Torn as Rip Torn. He even claimed he thought up Rock's moniker, although the credit really goes to Ken Hodge, a boyfriend of Rock's who acted as his very first agent.

If Willson didn't think an actor was cooperating and doing all he could to succeed, the agent could undermine him with rumors. "You wouldn't want him in a western. How about a tutu?" he'd say to a director, or "He's a good actor except for that drinking problem." In Rock Hudson, though, Willson could see his own stock rising. He launched a campaign to help Rock preserve his clean-cut image.

Willson first turned to famed Hollywood attorney Jerry Giesler for help. Willson and Hudson wanted to bar *Confidential* from publishing the story about some kind of gay "gang bang" involving Rock. Giesler explained that American law does not tolerate any "prior restraint" of the press. The only option Rock had would be to sue the magazine after publication. Willson reportedly told Giesler, "We've got to find a way" to stop the story.

And Willson did. He found his star a bride.

Willson didn't have to look far. His secretary Phyllis Gates already knew Rock Hudson. Phyllis was a Minnesota farm girl turned stewardess, turned junior talent agent. Petite and brunette, she was known for her down-to-earth quality and good sense of humor. She was learning about Hollywood and its ways from the expert Willson, but Phyllis did not catch on to the fact that she was part of one of the biggest publicity stunts of the 1950s until it was too late.

Hudson reportedly told author Armistead Maupin that he had been "forced" to marry Phyllis. She thought the courtship started naturally, though, with intimate dinners at little bistros off Sunset Boulevard. Rock could be quite sweet and sentimental, surprising her one night with a Christmas tree for her apartment. Phyllis thought she was at the center of a sudden but real romance, and when Rock asked for her hand in marriage, she said yes.

Henry Willson handled all the arrangements, at first wanting the couple to marry on a boat in the Caribbean. Phyllis Gates later learned that such an arrangement probably would have been illegal, preventing her from claiming any kind of real financial partnership with Rock. Phyllis had been raised a Lutheran, though, and she persuaded Willson to move the ceremony to the Biltmore Hotel in Santa Barbara, where a minister performed the rites. Rock Hudson and Phyllis Gates were wed on November 5, 1955. Neither set of parents attended. After the couple said their vows, the first thing they did was call Hollywood gossip columnists Hedda Hopper and Louella Parsons.

Rock and Phyllis honeymooned in Jamaica. Phyllis thought it bliss. Even their fledgling sexual relationship seemed good, although she hinted at a premature ejaculation problem that a doctor treated with a salve. There was one odd moment, though. She watched him showering and thought it would be playful to surprise him there. She removed her clothes and hopped in. A startled Rock chastised her and jumped out.

Back home at their redwood and glass house on Sparrow Lane in the Hollywood Hills, Rock devoured Phyllis's hearty meals of meat loaf and mashed potatoes. He would buy his new bride beautiful clothes and jewelry. Phyllis would be lulled into contentment, only to have late-night phone calls from young male "fans" disturb more than her sleep. Rock once made her hide in the bedroom while an old boyfriend came calling, hoping for some financial help.

Most of America believed the press reports about Rock Hudson and his bride. One magazine story, entitled "When Day Is Done—Heaven Is Waiting," quoted Rock as saying, "When I count my blessings, my marriage tops the list." Another, entitled "Trapped, Feeling No Pain," had Rock gushing, "Marriage has turned out to be all I hoped for and more. I'm just a whole lot happier."

Having Rock safely married off thrilled Universal. Its executives even threw a wedding brunch for the happy couple, with Phyllis the only woman in the room. The studio also wanted to capitalize quickly on the successful formula of *Magnificent Obsession*. In 1955 they again paired Hunter and Sirk, who in turn paired Rock Hudson and Jane Wyman.

They found another melodrama set in a small town. Oddly, it was loosely based on Henry David Thoreau's *Walden*, one of Sirk's favorite books. A shot of the book appears in a close-up, although the story of *All That Heaven Allows* doesn't seem much like Thoreau's tale of self-reliance. It focuses instead on a widow named Cary who falls in love with her young gardener, Ron Kirby. Her family and friends in town disapprove, so she ends the relationship. Later, she nurses him back to health from pneumonia, and it's implied that they will marry.

Again, Rock plays a "normal" guy. He moves through the frames in checked flannel shirts with the collar turned up, pruning Cary's trees, feeding deer, refurbishing an old mill into a rustic retreat for them. Ron shows her the natural delights of raising plants in the greenhouse and having an informal clam bake with friends, at which he opens a wine bottle with his teeth. Later, when the couple attends a stuffy cocktail party hosted by a small-town society maven, her nosy neighbor sneers, "So that's Cary's nature boy."

Sirk again employs windows and mirrors to dramatic effect. His wide shots flatten the space, creating almost a "postcard" look. As Cary and Ron stand in front of the picture window looking out at the snowy lawn and frozen pond, a deer makes its way over to them. The visual cliché reinforces the artificiality of the movie, the corny predictability of the modern romance.

Sirk meant the film's title ironically as well. He was astonished when the studio loved *All That Heaven Allows*, taking the title to mean that people could have whatever they wanted. "I meant it exactly the other way round," he said. "As far as I am concerned, heaven is stingy."

In one of the most famous scenes from any Sirk film, the widow's grown son has returned home from college for Christmas. He and his sister have expressed strong disapproval of their mother's relationship with a younger man. Earlier in the film, a friend has criticized her for carrying on with the gardener, telling her to find something more "suitable" to occupy a widow's time. The children buy Cary a television as a Christmas gift. A deliveryman wheels the set into the living room and Sirk pans in on it. Wyman, stunned and unsmiling, is reflected in the dead eye of the screen.

The camera comes closer until the image fills the frame, literally trapping Cary in the television. The deliveryman drones on about the companionship she can find there. "Drama, comedy, life's parade at your fingertips," he says. The implication, of course, is that the woman's real feelings and desires are troublesome and wrong, embarrassing to her children. She should satisfy herself with the artificial reflections she can see in the mirror of American television.

IN SIRK'S 1956 release *Written on the Wind*, Rock Hudson solidified his reputation for playing the moral straight man. The film tells a classic American story about a rich but unhappy oil family. Despite having everything money can buy, Kyle Hadley (Robert Stack) is rudderless and reckless. He drinks too much and doesn't know how to treat his beautiful wife, Lucy, played by Lauren Bacall.

Rock Hudson plays Mitch Wayne, Kyle's friend and business partner, the smarter, saner man always bailing him out of sticky situations. All strong jaw and stiff demeanor, Mitch is the son of a rancher. Like that of the gardener in *All That Heaven Allows*, the role of Mitch reinforced the idea of Hudson as naturally, innately masculine.

While his onscreen persona radiated normalcy, life at the real Hudson home grew curiouser and curiouser. The sex life that Phyllis Gates had regarded as satisfying, if a little boring and predictable, began to deteriorate. She once caught Rock dancing around the living room with his penis tucked between his legs. He acted as if nothing odd had happened. Later, he told her that "all women are dirty" and that their genitalia "remind me of cows." He asked that she shower before each bout of awkward lovemaking.

The tension between Rock's real life and the fantasy of his marriage seemed to grow, sparking dark moods and sudden rages. While in

Rome, the couple sat at an outdoor café on the Via Veneto. A young Italian man who knew Rock happened to walk by and joined them. Later, at the hotel, Phyllis expressed her frustration saying she didn't want to spend any more time with that "silly little fruitcake." Phyllis said he became so angered that he hit her, breaking her pearl necklace.

She was not alone in noticing a change in Rock. His friends saw a difference in him after the success of *Giant* (1956). He had earned an Academy Award nomination and had become what they called "Charlie Movie Star." He was obsessed with his privacy, offering increasingly evasive answers to interviewers and amusing himself by making up anecdotes. He even started refusing to give out autographs.

For Phyllis, though, her relationship with Rock Hudson cooled abruptly during his filming of John Huston's *A Farewell to Arms* in Italy in 1957. She became seriously ill with infectious hepatitis, and was hospitalized for a month at St. John's in Los Angeles. While Hollywood friends sent flowers and telegrams, her own husband remained suspiciously silent. The few times they talked by telephone, she begged him to come home. He said he couldn't interrupt the film's shooting. The ridiculous reports in the fan magazines tormented her further. She read fictitious items about how Rock would leave the set, followed minutes later by the sounds of a typewriter coming from his dressing room as he wrote his daily letter to his wife—but Phyllis said she never received any letters from Rock in Italy. Later, she learned that he had been involved with an Italian man during the five months on location and thus couldn't visit her in the hospital. Cruelly, the few gifts Rock brought home for her had been selected by this boyfriend, the very same man Phyllis had ridiculed on the Via Veneto months earlier.

Depressed and desperate to repair her frayed marriage, Phyllis sought help from a psychologist and implored Rock to do the same. He went only a few times and abandoned analysis. The relationship, even the genuine friendship they had shared, seemed lost. Convinced that Rock did not love her, had never loved her, she filed for divorce in April of 1958.

Rock and, of course, his agent Henry Willson urged reconciliation, but she was unmoved. Although Rock had told his friends that Phyllis was bisexual and some, including old boyfriend Jack Navaar, said they saw her in lesbian situations, Phyllis Gates denied it. She said Henry Willson planted the rumors as part of a "slander campaign" to win the public relations battle the divorce sparked.

Phyllis sued on grounds of "extreme mental cruelty." Anxious to have the marriage behind her, she claimed to have settled for a less than lucrative deal of $250 a week for ten years and the $35,000 house. Other reports suggested she hired *Confidential's* private dick Fred Otash to tape-record a conversation in which she and Rock discussed ways to "cure" his homosexuality. Allegedly, she then used the tape to bribe Hudson and get a better settlement. Whatever the case, she divorced at thirty-three and never married again. Strangely enough, twenty years after selling the first home she shared with Rock, Phyllis repurchased the Sparrow Lane house.

Although she went on to study at UCLA, Phyllis Gates found herself reduced to little more than a footnote in Rock Hudson's biography. The invitations to celebrity parties and premieres evaporated; her lifestyle changed dramatically while Hudson's career continued at its brisk pace. The late 1950s and early 1960s would see him perhaps at the peak of his popularity with Sirk's *Written on the Wind* and Hunter's light Doris Day comedies.

Beyond his success in the Hunter-Sirk films, Rock Hudson's ultimate achievement, sadly, may have been educating the public about AIDS. According to media analyst James Kinsella, Hudson's admission that he had the disease spurred a 270 percent increase in AIDS reporting by the end of 1985. His longtime affiliation with actor turned president Ronald Reagan, Jane Wyman's ex-husband, also furthered the cause of AIDS research and treatment. The Reagan administration had planned to cut funding for AIDS-related projects by $10 million, but they increased the budget to $100 million after learning of Rock's diagnosis.

Perhaps Rock found some comfort in the thirty thousand fan letters he received after announcing his battle with the fatal illness. Even the then up-and-coming pop chanteuse Madonna sent greetings. "To Rock Hudson, my heartthrob since childhood. Saying lots of prayers for you. All my love, Madonna." Too bad he didn't know who she was.

Rock died on October 2, 1985. After a memorial at which several hundred people drank margaritas, ate chili, and listened to a mariachi band, his ashes were scattered into the waters of the Catalina Channel. Phyllis Gates did not attend.

Nor did Douglas Sirk, for by then he had lost his sight. The man who had once directed "the greatest scene of going blind in the cinema" awoke one night and went to switch on the bedside lamp. "I thought the light had gone out," Sirk later explained to his biographer, Jon Halliday. "But it was my sight. It's goddamn ironic. Years ago, I made that picture about blindness—and now I'm blind."

By the late 1960s Sirk was virtually forgotten; he hadn't made a picture in over ten years. When he wasn't being ignored by critics, his *de luxe*, operatic movies were often mocked. Whenever Sirk's name came up among studio executives, the usual response was, "Are you sure you don't mean Kirk Douglas?" It would take another twenty years before filmmakers discovered Sirk as a master of Technicolor, music, and lighting. He lived long enough—he died in 1987, three months shy of his ninetieth birthday—to learn that his films were admired by directors as diverse as Rainer Werner Fassbinder, Jonathan Demme, and Quentin Tarantino, just to name a few. In fact, Tarantino, in his 1994 film *Pulp Fiction*, pays a sly homage to Douglas Sirk in a scene that takes place at a 1950s theme restaurant, Jack Rabbit Slims, complete with a Ricky Nelson impersonator and a waitress dressed as Marilyn Monroe (in the billowing skirt from *The Seven Year Itch*). John Travolta's character orders the "Douglas Sirk Steak," cooked, by the way, "bloody as hell."

CHAPTER 8

LEGAL ALIENS: EXPATS, ARTISTS, AND OSCAR LEVANT

IT'S IRONIC how popular Richard Burton became in Hollywood society with his carousing and his ability to quote reams of Dylan Thomas's poetry when Thomas himself was a complete flop and an embarrassment when he landed in Los Angeles the year before Burton.

The Welsh poet wore his "uniform," as he called it, a faded brown tweed suit with baggy trousers, and he carried a blue duffel bag with him wherever he went. The English screenwriter Ivan Moffat, who was an assistant to George Stevens when the director was adapting Theodore Dreiser's *An American Tragedy* for the screen, was waiting for the poet at the Los Angeles Airport. Moffat said that Dylan Thomas, with his sorrowful little bag, reminded him of the last scene of a Charlie Chaplin film. Like many writers who grew up on the glamorous image of Hollywood in the 1930s and 1940s, Dylan Thomas told Moffat that he wanted to meet a movie star. Moffat and Christopher Isherwood, another of Thomas's English hosts in Los Angeles, introduced the poet to Shelley Winters, who had recently been given the role of the factory girl in *An American Tragedy* opposite Montgomery Clift. Moffat says that Dylan pointed at her breasts and said, "Are they really real?"

She told him he could touch if he didn't believe, and so, very tentatively, with the index finger, he lightly touched her breast. It seemed to him substantiation enough. John Malcolm Brinnin, who wrote *Dylan Thomas in America* and was a friend of the poet's, said that he was told by Thomas that Miss Winters rebuffed him "in language which was as direct as a stevedore's." (Moffat says this is not so, and that she "liked him very much.")

Dylan Thomas was next invited to meet Charlie Chaplin. It was Isherwood who took Dylan up to the marble house in the hills where Chaplin lived. They were roughly the same size and both possessed "extremely fluid, rag-doll-like, quick emotion . . . striding about the enormous drawing-room together, talking and chattering." When Thomas said that no one back in Laugharne would believe that he had met his film idol, Chaplin sent off a cable to Dylan's wife Caitlin.

But the evening ended badly, with Thomas drunk and making a fool of himself. Moffat, comparing Thomas's drinking then and in London, thought that "in California he drank much more and it affected him in even greater proportion than before." In Los Angeles, there was a rougher, more insensitive side to his behavior, a disregard of other people's feelings. He let himself go in some way. Or perhaps it was his reaction to the rebuffs he began to receive from Hollywood society. Isherwood and Moffat asked Jean Howard if she would like to include the famous poet at one of her fabulous gatherings of Hollywood actors and producers, but she was not interested. Why have that short, disheveled little man when she could have Richard Burton reciting Thomas's poems instead? True to form, the greatest Hollywood hostess of the 1940s and 1950s preferred the illusion to the reality.

THE FAMOUSLY refined European sensibility of Hollywood began to slip away in the 1950s. In 1951, the last year of Arnold Schoenberg's life, a former pupil named Dika Newlin went to visit him in Brentwood and found to her amazement that the austere, august composer of *Moses und Aron* and *Pierrot Lunaire* "had now discovered television." Schoenberg claimed that he had bought a set just for the children—his younger son was still only nine—but Miss Newlin was not convinced. "No one was more enthralled than he," she observed, "as we sat in front of *Hopalong Cassidy* with our TV trays in our laps."

As more and more Europeans fled to America in the 1930s and

1940s, the great house for all German refugees in Southern California was that of Salka Viertel, Garbo's greatest friend and screenwriter, and her husband, Berthold. All German artists and intellectuals who got past Ellis Island in those days made a beeline for the hospitality of the Viertels. They all came—Dimitri Tiomkin and Bronislau Kaper from Warsaw, both very Polish and very nostalgic. Schoenberg and his wife came, and Otto Klemperer, then the conductor of the Los Angeles Philharmonic Orchestra (whose son Werner would play the comically sinister Colonel Klink in *Hogan's Heroes*, the television sitcom based on Billy Wilder's 1953 film *Stalag 17*). Silver-haired and charming, director Max Reinhardt arrived to stage *A Midsummer Night's Dream* at the Hollywood Bowl and later as a film for Warner Brothers.

But the European film community after the end of the war, after the Marshall Plan, did not feel the need to come to America. The French nouvelle vague, as much as they idolized and celebrated American cinema, would work at home in their own language. Truffaut, Bergman, Rossellini, Godard, and Antonioni didn't need America in order to make movies. Except for Billy Wilder, the 1950s were not kind to those European moviemakers who stayed in Hollywood, directors such Fritz Lang, Erich von Stroheim, Josef von Sternberg, and Jean Renoir.

After two brilliant decades in America, by 1956 Fritz Lang was shut out of Hollywood. Studio executives felt that European directors, with their foreign names, were too difficult and demanding. Their movies may have been *art*, but they didn't always make money. Lang would have to return to Germany to continue working. The case of Erich von Stroheim epitomized Hollywood's humiliation of its European directors. After he had gained a reputation for budget overruns and production problems on several of his movies, no studio would hire von Stroheim as a director. He had to rely on acting roles to support himself, which led to Billy Wilder's inspired casting of him as Norma Desmond's chauffeur, factotum, and former husband in *Sunset Boulevard*. (It was von Stroheim himself who suggested to Wilder that he be filmed "lovingly washing out Norma Desmond's underclothes," an idea suitably perverse for Wilder.)

Josef von Sternberg—the genius behind Marlene Dietrich's androgynous glamour—made one great Hollywood film noir in 1952, *Macao*, with Robert Mitchum and Jane Russell. Mitchum, Russell, and William Bendix resented von Sternberg's autocratic perfectionism and retaliated with a series of cruel pranks. They collapsed his tent while he was taking off his jodhpurs trying to get into his pajamas. They rubbed malodorous Limburger cheese on the engine of his car. Asked why they did it, Mitchum said that von Sternberg took himself and the picture too seriously. "It was just another crummy melodrama," he said at the time. "We weren't out to win the Pulitzer Prize or anything." Disheartened by this treatment, von Sternberg walked off the set and Nicholas Ray was brought in to complete the film.

Jean Renoir (son of Auguste, the Impressionist painter) was reduced to living in exile in Benedict Canyon, in the Hollywood Hills. In spite of the exquisite *La Grande Illusion* (1937) and *La Bête Humaine* (1938), Hollywood considered him virtually unemployable by the mid-1950s. "Renoir has a lot of talent, but he isn't one of us," Darryl Zanuck would say. Renoir, however, would have a prophetic dream, which he related to his friend, Salka Viertel. In Renoir's dream, he's in an airplane—the same one that had first brought him to Hollywood in 1940. "I saw myself . . . in Paradise," he told Salka, "beside Griffith, Charlie Chaplin, Lubitsch, and all the saints."

Salka continued to serve her Viennese chocolate cake to Aldous Huxley and Christopher Isherwood, to Charlie Chaplin and Oona O'Neill, to Ivan Moffat and his mother Iris Tree. Even Thomas Mann attended her soirées, Salka's Viennese cake hanging from his mustache. It was "sort of the end of the Hollywood intellectual era," remembered one of Salka's younger guests, "but we didn't know it yet."

"CALIFORNIA IS a beautiful prison," Man Ray wrote to his sister. "I like being here, but I cannot forget my previous life, and long for the day when I can return . . . eventually to France."

The great Dada-Surrealist artist and experimental filmmaker tried to adapt to Hollywood. Producer Albert Lewin became one of his closest friends, inviting Man and his wife to elaborate dinners at their home on the beach in Santa Monica. Man Ray admired how the Lewins had furnished their very modern-looking home with armless chairs on very short legs and a cocktail table "against which one barked his shins," so that none of the breathtaking ocean views would be obstructed, but nonetheless had completely filled the house with old books, deep cushioned seats, and Lewin's beloved collection of primitive art. At one of the more sumptuous dinners at the Lewins', Man Ray was seated next to Erich von Stroheim, who had recently played Gloria Swanson's cuckolded chauffeur in *Sunset Boulevard*. Man Ray told the imperious director how much he admired his performance in the film. He didn't feel that von Stroheim was simply playing a part, Man Ray added, but that he was portraying himself "as he might be in real life," especially in the film *Grand Illusion* by Jean Renoir, who it so happened was also a guest that evening. Von Stroheim waited for Man Ray to finish, then asked what he did for a living.

"I am a painter," Man Ray politely explained.

"A modern painter?" von Stroheim asked, adding that he hated modern painting.

Man Ray told von Stroheim that he never liked the word "modern," that he considered himself "simply of my time."

"How different he was from a man like Jean Renoir," Man Ray would later write about the encounter, "who also lived in another world than mine, with the background of his father's painting, with his fame as a film director—yet who treated me with tact, came to my exhibitions, and like Lewin, tried to find a place for me in his productions."

But it was not easy for Man Ray to ingratiate himself with the glove salesmen and accountants who ran the studios. He simply did not fit into their world. Man Ray had "ideas" and "theories" about his work which mystified the men who held his fate in their hands. Instead they sent their wives to him for lessons in photography and painting. "I accepted them willingly," Man Ray once said, "as it permitted me to continue expounding my thoughts without having to face a crowd."

Albert Lewin tried to find work for Man Ray in Hollywood, finally getting him a job on one of the last films Lewin made in America, *Pandora and the Flying Dutchman*. Lewin needed a color photograph of Ava Gardner in her period costume. "She was absolutely ravishing," Man Ray said of Gardner. "No film, I thought, had ever done her justice. And as a model, no one in my experience with mannequins and professionals surpassed her." Man Ray felt that Gardner posed for still photography as if before a movie camera. In fact, the portrait appears in the film as if it were a painting.

Lewin also made use of a chess set Man Ray had designed, insisting on its placement in a scene even after one of Lewin's fellow film executives wanted it scrapped. Man Ray had once observed how often painters figured in Al Lewin's movies—in *The Moon and Sixpence*, *The Picture of Dorian Gray*, *The Private Affairs of Bel Ami*—and how, in *Pandora and the Flying Dutchman*, the leading man, "besides being condemned to wander over the globe for eternity, is a painter who paints. . . ."

Despite his feeling that he had stumbled into the wilderness with no way out, the pace of Man Ray's final two years in Hollywood sped up "as if a crisis was approaching." "Households broke up and familiar faces disappeared"; new faces came upon the scene in quick succession, like Clifford Odets, who began to appear in Man Ray's life.

He began to spend a lot of time at Jean Renoir's "lovely house" in the Hollywood Hills. Man Ray, Renoir, and their wives had indoor barbecues after Renoir built a charcoal grill into the dining room wall. Nearby "he installed Gabrielle, his father's favorite model, with her American husband, Slade, a tall bearded man of great distinction." He would waltz with Juliet in the living room like "someone out of a painting by Renoir."

An old friend of Man Ray's married M. F. K. Fisher, and Man Ray and Juliet began to spend their weekends at their estate called Bare Acres. She could tell one "how to cook a wolf," to quote the title of her eccentric cookbook, and made a Burgundy beef stew that reminded Man Ray of Dijon.

"There was Galka Scheyer, onetime friend of Paul Klee, her house perched on no man's land at the top of the Hollywood Hills, crammed with the painter's works. Like a museum," thought Man Ray, "perched on a precipice."

May Ray would attend parties at the homes of Clifford Odets and Stravinsky. Invariably many of the guests were studio executives who would ignore the diminutive artist and make him feel like "a black sheep." He played furious chess games with Bertolt Brecht, usually losing to the intense playwright.

Man Ray, like Francis Picabia and many of his other contemporaries, was in love with the automobile, with speed. While in Hollywood, though, Man Ray began to develop "a dislike for all cars, including my own." The painter of those giant red lips across a beautiful sky began to notice an acrid pall hanging over the city of Los Angeles. Man Ray decided to live in Hollywood without driving. He and Juliet went out less often. They became more sedentary, and more isolated. For Man Ray, Hollywood began to lose its glamour.

MAN RAY was fond of remarking that "New York was always twenty years behind Paris in its appreciation of contemporary art, and California was twenty years behind New York."

Despite having spent a decade on the fringes of Hollywood, he (unlike David Hockney, for example, a generation later) never developed a regionalist sensibility. He was a transplant that did not take.

Man Ray's conflicted feelings about the movie business were complicated by the fact that he was still an outsider in the film industry. He had always been an iconoclast as a filmmaker, but a filmmaker who hadn't produced a movie since the 1930s. His lunches with movie executives at Romanoff's and the Brown Derby always disappointed him. They had no time for his theories of how movies should be made. And they were only interested in him as a cameraman or an editor, a concept that was anathema to Man Ray. He wanted to be involved in a film from its inception, like Arnold Schoenberg before him, who turned down an offer to compose the music for *The Good Earth* because he wasn't allowed to create an operatic score for all the dialogue. Man Ray longed for the day when "the production of film would be in the hands of one mastermind." His.

"I can't take this town anymore," Man Ray complained. When a new landlord announced his intention to raise the artist's rent, Man Ray calculated that a year's rent would equal two one-way tickets across the ocean, and he promptly made a decision: he and Juliet would leave for Paris on the next available boat out of New York.

When the couple held their annual Christmas season "open house and yard sale," it was clear he was getting rid of excess baggage and trying to raise some cash. Toward the end of the afternoon, several "objects of my affection"—artistic works that would one day become priceless—were unceremoniously thrust into people's hands or sold for a dollar.

"The die is cast," Man Ray wrote to his sister in February 1951. "We have reservations to sail for Paris on the 12th of March on the *De Grasse*." The night before his long journey, Man Ray told a friend, "The maturest people make mistakes."

On the day Man Ray left Hollywood, his landlord came over to say good-bye to his departing tenants. He told the artist that should he and Juliet ever choose to return, he could have his old studio back. Then the landlord turned his attention to more practical matters and asked Man Ray what he intended to do with his car, which had stood idle for so long in front of the house. The landlord offered to buy the car. Just before leaving for the airport, Man Ray, always on the lookout for the ironic detail, noticed for the first time the "discreet lettering" on the hood of the car: "Hollywood Supercharger."

AS MAN RAY and Juliet made plans to set sail for France, the Pittsburgh-born actor and dancer Gene Kelly was busy making arrangements to bring seventeen-year-old ballet dancer Leslie Caron to Hollywood from Paris. The vital, energetic dancer was becoming a powerhouse at MGM after his work as the star and codirector with Stanley Donen of *On the Town*. Kelly wanted Caron to star as the gamine Lise Bouvier in MGM's new Arthur Freed musical, *An American in Paris*. The musical would be a tribute not only to Kelly's choreography and director Vincente Minnelli's love of Impressionist painting but to George Gershwin's jazz-inflected orchestral suite.

Plans for *An American in Paris* had begun over a pool table at Ira and Lee Gershwin' s house on North Roxbury Drive, where Arthur Freed, a longtime friend of George and Ira's, was a frequent guest. There Ira agreed to sell Freed the film rights to George Gershwin's orchestral suite. Despite the presence of strong personalities such as Kelly, Minnelli, and Oscar Levant, the film's presiding spirit was George Gershwin. Film critic Andrew Sarris observed that if there was an auteur haunting *An American in Paris*, it was the ghost of George Gershwin. Agreements were made, Ira was hired as a consultant for the film, and Arthur Freed's Culver City machinery went into high gear.

Kelly had first noticed Caron dancing with the Ballet des Champs-Elysées in a Roland Petit production of *The Sphinx* he saw performed

Leslie Caron and Gene Kelly perform a graceful pas de deux in *An American in Paris*. Caron had rebelled against director Vincente Minnelli, cutting off her long locks just days before shooting began and inadvertently starting a fashion trend. *Courtesy of the Academy of Motion Picture Arts and Sciences.*

in Paris. Sitting on top of a huge pedestal was a girl in a black wig with long claws and heavy makeup. "She was the sphinx . . . and she moved," Kelly remembered, "very well." He was absolutely convinced that Caron was ideal for the part of the young Parisienne with whom his character, Jerry Mulligan, falls in love. Caron had absolutely no acting experience, but at Kelly's insistence, Vincente Minnelli and Arthur Freed gave Caron a screen test. The decision was unanimous.

Minnelli was "struck by the [young] girl's gamine quality. She was by no means conventional looking," he thought, "but her waif's appearance grew on you. The more you saw her, the more beautiful she became." And the seventeen-year-old Caron had a built-in advantage: she could dance.

Caron reluctantly left her bohemian dancer's life in Paris to come to Hollywood, accompanied by her eager American mother, Margaret Caron, whose living expenses in Los Angeles would be covered by MGM.

"Everything I knew about Paris, or had heard about Paris, would be incorporated wherever possible," said Minnelli. "Together we created a Paris so authentic that Frenchmen are amazed to discover the picture was filmed in the United States."

Typically, Hollywood was happier with its own studio re-creation of postwar Paris than it had been with having the real Parisians in its midst. Having ejected Man Ray and having failed to support the work of Magritte and other artists, MGM enthusiastically paid homage to French painters in *An American in Paris*, which swept the Academy Awards in 1951 and was named best picture, beating out, among other worthy contenders, *A Place in the Sun* and *A Streetcar Named Desire*.

A PART in the Technicolor musical was written for Oscar Levant, the highest-paid concert pianist of the 1940s. A leading interpreter of Gershwin's concert music, Levant was also one of the late composer's most ardent friends. In some ways Oscar Levant was the ultimate expatriate in Hollywood, although he was an American. Like Gene Kelly, Levant was born in Pittsburgh but spent most of his life in New York City before migrating to Los Angeles to find work composing for the movies. In his heart, the pianist and composer had never left the city streets. Levant would clomp down to his friends' Hollywood tennis courts in heavy shoes and a dark suit (a "subtly spotted business suit, suitable for all Fahrenheits") to watch a long line of tennis enthusiasts, from George Gershwin in the 1930s to Cornel Wilde in the 1950s. But Levant would never play, convinced that tennis was detrimental to his pianist's wrists.

Levant had never quite adjusted to life in Hollywood. When he did finally move to Los Angeles, he preferred the company of Europeans, such as writers Eric Ambler, Aldous Huxley, and Christopher Isherwood, and the composer Arnold Schoenberg, with whom Levant studied in the late 1930s and early 1940s. But now a new generation of Hollywood personalities was beginning to discover the aging and reclusive enfant terrible. They saw in Levant a figure of artistic integrity and independence, qualities the Hollywood establishment seemed to lack. He had not lost his power to entertain a gathering by the sheer brilliance of his conversation, either. From behind a permanent scrim of cigarette smoke, Levant issued some of the smartest, sharpest one-liners of his time. Of Joe DiMaggio's divorce from Marilyn Monroe, he said, "No man can be expected to excel at two national pastimes." Of Doris Day: "I knew her before she became a virgin." Of Zsa Zsa Gabor: "She's discovered the secret of perpetual middle age." But he came up with more than sarcastic bon mots. Joe Hyams, a writer and journalist who covered Hollywood for the *New York Herald Tribune*, befriended Levant and considered him "the most erudite man I've ever met."

One evening Elizabeth Taylor and her then husband Michael Wilding appeared on Levant's doorstep along with Arthur Loew Jr., scion of the famous theater chain, who brought his date, Joan Collins. Also present was the producer of *Giant*, Henry Ginsberg, and the film's young male star, James Dean.

After an evening of being entertained by Levant's scathing and iconoclastic wit, Joan Collins discovered that the Levants' eldest daughter, Marcia, had a huge crush on James Dean. Collins thought it would be amusing to surprise Marcia with her real-life idol.

"Marcia, Marcia, we're here to see you," Collins whispered to the sleeping girl. "Now come on, wake up. We have somebody who wants to meet you."

Marcia slowly awoke to the sight of James Dean lounging against her bedroom door. She screamed and put her head under the covers.

"It was a strange thing," Levant later wrote about the incident, "but seeing my daughter's room (filled as it was with pictures of the young actor) did not seem to please James Dean. On the contrary, it depressed him." Dean told Levant he felt crushed under the weight of such adulation.

After the other guests had left, Dean stayed and discussed music with Levant, who was impressed with the young actor's knowledge of composers such as Bartók and Schoenberg. Levant, one of the country's most famous neurotics by the end of the 1950s, loved *East of Eden* (1955). Levant would later recount that Nicholas Ray, the director of *Rebel Without a Cause*, told him he had set up a date for James Dean with a psychoanalyst, but three days before the appointment the actor was killed when he crashed his Porsche Spyder.

Collins was an occasional guest at the Levant home, and she invariably wore revealing outfits with plunging necklines, part of her English sex-kitten image. Her provocative attire did not go unnoticed by Levant. Observing that she always wore long, thick bangs that fell flirtatiously over her eyebrows, Levant was inspired to remark, "I have now seen every part of Joan Collins' anatomy except her forehead." But for all her provocative good looks, Collins was amazed by Elizabeth Taylor's beauty. She whispered to June Levant about Taylor, "Isn't she gorgeous! Isn't she beautiful!"

Levant remained friends with Elizabeth Taylor throughout her marriages to Mike Wilding, Michael Todd, and Eddie Fisher. "Always a bride, never a bridesmaid," Levant quipped about her. "Her five husbands have absolutely nothing in common—except her." Levant's remarks had not lost their sting.

ALAN JAY LERNER, whom Arthur Freed brought to Hollywood to write the screenplay for *An American in Paris*, once said that Freed began a sentence on Wednesday and finished it on Friday. A heavyset man who was always on a diet, Freed used to drift onto the set during the filming, his hands jingling the coins in his pockets, and not say two words. Despite his awkwardness, Freed knew how to get what he wanted, and he insisted that Lerner write in a part for Oscar Levant.

They decided that Levant would play Adam Cook, "a Dave Diamond type—a kind of perpetual expatriate composer living in Europe on the largesse of foundation fellowships." Freed "thought of no one but Oscar Levant for the part of Jerry's sidekick," Vincente Minnelli wrote in his memoirs. "Including Oscar in the film lent the enterprise a sort of legitimacy . . . though he would have blanched if I'd told him that."

Fred Astaire and Gene Kelly were both under consideration for the part of Jerry Mulligan—an American studying art in Paris on the GI Bill—but plans to include a lengthy ballet tipped the scales toward Kelly, who was more of a balletic dancer than Astaire.

At a studio party to welcome Leslie Caron to Hollywood, Oscar Levant met the French teenager who would be turned into an American movie star with her first picture. Levant's wife June was anxious to know what Gene Kelly's discovery looked like. "She looks too much like me as far as I'm concerned," Levant replied.

As preposterous as the remark sounded, there was truth in it. Caron did indeed look like a feminized, fetching version of Levant, with her full, pouty lips, round head, and wide, intelligent eyes. The resemblance would be borne out later in Amanda Levant, the daughter who looked the most like her father and would bear a striking similarity to Caron.

The French actress also shared Levant's rebelliousness and tended to balk at the demands of her studio handlers. She was now thrust into the male world of the MGM musical. "I was so revolted by all their emphasis on pink and lace, and their idea of femininity. . . . So I didn't play the game," she remembered. Her first act of defiance was to cut off her hair.

Caron thought her short hair looked great—modern and completely new. But Minnelli, Freed, and Kelly were all horrified. They stood around her, shaking their heads in disbelief at what the young actress had done. So shooting began with Leslie Caron sitting beside her hairdresser, who every now and then gave her hair a sharp tug, as if that would make it grow.

Levant's wife and three daughters visited their father on the set of *An American in Paris*. The girls were entranced by Caron, who was "so cute and friendly." Amanda Levant remembered being present while they filmed the Beaux-Arts Ball, Levant dressed in a cowboy suit and Caron wearing a little tiara with tiny stars suspended on wires that seemed to shoot off in all directions.

Andrew Sarris has observed that Vincente Minnelli was a director with "an unusual, somber outlook for musical comedy," belied, perhaps, by his glorious use of color. Real fulfillment and contentment always seem just beyond his characters' reach. In *An American in Paris*, despite a happy reunion of the lovers in the film's final ballet, there are several instances of "unresolved tristesse": Nina Foch as Jerry Mulligan's ill-treated, cast-off patroness; Georges Guétary's sympathetic role as the rejected suitor; Levant's status as a composer going nowhere, except in his fantasies. "I'm a concert pianist—that's a pretentious way of saying I'm unemployed at the moment. . . . I'm beginning to feel like the world's oldest child prodigy," are his first words onscreen.

There is pathos in Levant's Adam Cook, stemming perhaps from the fact that he is portraying a composer, the "racket" he had long ago given up. Levant shared with Minnelli something of the successful man's fantasy of "what could have been"—back in New York, Minnelli had once aspired to be a painter. Levant had been pigeonholed by the popular culture he had mocked, known more for his colorful personality than his artistic talents. "It's not what you are but what you don't become that hurts," he said.

For Levant, *An American in Paris* also had a haunted feel because it was yet another celebration of the late George Gershwin's music. Included in the movie were "(I'll Build a) Stairway to Paradise," the first Gershwin song that Levant had fallen in love with as a young accompanist in his sister-in-law's tap-dancing class, and "Love Is Here to Stay," the last, unfinished song George ever wrote, and one that Levant had helped Ira to complete after the composer's death of a brain tumor in July 1937. Performing those songs again was bittersweet. Levant had loved Gershwin, had honed his musical skills with him—and his wit: "Tell me, George, if you had it to do all over, would you fall in love with yourself again?" Yet his Gershwin connection always eclipsed Levant's solo efforts. "If it wasn't for George, I could have been a pretty good mediocre composer," he said, playing himself in *Rhapsody in Blue*, the 1945 movie about Gershwin's life.

In addition to his musical work, Levant also contributed some of his own lines to Alan Jay Lerner's screenplay for *An American in Paris*. He claimed credit for the remark, "It's not a pretty face, I grant you, but underneath this flabby exterior is an enormous lack of character," and reprised it elsewhere, but he also noted that Lerner was "apoplectic" when he learned Minnelli allowed Levant to write his own lines. Lerner, according to Levant, wasn't a "credit-sharer."

Arthur Freed was a Gershwin friend from the old days, as were

Minnelli and songwriter Johnny Green, who was the film's musical director and the head of MGM's music department. One of Green's prized possessions was an autographed picture of George Gershwin dated 1930. Green resented Levant's presence in the studio. He felt that while Levant had the public reputation of being Gershwin's closest friend, he himself had been no less a friend and confidant of the legendary composer. In a word, Green was envious of Levant's professional reputation as a Gershwin intimate, and whenever the two men worked together, sparks would fly.

They fought over what a "Gershwin sound" really meant and what Gershwin's musical intentions were. During the recording sessions for the Concerto in F, the "ego fantasy" scene, the two men locked horns. Freed leapt into the fray to defend Levant, humiliating Green in front of the studio orchestra. "Never was there a conductor so put in his place," Green remembered. "Freed hit me with every Sherman tank, every Louisville slugger in the place . . . because Oscar was It." Minnelli also tended to side with Levant in these debates. Luckily, perhaps, for the morale of the set, Green's responsibilities as head of MGM's music department forced him to leave most of the orchestrating duties to the more congenial Saul Chaplin.

One thing Freed insisted on from the first was that there would be no concert music in the film. "I don't want any lulls in this picture," Freed told the assembled collaborators during a meeting at MGM. The "Freed Unit" was redefining the movie musical, ensuring that the story be as strong as the music and at no point permitting the action to stop just to showcase a star turn. Levant, of course, felt differently, but it seemed that Freed only wanted him to play a medley of Gershwin's songs.

Levant first looked to Kelly for support but instinctively felt he would not get it. Kelly was gaining clout at MGM and wouldn't want to buck Freed. After Kelly rejected the idea of a concert sequence for the film, Levant walked dejectedly into Minnelli's office and collapsed into a chair. He then blurted out his idea: that he, Levant, be filmed playing all the instruments in the orchestra in a performance of the third movement of Gershwin's Concerto in F. At the conclusion of the piece, he's sitting in a box seat cheering his own performance. "That's a marvelous idea!" Minnelli enthused. He then called Arthur Freed,

The legendary pianist Oscar Levant (right) appeared with Gene Kelly in *An American in Paris*. Noted for his wicked wit, Levant appeared in more than a dozen films, always playing a version of himself. *Courtesy of the USC Cinema-Television Library and Archive of Performing Arts.*

reaching him just as he was leaving the Thalberg Building at MGM, and asked the producer to wait for them.

"Oscar's got a wonderful idea!" Minnelli told Freed. He described Levant's concept, which Oscar had dubbed the "ego fantasy."

"Had Oscar not come up with that idea," recalled Saul Chaplin, the film's orchestrator, "there's a chance that the Concerto might not [have been] in the picture, because that's how the picture was approached. . . . There's not a single number where somebody just stands by a piano and sings." It brought Levant much pleasure when, the following year, he heard through Freed that his "ego fantasy" was the French painter Raoul Dufy's favorite scene in *An American in Paris*.

When the film's final cut, completed in May 1951, was shown to the cast and crew, there was a great howl of pain from Levant. His final scene with Nina Foch at the black-and-white Beaux-Arts Ball had been edited out to make room for the seventeen-minute ballet.

Levant was crushed. "Some may believe Oscar was a personality and not an actor, but you couldn't have proved it by his vanity-wounded roar" when he realized this scene had been cut, Minnelli later wrote.

The missing scene would have rounded out Levant's character with the suggestion that Jerry Mulligan's jilted patroness would go on to sponsor Adam Cook. It was also an important scene for Nina Foch, one she believed contained her best acting in the picture—possibly her best acting of all her screen roles. In the scene, Foch (as Milo) has just been abandoned by Kelly (as Jerry Mulligan); she now realizes that any emotion he felt toward her was just a cover for his feelings for Lise. Foch has described the missing scene as providing a key to the character of Milo:

> The thing that makes Milo so touching was in this last scene at the black-and-white ball, where I get drunk because I realize that I've lost Gene, and I'm sitting at the table with Oscar Levant, talking about men and why men don't love me. . . . I'm just buzzing, about to be a weepy drunk, half-laughing, and suddenly up comes this truly lonely, lonely little girl whose daddy never loved her. That's not in the lines, but you can see that she's that kind of woman. A piece of confetti gets in my champagne glass, and I see it, take it out, and look at it. I look up; then I think about it, what it is that's in my glass. "Oh, it's a pill," and I take it like a pill. It's a beautiful moment.

Minnelli thought the scene detracted from the love story between Caron and Kelly, but its absence does leave a slight hole in the picture. The scene would have fleshed out the characters of the discarded patron and the hopeful composer. Sarris has speculated that it was excised because of Minnelli's devotion to his "morbidly beautiful *mise-en-scène*," and that the unresolved feeling we're left with at the end of the film is an expression of Minnelli's essential melancholy.

The reviews of *An American in Paris* were mostly ecstatic. The musical was a tremendous success, and it dominated the Academy

Awards the year of its release, nominated in eight categories. Lerner's original screenplay was nominated, as was Vincente Minnelli's direction. Saul Chaplin and Johnny Green won their Oscars for musical direction and orchestration (Green getting some of his own back at Levant, who wasn't nominated for anything). Arthur Freed was given the Irving Thalberg Award for the body of his work as a producer, and Gene Kelly was given a special award for his contribution to dance on film. But when *An American in Paris* was named best picture, the audience was noticeably surprised. No Freed production had ever been nominated for that honor before, and few in the industry had expected it to win.

Gene Kelly's gamble had paid off. *An American in Paris* had made Leslie Caron a movie star. Soon, fan clubs of young teenage girls sprang up across the country and MGM offered her a contract.

For Oscar Levant, the film's success was a mixed blessing. The overwhelming popular reaction to the movie furthered his public association with Gershwin's music at a time when his concert career demanded that he move beyond his image as the main interpreter of *Rhapsody in Blue*. And the film critics now typecast Levant as a Gershwin sidekick who could occasionally sit down to deliver a concert-level performance. Despite his great promise, they stopped wondering when Hollywood would give him a major part in a film.

Not long after Levant completed work on *An American in Paris*, he and his wife, June, joined Jerry Wald and his wife, Connie, for an evening out. The two couples were seated at a table at Chasen's, where Oscar regaled the Walds with stories about the making of his latest movie. George Jessel, the cigar-chomping vaudevillian who had recently become a Hollywood film producer, walked into the restaurant and made a beeline for Levant's table.

"Have you heard the news?" Jessel asked with a grave look on his face. "Al Jolson is dead." Jolson had died in San Francisco, in his hotel room, of a massive heart attack.

Oscar had never outgrown his idolatry of Jolson, for whom he worked as a pianist and sidekick on Jolson's short-lived radio show in the late forties. For Levant, Jolson would always represent the lost era of Broadway show business, when performers were reluctant to leave New York for California. He also represented the kind of complete, unquestioning self-confidence that had always eluded Levant—the absolute acceptance of one's own personality and even greatness.

From that night on, Levant couldn't bear to be in the same room with the old raconteur Jessel, whose very presence added yet another name to his ever-expanding list of forbidden words, phobias, and superstitions.

Levant was thrilled to have his friends with him in Los Angeles, out among the "suspicious-looking" palm trees, but as they began to die off or drift away, Levant himself became increasingly difficult and insulting. He would retreat, turning down more invitations than he accepted. Eventually a heart attack and mental disturbances made it almost impossible for him to maintain any meaningful relationships. He even avoided the piano. "It knows where to find me," he would tell people who asked if he still played. His wife soon realized that socially, in Hollywood, she was on her own.

Levant had always been an outsider in Hollywood, though he had moved there for good in 1947 and remained there for the next twenty-five years. He died in the summer of 1972 at his home on North Roxbury Drive, peacefully in bed, after practicing the piano. Candice Bergen had come to the house to interview him for *Esquire* on the day he died.

AN AMERICAN IN PARIS sparked Leslie Caron's career, but it also led to her being typecast as a kind of professional gamine in films such as *Lili* (1953) and *Gigi* (1958). Caron also was never completely at home in Hollywood. She befriended a young actor named Jack Larson, who would achieve fame in the 1950s playing Jimmy Olsen in the television series *The Adventures of Superman*. Larson, a close friend of Montgomery Clift, became Caron's escort in Hollywood. The pair took what Larson once described as "the young Werther approach to life," dressing all in black and reading French Symbolist poetry. A Hollywood hostess once asked the two young actors why they wore such somber clothing. "Because we're in mourning for our lives," Caron answered. Perhaps it was her reputation as an iconoclast that made her the obvious choice to play opposite George Peppard in *The Subterraneans*, the 1960 film based on the roman à clef by the ultimate Beatnik, Jack Kerouac.

Caron played Kerouac's lover Mardou Fox, who in the novel and in reality was an African-American. One of Kerouac's biographers noted how Caron "somehow managed to transport Gay Nineties coquetry into North Beach," the Beatnik enclave where the story was set. Towheaded Peppard was cast as Kerouac and Roddy McDowall played the wild poet Gregory Corso. Caron would later say that MGM wanted to "try something new" with its film version of *The Subterraneans*. "It was the new literature," she said. "It was the new style with the young people. It bombed."

Kerouac hated the movie and returned to the bottle, never fully recovering from his disappointment in the film version of his novel. Caron, however, did recover from *The Subterraneans*. In fact, she received an Oscar nomination for her role in the 1962 drama *The L-Shaped Room*.

She began to spend more time in France, eventually opening an inn outside Paris called La Lucarne aux Chouettes (loosely translated: "the Owl's Nest"). She never retired from acting, though, and recently had a small role in the Academy Award–nominated *Chocolat* and another in a television movie *Murder on the Orient Express*. During a publicity tour to promote *Chocolat*, Caron found herself reminiscing about her days at MGM in the 1950s. She told the New York columnist Liz Smith how the studio "coddled and pampered you to the point of keeping you totally childish and totally dependent. You were treated like an Oriental princess locked away in an ivory tower. And you were never alone. In the end, it was unbearably suffocating."

CHAPTER 9

LOVE AND HATE: *A PLACE IN THE SUN* AND *THE NIGHT OF THE HUNTER*

SHELLEY WINTERS waited at Schwab's Drugstore, the famous Sunset Boulevard spot where celebrities read the trade papers and filled their prescriptions for sleeping pills, and where hopeful unknowns waited to be discovered, drinking a float at the soda fountain counter. Her friends Sidney Skolsky and Winters's future roommate Marilyn Monroe soon joined her. Winters was newly signed to Columbia Studios, where she had steady work in small roles but was still waiting for a part with more than one line. Monroe, not yet twenty, was going by "Norma Jean Baker" and chauffeuring Skolsky, a gossip columnist, around in her old car since he'd never learned to drive. After lunch, the threesome headed out to the parking lot behind Schwab's. Skolsky pointed to a long, low building. "That's the Actors Lab," he said, explaining that it was a new Hollywood venture started by members of the famous Group Theatre. "Some of the best actors in the world teach there."

Monroe and Winters nearly flattened Skolsky as they ran to the building's front door. Monroe couldn't afford the tuition of twenty-five dollars down and fifty dollars for six months. But Winters signed up immediately for "intermediate" classes. She had studied "the Method" at the New Theater School in New York. And one of her first jobs ever was ushering at performances of the radical Group Theatre for a dollar a show. She had seen the power of their technique, which taught actors to rely on their own real, personal, and sensory experiences when performing scenes from plays and movies.

A groundbreaking acting troupe, the Group Theatre was founded in New York by Cheryl Crawford, Harold Clurman, and Lee Strasberg around 1930. It was the first company fully trained to work together as an ensemble. It also employed methods developed by Konstantin Stanislavski, a Russian actor and director who had explored the psychological aspects of performance in an effort to enable actors, as Clurman described it, to fuse "the technical elements of their craft with the stuff of their own spiritual and emotional selves." The Group Theatre also produced some of the most controversial and meaningful works of the day, such as Clifford Odets's leftist *Golden Boy*.

Although the troupe officially disbanded in 1941, meaning that it no longer performed as a single unit, its alumni continued the traditions and teachings, scattering to Hollywood or remaining on Broadway. Crawford, along with directors Robert Lewis and Elia Kazan, would found the Actors Studio in New York in 1947. They sought to create a kind of sanctuary, a place where actors could test themselves, take classes, and learn exercises to hone their talents in a supportive environment free from the scrutiny of critics.

Whether under the auspices of "the Group," "the Actors Studio," or "the Method," it all meant the same thing: a bold new kind of acting. And many of Hollywood's biggest stars of the 1950s embraced it, including Marlon Brando, Montgomery Clift, and James Dean. Marilyn Monroe would later take lessons, too, and Lee Strasberg's wife, Paula, would become her acting coach.

Monty Clift first encountered the Method in 1942, while working on a play called *Mexican Mural*. Robert Lewis, one of the Group's founding members, directed the play and used emotional-memory exercises and improvisation in rehearsals. Clift's curiosity was piqued, especially when he met Mira Rostova, a Russian émigrée and former stage actress. Clift and Rostova would have long talks about Stanislavski and the essence of art. She would later become his personal acting adviser and accompany him on the sets of his movies, to the chagrin of many Hollywood directors.

Shelley Winters didn't have a personal coach, though. So she took classes at the Actors Lab and watched rehearsals there of actors such as John Garfield and Lee J. Cobb. The lab filled an artistic void Winters had sensed since her arrival in Hollywood. But it gave the actress, newly signed to Columbia Studios, what she called "a rather schizophrenic approach" to film acting. The work she did at the lab looked nothing like the "acting" she was learning at the studio.

At Columbia, professional stylists tried to make Winters into a blonde bombshell, subjecting her to lengthy beauty treatments in which they dyed and straightened her hair. They even gave her a new hairline, which required painful waxing and electrolysis. In addition to her dancing and speech lessons, the studio also ordered that she take acting instruction from a young University of Michigan professor who spoke with a British accent. The acting classes, Winters remembered, included pasting Scotch tape onto her face so she could learn how to smile and emote without creating facial lines, thus maintaining a perfect image for the camera. Frustrated, Winters wondered how she could register emotion. Her instructor told her not to worry. When she needed to cry in a scene, someone from the makeup department would gently blow menthol into her face to force her eyes to water.

Winters longed to be more than a cookie-cutter starlet, however. She would get her first real opportunity to do some serious film acting in late 1949, when director George Stevens began production of *An American Tragedy*, later retitled *A Place in the Sun*. Based on the novel by Theodore Dreiser, it tells the story of an ambitious young man, played by Montgomery Clift, who strives to get ahead in his uncle's company. His plans for financial success and social acceptance, not to mention marriage to a beautiful and desirable woman, are thwarted when his first girlfriend becomes pregnant by him. Winters would play the role of Alice, that luckless shopgirl.

Her screen test for the film was the ambiguous rowboat scene in which Clift's character plans to murder his pregnant girlfriend, who then drowns when the boat accidentally capsizes. Stevens had given Winters the script only the night before. He urged her not to study it too much, telling her instead to visit factories and observe the girls who worked on the assembly lines; to ride buses in East Los Angeles and watch young women nearly asleep in their seats after a long day

Portrait of a love triangle: Elizabeth Taylor, Montgomery Clift, and Shelley Winters in 1951's *A Place in the Sun*. The film was nominated for best picture but lost to *An American in Paris*. *Courtesy of the authors.*

of mindless drudgery. "I did this for two weeks before the test," Winters said.

When she did glance at the script, Winters noticed a peculiar thing. In the script Monty Clift's character was named George Eastman. Stevens had given the doomed boy his own first name; in Dreiser's novel his name was Clyde.

Winters believed in Stevens as a director. One of his techniques was to have the actors rehearse the scene with dialogue, then, when the cameras began rolling, he told them to do the scene again without talking, using only their eyes and faces to communicate. Both Winters and Clift were students of the Method, and perhaps their experience with its emotional "exercises" allowed them to respond to such direction so well. Clift also followed Stanislavski's practice of intense concentration and would often focus so single-mindedly that he'd finish the scenes drenched in sweat. "Your body doesn't know you're acting," he told Elizabeth Taylor. "It sweats and makes adrenaline as though your emotions were real."

Stevens asked his actors to perform silent scenes because he felt that something had been lost when movies added sound. He believed that dialogue had somehow diminished the emotional scope of films, rather than broadened it. And much of *A Place in the Sun* relies on visual cues instead of spoken explanation. It was the opposing images, Stevens later told the American Film Institute, that interested him most in the movie, "Shelley Winters busting at the seams with sloppy melted ice cream . . . as against Elizabeth Taylor in a white gown with blue ribbons floating down from the sky. . . . Automatically there's an imbalance of images which creates drama." There are other visual allusions in the film as well, such as the neon sign outside George's rooming-house window that flashes "Vickers," the last name of Elizabeth Taylor's character, Angela, the woman he longs for. Later, when George and Alice go to the courthouse office to be married—only to find it closed—they stand beside a frosted glass door, "BIRTHS, MARRIAGES and DEATHS" written on the pane in stark black letters.

In keeping with Stevens's emphasis on the visual, some of the most moving moments in *A Place in the Sun* contain little or no dialogue. The fateful love scene between George and Alice is dominated by the play of light and shadow and the ambient sounds of Clift's heavy breathing, the falling rain, and the radio. Later, Alice is pregnant and alone, waiting for George to fulfill his promise to marry her. She walks to the mailbox, in her frumpy, baggy blouse and skirt, only to find no letter from him but a newspaper. On the front page is a photo of George and the glamorous socialite Angela frolicking on a speedboat over the caption "summer fun." Winters says nothing, but her pain and dejection are abundantly clear.

Winters also drew on her Actors Lab lessons during the scene in which she asks the doctor to "help" her. Written carefully so that censors would not object to the implied reference to abortion, the scene crackles with tension. The doctor makes small talk stiffly; Alice speaks quietly, trying to rein in her emotions. But she breaks down, almost yelling at the doctor, "I'm not married. I haven't got a husband." Winters, like all good Method actors, recalled her own past experience—twice she herself had faced unwanted pregnancies—so as to make her actions, and reactions, believable.

Shelley Winters would get her first Oscar nomination for the role. But her costar, Montgomery Clift, never liked her portrayal of Alice. He thought she played it "all wrong," that she was too obvious. She made the character "blubbery" and "irritating." Indeed, as time goes by and George still hasn't married her, Alice becomes shrewish and shrill. She interrupts him with a phone call from a bus depot during a Hawaiian luau at Angela's home. (Another Stevens visual cue, the gay party contrasted with the desolate depot.) She orders George to come pick her up and threatens to reveal their secret to the newspapers, thereby toppling him from his newly acquired social position. "I said now!" she says. "You're gonna marry me tomorrow or I'll phone the newspapers and then I'll kill myself!"

Stevens disagreed with Clift's criticism. He told Clift he was being too sentimental, that Alice's character was meant to be pathetic. Clift was known for his perfectionism, though. If the Method was a way for Shelley Winters to improve her craft, for him it was a way of life. He worked intensely with his coach Mira Rostova on the film. She stood so close to the camera that she sometimes ruined a take, her hand appearing in the frame as she gestured to Monty. Although he never threw her off the set, Stevens ignored Rostova's presence.

Clift, undoubtedly encouraged by his Russian adviser, argued endlessly with Stevens over the final moments of the film. As he's heading for the electric chair, Stevens wanted the actor to register some kind of horror, to appear afraid and overcome. Clift refused, saying a doomed man would never look that way. He would appear benumbed, nearly frozen.

Clift won the battle and his gaze, his haunted eyes in an immobile face, provides a memorable and disturbing finale. But he was disappointed and disillusioned with Stevens, calling him a "craftsman" rather than an artist and bemoaning his rigid attitude toward his actors. "George preconceives everything through a viewfinder," he said, a sentiment that James Dean would later echo, frustrated by his own experience with Stevens on *Giant* (1956).

Together with his Method muse Rostova, Monty had worked out every nuanced detail of his role in *A Place in the Sun*, turning Clyde, the unsympathetic social climber and murderer, into George, a complex, troubled, and essentially tragic hero. Richard Burton—trained for the London theater in a style completely opposite to that of the Method—thought that "Monty, like Garbo and Brando, had the extraordinary faculty for giving you a sense of danger. You were never quite sure whether he would blow his lines or explode." Perhaps that was what was behind the riveting power of Method actors.

But Clift and Winters performed too well. Their inspired portrayals helped change the meaning of Dreiser's classic story forever.

IT WAS long thought that the title of *An American Tragedy* was changed to *A Place in the Sun* because the original title sounded too dark and depressing for Hollywood. But the title was changed for a much more pernicious reason. The House Un-American Activities Committee had turned their attention, yet again, to Hollywood. Paramount was hoping that no one would notice that the socialist-leaning Dreiser had written the novel upon which the film was based, but Stevens told Ivan Moffat at Paramount that the title had to go.

Moffat had known George Stevens since the Second World War. They had served together in the famous film unit that had been among the first to enter Auschwitz and film the liberation of Paris. The war was often with them. One afternoon while taking a nap in his office on the Paramount lot, Moffat dreamt of Kaiser Wilhelm, of his famous 1913 speech in which he said Germany will have its place in the sun. Waking up with that phrase in his head, Moffat called Stevens and gave him the name of his movie.

Renaming *An American Tragedy* was only the first of many changes to come. Paramount rejected Stevens's original adaptation as being too un-American. But Anne Revere, who played Monty's evangelist mother in the film, thought that Stevens's original script was much more faithful to Dreiser's vision. It kept to the plot, following more closely the reports of the real killing and the resulting trial in upstate New York. "The characters in this version made perfect sense. They were almost archetypal," Revere said. "The murderer [Monty] was more frankly ambitious—conniving. Liz Taylor's part was originally a rich, spoiled, mean bitch. Shelley Winters was actually lovable. . . ."

All that was changed in the revision of the script: Monty's character becomes passive, hapless, and sympathetic; the rich society girl (Taylor) is so overwhelmingly beautiful that the viewer forgives Monty for plotting Winters's murder; and the factory girl herself (Winters) is so needy she becomes an irritating burden who deserves to be cast off. The film makes the wealthy characters the most sympathetic while the poor are characterized as unlikable. George, really a callous social climber, tears at our heartstrings—certainly not what Dreiser intended in his socialist critique of class conflict in America. Stevens turned Dreiser's novel into a love story, and most of Anne Revere's scenes as Monty's mother were cut. Revere would later be blacklisted after *A Place in the Sun*'s 1951 release, although her role in the film was not cited as a cause.

The film was a tremendous success, though, reported to be "the number 8 top grosser" in *Variety* and nominated for an Academy Award for best picture of 1951. Clift and Winters also earned Oscar nominations. But there was at least one Hollywood novelist and screenwriter with impeccable credentials who heartily disliked the film: Raymond Chandler. Writing to a friend in January of 1952, Chandler complained,

> I despised it. It's as slick a piece of bogus self-importance as you'll ever see. . . . *A Place in the Sun* never touches your emotions once. Everything is held too long; every scene is milked ruthlessly. I got so sick of starry-eyed close-ups of Elizabeth Taylor that I could have gagged. . . . And the portrayal of how the lower classes think the upper classes live is about as ridiculous as could be imagined. They ought to have called it *Speedboats for Breakfast.* And my God, that scene at the end where the girl visits him in the condemned cell a few hours before he gets the hot squat! . . . The whole thing . . . reeks of calculation and contrivance emotionally. . . . The picture was made by a guy who has seen everything and has never had a creative idea of his own.

The elegant writer of hard-boiled detective fiction was just as tough on Monty Clift, who, he wrote, "gives the performance of his career, which is not saying a great deal, since he had already demonstrated in *The Heiress* that he didn't belong on the same screen with first-class actors [Olivia de Havilland and the great Ralph Richardson]."

But perhaps Chandler just didn't "get" the new acting style, just didn't understand "the Method."

SHELLEY WINTERS and Marilyn Monroe, while unlikely intellectuals, wanted to learn all they could about their chosen profession, and not just from the Actors Lab. In late 1949, Charles Laughton was putting together a group of actors who would work on Shakespeare and study the history of the theater. Robert Ryan told Winters about the Sunday night meetings and asked the actress if she would like to meet Laughton and audition for the group. He told her to see as many of Laughton's pictures as she could and to be "myself at all times and tell him the truth about myself," especially her feelings of inadequacy.

Winters prepared by reading *King Lear* during a celebrity baseball game where she and Marilyn Monroe were cheerleaders. (Winters and Monroe were then sharing a cottage at the Chateau Marmont on Sunset Boulevard.) "Marilyn noticed the book, and even thought it was strange for me to be reading *King Lear* aloud to myself while being photographed by all the movie magazines." When Winters explained that she was preparing to audition for Charles Laughton's Shakespeare study group, Monroe asked if she could accompany her, saying she thought the corpulent Laughton "the sexiest man she'd ever seen."

Charles Laughton reciting Shakespeare to a roomful of adoring actors in his den in Santa Monica was about all the culture he was going to get out of Hollywood. In 1952 he had signed to appear with Bud Abbott and Lou Costello in *Abbott and Costello Meet Captain Kidd*, considered to be the nadir of Laughton's career and an example of the humiliation the great actor of the 1930s would endure in the 1950s.

Yet Laughton wasn't wholly ineffective in the slapstick comedy and turned in an enthusiastic performance, punctuated by pratfalls and funny walks. And although fans of the classically trained actor might have winced at seeing him in his underwear throughout most of the film, Laughton didn't seem embarassed. *Abbott and Costello Meet Captain Kidd*, in fact, may have provided a real opportunity for Laughton, since he would soon begin an important collaboration with the film's gifted cinematographer, Stanley Cortez.

Early in 1954, Charles Laughton was talking to James Agee, the screenwriter and novelist who would win the Pulitzer Prize for his autobiographical novel *A Death in the Family*. They were discussing a new book by Davis Grubb called *The Night of the Hunter*, which had just become a best-seller. It told the story of a corrupt preacher in pursuit of a stolen fortune. He ruthlessly hunts down two children who have the booty he's after, and kills their mother along the way.

Laughton was fascinated by the book's themes and by Grubb's rhythmic prose that conjured a dark southern world of insular communities, eerie church hymns, simple virtues, and complex vices. Critic William Wiegand described Grubb's work as "rich in local idiom" with "many of the qualities of the American folk song." Grubb contrasted what Wiegand called "the primal cruelty of some of the 'simple' people with the vast and helpless innocence of others."

Producer Paul Gregory had bought the rights to *Hunter* for $75,000 in December 1953, even before the book's publication, in hopes that Laughton would direct the film version. Laughton was immediately interested and thought Agee should write the screenplay. He offered Robert Mitchum the part of the evil preacher.

Agee at first seemed like the perfect candidate to adapt Davis Grubb's novel for the screen. The acclaimed author of *Let Us Now Praise Famous Men* had even successfully written a screenplay for *The African Queen*. But sadly, by 1954 Agee was an alcoholic in a tailspin, a fact that everyone in Hollywood—except Charles Laughton—knew. During the earliest discussions about *Hunter*, Agee often passed out drunk on Mitchum's couch. Mitchum felt a strange affection for this writer who chain-smoked and had terrible tooth decay. They were members of the same fraternity, Mitchum later explained to one of Agee's biographers, "the fraternity of the bottle."

Agee would spend the summer working on the *Hunter* script by the pool at the house on Curson Avenue. When he finished, he had created a 350-page monstrosity. It was not an adaptation but rather a "cinematic version" of the novel. He included extraordinary, some would say excruciating, details relating to the WPA and the Depression. He even specified newsreel footage needed to document the story's setting and added a number of elaborate, impractical montages. Mitchum understood what Agee was trying to do. He'd had some lean years during the Depression, too, had even hidden out in box cars and been rousted for vagrancy by the police. But the script was unusable. In the end, Laughton would write the screenplay himself, flourishing in his newfound position of sole creative authority.

Conversely, Mitchum at first seemed a strange choice for Laughton's leading man. The two men could not have been more different in tem-

Robert Mitchum, left, and director Charles Laughton pose at a Hollywood restaurant to promote their 1955 film *The Night of the Hunter*, based on the novel by Davis Grubb. *Courtesy of the Academy of Motion Picture Arts and Sciences.*

perament, appearance, and acting style. Laughton agonized over every nuance of every performance, driving to distraction such directors as Alfred Hitchcock (*The Paradine Case*, 1947) and Alexander Korda (*The Private Life of Henry VIII*, 1933). Korda once remarked, "With him acting was an act of childbirth. What he needed was not so much a director as a midwife." Laughton later suffered anguish on the set of 1962's *Advise and Consent* because he couldn't figure out how his character should walk. In contrast, Robert Mitchum seemed only to show up and say his lines; it's no accident that the subtitle of one Mitchum biography is *It Sure Beats Working*.

Mitchum, who made his debut in *The Story of GI Joe* in 1945, was a new kind of star. With a Weltschmerz formed back in the Depression-ridden 1930s before he ever came to Hollywood, Mitchum had been a stevedore and a ditchdigger; he rode the rails back when the homeless were called hobos. He even served time on a chain gang in Georgia on a vagrancy charge. You can't get more American that that.

Five years earlier, in February 1949, Bob Mitchum had served some sixty days in the Los Angeles county jail after getting caught in the act of snuffing out a marijuana cigarette. Perhaps the reason Mitchum's drug bust didn't derail his career was that his film persona was already that of a tough guy who had lived a hard life on both sides of the law. And that persona wasn't far from the man Mitchum really was. Unlike Laughton, who lived in fear of being publicly exposed as a homosexual, Mitchum had nothing to hide. Unlike Laughton, Robert Mitchum could not be blackmailed. Even Laughton's producer Paul Gregory was smeared in *Confidential* as having swindled his landlady out of $7500 by promising to marry her. But when *Confidential* wrote a smear piece on Bob Mitchum, the actor did the unthinkable: he sued.

"The Nude Who Came to Dinner" appeared in the May 1955 issue of *Confidential*, telling a wild story of Mitchum showing up drunk at a dinner party given by Charles Laughton and his wife, Elsa Lanchester. At one point Mitchum allegedly removed his clothes, smeared ketchup all over his body, and announced, "This is a masquerade party, isn't it? Well, I'm a hamburger."

Mitchum risked greater exposure by filing a libel suit against the New York–based magazine. The case was eventually overturned due to technicalities, but many believe that his actions led the way for other actors—Maureen O'Hara, Dorothy Dandridge, and Liberace—to file suits against *Confidential*.

MITCHUM WAS tall, manly, and heterosexual. Laughton was a self-hating homosexual: "I have a face like the behind of an elephant," he once said. Mitchum was taciturn; Laughton was witty, emotional, inventive. Mitchum grew up hard and poor; Laughton came from a comfortable middle-class family of English hotel managers.

But the extraordinary combination of these two men was a success from the start. "This character I want you to play is a diabolical shit," said Laughton.

"Present," replied Mitchum.

Laughton then cast his former Shakespeare student Shelley Winters, who had just been nominated for an Oscar for *A Place in the Sun*, as costar. Mitchum's first reaction was, "My God, Shelley Winters?" He agreed with Monty Clift's criticism of her portrayal of Alice Tripp, that she was too "downbeat" and "played her tragedy from the minute you see her on screen." Mitchum said, "The only part that Shelley's going to be able to do is float around convincingly with her throat cut." Later he commented that she "got what she deserved lying there dead at the bottom of the river." (Ironically, her character is drowned by her lover in both films.)

But producer Paul Gregory was enthusiastic about the idea of Shelley Winters in the role, as he could capitalize on her friendship with Laughton. "We can get her for $25,000," he told Mitchum. In Gregory's cables to the actress, though, he laid the praise on thickly, saying that he and Laughton were "thrilled to death" to have Winters on the project and that they wanted her "more than anything."

Mitchum trusted Laughton on casting and other decisions. He knew that Laughton could wring a powerful performance from Winters, and from him. "I never felt a keener sense of trying to please a director," Mitchum said. He also thought Laughton had a command of the material and helped his actors to understand it as well. "Charles Laughton is the only director I have ever encountered before or after the making of the film *The Night of the Hunter* who was really brilliant," Mitchum said.

Laughton, too, had a strong faith in Mitchum's abilities, often saying that he was "one of the best actors in the world." His praise is warranted by Mitchum's portrayal of the evil preacher Harry Powell. Speaking to a writer from *Esquire* during the making of the movie, Laughton described Mitchum as "literate and gracious, a kind man with wonderful manners. All this tough talk is a blind, you know. He's a very tender man and a very great gentleman. You know, he's really terribly shy."

The two men shared an instinctive bond despite their obvious differences. Each sensed the deep inner conflicts of the other. One day during filming, Mitchum became furious at the film's producer and urinated on his car. "Gregory had to buy a new Cadillac," Mitchum recalled. "Because, you see, I peed on the radiator and every time it heated up, it smelled, and so he had to sell it."

Laughton was appalled by Mitchum's behavior and called him up late one night. "My boy, there are skeletons in all our closets," Laughton said. "And most of us try to cover up these skeletons, or certainly to keep the door closed. . . . My dear . . . you drag forth your skeletons, you swing them in the air. . . . Now, I want you to get the picture. You simply must, Bob, stop brandishing your skeletons!"

But Laughton revealed his own secret to Mitchum. "I don't know if you know, and I don't know if you care, and I don't care if you know, but there is a strong streak of homosexuality in me," he told Mitchum one day as they drove along the freeway.

"No shit!" cried Mitchum. "Stop the car!"

Charles Laughton seemed to genuinely adore Bob Mitchum. But he also needed him to bankroll *The Night of the Hunter,* since Laughton and his partner Paul Gregory couldn't have financed it without his name. On the basis of Mitchum's star power alone, United Artists put up the relatively meager sum of $700,000. Laughton's reputation as a great actor didn't mean a thing to the money boys at United Artists, who knew that Laughton was nervous as a cat about his directorial debut.

LAUGHTON SOUGHT guidance from Davis Grubb, the author of the novel upon which *The Night of the Hunter* is based. The two began a fascinating correspondence in which both struggled to create an authentically American tale of greed. For Grubb, mired in the world of corporate advertising, Laughton's plans for the movie offered him a chance to reclaim his vanished childhood in West Virginia, a disappearing way of life. Nowhere is this more apparent than in one of Grubb's letters to Laughton, a letter once owned by the director Martin Scorsese. Grubb describes his search for a lost boat whistle. Like some Marcel Proust of the Ohio River, Grubb writes:

> When I was ten my mother took me on a trip on that great river lady from Wheeling all the way to Cincinnati. And in the nights of my

> childhood I heard the great 19th century packet flowing her way down the spring river through a thousand nights and the music of that whistle (you'll know when you hear it!) is like a chord from a Bach organ prelude. I called the Pittsburgh wharfmaster this morning and all he could tell me was what I knew—that the great boat had burned to the water's edge nearly a quarter of a century ago. He knew nothing of what had happened to her whistle. But, knowing rivermen as I do, I knew that the whistle had surely been salvaged and was being kept somewhere by someone who had loved its noise as, I imagine, old soldiers treasure the trumpets of Balaclava or Gettysburg or perhaps the horn of Roland.

Grubb presses the sea captain for more information about the great whistle and finally writes Laughton excitedly, "He knows where it is!"

> Years ago, loving rivermen saved it from the old boat where she had burned to her guards at the Pittsburgh wharf and they set the whistle up (Horrors! Ignominious fate!) on a sand tow-boat up the Kanawha River at Charleston.
>
> Captain Billy is making prompt arrangements about having the whistle tape-recorded for us. He understands this. He knows that no film has ever had a true steamboat whistle in it. He knows that this sound cannot be made in a studio. He knows that it must be recorded after having drifted sweetly across living water as shoreside ears would hear it.
>
> He thinks that I might scare the old rivermen if I called them and began talking money and movies and Hollywood.

Laughton's meticulous preparations for filming Grubb's novel gave the author the courage he needed to take another important step not just in reclaiming his past but in setting his future course. "This has been a week of resolutions," Grubb tells his director.

> I want to be absorbed completely in the realization of this story dramatically on film. I want to be a part of the job we all must do. I also want to finish my second novel (First Draft) by summer. To do both I cannot do my advertising job also. I have spent a week considering

> what to do. Today I resigned my position—effective May 15th. Now I am free to get at these two things unhampered. The three jobs were making me ill. The two jobs will merely prove invigorating and each will complement the others since both are about my river—my holy and blessed river.

Laughton made the world seem safe for poetry. His intense and unorthodox methods, his insistence that even a reprobate like Bob Mitchum was "deep down a great artist," brought out the poetic, the lyrical, even in an advertising man like Davis Grubb. "I am reading Stendhal," Grubb ends one of his long letters to Laughton. "He is so fine a writer that none of him rubs off on your hands to taint the work you are doing. Today has been the first warm spring day. Tonight is warm and I am unhappy because it brings back the secret of a woman I loved last spring who went away. So much for that. Please advise your writer. . . . Regards, Grubb."

IS THERE an image more terrifying than the sight of Robert Mitchum, playing an unregenerate parson, singing "Leaning on an Everlasting Arm" on horseback as he stalks two young children who are in possession of their father's fortune? Critic Pauline Kael said the "children's flight from the soul-saver is one of the most strangely dreamlike episodes ever filmed, a deliberately 'artistic' nightmare of suspense." She also called it "one of the most frightening movies ever made."

To capture the appropriate visual atmosphere for *The Night of the Hunter*, Charles Laughton sought inspiration from the films of D. W. Griffith, screening all of his movies at the Museum of Modern Art in New York. He thought they could help him create a world in which the evil came through "impressionistically," help him tell the "nightmarish sort of Mother Goose tale." Laughton found the films as powerful as ever, but he was stunned by the work of Lillian Gish. Her "unassailable virginity" moved him deeply, as did her strange ability to remain delicate yet indestructible. She was once described as "Kabuki-like," but Laughton's response to her was more than merely aesthetic.

Seeing her in *Broken Blossoms* in France just after the Armistice had been declared had forever changed Laughton. He remembered falling in love with her then. It was her very girlishness and passiveness, her lack of sexual threat, that seemed to have made such a strong impression. Perhaps to Laughton she symbolized the anima, the essence of his own feminine side.

The Night of the Hunter seemed at mid-century to span the strange history of American cinema, and nothing emphasized this more than Laughton's casting of Lillian Gish for the part of the spinster who turns her farm into an orphanage.

When, in her infinitely courteous way, she asked him why he wanted her in the film, he replied: "When I first went to the movies they sat in their seats straight and leaned forward. Now they slump down, with their heads back, or eat candy and popcorn. I want them to sit up straight again."

Their first meeting was slightly marred by the presence of a drunken James Agee, but he soon left them. Agee would remain with the film a while longer, but ultimately he did not write its script. What he offered was a vision, inspiring Charles Laughton to craft his own screenplay, salvaging it from the wreckage of the terrible disagreements between him and Agee.

For years the script would be passed off as Agee's own work. It even appeared in a collection entitled *Five Film Scripts by James Agee*, despite the fact that Laughton actually wrote it. For a first screenplay it is remarkably powerful, with fine structure and a consistent tone. Laughton, it seemed, had an innate understanding of how his film should look and sound.

Laughton's cameraman Stanley Cortez outdid himself with the moody cinematography, even inventing new ways to capture the desired effect, such as the scene of the child looking down from the hayloft to see the preacher in the distance. "The figure moving against the horizon wasn't Mitchum at all," Cortez later recalled. "It was a midget on a little pony. The lighting gave the illusion I needed, the feeling of mystery, of strange shadows."

In addition to the financial obstacles and artistic dilemmas Laughton and producer Paul Gregory faced, they also had to fight censors to get *Hunter* made. Joseph Breen, the head of the office that oversaw the strict film production code, had written Columbia chief Harry Cohn when he first saw *Hunter*'s script, advising that the film could not portray a minister as a murderer and a sex maniac. Breen stressed that the minister could not use passages of the Bible to justify his actions and even suggested it might be necessary to "change his vocation entirely."

George A. Heimrich of the National Council of Churches of Christ Broadcast and Film Commission lobbied Breen to quash the production, saying that the office was "considerably disturbed" by the movie. Heimrich then wrote a four-page letter to producer Paul Gregory, expressing his concern that the film's "distortions and misinterpretation" would "leave the impression with millions of theatre-goers that the *Lord* condones *killing for money*, that the Bible is a book full of killings . . . when the truth is that it is the *commandment* of the *Lord God* that 'thou shalt not kill.'"

Producer Paul Gregory tried to appease the church groups. Any reference to the "Reverend" was omitted, with the more generic term "preacher" used instead. And two hymns to be used in the movie would be changed to other songs that were not immediately identifiable as standard church hymns. But the Protestant Motion Picture Council still classified the movie as "objectionable," saying that "this study in human terror will be offensive to most religious people."

DESPITE ALL their efforts, despite its brilliant script, acting, direction, and cinematography, *The Night of the Hunter* was a flop.

Mitchum blamed producer Paul Gregory for the film's poor distribution by United Artists. According to Mitchum, the distributors "didn't care if he made any money at all as long as they made their money. So they simply buried the film."

It's unclear how much her cooperation would have helped *The Night of the Hunter*, but Lillian Gish also seemed to step back from the film when it was released in 1955. A rider to her contract had specified that she get costar billing, no less than third place, on all promotional materials for the film. But when she saw the poster, which apparently displayed only Mitchum's and Winters's names prominently, Gish's agent said she "blew her top." She had been scheduled to make some personal appearances as well as do guest spots on television shows such as *Ed Sullivan*, but after the poster dustup, she gave only one interview, to CBS's *Person to Person*.

A pensive Charles Laughton on the set of *The Night of the Hunter*. Despite innovative cinematography and fine acting, it was a commercial failure and Laughton would never direct another film. *Courtesy of the Academy of Motion Picture Arts and Sciences.*

For his trouble Mitchum did receive good personal notices. In the *New York Times* Bosley Crowther wrote: "The atmosphere of the sticks is intense, and Robert Mitchum plays the murderous minister with an icy unctuousness that gives you the chills. There is more than malevolence and menace in his character. There is a strong trace of Freudian aberration, fanaticism and iniquity."

The film was misunderstood in 1955, either treated as a thriller that wasn't thrilling enough or as a parable with a moral murkiness—but commercially it was a disaster.

In France, however, the film critics and future directors of the nouvelle vague—men like François Truffaut and Jean-Luc Godard—

thought Laughton's film a disturbing masterpiece, a great work. Truffaut described it as "immensely inventive . . . like a horrifying news item retold by small children. . . . I should hasten to add," Truffaut wrote, "that the preacher has 'love' tattooed on the fingers of his right hand, and 'hate' on the left, so you'll know that this is no ordinary film."

Writing in the influential French film journal *Cahiers du Cinema*, Truffaut drew attention to the fact that "screenplays such as this are not the way to launch your career as a Hollywood director. The film runs counter to the rules of commercialism; it will probably be Laughton's single experience as a director." Sadly, Truffaut was right. Another man might have overcome the bitter disappointment. But Laughton was too old and too tenderhearted. He was, in the words of more than one witness, destroyed by it. He had put all of himself into the film, and it was not wanted. From now on there would be no more great projects for Charles Laughton.

"He was one who worked privately with all the actors, understood their problems and worked patiently with each one," said Lillian Gish. "He was a wonderful man, and he gave a great gift to the world."

Robert Mitchum would always worry that Laughton had spent too much time editing *Hunter*, putting in "all those owls and pussycats" and softening the portrayal of the evil preacher. "I told him to leave the character to me. We were very good friends and he didn't want to make it too uncomfortable for me, so he reduced the effectiveness of the film, I think," Mitchum said in 1973. "It should have been right down the fucking line. Read the book. If it had been like that, it would have been for true."

CHAPTER 10

BELL, BOOK, AND SCANDAL: KIM NOVAK AND SAMMY DAVIS JR.

LIKE ALL great love stories, it was doomed from the start. He was black. She was white. It was the 1950s, and their careers both depended on the affection of a fickle, segregated America. Add one tyrannical movie mogul, a few mobsters, and a Vegas show-girl, and a full-fledged melodrama emerges. Almost.

Nearly fifty years later, the affair between actress Kim Novak and Rat Packer Sammy Davis Jr. remains an open secret, some-where between epic romance and lowly gossip. Before his death in 1990, Davis painted a picture of forbidden love, replete with danger and late-night rendezvous at a Malibu beach house. But Novak has never fully admitted that they were anything more than "good friends."

Whatever its true nature, their relationship was real. Whether they were friends or lovers didn't matter to Harry Cohn. The infamous dictator of Columbia Studios wanted the pair to split—and fast. When newspaper columnists across the country got wind of the affair in January 1958, Cohn mobilized a campaign to end it. He wanted desperately to save the career of his protégé Novak, who by the late fifties had established herself not only as the queen of the lot but as its golden goose as well. Cohn's tactics included mob threats to "put out Sammy's other eye," prodding Davis into a sham marriage to a black chorus girl.

But the breakup of Kim Novak and Sammy Davis Jr. marked a jagged fault after which nothing could be the same. Novak eventually would retreat from Hollywood altogether. An embittered Sammy Davis Jr. would spend the rest of his life trying to find love and acceptance, never fully embraced by white or black America. The end of the affair even might have changed Harry Cohn. He died of a fatal heart attack just after reviewing a thick packet of press clippings on "Kim and HIM."

WITH HER luscious body and icy blonde beauty, Novak looked like Columbia's answer to Marilyn Monroe. Indeed, her first roles for the studio featured her in fluffy comedies like 1954's *Phffft!* with Jack Lemmon. By 1956 she was the biggest draw at the box office, receiving more than thirty-five hundred letters a week in fan mail.

Something set Novak apart from the other leading ladies of her day, though. If they were bombshells, then she was a smoldering fuse. Pouty reticence and sleepy sensuality wafted from her like potent pheromones. Novak also had another, more peculiar gift. Viewers could almost project their emotions onto her smooth face, rather than see her character's feelings reflected there. Alfred Hitchcock must have sensed this when he cast her to replace Vera Miles as Madeleine/Judy in his 1958 thriller *Vertigo*. For although she was not his first choice for the role, Novak makes this creepy gem shine. Cool, coy, and eerily blank, she is utterly believable as the woman who lets Jimmy Stewart remake her into his own fetishistic fantasy, remaining unknown beyond her obvious and powerful beauty.

Novak's onscreen wariness was rooted in the real misgivings she had about being an actress. She came to California in 1953 as the aptly named "Miss Deep Freeze," demonstrating refrigerators on a sales tour for Thor Appliances. When the job ended, she and a girlfriend decided to visit Los Angeles instead of returning to their hometown of Chicago. "Do you know what we wanted to do in Hollywood? The only thing? We wanted to swim in the Beverly Hills Hotel pool," she said.

Novak chose to stay, saying she fell in love with the sunny climate. She rented a small apartment with the $500 she had saved from her work and registered with the Caroline Leonetti modeling agency. The account executive who first interviewed her thought she was "too over-

Kim Novak and William Holden in a torrid publicity pose for Josh Logan's 1955 film *Picnic,* based on the William Inge play. Columbia Studios chief Harry Cohn groomed Novak to replace Rita Hayworth. *Courtesy of the Academy of Motion Picture Arts and Sciences.*

weight" for regular modeling. Also, her looks were "too all-American." Swimsuits were "out, ditto evening gowns." In fact, Novak's card filed away at the agency wasn't promising: "Hands, marginal; legs, hefty; neck and face, flawless."

Novak always insisted that she never really wanted a film career, knowing too well her own limitations. "I could open a refrigerator door gracefully, that was it, period," she said. "I could see where a lot of time might go by before any movie studio would want a girl to open an icebox."

She wouldn't have to wait long, though.

Columbia's Harry Cohn wanted to teach his top star, Rita Hayworth, a lesson. Broke and brokenhearted, Hayworth had returned to the studio after a two-year self-destruction spree in which she married, then divorced Prince Aly Khan and lost her life savings of $300,000. She had completed *Affair in Trinidad*, the opulent *Salomé*, and *Miss Sadie Thompson*, but none of the films succeeded like those made before her sabbatical. Cohn and Hayworth had clashed constantly during the making of these films as well. He accused her of slacking on the set, while she blamed him for shuttling unrelated expenses to her personal production company.

Hayworth was slated to appear in Frank Capra's *Joseph and His Brethren*. She had remarried, this time to singer Dick Haymes, a control freak who micromanaged Hayworth's life down to her clothes and hairstyles. One afternoon Haymes marched into Cohn's office demanding to play the part of Joseph and threatening to yank his wife off the project. The film would never be finished, anyway, but an apoplectic Cohn responded by saying, "Pull her out. I don't give a damn. The next girl that comes through that door will be the queen of the lot."

And in walked Kim Novak.

Her name was Marilyn Novak, actually, and she had a bit more experience than Cohn's story suggests. The twenty-year-old had already appeared as a chorus girl in an RKO picture called *The French Line*. (Her one line: "Cannot give a canapé away.") But it doesn't matter if Cohn's colorful story is false, because the essence of it rings true. Cohn made her a star—his star—with all the blessings and curses only he could bestow.

"King" Cohn had a reputation for being the biggest bastard in Hollywood, a feat even then. Born to Jewish émigrés, he traded the oppression visited upon his Eastern European parents for an empire of his own. He didn't hide his affinity for dictators, either. He carried a riding crop and had a photo of Benito Mussolini on his massive, semicircular blond wood desk, a replica of the Italian fascist's own. Studio employees called the thirty-foot walk to Cohn's raised desk "the last mile."

Cohn, along with his brother Jack, had built Columbia up from a maker of one-reel comedies to a profitable and prestigious house of films like *From Here to Eternity* (1953). When Novak entered its gates, the studio had nineteen thousand employees and an annual payroll of $18 million. But the struggle to establish the studio had left Cohn "mean-spirited and greedy to the point of miserliness." Cohn had established an intricate spy network within his own company and he seemed to know almost instantly when an actor or actress was "transgressing" against him. "He became so powerful that paranoia and neuroses beleaguered him," said Cohn's personal assistant Max Arnow. "He was like a jaded Oriental potentate to whom everybody bowed and scraped. If they didn't, he erupted like a volcano."

Cohn did not see star quality in Kim Novak at first. He complained that she mumbled through her screen test. Producer and schmaltzmeister Jerry Wald, best known for his 1957 screen adaptation of *Peyton Place*, knew better. He told Cohn, "Don't listen, just look." The flickering image captured Kim leaning against a mantel with her arms stretched behind her, her assets suddenly apparent.

Cohn knew he would need a new love goddess to bring in the big-time cash. Even before the blowup over her husband, Hayworth's star was on the wane. As director George Sidney said, "The makeup didn't go on so easily anymore." With characteristic zeal, Cohn set out to mold her replacement. Novak fought him almost immediately, though, unsettled by the rapid and dramatic changes proposed for her.

Their first skirmish came over her stage name. Cohn chose "Kit Marlowe" for her, since Marilyn Monroe already had prior claim to Novak's given name. But Novak balked, believing "Kit" sounded too close to "kitten," as in the sexy type. She suggested "Kim" and Cohn relented. Then she argued to keep her family's Czech name of Novak, although Cohn disliked its ethnic tone. Cohn didn't appreciate her Bohemian background, allegedly calling her "that fat Polack" behind her back.

Though vulgar and uneducated, Cohn was a savvy businessman. He assigned to Kim a full-time publicist and Columbia's top makeup man. He put her on a rigid diet and exercise regimen. Cohn even hired fashion designer Jean Louis to create her wardrobe, one that complemented her ample bust. When he was finished, Novak had a new name, new capped teeth, and a new gimmick. Columbia publicist Muriel Roberts was browsing through an issue of *Vogue* magazine that touted lavender as the fashionable color in Paris that summer. Roberts decided to remake Novak's life into a "mauve symphony." From the light rinse on her newly cropped coif to her furniture and the ink on her lavender stationery, Novak became the princess of purple.

At Cohn's request, she moved into the Studio Club, a safe—and chaperoned—YWCA dorm that offered rooms and meals for $19.50 a week. She agreed when he demanded that she date only on the weekends, placing a guard outside the dorm to ensure her compliance. And Novak did her best in the roles the studio handed her, although she felt extremely self-conscious about her acting. Cohn had promised her a year of training before putting her in a major role, but three months later she was costarring with Fred MacMurray in 1954's *Pushover*.

To compensate for her inexperience, Novak prepared diligently for her roles. George Sidney directed Novak in three films, including 1957's *Pal Joey*, with Frank Sinatra and Rita Hayworth. He described her as a workaholic who depended on her directors for guidance. "She never wanted to go home. After a day's work, she'd want to sit and talk for hours and hours about the picture and what was underneath and how to do it," Sidney said. "She wanted to be good."

Rumors persisted that Novak couldn't act, though, that she threw tantrums and delayed shots by hiding in her dressing room. On location for *Picnic* in Kansas, with hundreds of local extras waiting, director Josh Logan was about to begin filming one of the climactic scenes when he realized Novak had disappeared across the lake. Using a megaphone, Logan yelled, "Kim, get your ass over here." Finally, he charged into her trailer and literally pulled her across the bridge in her beautiful dress, Novak protesting all the way, "I'm not ready. I've got my makeup." Logan stood firm. "Get in that goddamned boat," he said.

Novak became obsessed with having her hair and makeup perfect before she could begin working, worried that she couldn't live up to the media's portrayal of her as a sex goddess. Cohn bullied his fledgling star, too, amplifying Novak's anxiety. He would call her into his office and read out her bad reviews, repeating the especially hurtful phrases. "I made her. I can break her," Cohn could often be heard saying of his studio's new star.

Novak may have found a way to ignore Cohn's insults, but she never grew comfortable with her celebrity. She had worked in a Christmas card factory, clerked in a dime store, and groomed horses before coming to Hollywood. For her, acting was never a "real" job, one her immigrant, railroad-working father could be proud of. She didn't seem to have much ambition of her own, and she didn't like to play show pony, either. She resisted the requisite star turns at parties and nightclubs and the de rigueur pandering to Hedda Hopper, Louella Parsons, and Sheilah Graham, Hollywood's witchy triad of gossip columnists.

Director Sidney believes the press punished Novak for not obeying the unspoken rules of stardom and that she began to feel like a "prizefighter," battling her way through Hollywood. "I think she was a much better actress than the press wanted to give her credit for," he said. "I don't know, maybe if she'd gone to the Trocadero every night and all that, maybe they would have been kinder."

IF ANYONE had to fight his way through life, it was Sammy Davis Jr. For every door the multitalented entertainer opened on Broadway and on the Vegas Strip, two were shut in his face. In the late 1950s, the slick machine of the Rat Pack had not yet roared to life and Davis was at a turning point, struggling to hone his solo act in nightclubs and desperate for a movie career.

Born in Harlem to a chorus girl and a tap dancer, Davis literally grew up onstage. His grandmother cared for him until he was three, at which point his father, Sam Davis Sr., took him on the vaudeville circuit with his partner, Will Mastin, whom Sammy would always call "uncle" although they were not related. Innately gifted as a dancer and a fabulous mimic, Sammy even as a toddler proved the most popular member of the Will Mastin Trio.

World War II interrupted the trio's touring and would mark one of the most traumatic chapters in Sammy's life. He would not see combat, but was forced to battle white soldiers at a Cheyenne, Wyoming, base.

Sammy Davis Jr. performs at Ciro's nightclub in March of 1955, just after he lost an eye in a car accident. Celebrities packed the club to see his Oscar-night show. Not long after, Davis would begin a brief affair with the actress Kim Novak. *Bettmann/Corbis.*

Before transferring him to the special-services branch, the Army ordered Davis to repeat basic training several times. While stationed at Fort Francis E. Warren, Davis endured endless racial taunts and beatings.

But Sammy could always reach people as an entertainer, and in 1951 he got one of his biggest breaks. The Will Mastin Trio Featuring Sammy Davis Jr. debuted at Ciro's in Los Angeles. A favorite spot of Hollywood hipsters, the club was especially full that Academy Awards night. Set to open for singer Janis Paige, the trio had been given only twenty minutes on stage, with stiff warnings not to take more than two curtain calls. Sammy Davis Jr. never could refuse a cheering crowd, though, and the trio performed for two hours, rooted on by celebrities like Clark Gable and Humphrey Bogart. For a punchy encore, Sammy performed some of his impressions of white stars like Frank Sinatra and Jerry Lewis.

"From that point on, Sammy went like a meteor," said Arthur Silber Jr., a longtime friend whose father was the trio's agent at the time. "Janis Paige was a good-looking actress with a mediocre singing voice, starring at Ciro's because she was married to Errol Flynn. And Sammy went on and did his thing and just blew her right out the door. All he had to do was dance. . . . And from there he went to the Chez Paree [in Chicago] and it kept getting bigger and bigger. Miraculous shows."

Sammy's lush talent seems hard to describe today. Perhaps the Sammy of the 1970s and 1980s—the corny, flashy-ring-wearing, hep-cat talking Candy Man of contemporary memory—has eclipsed the startling genius of his live performances. He improvised everything, save for two rehearsed numbers at the top of his shows.

"You'd be sitting in the dark and suddenly the music would cut through the whole thing and it was exciting, it was thrilling. It was almost a sexual thing. You could feel it in your stomach," said Davis's friend Burt Boyar, who along with his wife, Jane, cowrote Davis's autobiography. "Whatever he did, it was always different. He never even had his clothes planned. Everything was totally spontaneous. There was nothing that happened yesterday. It was all fresh. I watched Sammy's shows hundreds of times and I never, never was disinterested ever once."

Sammy's personal success also spurred societal change, however incrementally. By 1954 the New Frontier hotel in Las Vegas paid the Will Mastin Trio $7,500 a week and provided each member with a suite. Just a few years before, black performers could not stay at the hotels where they headlined, forced instead into ramshackle rooming houses on the west side of town. Blacks were not welcome in the casinos, either. "Now they wanted us so much they were breaking their rules. We were bigger than Jim Crow," Davis recalled in his autobiography *Yes I Can.*

Even disaster could not slow Davis's growing popularity. In November 1954, he lost an eye after injuring it on his Cadillac's conical steering-wheel ornament in a crash. The drama of the accident generated sudden sympathy for Sammy, as hundreds of Americans sent get-well telegrams to his San Bernardino hospital room. A few months later, in March of 1955, Sammy made a triumphant return to Ciro's, a silk eye patch still covering the damaged left socket.

Again, applause served as a balm for his hurts. As Sammy remembered it:

> From one end of Ciro's to the other were the giants of the motion picture industry—the Cary Grants, the Bogarts, the Edward G. Robinsons, the Spencer Tracys, Gary Coopers, Jimmy Cagneys, Dick Powells—standing and applauding. I saw tears rolling down June Allyson's cheeks. . . . Their faces held expressions of warmth and elation that you expect from your own family, as though they were taking personal pride that I was back, like it was their joy as much as my own. Never had I felt so much a part of show business.

A starring role in a Broadway musical created just for him by Jule Styne and George Gilbert followed. Although the show garnered lukewarm reviews, Sammy kept *Mr. Wonderful* running for a year. His inspired performance only highlighted another problem, though. His father and "uncle's" style of singing and dancing looked increasingly old-fashioned beside that of the ultramod Sammy.

"They no longer should have been on the stage with him. It was bad show business. Sammy would never, never—he would not hurt their feelings. He just kept smoothing it over," Boyar said. Sammy's father retired during *Mr. Wonderful*, but Will stayed on. Even after he was no longer in the act, it was still billed as the Will Mastin Trio Presents Sammy Davis Jr. Will Mastin would travel with Sammy and be given his own dressing room. He would bring his costumes and makeup and set up his whole dressing table, even though he would never set foot onstage. Show business had become a sickness that Mastin couldn't shake.

Hate undermined Sammy Davis's happiness, even as he reached the rarefied circles of stardom. One night, after a performance of *Mr.*

Wonderful in New York, he went to the chichi El Morocco for the first time and got a chilly reception. "It was a very, very bad experience. They were not at all pleased to see him despite the fact that he was starring on Broadway and defeating the critics," said Burt Boyar. Instead of seating him with the other patrons, the maître d' gave Davis and the Boyars a table on the other side of the dance floor, in an empty section of the club.

"As you pass the dance floor and the banquettes there, you're suddenly on the wrong side of the room. I'll never forget it," Boyar said.

> John Perona was the owner and he was like the arbiter of New York society in a very cheap sense—café society—and he was in the kitchen staring out through the window of the swinging door, just staring at Sammy and the idea of a black man in this place. Every hooker ever and Bob Harrison, who published *Confidential*, was a regular. All these very bad people were there but the fact that Sammy was there just threw him completely.

Although he continued to fill nightclubs, a film career initially proved elusive for Sammy Davis Jr. With the exception of a few television roles, he would not get significant work in movies until he had the pull of Frank Sinatra behind him, and then it was only bit parts in clunkers like *Ocean's 11*. Davis had dreamed of being a serious film actor, but the racial barrier proved too difficult to overcome.

He would never let it show in public, but the frustration, combined with the incessant slurs and slights, took its toll on Davis. "He would come out of the stage door having had six standing ovations and somebody would yell, 'Nigger,'" Boyar said. "There would always be something that would just cut through it all, that would just knock him down."

THE COSMIC CONNECTION of the reluctant movie star and the starstruck entertainer at first seems unlikely. But by the late 1950s, both Kim Novak and Sammy Davis Jr. deeply resented their circumscribed worlds, his defined by racism and hers by sexism and Harry Cohn. What they shared gave the relationship instant earnestness.

"We weren't dealing with *The Newlywed Game* or *The Dating*

Game," said Tony Curtis, who introduced the pair at a party he gave with his wife, Janet Leigh, in 1957. "They spent an evening together deep in thought, deep in talk."

A gossip column reported on the party the next day, noting the couple's tête-à-tête. When Sammy Davis called to apologize to Kim Novak, she told him that the studio "didn't own her" and invited him over for an intimate spaghetti dinner. A cloak-and-dagger drama ensued, with Sammy traveling to her house in the dark. After synchronizing watches with his friend and driver Arthur Silber to ensure a quick exit, he ran a breathless block to Novak's door.

They later rented a house in Malibu for clandestine meetings by the sea. To avoid being seen by anyone, Davis would lie on the floor of the car with a blanket over him while Silber drove. Silber often acted as a go-between for the couple, a witness to the daily machinations of keeping a romantic secret.

Silber had seen Sammy with "hundreds of white girls," including stars such as Ava Gardner. But he knew this was different. Sammy had a private telephone installed at the Sands Hotel in Las Vegas so he could take Novak's calls. "I just knew this was big trouble," Silber said.

Many people saw the relationship cynically. A torrid love affair with Novak would have garnered press attention for Davis at a time when he needed to establish himself as a star in his own right. For Kim Novak, a relationship with a black man would have flaunted her independence from Harry Cohn.

"She was rebelling against Harry Cohn. That's why she went out with Sammy, no question about it," said journalist James Bacon. ". . . She always said they treated her like a piece of meat when she was under contract at Columbia."

Sammy acknowledged that both he and Kim were strangely charmed by the explosive effect their relationship might have on Hollywood. "Through me she was rebelling against the people who made rules for her. And wasn't I doing the same thing? We'd spent a few hours in each other's company at a party. . . . I was impressed with the glamour of a movie star and she was impressed by my talent," he said. "But when it was forbidden, we became conspirators, drawn together by the single thing we had in common: defiance."

Davis told his coauthors, "With the indignities, the injustices, the nastiness, the racial abuses, I got to the point where I wanted to get the whitest, most famous, whitest chick in the world and just show 'em."

Kim Novak later described their relationship as a kind of liberal manifesto brought to life. On a promotional tour for the rerelease of *Vertigo* in 1997, she said,

> I was a gentile raised in a Jewish neighborhood—always being shoved in the snow or having rotten pies pushed in my face—so I identified with him as a minority. I could tell he was in love with me as he was so nervous taking pictures of me that he forgot to take the lens cap off. It was so sweet, you know, "Oh, you're a white girl and you talked to me." I knew how he felt.

Burt Boyar also insists that Sammy and Kim were lovers as well as good friends.

"I think they had a sexual relationship," Boyar said. "You don't hide on the floor of a car and then finally hate yourself for it just to say, 'Let's have tea.' "

The one event that ultimately called attention to their relationship, in fact, offers the most clues as to how serious it had become. Unable to leave the Sands Hotel in Las Vegas because he had to perform, Davis asked his friend Arthur Silber to find Novak, who was visiting her parents in Chicago for Christmas. The urgent message: "I love you."

The devoted Silber took a red-eye flight to Chicago. Soon after arriving, he learned that Sammy would be joining him after all. Silber was puzzled, wondering how Frank Sinatra could have let him out of his engagement at the Sands. But Sammy went to Chicago anyway. "It was the most ridiculous, ludicrous thing. I mean, all this for five minutes? It was just how deep this affair went," Silber said. "Sammy and I came back home the next morning. It was close—by the time our car arrived at the Las Vegas airport, Sammy's dance shoes were at the stage door, he slipped on his dance shoes and went right onstage."

Davis supposedly wanted to meet Novak's parents to tell them in person of his intention to marry their youngest daughter. His ardent haste may have cost him any kind of relationship with Novak, though, because news of the affair was leaked to reporters as the Sands Hotel booked a last-minute replacement for him.

In New York for the holidays, Harry Cohn met with friends and supporters at a memorial dinner for his brother, Jack, who had died the year before. The real occasion was the success of Columbia, though. In 1957 the studio had released forty-six films, including the Oscar-winning *Bridge on the River Kwai*. And in the three previous years, Kim Novak's films had helped Columbia earn more than $10 million in clear profits. Several Columbia executives remarked that they had never seen Harry Cohn so content. He seemed almost gracious as he sat among the rich and the powerful who had come to honor the memory of Jack Cohn. But in fact they had come to honor Harry—"Harry the survivor, Harry the omnipotent."

In the middle of the dinner, a young marketing executive slipped into the room. His face was ashen as he edged behind Harry's chair in the ballroom and leaned down to whisper something in his ear. Several executives noticed that the boss's hands were shaking as he pulled himself up out of his chair and brusquely left the dinner.

Back in his suite at the Sherry Netherland Hotel, Cohn gulped a handful of nitroglycerin pills and splashed water on his face. Then he called Evelyn Lane, his assistant in Hollywood.

"I'll be coming back tomorrow morning," he said. "Meet me at the airport." After sleeping fitfully for two hours, he grabbed the phone. He had to tell somebody—it was too distressing a secret to keep to himself. He finally located his assistant Max Arnow at a party in Beverly Hills.

"Max," he said, "we've got a disaster on our hands." Arnow's mind raced. Somebody must've died, Arnow thought to himself, but then he would already have heard about it.

Harry ended the suspense by breaking in: "It's Kim, Max. She's fucking that colored Cyclops, Sammy Davis."

Max Arnow scoffed at the idea. "Impossible," he told his boss. "We've had private detectives following her for three years now. I would've known."

"But you didn't have her followed in Chicago, Max. You didn't have her followed when she went home."

Less than two hours after the Cohn-Arnow phone conversation,

Dorothy Kilgallen wrote in her *New York Journal American* column, "Which top female movie star (K.N.) is seriously dating which big-name entertainer (S.D.)?"

The next morning Harry Cohn had his first heart attack while flying back home to Los Angeles. Tests later indicated that Cohn had in fact suffered two heart attacks: one just after the formal dinner when he was informed about Kilgallen's column, and the other in the airplane over Colorado. Cohn's doctor ordered him into the hospital, but he refused.

Kilgallen's column started an avalanche of Kim and Sammy news in the first week of January 1958. On January 1, Kilgallen wrote, "Studio bosses now know about K.N.'s affair with S.D. and have turned lavender over their platinum blonde." On January 2, Irv Kupcinet of the *Chicago Sun-Times* wrote, "C'mon Kim, give us the lowdown. Who's S.D.? Who's the new man in your life, and why is your studio so angry?" (Kupcinet in 1985 claimed to have verified a marriage license, tipped off by sources close to Novak.) And the *London Daily Mirror* came right out with, "Kim Novak is about to become engaged to Sammy Davis, Jr., and Hollywood is aghast."

The Negro press were just as outraged. "Sammy Davis Jr., once a pride to all Negroes, has become a never-ending source of embarrassment," wrote *Jet* magazine:

> The legend of Mr. Davis' amours trips gaily from one bedroom to another, leering out at us from the covers of endless scandal magazines, dragging us all through the mud along with him. . . . Mr. Davis has never been particularly race-conscious but his current scandal displays him as inexcusably unconscious of his responsibility as a Negro. Look in the mirror, Sammy. You're still one of us.

Confidential had a field day. After all, the Davis-Novak romance fit one of their most popular themes: interracial love affairs. Curiously, something about the pressures being brought to bear on Davis and Novak must have touched the jaded hearts of *Confidential*'s writers, for they described the affair in sorrowful terms: "This is the tragic love story of the century," their coverage began, followed by an allusion to *Romeo and Juliet*. "Sammy Davis couldn't give up the Negro race. Kim Novak couldn't give up the white race." Ordinarily given to sensationalizing—and moralizing about—interracial love affairs, the scandal magazine sympathized with the lovers and painted Hollywood society, the studios and talent agencies, and especially Harry Cohn as the villains of the piece. "People were becoming more cruel," *Confidential* wrote. Even Frank Sinatra, Davis's close friend, was depicted as a hypocrite in the affair.

"Sammy received pressure from his friends, too," disclosed *Confidential*:

> Frank Sinatra . . . called and said, "Sammy, you're making a serious mistake." It is reliably reported that Sammy lost his temper at Frankie, telling him, "You're a hell of a one to talk. You invented mistakes. You get away with murder and people love it. If I tried a tenth of what you do, they'd hang me in the morning."

Ever since Dorothy Kilgallen broke the story, Harry Cohn felt the pressure from Columbia's New York executives, members of the corporation board, and even a few major stockholders. Kim Novak was a valuable commodity and the studio couldn't afford to lose her. Furious at his failure to rein in his star on his own, Cohn called on the men who had made a business of "cleaning up" unexpected messes: the true gangsters of Hollywood.

Cohn told the hired thugs to drive Sammy out into the desert and threaten to "put his other eye out," and thus end his show business career, unless he stopped seeing Kim Novak.

Even the underworld has boundaries, though, and Cohn found himself in a power play with the dons of Chicago and Las Vegas. They guarded their investment in Sammy Davis and his profitable casino shows as closely as Cohn did Kim Novak and her movies.

"I was there when the phone call came," said Silber, who remembered how a worried Davis turned to legendary mafia boss Sam Giancana for help. "Virtually it came down to a quote. Sam says, 'We can protect you here, in Chicago, in Vegas, but we can't do anything about Hollywood. Stay out of Hollywood until we get this settled.' "

Despondent and afraid, Sammy Davis Jr. barricaded himself in his suite at the Sands Hotel in Las Vegas. His hobby of collecting pistols and playing "quick draw" with his old friend now became serious forms of self-defense. For the first time, they loaded their guns with real bullets, never knowing who might be in the next room.

Although Davis was probably not in real physical danger, the syndicate needed Sammy to find a way to cool Cohn's temper and quiet the screeching press. "Nobody was going to kill him. No member of any mob or any mafia was going to do anything to hurt Sammy Davis Jr. He was too valuable," said Burt Boyar. ". . . What they did is they said, 'Come on Sam, we're in a bind. You know nothing is going to happen with us, but take the heat off.' "

The mobsters so notorious for settling scores among themselves finally came up with a plan. Sammy would marry a black woman, reap the press benefits, and then pay her off for a quickie divorce. Everybody would be happy—the white press, the black press, Harry Cohn, everyone except Sammy and Kim.

Back at the Sands, Silber watched as Davis flipped through the pages of his address book. He found her in the W's. A pretty chorus girl who worked at the Silver Slipper, Loray White had dated Davis a few times before. Davis sat her down and offered her a deal. He'd pay her to marry him. She'd enjoy all the rights of Mrs. Sammy Davis Jr., and at the end of the year, the marriage would be dissolved.

Sammy Davis Jr. and Loray White were married on January 10, 1958, in a small ceremony at the Sands Hotel. Harry Belafonte was best man. Loray's daughter from a previous marriage was flower girl. Sammy had been so nervous that he spelled her name "Leroy" on the marriage license application. Sammy and his wife posed for photographs next to the three-tiered wedding cake, with its sugar swans and glittery ribbon spelling out "happiness." But after the photos ran on the front page of some black newspapers like the *Chicago Defender*, Sammy and his wife rarely saw each other. Their marriage went unconsummated. Sammy didn't even sleep at the Hollywood Hills house he rented for his borrowed bride, preferring instead to live with his grandmother.

Kim Novak disappeared from view briefly after Davis married. By the time she returned to Columbia for the filming of *Bell, Book and Candle* with Jimmy Stewart at the end of January 1958, it was almost as if the whole thing had never happened. Novak refused to comment on her relationship with Sammy Davis Jr. at all until the mid-1980s. "It was a very dangerous relationship then—a white woman and a black man, no matter his status, simply didn't mix publicly," she said. "I was suddenly in the eye of the hurricane. Harry Cohn was infuriated. My agent told me my career would be over if I continued to see Sammy. Some of my friends wouldn't even return my phone calls."

Sammy Davis Jr. and Loray White quickly and quietly divorced a few months after they married. For her trouble, White got $25,000 in cash, plus about $10,000 in clothes and shoes she had bought in a shopping frenzy just after the wedding. "It was strictly a short-term situation, it was like a booking," Davis biographer Boyar said. "It was something he had to do and he did it."

HARRY COHN had a premonition that he would die when he reached the age of sixty-seven. All the Cohns died at that age, he said, and when his brother Jack, then sixty-seven, died suddenly after a routine operation, Cohn's fatalism deepened.

He hadn't suddenly turned melodramatic. Several years before, he had been treated for throat cancer. Almost everyone knew why he had been hospitalized, but Cohn, like Mayer, never discussed his illnesses. In any case, after several operations he appeared to have beaten it and returned to the studio, but he was distracted, enervated, even conciliatory—he was not the same man who had once struck terror in the hearts of his employees, and of whom Hedda Hopper, J. Edgar Hoover's favorite aging gossip columnist, once said, "You have to stand in line to hate him."

"I certainly saw a change in those last years," said his nephew Robert. The studio was no longer a fiefdom where Cohn could order his employees to make the pictures he wanted. Like all studio heads, he now had to contend with independent producers and pricey talent.

Two months after Cohn was first told about Kim Novak and Sammy Davis Jr.'s love affair, he and his wife flew to Phoenix for their annual vacation at the Arizona Biltmore Hotel. He was dressing for a reception he was to host later that evening when he admitted he felt queasy. At dinner he took six nitroglycerin tablets—his prescription called for one—and his wife arranged for a wheelchair to be brought to the table. Cohn waved it off and left the dining room on his own, but his wife cancelled their reception, ignoring his wishes.

The next morning, February 27, 1958, he was carried to an ambulance and rushed to St. Joseph's Hospital. "Too tough," he told his wife, who sat beside him. "It's too tough." He died of a coronary occlusion before reaching the hospital. He was sixty-six years old.

His wife, Joan, would always believe Novak caused Cohn's death, as did some Columbia executives. *Confidential* reported that "several executives still needle Kim with words to the effect that this romance killed Harry Cohn." However, when the news of Cohn's death was brought to her on the set of *Bell, Book and Candle,* Kim Novak was the only one who wept.

Although in his will he had requested no funeral, Cohn got a Hollywood send-off even he might have thought was in bad taste. It took place not in a church or synagogue but on the Columbia lot, in two sound studios arrayed with plastic plants and faux stained-glass windows aglow from hidden spotlights. Danny Kaye gave the eulogy. Scheduled on a Sunday so no one would miss work, more than two thousand stars and staffers attended the funeral, inspiring Red Skelton to quip, "Well, it only proves what they always say—give the public what they want to see, and they'll come out for it."

For Kim Novak, a more fitting sentiment might have been St. Teresa of Avila's: "More tears were shed over answered prayers than unanswered ones." Without Cohn around, she regained control of her personal life but lost the strong force that had guided her career. The tyrant who had manipulated Novak had also chosen her parts carefully. When he was gone, so were the challenging scripts like *Vertigo* and *The Man with the Golden Arm.* Instead, the 1960s found Novak showing ever more skin, floundering in increasingly forgettable films like *Kiss Me Stupid, The Legend of Lylah Clare,* and *The Amorous Adventures of Moll Flanders.*

She moved north to Carmel, California, receding almost entirely from public view by the early 1970s. Cocooned in her privacy, Novak married a veterinarian, raised llamas, played guitar, and painted—but only rarely accepted film roles, such as in 1980's *The Mirror Crack'd.* Ten years later, believing she had "unfinished business" with her acting, she reestablished contact with her agent and in 1991 played a mentally ill woman dying of cancer in Mike Figgis's *Liebestraum.* Her comeback was short-lived, however, and she quickly returned to her reclusive ways. Today she lives in Oregon and for almost a decade has been working on an autobiography.

Sammy Davis Jr. had his own demons. Instead of withdrawing to the country, though, he began a frenetic touring schedule that would continue almost through the rest of his life. While Kim Novak's career slid south through the 1960s, Davis's flourished as the Rat Pack's "Summit at the Sands" ushered in the baroque phase of American cocktail culture and live lounge entertainment.

IN 1960 Davis married Swedish actress May Britt. He postponed the wedding until after the presidential election so Frank Sinatra could be his best man. Sinatra had stumped tirelessly for John F. Kennedy, and pollsters worried about how Davis's marriage to a white woman would play to voters.

Together, Davis and Britt would later have a daughter and adopt two sons. The marriage wouldn't last, though, with Davis on the road while his wife raised their children. By marrying the blonde actress, Davis had further alienated himself from blacks. He could never win, it seemed. He had spent the first half of his life making himself loved by whites. As the civil rights movement changed the cultural landscape, he would spend the second half of his life trying to bridge the gulf that had grown between him and black America.

It would not be easy for Davis to change his image, however, because he wanted so much to be adored—even by Richard Nixon. The president surprised Sammy on stage once in Florida. After Nixon gushed about what a big fan he and Pat had become, Sammy affectionately embraced him. The infamous "Nixon hug" didn't win him any friends among blacks or liberal whites.

Although too much was made of the minor incident, Davis did go on to visit Nixon's White House. After sleeping in the president's private wing, he had breakfast with Nixon, the two of them still in their bathrobes. He had campaigned for Kennedy but political loyalty paled next to the sheer glamour, and legitimacy, of hobnobbing with the leader of the free world.

When blacks in the press criticized Davis, he increased his efforts on behalf of African-American causes. He hoped his remarriage to a black dancer and choreographer named Altovise Gore would receive a gentler response and, in a small way, mend some fences. But his third marriage was an unhappy one, too.

In the 1970s, Arthur Silber went back to work for Sammy and

noticed profound changes in his personality and behavior. On a tour of Australia, Sammy collapsed several times from sheer exhaustion. He was drinking too much and staying in his room all day. "He just withdrew into himself, like closing the door to keep out the bad weather," Silber said. "I knew in my heart of hearts that Sam was hurting and that he was lonely as he could be."

Sammy began having problems with his throat around 1988. People around him became concerned when he started canceling concert engagements and dates in Vegas. His agent, Sy Marsh, took him to a specialist who found that his constant smoking and singing had caused inflamed nodules on his vocal cords. Sammy liked to inhale in the middle of a song and then exhale with the note pouring out. Nat Cole warned him, "Don't do that. You're burning your vocal cords with all that heat—you're making it worse." But nothing could stop him—he did it for the theatrical effect. "The drinking I can handle," he told Sy Marsh, "but the cigarettes are my crutch. Just to walk out on the stage each night is a tremendous challenge."

Within two years Sammy developed throat cancer. When the doctor told him he needed surgery to live, he knew it would mean he'd never sing again. Sammy decided not to have the operation.

Amazingly, his voice actually improved in the last years of his life. "It was stunning," Boyar remembered. "Here's a man dying of throat cancer, and his voice was glorious, like a nightingale. It was almost unreal."

SAMMY DAVIS would see Kim Novak one last time at Cedars-Sinai Hospital in Los Angeles. They sat together and talked in his room. Sammy had sent someone to his house to retrieve his beautiful silk robe and silk pajamas. Even though he was ailing, he still wanted to be dressed to the nines for her.

Sammy died on May 16, 1990. Murphy Bennett, Sammy's valet and probably his closest friend for over forty years, would often visit his grave at Forest Lawn Cemetery. Each time, he would stop on the way and buy a single white rose. Sammy had always given Kim Novak white roses, and now Bennett placed the flower on the headstone, as if the actress herself had come to pay her respects.

CHAPTER 11

A COOKIE FULL OF ARSENIC: *SWEET SMELL OF SUCCESS*

WHY HAS *Sweet Smell of Success*, rejected by audiences in its day, reemerged in all its low-life glory? What is it about this movie that lives up to its hype as "the film that will never be forgotten, or forgiven"?

The story of a press agent named Sidney Falco and a power-mad gossip columnist named J. J. Hunsecker, *Sweet Smell of Success* did for New York what *Sunset Boulevard* did for Hollywood. Among the film's many pleasures are James Wong Howe's low-angled, chiaroscuro cinematography, making *Sweet Smell* the first and possibly the best film to capture the look and feel of New York City. Howe shot his subjects from low angles so they always seemed to be "knifing up, as if poised for the kill." The city is awash in brilliant shadows—everything gleams, as if drenched in acid rain: the enormous neon signs above the great buildings, even the newsstand holding down its corner of the sidewalk in front of Nedick's. At one point, Hunsecker watches a drunk being bounced from a nightclub and turns to Sidney Falco and says, "I love this dirty town." *Sweet Smell of Success* is a corrosive valentine to New York, embracing its energy and its clashing ambitions.

But what cineasts really love about this film is its biting dialogue, written by Ernest Lehman and that most miserable of urban geniuses, Clifford Odets. Where else would you hear a sinister cop utter the words, "Come back here, Sidney. I want to chastise you"?

The Sturm und Drang of bringing Ernie Lehman's tale to the screen had a nearly lethal effect on a number of its players. It made Lehman so ill he had to leave the project—and the country. It deepened the melancholia of the great Odets. It almost sent Susan Harrison, the fragile actress who played Hunsecker's sister, over the edge. And it helped to derail the career of its brilliant director, Alexander "Sandy" Mackendrick.

It's a toxic little film, impeccably made—a veritable "cookie full of arsenic." Conceived in 1949 by an unhappy press agent who only wanted to be a novelist and a screenwriter, the "novelette" was Lehman's attempt to expiate his guilt over being one of the little guys feeding the big columnists the stuff that made men like Walter Winchell more powerful than presidents. He had tackled the theme earlier in a short story published in *Collier's* called "Hunsecker Fights the World."

Burt Lancaster plays the villainous J. J. Hunsecker, recognized by all audiences—then and now—as a swipe at Winchell, though Lehman claims he went out of his way to make Hunsecker as different from Winchell as he possibly could. ("Winchell never played golf," Lehman points out. "I put all those golf trophies in Hunsecker's study!") But Hunsecker *is* Winchell: an unscrupulous, power-mad gossip columnist for the *New York Globe* with sixty million readers who rules his empire from a table at '21' (Winchell's was table 25 at the Stork Club). Lancaster portrayed Hunsecker as a tight-lipped monster, "the first heartless titan in American film." He's obsessed with his own power, destroying careers on a whim, using his column to bludgeon his enemies and friends alike. But then he has no friends, just the lackeys and hangers-on like Sidney Falco who suck up to him, the press agents whose livelihood depend on getting their clients mentioned in Hunsecker's column. "You're dead, son. Get yourself buried," are nearly the first words that come out of Hunsecker's mouth.

What drives the plot is Hunsecker's obsession with his sister, a fragile doll in an oversize mink named Susie, and his desire to break up Susie's romance with a jazz guitarist named Steve Dallas, played by the gleamingly clean-cut Marty Milner. (This was another element that was too close to be a coincidence: Winchell was obsessed with his beautiful daughter Walda to the point of ruthlessly hounding her boyfriend, William Cahn.)

Enter Sidney Falco, press agent on the make and uneasy protagonist of this weird morality tale, played by Tony Curtis in arguably the greatest role of his long career. Falco is Hunsecker's lapdog—he'll do anything to stay in the columnist's good graces: lie, cheat, pimp his girlfriend, and finally destroy Steve Dallas by libeling him as a pot-smoking Communist in order to help Hunsecker break up Steve's romance with his sister. When Hunsecker says to Falco, "I'd hate to take a bite out of you, Sidney, you're a cookie full of arsenic," Falco just smiles. It was a hell of a role.

IN SOME WAYS Ernie Lehman was not a typical press agent. He was probably the only press agent in history who had been raised by an Austrian nanny. Born to a wealthy family in Woodmere, Long Island (one of the "five towns"), Lehman saw his parents lose their home during the Depression. Shy and high-strung, Lehman had the nervous system of a whippet. He also had moral qualms about his livelihood. "I knew Winchell. I was the guy on the other end of the phone. He'd go into a thirty-minute tirade about Ed Sullivan, then he'd say, 'Who is this?' The nicest thing you could do was to keep someone out of that world."

"We were a frightened bunch of people," Lehman said about the cadre of press agents and writers who fed the columnists and made the rounds of all the nightspots in New York in the forties: '21,' El Morocco, the Stork Club, the Beachcomber. "We knew our lives were in the hands of a small group of columnists. It's hard to believe they were that important in those days. There were three in the *Daily News*. There was Nick Kenny and Walter Winchell in the *Daily Mirror*, there was Louis Sobol and Dorothy Kilgallen in the *Journal American*, there was Lucius Beebe in the *Herald Tribune*. There was George Ross in the *New York World Telegram*. There were Sidney Skolsky and Ed Sullivan. . . ."

Lehman was still living with his parents on East Seventy-fifth Street when he was immersing himself in the world of *Sweet Smell of Success*. Looking back on that whole episode, Lehman says that he "was fearful" when he quit his job, rented a cottage in Provincetown with his wife, and began writing his hundred-page novelette. "I knew I was playing with fire."

Irving Hoffman was the chief press agent for whom Lehman worked as leg man and writer of items. "Irving was a celebrity, really," Lehman recalled, "and he was one of the few men who could stand up to Winchell, tell him where to get off." Hoffman was tall, physically imposing—"a great talker and phone man." He was extremely nearsighted and wore glasses. He wore a camel's-hair coat. He was a star in his own right, a friend of J. Edgar Hoover's. He had his own power, including a column in the *Hollywood Reporter* with the highbrow title "Tales of Hoffman." Ernie Lehman contributed to those columns, including a segment that appeared every Monday called "Last Week on Broadway."

Like Sidney Falco, Hoffman read the galley proofs of Winchell's column the night before it appeared in the paper. So when he read the manuscript of Lehman's novelette, which would be published in *Cosmopolitan* under the title "Tell Me About It Tomorrow" (Herbert Mayes, *Cosmopolitan*'s story editor, didn't want the word "smell" to appear in his magazine), Hoffman was furious. "Ernie," he asked, "how can you do this to me? Everbody's going to think I'm Sidney! Everybody's going to think Hunsecker is Winchell! You have things in here that only somebody who's close to Winchell would know!"

There *were* similarities: the reading of Winchell's column in galleys the night before, Falco's apartment-cum-office, which was very much like Hoffman's. ("I used to visit Irving's office," Lehman recalled. "He would hand the phone over to me so I could hear Truman Capote's voice.") A bedroom lurked behind the front desk, where on at least one occasion Lehman had to knock off a theater review to the sounds of moans and bouncing bedsprings coming from behind the door. Hoffman was a world-class womanizer, a fact confirmed by Ernie Lehman's longtime friend the producer David Brown, who has known the writer since they were boys together on Long Island.

Brown was the editor in chief of *Cosmopolitan* when Lehman's novelette appeared in the magazine. Brown believed that "Hoffman suffered from satyriasis—he was the male equivalent of a nymphomaniac."

But there was one important difference between Sidney Falco and

Irving Hoffman: Hoffman didn't suck up to Winchell. And Hoffman didn't cringe. Hoffman wielded his own power. Ernie tried to explain this to his former boss, but it didn't matter: "Irving had a right to feel betrayed," Lehman would later say. In fact, out of respect for Hoffman he made several small changes in the manuscript: having the secretary address Hunsecker differently, for example, because Winchell's secretary, Rose Bigman, always addressed Winchell as "chief." But Hoffman was not assuaged. "For a year-and-a-half, he didn't talk to me," Lehman said. "We had a complete break."

Hoffman was right—everyone did read *Sweet Smell of Success* as an attack on Winchell, and that's why, at first, no one in Hollywood would touch it. Lehman's agent in Los Angeles, George Willner, attempted to sell the story before it even appeared in *Cosmopolitan*. He wrote to Lehman in Provincetown in June of 1949: "The big problem still remains the resemblance to Winchell. I went to all the places where I thought it would do some good, but I still ran up against the same problem. . . . I'll say one thing for your story, it set this town on its ear. And Ernest Lehman's name is probably as well known out here now as any of the top ten or twelve writers."

Ironically, it wasn't the manuscript of *Sweet Smell of Success* that brought Lehman to Hollywood but his estranged mentor Irving Hoffman. Hoffman finally wanted to make up with Ernie. They were brought together by a mutual friend, a press agent for Artie Shaw named Sidney Garfield (who, by the way, would lend his name to Sidney Falco). As an olive branch, Hoffman offered to give Lehman a plug in his column. Better yet, he let Lehman write the whole column himself:

> The world I want to see on film is the world of Toots Shor's at lunch-hour, Sardi's at 11 of an opening night, Lindy's at 2 o'clock of any morning. . . . [T]he world of Winchell and Wilson, Sullivan and Sobol . . . of columnists on the prowl for items, press agents on the prowl for columnists. . . .

Lehman ended his pitch with, "Now I may be wrong (and I don't think I am), but just off his past performances I would say that Ernest Lehman is the guy who can write that kind of picture. . . ."

Two weeks later, Paramount called.

And none too soon: Lehman had become a pariah at Lindy's, the Stork Club, '21'—places he had formerly plied his trade. Press agents got up and left the table when Ernie Lehman entered the room.

THE PRODUCTION COMPANY of Hecht-Hill-Lancaster could be a treacherous place to work. Harold Hecht was a small ex-hoofer and former literary agent. At one point in his career, he had been a dancer for Martha Graham. Tricky and clever, Hecht laughed and drank a little too much. The skinny on Hecht was that he was very affable, but don't turn your back: he was given the nickname "the Mole." Victor Navasky described him as "a denigrating informer" in *Naming Names*, his book on Hollywood and the House Un-American Activities Committee. One story told about him is that when he was called before HUAC, he brought in one of Hecht-Hill-Lancaster's screenwriters, Roland Kibbee, to help him prepare a statement to be read before the committee. But right after Hecht read the statement, he named Kibbee as a Communist.

Burt Lancaster had just appeared on Broadway in *A Sound of Hunting* when he met Harold Hecht in 1945. Hecht, six years Lancaster's senior, had already spent twenty years in show business, but with modest success. He set himself up as Lancaster's agent, recognizing the actor's immense potential. Lancaster's brief show business career before his stint on Broadway had been in a failing trapeze-and-gymnastic act, but his sheer physical presence was overwhelming. His shadow fell over you before he even entered the room.

An inducement for Lancaster to go in with Hecht was Hecht's idea of forming their own film production company—something unthinkable for a mere actor at the time. "Here we were," Hecht told Lancaster's biographer, "a couple of bums without a quarter between us, discussing producing our own pictures."

James Hill, the third partner in Hecht-Hill-Lancaster, was perennially boyish. He was a page at NBC before becoming a contract screenwriter at MGM. People wondered why he was made a partner in the company. The truth was, Jim Hill was "Burt Lancaster's boy," according to screenwriter Julius Epstein. It had been Burt's idea to put Hill's name between those of Hecht and Lancaster; Jim Hill would come between the two partners in other ways. Hill provided a buffer between the two men, who were often at each other's throats. In return, Lancaster procured women for Hill, and not just any women—movie stars. Hill made fun of men who were reduced to sleeping with their secretaries. In February of 1958, at the age of forty-one, Hill would marry Rita Hayworth—her fifth marriage, and his first. The marriage would only last three years.

When Hill first came to work at the Hecht-Lancaster building they owned on North Canon Drive which had formerly housed the William Morris Agency, he noticed the intense rivalry between the two partners. "Harold and Burt," Hill recalled in the last interview he would give before suffering a stroke in 1999, "had as strange a relationship as you could get. People were frightened of Burt, and he never did anything to make people un-frightened of him." Another friend described their relationship as "a Freudian can of worms." Not only was Lancaster capable of verbally brutalizing Hecht, he once lifted his partner into the air and threatened to throw him out the window. The contention between them stemmed from Hecht's desire to "get out from under Burt's shadow," Hill believed. Lancaster wasn't just a company figurehead, he was an active and involved partner.

Ernie Lehman knew that "Burt had the power. He was the famous movie star. He had the money, which Harold Hecht didn't have. . . . In terms of publicity and power, Burt Lancaster had both. Hecht was the nobody." Hecht resented Jim Hill's presence in the company, but he wasn't about to go up against Lancaster. "It was old-fashioned jealousy," Ernie Lehman believed. Once Jim Hill became involved in the making of *Sweet Smell of Success*, Harold Hecht lost all interest in the film, although he had been the one who originally angled for the rights.

Long before the production company acquired *Sweet Smell*, Hecht-Hill-Lancaster hired Lehman to work on a script for another project. But from the minute he walked into their plush offices—complete with an aviary of twittering finches that seemed to fall silent whenever Lancaster passed by—Lehman took a dislike to his surroundings. "They were profligate," he remembered. "They spent money on everything—$12,000 remodeling the executive washroom." The partners also maintained a luxurious apartment on Wilshire Boulevard for their trysts, replete with gold-plated dinnerware and a Utrillo hanging in the hallway near the bathroom; the antiques and hundred-dollar ashtrays still had their price tags attached to them.

Lehman's first encounter with Burt Lancaster didn't do much to change his mind:

> I was sitting with Harold Hecht. The door opened and in walked a towering, impressive figure. He was zipping up his fly and smiling proudly, saying, "She swallowed it." That was my introduction to Burt Lancaster. I called my agent and said, "I'm not going to do this picture. Get me off of it." Harold Hecht pleaded with me. He got down on his hands and knees and said, "Please don't leave, or Burt will blame me."

But Lehman did leave, and when Hecht first tried to persuade him to adapt his novelette for a Hecht-Hill-Lancaster film, Lehman refused, although they were the only producers in town with the courage to make the film. Frankly, the trio scared him—there was a whiff of violence about the place.

Lancaster was rumored to have beaten up his current girlfriend, a telephone operator in the building. "He was known to be violent with women," confirms Lehman. *Confidential* published an article in 1955 with the headline "The Secret's Out About Burt Lancaster." Francesca De Scaffa, who was rumored to be a former mistress of the Shah of Iran and a paid informant for *Confidential*, offered the story to the magazine. She had met with Lancaster to angle for a role in the 1954 film *Vera Cruz*, but she claimed that when she turned down his sexual advances, he attacked her, ripping the sleeve from her $400 Jacques Fath dress. "Things went from waltz time into a tempo four times faster than the mambo," the tabloid reported in their signature style. "Burt's tendency towards clobbering cuties is rapidly becoming no secret at all among dames in the know in Hollywood. . . ."

"The place was rife with womanizing," Lehman remembers. Early on, the screenwriter was invited to a meeting with the three heads of the company, the subject of which was "Who can we find to become our official procurer?"

"I'm ashamed to say," Lehman said, "that I was a part of this meeting. There we were, scratching around for women. They were the most corrupt group. I really sank into the depths when I decided to work with them."

Lehman remembers being in Palm Springs with his wife when Harold and Jim tried to persuade him to join them in Acapulco, where Hecht had two women waiting. "I said no, absolutely not. And to this day, I can't figure out why they did that. Here I was, married with two young children—my wife was in the next room. What were they trying to do by exporting me to Acapulco? What were they planning to do while I was away? It was very strange."

Paddy Chayefsky was adapting his television play *Marty* for the production company at the time. He and Lehman would go on long walks together and trade horror stories. "I seemed to be surrounded by evil," Lehman believed. "But they were the ones who felt a great affinity for *Sweet Smell*. They dug it. Nobody else did, really. The film could only have been made by Hecht-Hill-Lancaster." It was the unexpected success of Chayefsky's *Marty* that led Lehman to change his mind about signing over the rights; the film won four Academy Awards, including the 1956 Oscar for best picture. "When *Marty* won the Oscar, I finally said yes," Lehman recalled. "But on the condition that I also direct the picture."

TONY CURTIS hounded Burt Lancaster for the part of Sidney Falco, the weaselly press agent who long ago threw his moral compass into the East River. Lancaster had been impressed with Curtis during the making of *Trapeze* the previous year, the sawdust-and-sweat circus drama in which the two men were teamed for the first time. The pairing of Lancaster and Curtis as trapeze artists who fall out over Gina Lollobrigida was highly successful: there was more chemistry between the two men in tights than between either man and the girl. The two handsome actors had walked off with the picture—on their hands.

Tony knew he was born to play the streetwise Falco. "All they had to tell me was New York. I was raised in that city. I should have done *Sweet Smell* the first movie I ever made. Instead, Universal put me in bloomers with a scimitar, with big-breasted girls up against my chest. That seemed to satisfy everybody." Up till then he had swashbuckled his way through numerous "tits and sand" movies like *Son of Ali Baba*

Tony Curtis as Sidney Falco and Burt Lancaster as J. J. Hunsecker, plotting at '21' in a scene from 1957's *Sweet Smell of Success*. Hunsecker's character was based on columnist Walter Winchell, then in the twilight of his career. *Photofest.*

and made lots of money for Universal, who had transformed a rough-cut Hungarian Jew from Brooklyn named Bernard Schwartz into a brilliantined teen idol who called himself Antony Curtis. *Sweet Smell of Success* would reverse that transformation.

For the role of J. J. Hunsecker, Hecht and Lancaster immediately thought of Orson Welles. But when Lehman began working on the first of several drafts of the screenplay, Lancaster would attend story conferences, reclining on a large green sofa in his sumptuous office. "He was fascinated," Lehman remembered. "It's like he smelled that this could be a different role for him—no hero. One day, Burt just said, 'I'm going to do it.' That's when it became a bigger venture, more important."

With Lancaster now slated to appear in the film, Lehman's sensitive stomach began to give him trouble. "It bothered me a lot," he said. "They used to make jokes about it. I remember at a meeting we had one day when Burt looked at me, and he said, 'I can see us all standing around Ernie's grave, and there's a stomach tree growing out of it.' And the three of them laughed. This was the atmosphere I was working in. This was no John Houseman or Billy Wilder." Lehman had written his novelette as an atonement, "having done some pretty terrible things as a press agent." Now he felt he'd entered a whole new level of corruption.

When United Artists put up the funds to produce the picture, Hecht seized the opportunity to fire Lehman as the film's director. The ostensible reason was that Lancaster's first directorial effort, on *The Kentuckian* (1955), had lost money for United Artists, but the truth was, "We were never gonna let Ernie direct!" as Jim Hill explained forty-two years later. In fact, Hill believed that "Ernie didn't want to work on the picture at all, or he wouldn't have made a demand like that." Tony Curtis confirms this. "We were talking about getting Orson Welles to play J. J. Hunsecker. They're gonna let Lehman, who's never directed a movie before in his life, direct Orson Welles? They did that, I feel, because they wanted to get the property. That's the only reason."

Lehman was crushed when Hecht called him into his office. He went to his agent, Lew Wasserman, and said, "'Lew, I have terrible news for you.' And Wasserman said, 'I already know.' That was the trouble with MCA in those days, because Lew Wasserman was also *their* agent! So they made me a producer instead of the director. I kept getting more and more pain in my gut, and more and more stress. And that's when they chose Alexander Mackendrick. Sandy was already there on another project, so they asked him to direct *Sweet Smell*. It seemed an unlikely choice. What the hell would he know about the world of Broadway and New York night life? He was from Scotland for god's sakes!"

IN A WAY, Alexander "Sandy" Mackendrick was coming home when he flew to America in 1956. Although he had grown up in Glasgow and worked in England, he was actually born in Boston of Scottish immigrant parents. When his father died in the Spanish flu epidemic of 1918, it was clear that the experiment of living in America just hadn't worked out. The family returned to Scotland and Mackendrick was brought up by his grandparents. (Mackendrick was fond of telling people that he was actually conceived in Hollywood though born in Boston, so his "mistrust of Hollywood was prenatal.")

Mackendrick had made his reputation directing two of the classic Alec Guinness comedies for Britain's Ealing Studios, *The Man in the White Suit* (1951) and *The Ladykillers* (1955), considered the apotheosis of the Ealing style. His background was in design; he was a wunderkind for the advertising agency J. Walter Thompson before being hired to create storyboards for Ealing, which he then parlayed into directing. His comedies are known for their dark-edged humor ("Where there is comedy he rims it in black," wrote one critic). His friend Alec Guinness described him as "a man of great charm, but of astonished outrage at the wickedness of the world."

Soon after *The Ladykillers* was made, Michael Balcon sold Ealing Studios to the BBC and Mackendrick sought his fate abroad. "He got a call from his agent one day asking him to come out here and talk to somebody at Paramount," remembered Mackendrick's widow, Hilary, whom the director had met while working at Ealing Studios. "It was all rather mysterious, so naturally he was intrigued." Mackendrick, used to the camaraderie of Ealing, turned down offers from big studios like Paramount and producers like David O. Selznick, deciding instead to sign with Hecht-Hill-Lancaster, where he would direct an adaptation of George Bernard Shaw's *The Devil's Disciple*.

Hilary and Sandy Mackendrick settled into a rented house on South Rodeo Drive. The Ealing Studios had provided its crew with a quart of bonded whiskey a day during shoots, and Mackendrick's biggest complaint about Hollywood at that time was its lack of pubs.

During daily conferences with Mackendrick, Lehman quickly recognized the Scottish director's brilliance. "His words just tumbled over each other; I couldn't quite follow him at times. He was too bright for me, too fast. Working with Sandy was great, but at the same time, stressful. You had the feeling he wasn't even listening to you because his mind was going so fast."

After one particularly rough story conference, Lancaster walked Lehman out into the hall and put an arm around his shoulder. "We're going to start shooting next week in New York," he said. "You're going to have to do some rewrites behind the camera."

"OK, Burt, but first I'm going to have to go see my doctor."

Lehman was really suffering. His friend David Brown, then living in Hollywood and working as an executive at Twentieth Century Fox, drove him in his Mercedes sports car to Cedars of Lebanon Hospital. "When I woke up the next morning," Lehman recalled, "the doctor was seated next to my bed. He said, 'Ernie, we've looked up there with a sigmoidoscope, and you're not going back to work. In fact, you're leaving the country.'"

When the doctor called Harold Hecht to say that Lehman was leaving the picture, Hecht hung up the phone and turned to his partners. Two of them spoke at the same time: "I hope the son of a bitch dies."

Lehman traveled to Hawaii and then on to Samoa and Tahiti. "I went native," he said. "One day I was lying there by myself on a beach, and suddenly I sat up and realized, 'My god, they're shooting a picture in New York called *Sweet Smell of Success.*' I'd forgotten all about it."

IT WAS Sandy Mackendrick's idea to bring in Clifford Odets, whom he had hero-worshiped from afar. Odets was already adapting A. B. Guthrie's 1949 novel *The Way West* for Hecht-Hill-Lancaster. Odets had never gotten over the triumph of having five plays running simultaneously in New York in 1935, when he was only twenty-nine, including *Waiting for Lefty* and *Awake and Sing*. "The poet of the Depression" was stocky and handsome, with wild blond hair that haloed his head like Einstein's. "He used to be wonderful to observe at parties," Tony Curtis recalled. "He had an old tuxedo with a vest and he had a very beautiful look about him in those days. No one looked as elegant as he with a martini in his hand. He had a great deal of fire and lust and drive." Odets took many women to bed, including the movie star Luise Rainer, whom he married in 1937.

It had taken the Depression to make Odets a great success and to give him his raison d'être, writing plays for the common man in an era of drawing-room comedies. He left a year later for California, where he accepted Hollywood's lucre but spent the rest of his life being branded a hypocrite for abandoning the leftist views of his great early plays. It was an opinion the playwright shared, torturing himself with his own sense of betrayal.

Arthur Miller spent some time with Odets in Hollywood six years after Odets had been a friendly, though captious, witness for HUAC during the McCarthy bloodletting. Finishing the screenplay for *Sweet Smell* would give Odets a way of striking back at what had been a public humiliation. Arthur Miller described the embattled playwright as typifying "what it meant to survive as an artist in America. There was something so utterly American in what had betrayed him—he had wanted everything." He compared Odets to his wife Marilyn Monroe: "Like her, he was a self-destroying babe in the woods, absentmindedly combing back his hair with a loaded pistol."

Harold Clurman, one of the founders of the Group Theatre, which had launched Odets, kept exhorting the playwright to leave Hollywood and return to New York. But Odets knew that the theater world he had known in the thirties no longer existed. Even with his tremendous early success, he could not have supported himself as a playwright. As Arthur Miller observed, there was little to return to: "only show business, and some real estate."

In 1936 Odets had predicted that "in a few years the movies will have developed into the most important artistic medium the world has ever seen, and it's high time playwrights found out about them."

But twenty years later, when he was signed to finish Lehman's script, Odets was living in reduced circumstances—divorced from his second wife, driving a dusty old Lincoln, and caring for his two young children. A gifted painter and collector of works by Klee and Matisse, Odets was forced to sell a number of his paintings just to survive.

Tony Curtis remembered his first meeting with Odets at the offices of Hecht-Hill-Lancaster. "He used to call me 'boychick,' right from the start." There was a kind of bond between Odets and Curtis—the playwright may have seen in the younger man a reminder of his own youthful urban beauty, now rumpled and fading. "The picture is loaded with little references to my looks," Curtis points out, "'the boy with the ice cream face,' and Rita, the cigarette girl, calling me 'Eyelashes.'"

One of the things Odets did was to give Curtis the key to Sidney Falco. He said, "Don't be still with Sidney. Don't ever let Sidney sit down comfortably. I want Sidney constantly moving, like an animal, never quite sure who's behind him or where he is." Curtis took Odets's suggestions to heart and gave what many consider to be his breakthrough performance.

There's sweet irony in the fact that Curtis went back to his roots—back to being Bernie Schwartz—to unleash that character on the world. Falco's little aria on success, delivered to his lugubrious secretary while he's changing clothes in his cramped bedroom behind her desk, could easily have been Curtis's credo as well: "Hunsecker is a golden ladder to the places I want to get. Way up high, Sal, where it's always balmy and no one snaps his fingers and says, 'Hey, shrimp, rack the balls!' . . . [F]rom now on, Sally, the best of everything is good enough for me. . . ."

"I was really astounded by the twist of it," Curtis said about playing Falco. "I was able to grace the part with little physical innuendoes. Not for nothing, I wanted to make him an excellent athlete, growing up in the streets of New York, playing stickball. He punched, he boxed, he did everything, always on his feet, always moving."

Both Mackendrick and Lehman thought that Tony Curtis was "miraculous" as Sidney Falco. For Curtis, *Sweet Smell* opened doors; other brilliant roles would follow: *The Defiant Ones, Some Like It Hot, The Great Impostor*, and *The Boston Strangler*. And behind all those roles was Sidney Falco: "In all the films I've done, I've never lost Sidney. And I don't want to lose him."

In contrast to Falco, J. J. Hunsecker hardly seems to move—he's usually shown sitting, at his table in '21,' at his desk writing his column, in a studio waiting to tape his television show. In one early draft of the script, Lehman even put Hunsecker in a wheelchair, tended to by a male nurse named Sam. Ambition moves, power stays put.

One of cinematographer James Wong Howe's challenges on the film was to transform the robust Burt Lancaster into a tense, bespectacled ghoul. How do you take this big man and shrink him? His solution was to use the glasses to create a man who wasn't physically powerful, though he had a violent presence. The horn-rimmed glasses are one of the elements that make Lancaster's performance so chilling. Lancaster wore glasses in real life, and he fought with Mackendrick about wearing them in the film. But Mackendrick won this battle, and James Wong Howe—who had photographed Orson Welles in *Citizen Kane*—used the glasses as "a focal point for the light." The shadows cast by the glasses onto Burt's face gave him the skeletal look of a walking corpse. It's as though Hunsecker is already a dead man, his soul long since squeezed out of him by the machinery of power. "Match me, Sidney," he says to Falco from his throne at '21,' in his sadistic little game of domination and submission.

HOWE IS rightly credited with the movie's dazzling evocation of Broadway's nightlife. Filming inside '21' was impossible, so interiors were shot in Hollywood at Goldwyn Studios' Soundstage 8—they spent $25,000 just re-creating '21' with movable "wild walls" to make way for Howe's camera. Howe had the walls smeared with oil to make them gleam. To capture the smoky atmosphere of New York nightclubs, sets were built two feet off the ground and smoke pots placed underneath so that Howe could "light the smoke."

Production moved to New York City to begin shooting, bringing Odets with them to furnish script changes on location. Hill and Odets traveled east on the 20th Century Limited because Odets thought he could get a lot of writing done on the train. They got as far as Chicago, however, and Odets still hadn't written anything. Hill had to resort to devious methods to get Odets to work on the script: like scribbling an unusable scene himself and saying, "Let's give this to Sandy." Hill knew that Odets "had great pride in his work. He would sometimes write the same scene eight times before he'd let you read it."

But there was another problem. Odets didn't seem to realize until Chicago that they were going on to New York. He complained to Hill, "For Christ's sake, I can't go to New York! I can't face those people!" He was referring, of course, to the theater people he had left behind, who by now considered him a defector: Harold Clurman, Stella Adler, and other founding members of the Group Theatre who had remained hostile to Odets.

Meanwhile, Mackendrick was frustrated by the lack of a finished script. In Los Angeles Odets would write all night and slip his script changes under Sandy Mackendrick's door each morning. When Mackendrick read the sheets, he had mixed feelings about Odets's sizzling dialogue, worried that it would "sound stagy." But Odets reassured him: "You're probably worried that the dialogue is exaggerated and may sound implausible. Don't be. Play it real fast—and play the scenes, not for the words but for the situations! Play them on the run and they'll work just fine."

By the time shooting finally began in New York, things had become chaotic. "One of the most frightening experiences in my life was to start shooting in the middle of Times Square with an incomplete script," Mackendrick has said. It was the winter of 1956, and it was particularly bitter. The production manager, Richard McWhorter, remembered, "God, you needed all the clothes you could pile on, and you were still cold." To add to the chaos, the mimeographed sheets of Odets's script were often distributed to the cast and crew *after* the scene had been shot.

Then, one night early in the production, Tony Curtis noticed that Clifford Odets was missing from the set. He asked Jim Hill where Clifford was, and Hill said, "We've got him locked up at the Essex House." And sure enough, Curtis remembered, "there was bleary-eyed, stiff-haired Clifford, sitting in his pajamas on a couch, with papers—typewritten, handwritten—all over the joint. I said, 'Let's go out for dinner,' and Jim Hill said, 'What, are you nuts?' They wouldn't let him out until he had completed more work on the script."

Eventually Hill allowed Odets to leave his hotel room and come down to the location shoot in Times Square. They made room for him and his typewriter in one of the prop trucks. "I remember," said Curtis, "it was about three or four in the morning, and it was cold, bitter, and miserable. Between shots, I was strolling around, and I heard this 'tik-tik-tik' coming from inside a prop truck. So I go and look in, and there's Clifford Odets, sitting in an overcoat, huddled over his typewriter. I said, 'What the hell are you doing here this time of night?'"

He said, "I've got to finish this sequence. You have two more days shooting here, and I've got to get it done."

Tony joined him in the truck, sitting at the playwright's feet. He suddenly looked up, and Odets said to him, "Come here, kid. I want to show you something. Look at what I'm writing."

"I see he's just typed out, 'The cat's in the bag, and the bag's in the river.' It took my breath away, right from his brain to my brain. He wrote it as we were shooting it."

Sandy Mackendrick would note years later, "There never was a final shooting script for the movie. . . . It was all still being revised, even on the last day of principal photography. It was a shambles of a document."

But a bigger problem on the set was the power struggle between Mackendrick and Lancaster. They both wanted to be the man in control. Sandy was the director, but Burt was the central figure of the production; he was the one who was really in charge. Lancaster would go behind Mackendrick's back, for example, to give Marty Milner direction on how he should play the role of Steve Dallas. Mackendrick would later observe, "The hysteria of that production was the edge of fear. I was working from moment to moment. . . ."

Curtis recalled how Sandy insisted on absolute silence on the set, or he wouldn't shoot. To Sandy, the set was a cathedral. "Even if everything went perfectly," Curtis said, "he would still want to reshoot. In the middle of a scene, he'd yell 'shut up!' Everyone tiptoed around him on that set. Burt would get mad because they couldn't afford all that reshooting." Mackendrick in fact did an epic number of takes of the scene in which Hunsecker watches a drunk being bounced from Club Pigalle. They did it over and over and over again, going all night long, and then Mackendrick said, "Print takes 1 and 2 and let's wrap!"

Burt was furious: "Remind me to pay somebody to take the little Limey's legs off."

Elmer Bernstein, who composed the film's powerful, jazzy score, confessed to the director James Mangold (*Cop Land*), "The combination of people on that movie—Hecht, Lancaster, Odets . . . was a snake pit. There was a cultural distance between Burt and Sandy. It was like Sandy's heart beat at a different rate."

"Burt was really scary," the composer recalled. "He was a dangerous guy, he had a short fuse, he was very physical. You thought you might get punched out. . . . It was a miracle that [Sandy] finished that film. In fact, I think that film is what finished Sandy." Lancaster would later admit with a grin that Mackendrick considered him "pure evil."

Their biggest power struggle, however, would be over the ending of the movie. The film critic and screenwriter F. X. Feeney, who would later befriend Mackendrick, knew that "Lancaster was adamant about ending the film in a certain way, which Sandy was opposed to." Mackendrick had been warned by Alan Crosland, the film's editor, that Lancaster intended to take over the film and reedit it. "Sandy was at his notepad trying to figure out how he could do it *his* way, when a big shadow fell over him—it's Lancaster. He had to come clean about what he was doing, and he ultimately had to shoot the scene in two different ways, and cut the final ending on his own, behind Lancaster's back."

The dilemma was, in part, whether to end with Sidney Falco getting beaten up by the sadistic cop Harry Kello—ominously portrayed by New York character actor Emile Meyer—or to end with Susie Hunsecker rejecting her brother, walking out into the first shaft of sunlight that appears in this otherwise dark film. Jim Hill and Burt Lancaster cut the final scene in reverse order, but when they screened it, they could see it wasn't working.

"So Sandy tells them," Feeney explained, "'I've cut the film this way, why don't you look at it?' In a kind of grudging spirit, they all sat down, and Sandy had the rare satisfaction of watching them sink in their chairs and kind of get it—they actually got his ending."

Neither ending, however, satisfied Ernie Lehman, who disliked the scene in which Susie is saved from throwing herself over the balcony of her brother's penthouse apartment. (Hunsecker keeps her like one of those caged finches, in a little bedroom just off his study.) Lehman had originally written a similar ending, but he changed it to give her character more strength and cunning. Mackendrick, however, felt that the story "needed someone to bring death into the room" so that Falco and Hunsecker can finally be toppled.

When Lehman returned from Tahiti, Sandy called him and said, "Come down, I want to show you the rough cut." Lehman was dazzled by parts of it but disappointed by the ending, especially the suicide attempt. He suspected that "it had to be my stupidity in telling them about the ending I had originally written and thrown out."

THE ROLE of Susie Hunsecker went to an eighteen-year-old actress from the Bronx with no professional experience. Susan Harrison had been a former waitress at the Limelight, a Greenwich Village coffeehouse, and a model in the garment district. She had the delicate, frightened look of a startled deer. At five foot seven Susan was a willowy, nervous girl with brown eyes and light brown hair who smoked incessantly. Describing herself as "a person with moods," she struggled to hold on to the thread of her identity in the crucible of Hollywood. When Susan was thrown into the tough, womanizing partnership of Hecht-Hill-Lancaster, a number of the cast and crew feared she wasn't going to make it. The fragility she conveyed onscreen was not an act.

"I heard the whispers that I was neurotic, difficult, an oddball," she

Susan Harrison made her film debut in *Sweet Smell of Success*, but her career was short-lived. She was in the news again in 2000, after her daughter Darva Conger married Rick Rockwell on Fox TV's infamous show *Who Wants to Marry a Millionaire? Photofest.*

would later say. "I wore long hair, black stockings, and oversized sweaters. I didn't know what I was doing in front of the camera, but they all said it looked good."

In preparing for her climactic scene, Mackendrick told the young actress, "Here, Susan, is where you lock yourself in your room. What would you want to do before you committed suicide?"

Feeney remembers Mackendrick telling him that Susan "admitted to a fascination with high buildings—she had an impulse to throw herself off. Sandy said, 'Just give us that,' but he saw something in her that was a little frightening. He was genuinely prescient about people."

What Mackendrick didn't know was that shortly before beginning work on the film, Susan Harrison had fallen during a photographic shoot that Hecht had arranged with the German-born photographer Peter Basch. It was in a private house behind the Chateau Marmont in

West Hollywood. Susan, who stepped on an unsupported section of roofing and fell ten feet to the concrete porch below, later admitted that her fall "might have been a veiled suicide attempt. I thought, deep down, of killing myself because I was very depressed. . . ."

Peter Basch remembers the event, and he vividly recalled Susan Harrison's unusual beauty. Basch has photographed many ingenues, including Tuesday Weld, Jane Fonda, and Natalie Wood when they were barely in their teens. "What I found fascinating about her was that she was not the girl-next-door," Basch recalls. "She was a young woman with a strong erotic component, she could have worked all over Europe. The Italians would have loved her." Susan was so luckless that not only did she fall ten feet to a cement floor, the ambulance called to rescue her crashed on its way to the house. Her injuries were slight, though she ended up suing Basch and the owner of the house, urged on by her husband, a phony Frenchman to whom she was married for six months. "Her choice of men—I think that's what tripped her up, finally," said Basch.

When Sidney Falco tells Susie Hunsecker in the final scene of the film, "Look at yourself, you're nineteen years old, just a kid, and you're falling apart at the seams . . . with a fatality for doing wrong, picking wrong, and giving up even before you start to fight . . . ," he could have been speaking about Susan Harrison herself. It was one of those many moments in *Sweet Smell* where the line between life and art is blurred.

Curtis knew that "working with those guys was tough. We all came in with barrels loaded, we all came in to fight. Susan had no experience at all, so we drove her down into nowhere. She seems lost in the film."

THE FILM premiered on June 27, 1957, at the Loew's State Theater in New York, with Walter Winchell, the most powerful gossip columnist in America, pacing nervously across the street. Winchell was waiting for a handful of his spies to reassure him that the movie was going to be a flop. And indeed it was. The public hated it. Earlier, when it was screened by a Northern California audience, one viewer wrote on her preview card: "Don't touch a foot of this film. Just burn the whole thing."

Hoffman—like Winchell—refused to see it. Instead, he paced the theater lobby. When the movie was over, he exhorted the departing audience, "It's a bunch of crap—don't believe a word of it!" Winchell, on the other hand, displayed his "sheer egotism" when he called up rival columnist Louis Sobol after the novelette was first published and said, "Hey, did you read what Ernie Lehman wrote about you?"

But the film that's now regarded as a delicious morality tale is still credited with destroying Winchell's reputation.

And this stylish, black-and-white film refuses to go away. Its sly influence has cropped up in the work of directors as diverse as Martin Scorsese, Barry Levinson, the Coen brothers, and Paul Thomas Anderson. "It was such a tough film," Scorsese has said. "It was vibrant, alive, the images of New York, the location work were all brilliant. It was a world of operators I knew very well."

There were a number of reasons why *Sweet Smell* failed at the box office, the first financial disaster suffered by Hecht-Hill-Lancaster. The movie was just too cynical for the times—in 1957 America was in no mood to see a film about its dark side. And the public wasn't ready to see two popular stars, Curtis and Lancaster, cast as villains. They had been so likable in *Trapeze*. One film executive marveled that the film seemed to have been made "almost in defiance of the box office."

The Hollywood reporter Ezra Goodman accompanied Hill, Hecht, and Lancaster to San Francisco for a preview of the film. After the screening, Hecht approached Goodman and asked him what he thought of the picture.

"I told him that I thought it was poor. Hecht was overjoyed. His face broke out into a wide Cinemascope smile, and I became his buddy. *Sweet Smell* was a flop and lost a great deal of money, but Hecht was happy." Ever since Jim Hill had been made a partner in the company and ended up getting the producer's credit on the film, Hecht was glad to see it fail. Three years later, Hecht-Hill-Lancaster would dissolve their partnership.

At a party at Jim Hill's apartment after the preview, Lehman sat at a table with Burt Lancaster. Burt turned to him suddenly and said, "You weren't that sick, Ernie. You didn't have to leave the picture. I ought to punch you in the jaw right here and now."

Ernie said, "Go ahead, Burt. I need the money."

"They resented me," Lehman felt. "They considered me an enemy in their midst. I never saw Clifford again. He was off on another picture. They got rid of everyone."

One of the people they got rid of was Sandy Mackendrick, two weeks into the making of *The Devil's Disciple*, the film he had initially been hired to direct. Lancaster claimed that Sandy was just taking too long, driving up the budget. "Sandy was a very brilliant man," Lancaster explained, "but we hadn't the time or the money for him. That's the truth." Hilary recalls that "he was let go from *Devil's Disciple* after he had already shot sequences with Laurence Olivier. . . . [H]e had no idea why it happened. He was particularly annoyed that Harold Hecht did not speak to him personally, but sent in the production manager. It was very crushing for him. He became depressed." It's possible that Sandy was being made a scapegoat for the box office failure of *Sweet Smell of Success*, despite the critical appreciation of the film and the fact that it made *Time*'s and the *New York Herald*'s ten best lists for 1957.

The Mackendricks returned to England, where Sandy made a few more films before they came back to Hollywood to live in 1969. He had spent ten years in England developing *Mary Queen of Scots*, which he felt would have been his masterwork, only to have Universal cancel the project. His last film would turn out to be a silly 1960s comedy with Tony Curtis and Sharon Tate called *Don't Make Waves*, but it was plagued by problems—including the death of a stuntman—and Sandy had had enough. He had come to the conclusion that in Hollywood, "the deal is the real product; the movie is the by-product of the deal." When the California Institute for the Arts began looking for someone to head up its new film program, they asked Mackendrick. He accepted, and became its longest-serving dean and a much loved teacher from 1969 to 1978. The Mackendricks' home just off Santa Monica Boulevard became something of a haven for the director's favorite students, such as F. X. Feeney, and former cronies from Mackendrick's days at Ealing, such as Peter Sellers and Alec Guinness. Sadly, he never made another film. "Without him," Anthony Lane wrote in *The New Yorker*, "the landscape of cinema has grown dimmer."

"He was cynical, cynical about everything," Hilary said. "He took to calling *Sweet Smell* a piece of hokum, but that was his nature. He just couldn't bring himself to acknowledge that he had made a masterpiece." Hilary Mackendrick, a statuesque woman with porcelain skin, now spends much of her time as chair of the Archive Committee of the British Academy of Film and Television Arts in Los Angeles, devoted to preserving the legacy of the British movie colony in Hollywood.

In 1965, eight years after the film was released, Susan Harrison sued Harold Hecht for $25,000, claiming that Hecht had fraudulently seduced her into abandoning her contract with Hecht-Hill-Lancaster. After that, she seemed to just disappear. Except for a teen exploitation flick, she never made another film in Hollywood. In October of 1965, Harrison was given a ninety-day suspended jail sentence by a Superior Court judge in Los Angeles for child neglect, when she failed to give her two-year-old son urgently needed medical attention. The boy, Daniel, sustained brain injury when he fell from a high place.

Walter Winchell, who had refused to even see the film or punish Ernie Lehman in his column, ignored all references to *Sweet Smell*—except to report its failure at the box office. "I don't deal with the Lehmans of the world," he said magisterially when asked why he didn't retaliate against the film in his column. It wasn't until the end of the year, nearly six months after its run, that Winchell acknowledged the film at all, reporting matter-of-factly that "Hecht-Hill-Lancaster would stand to lose $500,000. . . ." But as Winchell's latest biographer Neal Gabler wrote, Lehman's novelette and Mackendrick's movie had "helped sully Winchell's name forever." He lived another fourteen years, long enough to see his power and influence evaporate. David Brown described his last encounter with Winchell: "It was at Danny's Hideaway. He was all alone in the booth, surrounded by his clippings. He had totally abandoned his column, he had been fired, but he still had that incredible ego. At his funeral, you know, nobody was there who wasn't paid to be there."

As for Odets, he continued to work on films, often uncredited. He had always been a cynic about the sweet smell of success, particularly in the film industry. "Hell," Odets once said to Burt Lancaster, "you can get killed just yearning for Hollywood."

Odets was hired to write *Wild in the Country* for Elvis Presley, but when he had Presley's character commit suicide at the end of the picture, he was forced to rewrite the ending. He did so: he needed the money. "Everything he was against at the beginning of his career," observed his friend Oscar Levant, "he wound up doing himself."

Odets lived six more years after the release of *Sweet Smell of Success*. Just as he had accepted the inevitability of movies, he accepted the inevitability of television, and agreed to be head writer for *The Richard Boone Show*. But when a stomach complaint turned out to be cancer, Odets was hospitalized. While in the hospital, he was convinced that all his nurses were trying to poison him. He also had his psychiatrist flown in from New York, and he proposed marriage to her on his deathbed. All his old friends from Broadway, the ones he had avoided during location shooting in New York—Harold Clurman, Elia Kazan, Stella Adler, Lee Strasberg—now showed up at his bedside to pay homage to their former golden boy.

"He gave me his hand to hold," Elia Kazan later wrote about his old friend. " . . . [H]e beckoned to me to lean closer, and he whispered—I remember the words well—'Gadg! Imagine! Clifford Odets dying!' "

His death received modest notice in the press: *Time* magazine traduced his long career to a flippant announcement, "Odets, where is thy sting?" But Odets, near the end of his life, had written his own epitaph: "That miserable patch of events, that mélange of nothing, while you were looking ahead for something to happen, that was it! That was life! You lived it!"

Odets was to suffer one more indignity. It was revealed shortly after his death that the Pulitzer Prize committee had chosen Odets's last play, *The Flowering Peach*, for the 1954 prize, but they were overruled by the advisory committee, and the award went instead to Tennessee Williams's *Cat on a Hot Tin Roof*.

Ernie Lehman would go on to have a spectacular career as a screenwriter in Hollywood, writing the screenplays for *North by Northwest*, *West Side Story*, *The Sound of Music*, *Who's Afraid of Virginia Woolf?*, *Hello, Dolly!*, and Hitchcock's last film, *Family Plot*. It's now been over twenty years since Lehman's last film, *Black Sunday*, written for director John Frankenheimer. David Thomson, writing in his *Biographical Dictionary of Film*, eloquently lamented Lehman's long good-bye, wondering if Lehman "may have been writing away (like Billy Wilder) on screenplays that are smart, funny, and beautifully constructed, only to be told that no one has the patience for movies like that anymore."

Lehman has outlived all three of his nemeses, Harold Hecht, James Hill, and Burt Lancaster, who had once imagined standing over the screenwriter's grave. Two weeks shy of his eighty-first birthday, Burt Lancaster had a fatal heart attack in his Century City home. He had suffered a stroke in 1990 while visiting the actor Dana Andrews at the John Douglas French Center for Alzheimer's Disease. This physically powerful actor who had begun his film career in *The Killers* and was practically a force of nature onscreen—who had once dominated Hecht-Hill-Lancaster by his sheer physical presence and the threat of violence—ended up confined to a wheelchair, his speech impaired, after suffering several heart attacks. Hecht, who died in 1985, and Lancaster are both buried in Westwood Cemetery, near the grave of Alexander Mackendrick. "Poor Sandy," his widow Hilary says. "Hecht is buried to the left of him, Lancaster to the right." James Hill was the last to go, dying in a nursing home in 2001.

Ernie Lehman has continued to draw in the sweet smell of success (a phrase, incidentally, that will enter a new edition of *Bartlett's Familiar Quotations*, keeping company with the words of Heraclitus and Yogi Berra). He has found a new demand for the stories that began his career as a magazine writer a half century ago. Publisher Peter Mayer and his Overlook Press have brought *Sweet Smell of Success and Other Stories* back into print for the first time since 1958.

Finally, *Sweet Smell of Success* has come home. It returned to New York as a Broadway musical in the spring of 2002, with a cadre of talent that would make Sidney Falco weep with envy. The effort to bring *Sweet Smell* to Broadway was spearheaded by Lehman's boyhood friend David Brown, with a book by playwright John Guare (*Six Degrees of Separation*) and a score by Marvin Hamlisch (*A Chorus Line*) and Craig Carnelia. British director Nicholas Hytner (*The Madness of King George*), who has always admired the look of Alexander Mackendrick's film, directed. While listening to a tape recording of the Hamlisch-Carnelia score in his living room in Brentwood, Lehman was moved to tears. "I don't want to oversell it," he said, "but I think it's a marvelous work."

It has always been David Brown's dream to make *Sweet Smell* into a Broadway musical. "After all, it's a fable. And a musical lends itself to fable. We are now living in a tabloid era—not the era of wonderful nonsense," Brown believes, "but an era of character assassination, of instant celebrity. In my view, it was all invented by J. J. Hunsecker."

As for Ernie Lehman, who in 2001 won an Oscar for lifetime achievement, he's remaining on the West Coast, content to stay away from this new incarnation of the novelette he wrote fifty years ago in a Provincetown bungalow. "I wrote the novel, the screenplay—it's theirs now," he says. "I'm staying away from it. I just hope they have a good press agent. Maybe Sidney Falco will get the job."

CHAPTER 12

THE HOUSEWIFE AND THE SWEATER GIRL: HOW *PEYTON PLACE* SAVED LANA TURNER

HOLLYWOOD DIDN'T KNOW what to make of Grace Metalious. She could be crass, even crude. While the movies celebrated female perfection, she embraced a kind of antiglamour, unembarrassed by her weight problem and her ugly wardrobe. But Metalious had written *Peyton Place*, a phenomenally best-selling novel, and Hollywood couldn't wait to make the film version. And, ironically, this story written by a homely housewife would revive the career of one of Hollywood's most beautiful and glamorous stars—Lana Turner.

It is hard to imagine the effect *Peyton Place* had on popular culture today, when song lyrics are embarrassingly explicit and there's nudity on prime-time television. But in September 1956, Metalious's novel detonated the myth of wholesome small-town life and the neo-Puritan ideals so many Americans seemed to embrace after World War II. In the course of one hefty potboiler, Metalious details two rapes, four seductions, two unwed pregnancies, two abortions, and the murder of a rapist by his victim, who also happens to be his stepdaughter. And all of it in the florid, deathless prose of a dime-store romance. "Indian summer is like a woman," Metalious begins. "Ripe, hotly passionate but fickle, she comes and goes as she pleases so that one is never sure whether she will come at all, or for how long she will stay."

It was the novel that "lifted the lid off a respectable New England town." Libraries barred it from their shelves. Canada refused to import it. South Africa banned it, too, until 1978. Critics like the *Christian Herald* wrote, "This is a bad book—quite beyond redemption. A novel so obscene should neither have been written nor published." Letters to the editor in hometown newspapers called Grace Metalious "a dirty writer." A fruit stand owner in her own town even accused her of writing nothing more than a compilation of items from such scandal sheets as *Confidential*, *Exposé*, *Hush-Hush*, and *Top Secret*.

Grace Metalious was often hurt by the criticism, especially when her children were ostracized at school. But publicly she put on a brave face. "If I'm a lousy writer, a hell of a lot of people have got lousy taste," Metalious said wryly (and often). Indeed, the furor over her book only fanned the flames of its success. In Nashua, New Hampshire, 500 copies were sold in two weeks. Across the country, a total of 60,000 copies had been sold in only ten days. Soon hardcover sales would rocket to more than a quarter of a million copies. The paperback would sell more than ten million copies and Metalious's first novel would soon be translated into nine different languages, making it one of the most successful novels of the twentieth century.

Peyton Place shocked polite society because of its frank tone and bold subject matter, but the fact that a young housewife had penned it was almost more scandalous. By the mid-1950s, "Rosie the Riveter" was long retired. Women had left their wartime posts in factories and offices and were back where they supposedly belonged, in the home as full-time mothers. While other women cooked and cleaned, though, Grace Metalious banged out poems and short stories on an old typewriter. She complained that making dinner took time away from writing, so her family lived on quick and easy spaghetti. Husband George often took care of the children and did the dishes, especially when Grace became engrossed in writing the new novel that would make her famous.

One day at the public library, while other mothers attended story hour with their children, Grace Metalious pulled down a copy of *The Writer's Handbook*. She selected a literary agent at random, choosing him only because he had a French-sounding name and she had French-Canadian roots. Jacques Chambrun, who had also represented

Metalious's favorite author, W. Somerset Maugham, read her anguished five-page letter and accepted the novel *The Quiet Place*. Six publishers rejected it. By then Metalious had finished the work that she thought was even better than the first, however, *The Tree and the Blossom*, later known as *Peyton Place*. It too was rejected by five publishers before Julian Messner, Inc., bought it.

Grace Metalious signed the contract one summer day in August 1955. She received a $1,500 advance. Her publisher, Kitty Messner, was the epitome of the sophisticated New York professional woman. Grace remembered her beige pantsuit, the white carnation in her lapel, the way she looked so cool and fresh on that scorchingly hot day.

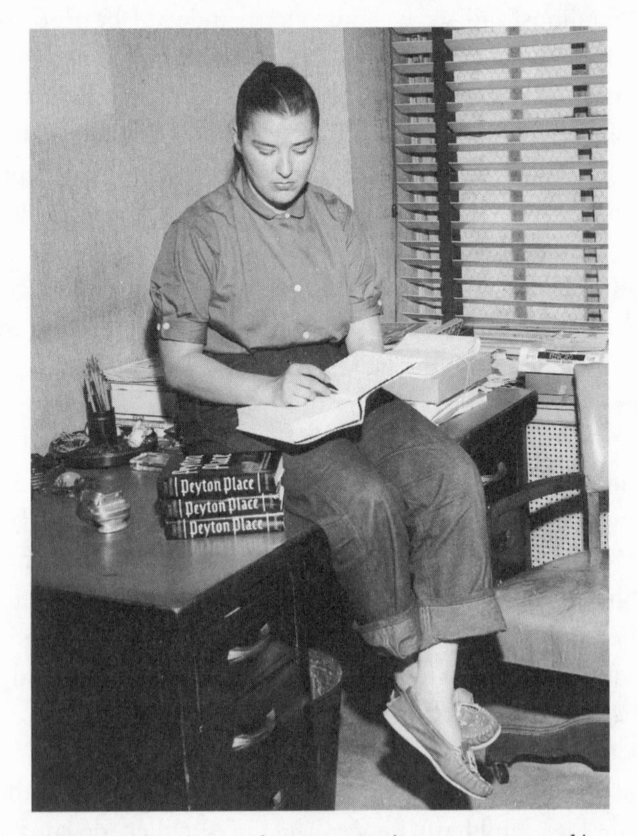

New Hampshire housewife Grace Metalious signs copies of her best-selling novel, *Peyton Place*. Producer Jerry Wald bought the film rights just a month after the book's 1956 publication. *Photofest.*

"Me, well you know what the heat does to me," Metalious said. "My armpits itched. I stuck to the chair and my hair was limp as hell."

The trio went out to '21' for a celebratory drink. Grace would always remember that very cold melon daiquiri. "I was an author with a contract. I had a French agent and a lady publisher. I was in 21," she said. "I had arrived."

That moment of civilized reflection passed quickly, though. Indeed, the power of *Peyton Place* to offend conventional sensibilities was surpassed only by Metalious herself. Her outspokenness did not win her any friends among her neighbors. During a television interview she said, "New England towns are small and they are often pretty, but they are not just pictures on a Christmas card. To a tourist these towns look as peaceful as a postcard picture, but if you go beneath that picture, it's like turning over a rock with your foot! All kinds of strange things crawl out."

Neighbors buzzed about her lack of homemaking skills, too. She was a notoriously poor housekeeper and agreed that, as was said of her in childhood, she "only had to be in a room five minutes to make it look like a pig sty." Howard Goodkind, Metalious's editor, visited her at her home in Gilmanton, New Hampshire (population 754), just a few weeks before *Peyton Place* hit bookstores. He had to step over a pile of garbage to enter the asbestos-sided shack she'd nicknamed "It'll Do." Inside, there were dirty dishes everywhere and flies hovering over open jars of peanut butter and marshmallow, lunch for her three children. When she wasn't home, she was a fixture at the local Rod and Gun Club, where, without her husband around, she could "drink everybody else under the table."

Grace Metalious didn't look like June Cleaver, either. A 1956 *Cosmopolitan* article described her as a "big woman" who "doesn't seem to worry about being overweight nor does she have any of the usual feminine worries about clothes and appearance." She wore her long hair held back in a ponytail by a rubber band. The standard uniform for her five-foot-four, 145-pound frame was a man's shirt, untucked, and a pair of dungarees.

"I think diets are stupid," she said. "I don't wear nylon stockings or girdles. I don't waste any time shopping when I'm in New York. These Fifth Avenue stores are strictly for jerks."

Perhaps as a way of protecting herself from the unending barbs, Grace Metalious concocted little biographical fictions that persist to this day. The child of French Canadian parents who had settled in New Hampshire, she claimed to be born Grace Marie Antoinette Jeanne d'Arc de Repentigny. Although the linking of a French queen and a peasant heroine in one unwieldy name says much about the two faces of the *Peyton Place* author, her birth certificate reads simply, "Marie Grace Repentigny."

She liked to tell a story about her marriage to George Metalious at seventeen, how the whole town suspected it was a "shotgun wedding." Exactly nine months after the ceremony, she said she threw a huge party to prove the gossips wrong, to show that her stomach was "flat as a pancake." It's a funny story about a plucky young woman. But the fact is that daughter Marsha was born seven months and three weeks after the wedding. Like her mother before her, she was one of thousands of young women of her day who "had to get married."

Her most calculated exaggeration came just before the release of *Peyton Place*. When her editor and a public relations man visited her in Gilmanton, New Hampshire, Metalious mentioned that her husband's contract as school principal was up. Although the school board had been talking about ousting George Metalious months before anyone had even heard of his wife's racy book, newspaper headlines suddenly sang out, "Teacher Fired for Wife's Book: Gossipy, Spicy Story Costs Him His Job." A best-seller was born.

But Grace Metalious's little lies were more than gimmicks. They reveal how deeply ambivalent she felt about small-town life. She wanted to lash out at provincial persecutors who could ruin a woman's reputation with a rumor or fire a man for no good reason. Yet she wanted to be accepted by them and feared being thought of as less than a normal woman because she didn't fit the 1950s mold of how a wife and a mother should look or behave. Grace Metalious, raised by a single mother in a working-class section of Manchester, New Hampshire, wrote from an outsider's perspective and despised any form of snobbishness. But she was also achingly ambitious and longed for the better life that literary success could provide.

For a while, the roughly $400,000 in profits from *Peyton Place* did make things better for the Metaliouses. Grace bought a new car and a new nine-room Cape Cod–style house on a large parcel of land outside Gilmanton. Soon, though, success would exact its own kind of price.

Lured by the enormous popularity of her novel, Hollywood producer Jerry Wald wanted a piece of the action. Less than a month after its publication in 1956, he offered $250,000 to make *Peyton Place* into a movie for Twentieth Century Fox, with $75,000 up front. Considering the profits he saw from it, though, Wald bought Metalious's novel for a song and bragged about his good judgment for years.

In January 1957, Grace Metalious was newly separated from her husband of sixteen years. More fodder for the town "ax mouths," she mused. With her new boyfriend at the wheel of her white convertible, she and her three children set out for Hollywood. She was on her way to serve as a "story consultant" for the film version of her novel and thought her brood could have a little fun along the way. From New Hampshire they drove to Virginia and then across the broad, flat nowhere of middle America. At Las Cruces, New Mexico, Metalious treated her children, her beau, and herself to western outfits. By the time she arrived at the Beverly Hilton in Beverly Hills, the shiny convertible was a dusty beige and their western getups looked the worse for wear.

A lesser woman would have been intimidated, pulling up to the swank hotel at nine o'clock on a Saturday night, the lobby full of glamorous people in formal evening dress. But Grace Metalious pretended her clan was a family of Texas millionaires and, with a false southern accent, feigned surprise when she found indoor plumbing in her huge suite.

In Hollywood the writer got the star treatment, riding in limousines and enjoying fancy dinners at famous restaurants. Twentieth Century Fox provided a private screening of any film she wanted and Metalious watched *On the Waterfront* in wonder. She also met celebrities like blonde bombshell Jayne Mansfield, leading man Cary Grant, and *Dragnet* star Jack Webb. One of her favorite moments was lunching with Frank Sinatra. He responded to her more than most of the Hollywood types and she appreciated it, describing him later as a wonderful conversationalist.

The Metalious children also got into the act. Fox executives arranged for six-year-old Cindy to meet Roy Rogers's horse Trigger. Marsha, thirteen, thought she had landed in teenybopper heaven. She met clean-cut smoothy Pat Boone and positively "swooned" upon meeting Elvis Presley, whom she thought was "gorgeous." Nine-year-old Mike was disappointed, though, when Fox couldn't arrange a meeting with Marilyn Monroe because she worked for another studio.

Despite all the attention and the staged publicity photos, however, Jerry Wald had no intention of letting the New Hampshire housewife write the script for the film version of her novel, nor even serve as any kind of real consultant. Grace Metalious soon felt betrayed and out of place in Hollywood.

One day she watched as Wald auditioned actresses. She thought the spectacle was disgusting and was disturbed by how the producer treated the women "like cattle," barking out orders. "Walk, turn around, lift your skirt, don't call us, we'll call you." But Metalious found the women themselves equally strange and obscene. She called Hollywood a "flesh market" where all the women were blondes, brunettes, or redheads. "In all my time there, I didn't see one single woman with plain brown hair," Metalious said. "Neither did I see one who could be presumed to wear a size 32-A brassiere."

Grace Metalious was also disillusioned by how tame Hollywood seemed. She felt people there were "dead in the head" and thought her own New Hampshire town had more real scandal. She thought Hollywood was a very strange place, governed by people in constant fear of losing their jobs or their status. She thought the atmosphere was "dreadful," but most upsetting to her was how her book fared in Hollywood.

Instead of using Grace Metalious, Wald brought in screenwriter John Michael Hayes. Hayes was well respected in Hollywood for his many collaborations with Alfred Hitchcock, including *Rear Window*, which had won him his first Oscar nomination in 1954. Hayes also wrote serviceable scripts for the soapier dramas, though, such as 1953's *Torch Song*. But in spite of his good reputation, Hayes immediately offended the fiery author of *Peyton Place*. Wald first introduced him to Metalious at Romanoff's restaurant. Hayes then asked her the question she most hated. Was *Peyton Place* her autobiography? "I beg your pardon," Grace asked, hoping Hayes would back off. He repeated the question. Grace threw her Bloody Mary in his face.

She did sit in on one "story conference," though. She thought the writers and assistant producers were joking when they suggested singer

Pat Boone for "the good boy in the book." Grace joined in the conversation, suggesting facetiously that Pat could sing the "Peyton Place Blues." She soon realized that the studio executives were serious about Boone. She fled Hollywood for home, knowing that movie producers would turn her hard-won novel into something "saccharine." It would clean up all the raw emotion and dark truths of *Peyton Place*, turning her story into everything she had fought against in writing it.

GRACE METALIOUS couldn't have known what she was getting into with Jerry Wald. But anyone in Hollywood could have told her what Wald had planned for *Peyton Place*.

Wald was one of the band of producers who inspired Budd Schulberg's *What Makes Sammy Run?*, a 1941 novel that takes a satiric and stinging look at a young hotshot producer who is long on ambition and short on ethics. Wald, fat and fond of wearing Hawaiian shirts, had been a producer since the mid-1940s. Frustrated by Columbia's Harry Cohn, the fearsome studio chief who kept shooting down Wald's ideas, he moved to Twentieth Century Fox in 1956.

At Fox, Wald began work on *Sons and Lovers*, an adaptation of the D. H. Lawrence novel which won him an Academy Award when it was released in 1960. He was most famous as a producer of "women's pictures," though. These were films about "relationships" and they had substantial parts for women. They often had less than subtle messages about the ideal roles women should play in society, too. As Grace Metalious sensed early on, they tended to be sappy and overblown. Wald also had a reputation for butchering the original stories that made his films possible.

Wald was an oddity. He preferred to buy classic literary properties, but as an article in *Esquire* once noted, "because of some integral gaffe in casting or script or treatment, they are often no better than the standard Hollywood hash that everyone else is turning out."

In 1950 he made a film of Tennessee Williams's play *The Glass Menagerie*, which Hollywood acknowledged was a serious and meaningful artistic endeavor. He cast Gertrude Lawrence in the leading role because she had shone in the Broadway version of *The King and I*, but the picture bombed. He later made a similar casting mistake with *The Sound and the Fury*, a 1959 film version of William Faulkner's novel.

He had a good script, and Wald himself had studied Faulkner's work, but with Yul Brynner as the lead, it seemed almost destined for failure.

In the film version of *Peyton Place,* released in 1957, Wald's signature staginess produced a story somehow both melodramatic and bland at the same time. It's true that screenwriter John Michael Hayes had to contend with the Hays Office, the arm of the Motion Picture Producers and Distributors of America that set a strict production code designed to cut down on sex, violence, and any kind of moral turpitude. The code, instituted in 1922, prohibited everything from swear words to couples seen in bed together (even married couples had to be shown in twin beds). The code also spelled out bizarre formulas of "compensating values," dictating that any kind of vice or evil could only be shown if in the end the "good" characters were rewarded and the "bad" characters were punished or, better yet, converted.

These rules, of course, presented some challenges in telling the story of *Peyton Place*. But the resulting film cut the heart out of Metalious's novel. Although most of the main characters made it into the film, they were significantly changed to meet 1950s standards of morality.

In the book, for instance, Rodney Harrington is the son of the powerful mill owner and a handsome cad who tools around town in a brand-new car. He knocks up his girlfriend, who extorts money from him. Later, he meets his maker when a truck runs him over as he tries to cop a feel from another girl. But in the movie version, Barry Coe plays a decidedly less dangerous Rodney. He elopes with the girlfriend (Terry Moore), who never becomes pregnant. Rodney's wealthy father is about to disown him when he is drafted. The family reconciles and Rodney ends up honorably "killed in action" in World War II.

Selena Cross, the dark beauty of Metalious's *Peyton Place,* becomes fresh-faced, blonde Hope Lange. She doesn't need an abortion, which she begs Doc Swain for in the novel, but instead suffers a convenient miscarriage.

Diane Varsi is perfectly fine as the first naive and then disillusioned Allison. Just twenty years old, Varsi already had a one-year-old daughter and two broken marriages behind her, and those real-life troubles may have informed her work in *Peyton Place*. Hollywood columnist Hedda

Hopper chose her as a "New Face" for 1958, noting that she "looks innocent but is hotter than a gatling gun." Yet the movie version of the novel significantly reduces Allison's part in the story. The book character that most resembles Grace Metalious, Allison flees the small town to become a writer in New York. Her career and adventures there take up a major part of the book but are barely mentioned in the movie.

The most noticeable difference between the book's characters and the film's can be seen in Michael Rossi (Tomas Makris in the book). Grace Metalious wrote the high school principal as a strong Greek man who was handsome in an "obviously sexual way." He and a repressed and repressive single mother, Constance MacKenzie (a role Lana Turner made famous), share a sizzling midnight swim in which he rips off her bathing suit. Then he kisses her mouth "brutally, torturously, as if he hoped to waken a response in her with pain that gentleness could not arouse." Later, he carries Constance up the stairs to her bedroom, where he throws her down and ravishes her.

In the movie, Lee Philips plays a mild-mannered, milquetoast Mike, about as sexy as somebody's cousin. He and Constance hardly share a kiss. They have their first date at a Labor Day picnic. Later, he invites her to help him chaperone a high school dance. Not exactly the stuff of a steamy romance. The scenes are lame and Philips's wooden acting doesn't help. Like most critics, Grace Metalious thought he was "terrible."

More importantly, though, *Peyton Place* the movie lacks the powerful message of the novel. The story that one book reviewer compared to the work of Sherwood Anderson, John O'Hara, and Sinclair Lewis is reduced to something sentimental and meaningless. One critic wrote that the film ignored the essential theme of the book, how hypocrisy and cruelty can poison a small community. Bosley Crowther, reviewing the film for the *New York Times*, wrote, "There is no sense of massive corruption here."

When she saw the movie, Grace Metalious said she "could do nothing but weep." She felt worse when she learned that most critics said they preferred the movie. As Jack Edmund Nolan wrote in *Films in Review*, the *Peyton Place* script had "transformed a worthless, and dirty, book into a good film." Metalious retreated to her New Hampshire home. She produced a few more novels, including a sequel to *Peyton Place*, but never matched the staggering success of her first work. She floundered in debt and despair and died of an alcohol-induced liver disease on February 25, 1964, less than ten years after she broke into publishing.

The film *Peyton Place* proved to be as wildly popular as the book. In 1957 it set movie theater attendance records everywhere. And it was nominated for a slew of Academy Awards, including best picture, best direction, best photography, and—most insultingly—best screenplay. Hope Lange as Selena Cross, Diane Varsi as Allison MacKenzie, Arthur Kennedy as the evil Lucas Cross, and Russ Tamblyn as the loser turned paratrooper Norman Page were also nominated for Oscars.

UNDOUBTEDLY THE biggest winner from the movie version of *Peyton Place* was Lana Turner. For her star turn as Constance MacKenzie, Turner received a nomination for best actress. It was the only time the Academy ever recognized her work, and her performance, in a role she originally didn't want, revived an increasingly lackluster career.

The "sweater girl" who was discovered at fifteen while playing hooky from Hollywood High had blossomed into one of its most glamorous stars. By 1957 Lana Turner had appeared in more than forty films. Unfortunately, most of them were forgettable flops like *Latin Lovers* (1953), and in 1956 her contract with MGM was not renewed. The former Julia Jean Turner was undeniably beautiful but sometimes awkward on camera, inspiring Tennessee Williams to quip, "Lana Turner couldn't act her way out of her form-fitting cashmeres."

But the star whose image graced the lid of many a flyboy's footlocker during World War II could scorch the screen when given the right role. Turner was oddly wrong in conventional romances and costume dramas. Instead, she shone in slightly more unseemly parts, especially ones where women made bad choices, often with men, in order to achieve stardom or stability.

One of her best performances came in 1946 in a film noir adaptation of the James M. Cain novel, *The Postman Always Rings Twice*. With her platinum blonde hair and shimmery white wardrobe, Turner exudes a frosty sexiness as Cora, the ambitious wife of a roadside diner owner (played by Cecil Kellaway). Sparks fly when John Garfield answers the prophetic ad for "Man Wanted." She and Garfield plot to kill her husband and take over the business. As she says repeatedly in the film, Cora wants to "make something" of herself. Even as she and Garfield steam it up with desperate love scenes, followed later by anguished arguments, Turner holds Cora carefully in control, making her much more than a mere femme fatale.

The Bad and the Beautiful was another of Lana Turner's best pictures. The 1952 classic directed by Vincente Minnelli cast her as a starlet turned alcoholic, taken advantage of by producer Kirk Douglas. Minnelli worried that she wouldn't be able to handle such a demanding role, but she held her own.

Turner and trouble were perfect together, onscreen and off. In fact, her lifetime of failed relationships and heartache seems almost predestined. Her mother was just fifteen when she ran away with twenty-four-year-old John Virgil Turner. A gambler and a bootlegger, he was murdered after a crap-game win when Lana was just nine years old.

Born in Idaho, she lived in a series of foster homes after moving to California with her mother, who seemed incapable of caring for her full time. Eventually, Mildred Turner found work as a hairdresser and she and her daughter lived together again. But the abuse and Cinderella-like working conditions in the foster homes, coupled with the terrible loss of her father, created an unending sense of longing in her even after reuniting with her mother. "The shock I suffered then may be a valid excuse for me now," she said many years after her father's death. "It may explain things I myself do not understand."

When Jerry Wald began casting *Peyton Place* in 1957, Lana Turner was thirty-seven years old and in the middle of divorcing her fourth husband, former Tarzan actor Lex Barker. Gossip columnists reported that the marriage ended over a fight in a parking lot. Years later, her daughter Cheryl Crane would reveal the real reason in an autobiography: that Barker had raped his stepdaughter repeatedly. The abuse began when Cheryl was ten years old. She was thirteen before Turner found out about it, giving Barker twenty minutes to clear his things from her Beverly Hills home. But his crime, along with Turner's two abortions and a 1951 suicide attempt, never made it into the headlines. Instead, executives at MGM would spread stories that she had needed an "emergency appendectomy" or had to be hospitalized for "exhaustion."

Actors and producers in Hollywood knew better, though. Ever since *Hollywood Reporter* publisher Billy Wilkerson had "discovered" a fifteen-year-old Lana sipping a Coke at the Top Hat Café, gossip columnists had dubbed her "the Nightclub Queen." She would appear with a different man every week for months at a stretch. "I liked the boys and the boys liked me," she said. Everyone from Robert Stack and Fernando Lamas to Mickey Rooney and Tyrone Power took a turn on her arm as she partied around the clock at places like Ciro's, the Cocoanut Grove, and the Trocadero. "She was amoral," an MGM executive once said behind her back. "If she saw a stagehand with tight pants and a muscular build, she'd invite him into her dressing room."

Word got around about Lana's lascivious ways. When she was at MGM, studio boss Louis B. Mayer had called her on the carpet in his cream-colored office suite. He leapt from behind his desk and shouted, "The only thing you're interested in is . . ." He pointed at his crotch. She was a natural target for *Confidential* magazine, and the scandal rag took a wholly characteristic glee in her romantic disasters, crowing in 1956, "She doesn't exactly slug men and carry them home. But when they get there that noise you hear later is husbands—busting out of the boudoir!"

The article went on to catalog her various failed relationships and marriages, seven in all, and dubbed her "the jilted-est girl in Hollywood." As it moved from Artie Shaw to Lex Barker with snappy transitions like "it wasn't long before Lana's glands got to working again. . . ." *Confidential* offered other spicy little details. It alliteratively alluded to how Steve Crane couldn't keep up with "Lana's uncontrolled urge for high living, liquor, love and late hours." It also noted that the house she shared with third husband Bob Topping "boasted the one and only bidet in the movie colony," adding sarcastically, "but a house needs more than a bidet to be happy."

Even in 1957, when the bombshell baton was being passed to younger stars like Marilyn Monroe, Turner's reputation remained intact. Twentieth Century Fox fought Wald on his choice of her as leading lady in *Peyton Place*. The studio wanted Olivia de Havilland or

Jane Wyman as Constance, but Wald insisted. She was the only real star in the film and he knew she would bring a certain raw sensuality that an actress like Wyman couldn't conjure. As *Time* magazine once said about Turner, "In any posture, Lana suggests she is looking up from a pillow."

Lana herself needed some convincing before taking the *Peyton Place* role, however. She thought she was too young to play anyone's mother. Jerry Wald and director Mark Robson spent five hours trying to persuade her to play Constance MacKenzie. They finally won her over by pointing out that Joan Crawford had reinvented her career by playing the mother in Wald's production of *Mildred Pierce*, a role for which she had won an Oscar in 1945.

Lana Turner as Constance MacKenzie may have been the film's truest interpretation of a character from the novel. Her chilly pride suited the prissy prettiness and paranoia of Metalious's small-town dress shop owner. Turner's own life also added depth to her portrayal of Constance, as issues of illegitimacy and single motherhood swirl around the character and her daughter. In *Peyton Place*, Constance MacKenzie runs away to New York, where she gets involved with a married man and becomes pregnant by him. When he dies, she returns to New Hampshire and vows to keep the details of Allison MacKenzie's birth a secret.

Turner also had a less than legitimate liaison. After a short-lived marriage to bandleader Artie Shaw, she wed restaurateur Steve Crane in 1942, only to discover five months later that his divorce from his first wife was not final. The couple split, but, six months pregnant with their daughter, Turner legally wed Crane in 1943 in a shabby Tijuana ceremony. A year later, she sued for divorce.

Like her *Peyton Place* alter ego, Lana Turner did not want her daughter to grow up too fast. While Constance MacKenzie rules her daughter strictly and steers her away from the sexier offerings in her dress store, Lana Turner went to more bizarre extremes. She called daughter Cheryl "the baby" well into her adulthood. She dressed her in pinafores until junior high school and insisted that a nanny bathe Cheryl nightly even after the girl began menstruating. She once slapped a thirteen-year-old Cheryl for allegedly "flirting" with Turner's then boyfriend, young actor Michael Dante. She screamed that

Cheryl was running wild and going to get a reputation. "I have eyes, I can see what you're doing," she ranted. "Smiling that way. Wiggling your bottom."

In the book as well as the film of *Peyton Place,* Constance MacKenzie also obsesses about her daughter's chastity, worried that she'll get in trouble the way her mother did. One embarrassing scene features Allison's first teenage kissing party being broken up by her mother, who turns the lights on in the darkened room and scolds her daughter and guests mercilessly. Another scene in the film shows Allison humiliated again as her mother questions her about a swim she took with a boyfriend. A busybody neighbor had spotted another couple skinny-dipping and had mistaken the girl for Allison. Constance slaps her daughter's face as the girl insists she did nothing wrong.

Watching the scenes today is excruciating, pointing up the era's rigid moral code and the pervasive sexual dysfunction it must have created in young women. It seems even stranger and almost painfully ironic that one of the day's sexiest stars, known for her lustiness, should deliver such messages. Taken in the context of the sexual trauma Turner's own daughter suffered around this time, though, the scenes are rather creepy, both strident and sad. The wild gleam of mother-bear protectiveness in Turner's eyes looks, momentarily, real.

Cheryl Crane recognized the weird similarities between her own life and *Peyton Place*. During the Hollywood premiere of the movie, she cried during "the slapping scene." But something else disturbed her even more. "They were all too familiar, those icy, dangerous looks Mother gave, the imperial manner and tight-assed way of crossing a room, the way she would turn and punch home a line," Crane would write later. " . . . The techniques Mother used to intimidate and control me came not from a well of feeling but from her bag of actress tricks. To her, life was a movie. She did not live in reality."

Just as it had for other Hollywood actresses of the 1950s, though, Lana's having a daughter helped ensure that the public saw Lana as a "normal" woman, with normal feminine responsibilities and desires. Almost every Hollywood actress reported at one time or another that motherhood was her most important role. Magazines reported things like, "As soon as she gets home, Lana always scrubs her face and removes all lipstick so she can kiss the bambino all she wants." Shortly after her birth, *Photoplay* ran an article "by" Cheryl. "Sometimes I wonder what the nurse is for—because Mother likes to do everything for me," it said. In truth, Cheryl was almost a year old before her own mother bathed her.

Like many other celebrity children of the 1950s, Cheryl rarely saw her mother. On the few occasions they were together, Cheryl would reach out to hug and kiss her flawlessly styled mother. Turner would gently push her away. "Sweetheart, the hair," she said. Cheryl would lie in bed at night looking up at the phosphorescent stars stuck to the ceiling. On a shelf stood her three-foot-high, lifelike Lana Turner doll that a fan had sent her, but the real Lana Turner almost never made an appearance to tuck her daughter in.

Mother and daughter would soon find themselves forever bonded by one horrific moment, though, and forever at the heart of one of Hollywood's most enduring scandals.

After Lana Turner separated from Lex Barker in 1957, she quickly replaced him with an equally loathsome companion. Johnny Stompanato was a gangster linked to mob boss Mickey Cohen. He was known in Hollywood as a "Handsome Harry," for his habit of wooing rich women and "borrowing" their money. He liked to wear his shiny silk shirts open to the navel. And there was a rumor that he had earned the nickname "Oscar" because his penis was as long as the coveted statuette.

Stompanato was also a manipulative bully. He pressured Turner constantly to help him break into a career as a movie executive. She refused. When she finished filming *Peyton Place*, he visited her in England on the set of *Another Time, Another Place*. He tried to strangle her when she again declined to ask that he be named executive producer of her next film. He was promptly bounced from the country after the attack (and a minor dust-up in which Turner's costar Sean Connery decked the thug in lizard shoes). Stompanato's frustration with Turner grew more intense when *Peyton Place* became a hit, however.

On March 24, 1958, Hollywood gathered for the thirtieth presentation of the Academy Awards. Produced by none other than *Peyton Place*'s Jerry Wald, the show featured the overlooked Burt Lancaster and Kirk Douglas singing "It's Great Not to Be Nominated." Another duet paired Mae West and Rock Hudson for a hot version of "Baby, It's

Cold Outside." It was the last year the ceremonies would take place in the Art Deco glory of the Pantages Theater. And it was the first time Lana Turner would appear on live television, without a memorized script, and in front of fifty million viewers. She felt understandably nervous, and excited about her first and only best actress nomination for *Peyton Place*. Turner knew that her career could get a big boost from winning an Oscar. It might restore her name to its rightful place, above the title in movie posters and opening credits.

Cheryl Crane remembered sharing the special night with her mother. For the first time, at fourteen, she was allowed to wear a glamorous evening gown and high heels. She also had a taste of her mother's obsession with image. As they rode to the ceremony in their limousine, Lana told Cheryl she didn't want to see her with a cigarette in hand, especially if photographers were around. So often denied her mother's attention, Cheryl took a cynical view of this advice. Since her role in *Peyton Place*, Lana "liked to play real-life scenes with me that showed special maternal concern," she said.

Even jaded Cheryl was impressed with her mother's performance at the Oscars, though. As expected, Turner lost the award to Joanne Woodward for *The Three Faces of Eve*, but was quite gracious and held court afterward at the Beverly Hilton. Hollywood's new crop of stars, such as Woodward, Sophia Loren, and Kim Novak, surrounded her. Her friendly rivals Rita Hayworth and Ava Gardner were home watching television and soon would retire. Yet Lana Turner still commanded the room's attention, bridging the Hollywood generations. She didn't bring home the award, but she did savor this high point of her long career.

A few hours later, Turner returned to her bungalow at the Bel Air Hotel. Johnny Stompanato was waiting for her there in the dark bedroom, seething with rage. He berated the star for taking her mother and daughter to the ceremony instead of him—and then he beat her up. "I was still wearing my jewelry, and the bitter irony of a battered woman in diamonds struck me like another blow from John's fist," Turner later wrote in her autobiography. "And the incredible contrast of the evening—the exhilaration of the Awards ceremony and the love I'd felt from everybody, their encouragement and approval. To go from that to this. . . ."

The irony was not lost on Cheryl Crane. A few days after the incident, her mother confided in her, telling her how she feared the gangster and needed help. Crane urged her mother to go to the police but she refused. "No one must know," Turner said. She worried that Stompanato's gangster cronies would find a way to hurt her or her family. And she didn't want her love life played out in the press again.

On the first of April 1958, Lana Turner and her daughter moved with Stompanato to a big house on North Bedford Drive in Beverly Hills. Laura Hope Crews had built the neo-Colonial house with money she earned from playing Aunt Pittypat in *Gone With the Wind* and Turner hoped it would provide a fresh start for the fractured family.

But three days later, on Good Friday, she and Stompanato clashed again. Turner had learned from a mutual friend that the gangster was thirty-three years old, not forty-three as he had told her. This meant that Turner was five years older than her boyfriend and she was very angry. As she neared forty, she had grown increasingly sensitive about her age. "He's making me seem like one of those old has-beens you see around who pay for young men," Turner wailed to her daughter.

When Stompanato came home that night, Turner told him their relationship was over and threw him out. He became enraged, cursing and grabbing Turner. Cheryl, hiding out in her suite with its brand-new Princess phone and television set, tried to ignore the ruckus. But when Stompanato threatened to kill her mother, she left the term paper she was writing about the body's circulatory system and ran to the kitchen in her pink mule slippers. She grabbed an eight-inch carving knife, intending only to scare him and force him to leave. She climbed the stairs again to her mother's room and banged on the door.

As the gangster lunged out, he "ran on the blade," as Cheryl remembered it. The knife, purchased by Stompanato and Turner only a few hours earlier when they were fixing up the new house, punctured his kidney and aorta. He made a gurgling sound and died on the carpet.

A coroner's inquest into Stompanato's death found that it was a justifiable homicide. The district attorney did not charge Cheryl Crane with the crime. But he felt that Crane had never had a true home with her mother or her father, and after she'd spent three weeks in Juvenile Hall, the court declared her a ward of the state. It ordered her placed in the custody of her grandmother.

The trauma lingered, though. After running up speeding tickets and getting in trouble at nightclubs, Cheryl Crane landed in reform school for another eleven months. She returned to her grandmother only to run away twice. At seventeen, her frustrated family sent her away to the Institute of Living, an elite sanitarium in Hartford, Connecticut. When her mother told her, incorrectly, that the court had extended her wardship by a year, she tried to kill herself by smashing her fists through a window. She spent weeks afterward in a fog of sedatives.

Crane would attempt suicide once again, mixing a potent cocktail of alcohol and sleeping pills. But after a hospital stay, she changed her life and became a partner in her father Steve Crane's Los Angeles restaurant, the Luau. She and her mother reconciled later in her life, eventually forging a kind of friendship.

When Cheryl Crane chose to write a memoir in 1988, Turner worried that it would read like another *Mommie Dearest*, Christina Crawford's harrowing account of her troubled childhood which did a hatchet job on her adoptive mother. But Crane dismissed those concerns. "Mom wasn't around that much in my life for a *Mommie Dearest*," Crane said. "She qualifies perhaps for a long cameo role."

After the Stompanato murder, Lana Turner feared she would never again work in Hollywood. Certainly the ensuing media storm did not help her in some circles (although it did boost *Peyton Place* ticket sales by 32 percent). *Time* magazine described her as "the Sweater Girl whose feckless pursuit of happiness became men's-room talk from Sunset Boulevard to Fleet Street." While Turner tried to convince the authorities and the public that she was a battered woman and that Stompanato had deserved to die, Mickey Cohen had other plans. The man *Time* described as "the runty gambler" broke into his old colleague's apartment and stole dozens of letters to Stompanato from Turner. The letters ended up on the front page of the *Los Angeles Herald Examiner* and were reprinted worldwide, more than four hundred column inches in which she calls him "Daddy" and "Honeypot" and writes, "I miss you, want you and ache for you." Stompanato's letters in return were even more embarrassing. "You know Baby, I'm so lonesome for the touch of you I could die," he wrote. "I try to think back of when you were here and those precious minutes I wasted when my lips were not on yours."

Even Lex Barker took a turn kicking at Lana when she was down, accusing Cheryl of being "two-faced." He blamed the girl, in print, for his divorce from Lana. He claimed to have warned his ex-wife to "watch out for Cheryl," predicting, "that girl will end up involved in great trouble."

One Hollywood producer, though, would soon regard Lana Turner's troubles as box office gold.

CHAPTER 13

LANA, THE SEQUEL: *IMITATION OF LIFE*

SOMETIMES HOLLYWOOD is a mirror, and no one saw her life reflected in it more than Lana Turner. Just as the lurid press coverage of Johnny Stompanato's death was ebbing, she starred in *Imitation of Life*, a film that weirdly mimicked her rise to stardom and her troubled relationship with her daughter. The film opens with the oversize title, the frame slowly filling with hundreds of "diamonds," hinting at the parade of false values and empty histrionics to come. The glamour, though, is real. Producer Ross Hunter wanted Turner as the film's star because he knew she could carry the glitzy melodrama. And he wanted her precisely because of—not despite—her part in one of Hollywood's most sensational scandals.

The producer had come to Hollywood in the 1940s as Martin Fuss, and after adopting a sexy new moniker, Ross Hunter appeared in a string of B movies. Hunter gave up, though, when a director told him he had only three facial expressions: "blank, blanker, and blankest." He signed on as a producer at Universal in 1953, determined to bring back a kind of glossy glamour to the movies. Hunter's vision meant giving moviegoers "a chance to dream, to live vicariously, to see beautiful women, jewels, gorgeous clothes, melodrama."

Hunter claimed he transformed the mostly B actor Rock

Hudson into a star in *Magnificent Obsession* (1954) just by putting him in a tuxedo. He credited himself with glamming up Doris Day's girl-next-door image, too, by covering her freckles and giving her a new hairdo before pairing her with Hudson in 1959's *Pillow Talk*.

Turner needed no tutoring on how to be glamorous, and Hunter thought she would add sparkle to *Imitation of Life*, a remake of a Fannie Hurst weepie about two single mothers. One is a white woman who, like Turner herself, sacrifices her daughter's love for a successful movie career. The other woman is her black maid, Annie, whose headstrong, trying-to-pass-for-white daughter rejects her affection. Hunter inked a deal with Turner just six weeks after the Stompanato murder, wooing her with the perks she had once enjoyed at MGM.

Director Douglas Sirk remembered how persuasive Ross Hunter could be. "He was tremendously successful—very charming. 'Oh, but it's a crude charm,' someone said. Yes, but in Hollywood, who will notice if you have a subtle charm?"

Catering to the clotheshorse in Lana, Hunter had Jean Louis design all thirty-four of her outfits. According to the film's production notes, the wardrobe was valued at $78,000, making it "the most expensive wardrobe ever to gown a star in Universal-International history." Hunter had limousines waiting for the actress, filled her dressing room with flowers, and even hired someone whose sole job was to play records to keep her relaxed. Also "adding lustre" to Lana and the production were the $1 million worth of jewels loaned to the studio by Laykin et Cie. The production notes gleefully tick off the pieces, including a $240,000 set of Russian emeralds and diamonds, a $50,000 star sapphire set, and a $127,000 15-carat diamond set. "Two armed guards stayed near Lana every minute the fabulous gem collection was in use," the notes detail.

But Turner would have taken the job, even without the niceties. She needed it. After her and Cheryl's legal problems, she was in debt and couldn't turn down a job that paid $2,500 a week, although it stung that the figure was exactly half her old MGM salary.

Imitation of Life, released in 1959, played to the millions who had read every word of the Stompanato coverage. Fans would recognize the strained mother/daughter relationship in the movie as similar to Lana Turner and daughter Cheryl Crane's. And the plot twist that has film daughter Sandra Dee fall in love with her mother's boyfriend pandered directly to the rumors that Cheryl Crane had an affair with Stompanato and killed him out of jealousy.

Indeed the filming was difficult for Turner, especially the lavish funeral finale. She dreaded the scene, especially when Sara Jane, racked by remorse, throws herself on her mother's casket. The moment is supposed to remind Turner's character of her own troubled relationship with her daughter, but it served the same function for Lana herself.

Sirk laid it on thick for the scene, hiring Mahalia Jackson to sing "Trouble All the Way" and filling the church with fresh flowers. The sight of the casket, laden with perfumed gardenias, "had wakened unexpectedly all the crushing thoughts of death I had been trying to suppress," Turner said. She became hysterical and ran to her trailer sobbing. After a sobering slap from her hairdresser, Turner reined in her emotions and returned to the set.

Cheryl Crane thought director Douglas Sirk took the real-life parallels a bit too far, though. He had filmed a graduation scene at her junior high school. The daughter gets a pony for a gift, just as young Cheryl did one birthday. It "made me feel used," she said. "The happy ending made me sneer."

Imitation of Life redeems itself somewhat by confronting rather gracefully the thorny issue of race. It was 1959, just before the decade in which America's most bitter battles over the subject would be fought, and Susan Kohner and Juanita Moore positively shine as the trying-to-pass daughter and long-suffering mother. With her dark moods, exotic looks, and palpable longing to fit in, Kohner is infinitely more exciting to watch than the daffy Sandra Dee. "The only interesting thing is the Negro angle," director Sirk later said of his melodrama.

It is strange to watch Kohner, though, knowing she is not black but the daughter of Lana Turner's German film agent, Paul Kohner, and Mexican movie star Lupita Tovar. Even in the 1934 version of *Imitation*, a light-skinned black named Fredi Washington had played the Sara Jane role. Hunter and Sirk had tried to find a black actress but were unsuccessful. They interviewed one hundred "Negro" actresses and searched two continents before settling on Kohner, whom they called "an ideal choice." In fact, she was a fine young actress, debuting in 1955's *To Hell and Back* as Audie Murphy's Italian girlfriend and then playing opposite Sal Mineo in *Dino* (1957).

Juanita Moore also steals the show occasionally as the warm and sympathetic maid, Annie. At thirty-six, she had appeared in films such as *Lydia Bailey* (1952) and A *Band of Angels* (1957). Ebony Showcase in Los Angeles also featured her in Jean-Paul Sartre's *No Exit*. She was a singer as well, performing once at the Moulin Rouge. Ironically, in the film, her daughter runs away to pass as white and get a job at the Hollywood version of the Paris club.

Also of note is Robert Alda as Laura's theatrical agent. *Imitation of Life* marked the first time Alda had appeared on a soundstage in more than ten years. After starring as George Gershwin in the biographical picture *Rhapsody in Blue* (1945), Alda had left films for Broadway.

But Lana Turner was the undisputed superstar of the film. She exudes her familiar brand of brittle beauty and remains strangely distant, even in the film's most overwrought exchanges between mother and daughter. In fact, her performance was called an "imitation of acting" by a few critics. Others, however, relished the very falseness of Lana's performance. "With most stars, the point is to disguise the manufacturing," critic Richard Dyer said. "With Turner, part of the fascination is with the manufacture itself—with her, it is actually beguiling to see the strings being pulled."

Campy as it was, *Imitation of Life* was the biggest moneymaker of Lana Turner's career because she had gotten an unusual profit-sharing deal with Universal. And *Imitation of Life* generated more revenue for the studio than any other previous film in its history. (Hunter said in an interview that it made "way over $50 million.")

Imitation of Life was a high-water mark for the old-fashioned "women's picture." Arguably, it also signaled the peak of Lana Turner's career and offered a baroque finale to the ten-film partnership of Douglas Sirk and Ross Hunter. Sirk was ready to end their alliance, feeling that Hunter hindered his creative efforts at times. He had grown tired of Hunter's imploring him, "Doug, Doug, make them weep! Please make them weep!" He had tired of being interrupted while directing a scene to hear, "I want five hundred handkerchiefs to come out at this point."

WHEN *Imitation of Life* became Universal's most successful picture, it made Sandra Dee a household name. Dee played a girl desperate for her mother's love in *Imitation*, and Ross Hunter said she soon "became every mother's dream." After the soapy melodrama Universal couldn't open a movie starring Sandra Dee and not make money, no matter how bad it was.

Dee, so sweet she caused cavities, was another Ross Hunter production. He claimed to have discovered the quintessential teen angel when she was fourteen, standing on Park Avenue in New York. He did not know that Dee was really twelve years old. He saw only the box office potential in her virginal good looks. Hunter described her as "a sophisticated baby," knowing that her pert persona was a perfect fit for 1950s Hollywood.

Petite and blonde, Sandra Dee inspired girls across the country to imitate her style. In *Imitation of Life*, Sandra's character wears a graduation dress designed by Jean Louis. To promote ticket sales, Universal ran ads telling mothers they could get a free sewing pattern of the dress if they sent in two tickets to the film. In the first month, the studio gave out fifteen thousand patterns and soon had to stop because they couldn't meet demand. When Cheryl Crane, Lana Turner's dark-haired daughter, saw *Imitation*, she wailed that Dee "looked more like Mother than I did." But like Cheryl, Sandra Dee had her own sad story behind the celluloid image.

Born Alexandria Zuck in Bayonne, New Jersey, she never knew her father. Her mother worked as a secretary to support herself and her daughter. "Everything was great until the third grade, when something freaky happened to me. I developed a bust," Sandra Dee said years later, still sounding like a teenager. The early onset of puberty proved traumatic, as her mother forced her to camouflage her breasts by taping them down under her little girl dresses.

In 1950 Sandra Dee's mother remarried. Sandra went along with the couple on their honeymoon to Atlantic City, where her new stepfather insisted she sleep in bed between the newlyweds. The man, who claimed, "I'm not marrying your mother, I'm marrying both of you," soon began to sexually abuse the girl.

Sandra Dee never knew a normal childhood. In addition to having a disturbingly adult relationship with her stepfather, she held down a serious job as a model for advertising agencies and magazines. After her stepfather died, she became her mother's main source of income. In fact, she made more than $75,000 a year, much more than she would later earn in her first years in movies. Ever the codependent, Dee said she took Hunter's offer to bring her to Hollywood because she worried that her mother was deeply aggrieved over the loss of her husband.

With her mother in tow, Sandra Dee landed in Hollywood in 1957. In a December issue of *Modern Screen*, nestled among holiday items that included recipes for Rock Hudson's Buttered Rum and Ann Blyth's Jell-O mold, Dee received one of her first publicity boosts. "I nominate for stardom Sandra Dee," Louella Parsons wrote in her column.

"She's the cutest 98 pounds of blonde pertness and cuteness to come along since Shirley Temple was 15 years old," Parsons gushed. "With her blonde hair and wide eyes, she looks like a doll. . . . This elfin little girl is really on her way to stardom."

The column describes her debut in MGM's 1957 release *Until They Sail*, which starred Paul Newman and Jean Simmons. Parsons asked Dee about her first screen kiss, shared with young John Wilder. Dee laughed and said, "It just comes natural for me, I guess I liked it." Dee's history of abuse, though, and the fact that she was only twelve, had made her extremely nervous about the scene. The script called for her and John to walk down a path, stop at a certain tree and kiss. Every time she approached the tree, she would say she urgently needed to use the bathroom. Finally, a woman in the crew asked if she had a urinary tract infection. Dee said she had never been kissed before, an artful and believable lie.

Dee also had another secret she had brought with her to Hollywood. She was anorexic and had lived on a lettuce diet for almost a year before Hunter discovered her. Even in the first mentions of Dee in the gossip columns, reporters fawned over her petite figure and noted her bizarre eating habits, although no one thought it was dangerous. "Day after day, her lunch is a hard-boiled egg and half a head of lettuce—with a teaspoon of vinegar when she feels reckless," read one newspaper account.

On the set of *Until They Sail*, her eating disorder took its toll in an obvious way. Her kidneys shut down from lack of protein. She could not eliminate the toxins from her body through urination and her body began to swell. In a matter of minutes, the twelve-year-old actress became so bloated that she split the seams of her pants.

Dee said she was an "80-pound child who looked like an elephant from the waist down." Diagnosed with acute edema, her doctor force-fed her proteins. It wouldn't cure her compulsive dieting, though.

Eating disorders were nothing new to actresses, of course, and Dee soon learned how to purge as well as starve herself. While waiting at a salon for a massage, she overheard someone telling Kim Novak how to lose weight by drinking Epsom salts dissolved in water. The salts would act as a powerful laxative. A few months later, Dee passed out on her bedroom floor. She had to be hospitalized because this regimen had depleted her body of potassium.

Any kind of long-term treatment for the clearly troubled teen would have been unheard of at that time. Besides, Ross Hunter had big plans for Sandra Dee.

Hunter had loaned her to MGM for *Until They Sail* because his own studio, Universal, did not see the potential in her that he did. Universal's executives thought Dee hadn't developed enough physically yet and didn't want to put her under contract. Hunter said he would personally hold her contract for a year, but he never told Dee about the arrangement, wanting her instead "to think she was under contract to a studio because that was the glory, being under contract to a studio, not a particular producer."

Dee had acted only in a few television commercials, but she performed so well in her first film that Universal signed her. She would have the lead role in 1958's *The Restless Years*. Ross Hunter claimed that it did better than a Cary Grant–Sophia Loren film in some markets, and it launched Dee as a star in her own right. But it also made her increasingly isolated. After her first two movies, Dee became one of the last contract players at Universal. When she wasn't tutored on the set, she would often be the only student in a studio classroom with twenty-nine empty desks.

Because she was a minor, the law required Dee's mother to travel everywhere with her and supervise her on the set. The arrangement made for a stifling reversal of roles. In New York, Dee served as a surrogate parent, supporting her mother financially and emotionally. In Hollywood, Dee was treated like a child again by a mother who

Lana Turner (right) and Sandra Dee in a scene from 1959's *Imitation of Life*. The film exploited the salacious buzz around a real scandal: the death of Turner's gangster boyfriend Johnny Stompanato at the hands of her daughter, Cheryl Crane. *Courtesy of the Academy of Motion Picture Arts and Sciences.*

wanted to live vicariously through her. "My mother wanted a cripple," Dee said bluntly. "She didn't want me to fly. [If I was] before a camera she was fine. She would never butt in there, but otherwise she would just glom onto me."

John Saxon, who starred with Dee in 1958's *The Reluctant Debutante*, remembered the joy of shooting in Paris. He explored the city, eating dinner at a different restaurant every night. But Dee never joined him and, as he remembered it, never left the hotel.

Sandra Dee kept a diary of the shoot. "My goodness, I don't know what it is, but I just can't seem to get enough sleep. Today I got up around 3 p.m., had breakfast, then met my tutor, hairdresser and makeup man. . . ." she wrote. " . . . Boy are the French friendly. They talk to you on the street, which at first seemed rather strange, but now I realize they are warm and friendly."

Within three days, though, Dee's mother began correcting her spelling in the diary and adding false entries that were supposed to be in the young actress's "voice." One of her entries read, "Today, made many new friends. There are a lot of Russian people working here. And they found out I was of Russian parents and so Mother had fun speaking Russian. I'm sorry to say I don't speak fluently at all, but understand it all. My first performance age twenty-one months was in a Russian play at church."

Ross Hunter wanted to market Dee's image to teenagers and loaned her out to Columbia to make *Gidget* in 1959. The film "added a completely new dimension to Sandy," Hunter said. "No matter how sophisticated she may have been in some of the other pictures, she was one of the kids, and they fell in love with her and with *Gidget*, then with *A Summer Place*."

The cruel irony, though, was that Sandra Dee didn't know any teenagers. She never had a boyfriend or went to the prom. For publicity, the studio had to fabricate dates for her with young actors such as Sal Mineo and Johnny Wilder. Even on movie sets, Dee only got to know the adult actors. Teenybopper extras would come for one or two scenes and then be gone forever. As she told *Newsweek* in 1959, "I've never had any friends, but it's like strawberry shortcake. If you've never had it, how can you miss it."

The confectionary comedy and the good-girl-in-trouble saga of teenage love and unwanted pregnancy established Sandra Dee's reputation as America's new sweetheart. Troy Donahue, her hunky costar in 1959's *A Summer Place*, described her unusual quality of being both ladylike and girlish. "It was as if she were always wearing white gloves. But she wasn't," he said. "I had the feeling she had Mary-Janes on. But she didn't."

Ross Hunter knew he was manufacturing a star. ". . . We created the monster, if the truth be known," he said. "We wouldn't let her out of her house unless her hair was done and unless she wore a beautiful dress and unless her makeup was lovely."

Sandra Dee began to feel like the property of her suffocating mother and ambitious producer. It was obvious even to her costars. Troy Donahue sensed some days that she wanted to be somewhere else, that she might have wanted a different life. But she was "a commodity. . . . [S]he had become too important to let go of."

Without Douglas Sirk to direct and with an almost laughable lack of irony, Ross Hunter used Sandra Dee and the same extravagant formula of *Imitation of Life* to pump out losers like 1960's *Portrait in Black*. Lana Turner also resurfaces in *Portrait*, decked out in increasingly ornate and over-the-top Jean Louis gowns and jewelry that included a $37,000 pair of earrings. One scene shows her in a turban looking a little too much like scary Gloria Swanson in *Sunset Boulevard*. But Dee once again played the dutiful daughter and Turner doggedly reprised her role as an adultering murderess.

Dee would soon find a way to drop out of Hollywood, though. The world thought she was eighteen when she eloped with twenty-four-year-old singer Bobby Darin in 1960. In reality, she was only sixteen when she stood before a justice of the peace at four in the morning, then ate her wedding meal at a Newark, New Jersey, diner.

After a series of miscarriages caused by her severe eating disorders, Sandra Dee and Bobby Darin had a son, Dodd. By the end of the 1960s, Sandra Dee would be divorced and drinking up to a quart and a half of alcohol a day. She made fewer and fewer films. She had been too successful at playing "good girls," a victim of Ross Hunter's celebrity alchemy. Her image had grown brittle, encasing her like an iron maiden. It prevented her from aging gracefully and from taking on more adult roles. She would disappear almost completely in 1970. Bobby Darin died of heart disease in 1973. Later in the decade, she would find herself parodied onscreen, a running joke in *Grease* as

Stockard Channing sings, "Look at me, I'm Sandra Dee, lousy with virginity." As Dee told a Newark newspaper, "I feel like a has-been that never was."

Dee, a virtual recluse, at one point claimed, "I haven't been out to eat in three years." But even later, when she came clean about her less than perfect past, America's former sweetheart worried about what her fans would think. "I hope they aren't disappointed," she said. "At least they'll know the truth."

CHAPTER 14

SHEER BITCHERY: LOUELLA PARSONS, HEDDA HOPPER, AND SHEILAH GRAHAM

IN THE MALE-DOMINATED world of 1950s Hollywood, a small group of women wielded enough power to make even studio chiefs shiver with fear. These women weren't producers or censors or their wives. They were gossip columnists, snarky scribes who could make—or ruin—a career with a mere phrase.

Louella Parsons, Hedda Hopper, and Sheilah Graham each had her own syndicated column with a circulation in the millions. Plied with extravagant gifts and fat salaries, they lived among the stars they chronicled and cultivated their own growing rivalry. Each woman had reinvented herself, battled her way to the top. But each also had a life that couldn't withstand the scrutiny they practiced in print.

Louella Parsons had two secret divorces before taking up with an alcoholic named Dr. "Docky" Martin, known in Hollywood for his discreet treatment of celebrity venereal disease. As a young stage actress, Hedda Hopper had married an aging Lothario who humiliated her with his dalliances. Embittered by him and her failed movie career, Hopper filled her fountain pen with acid and waged her own war against Communism. Sheilah Graham, though, was perhaps the most glamorous of the captious columnists. The former orphan Lily Sheil transformed herself into a showgirl and a social butterfly in London's smartest sets.

Presented at court before coming to America, she became a hard-nosed reporter and the last lover of the tortured Jazz Age novelist F. Scott Fitzgerald.

Despite the dramatic changes in Hollywood, from the end of the studio system to the rise of television entertainment news, the columnists still wielded considerable power in the 1950s. Unlike the fly-by-night writers and the blackmailed and paid informants of *Confidential*, they were part of the Hollywood mainstream. They often lived as well as the stars, or at least in the same neighborhood. Louella Parsons and Sheilah Graham lived on Maple Drive in Beverly Hills, around the corner from Danny Thomas and around the block from a young Elizabeth Taylor and her parents.

Since the silent film era, the columnists had become an accepted part of doing business in Hollywood. Studios hoping to rein in a reckless partier or even a tacky dresser, for instance, might tip a columnist who would gently—or not so gently—scold them in print. Celebrities thus tried to stay on good terms with Graham, Parsons, and Hopper. When authorities asked Bob Hope whom they should contact in case he was hurt or killed entertaining the troops during World War II, he joked, "Louella Parsons. She'd never forgive me if she wasn't the first to know." Lana Turner, who really could never win with them, described the way celebrities had to "kowtow" to columnists. "They took bribes and gifts and played favorites, and God help you if they ever got mad at you," she said. " . . . Be nice to Louella, she's in a bad mood. Go be sweet to her, make her laugh. If you didn't do it, she'd get on your back in her column and never get off."

As Peter Sellers told the *Hollywood Reporter*, "To make these female gossip columnists happy, you've got to wear a suit made out of the stars and stripes; hang a placard around your neck saying, 'I love Hollywood'; take them out to dinner; buy them roses; wipe the dust off their shoes and declare, 'I love you. I love you all!' "

Each Christmas all Hollywood would shower gifts on the columnists, hoping to curry favor with a stack of handbags, radios, cigarette lighters, china, and enough liquor to supply a year's worth of parties. Sheilah Graham's daughter remembered her mother receiving so many things that she wrapped some of them to be given out as gifts to friends throughout the year. A producer reportedly learned the hard way that gift-giving could backfire, though. After playing Hedda and Louella quite well against each other, he bought each an expensive handbag and had it sent over with a note. Somehow, the deliveries got mixed up. Hedda got a message for Louella and vice versa. Hedda Hopper phoned him and laughed it off, but Louella was furious. Another gift mix-up left Hedda Hopper with two cut-crystal decanters, one engraved with "HH," the other with "LOP," Louella's initials. When the gift-giver asked for it back, Hedda refused. She thought it too good a conversation piece; it would be too much fun to ask guests, "Would you like some Jack Daniels out of Louella's bottle?"

To avoid bad press and to massage their egos, celebrities also included columnists in social events like weddings and birthday parties, or at least gave them the impression that they were included. In an issue of *Modern Screen* from summer 1950, for instance, Sheilah Graham and her children visited with Elizabeth Taylor, who had just returned from her honeymoon with first husband Nicky Hilton. In the article, Graham writes of her close relationship to Taylor: "For more than five years, I've been a neighbor of the Taylor family. . . . We've been good friends. In the summer we've been beach neighbors at Malibu. I watched Elizabeth grow up, chatted with her over the back fence."

Bribing columnists with gifts and special treatment, then, was almost a necessity. Hedda Hopper jokingly referred to her home on Tropical Drive in Beverly Hills as "the house that fear built." Samuel Goldwyn once commented that Louella Parsons was stronger than Samson. "He needed two columns to bring the house down," he said. "Louella can do it with one." Years after their retirement, the mention of a columnist's name could still stir anxiety. When approached in the 1970s by a biographer to talk about Parsons, actress Lola Lane declined. It would be professionally imprudent, she said. She had last appeared in a film in 1946.

Like the actresses they followed in their columns, though, each writer had a unique story behind her success. The columnists, too, edited and changed their biographies to add spice and subtract years from their ages. At a time when few women worked outside the home, they were trailblazers, earning salaries higher than those of many studio players. Rivals among themselves, Parsons, Hopper, and Graham also possessed a kind of singular ambition to rise above their difficult pasts by any means necessary.

LOUELLA PARSONS was arguably the queen bee of the Hollywood hive. Not only did she practice celebrity journalism, she virtually invented the genre.

She began her career as a reporter for the *Dixon Star* in Illinois, an unusual post for a woman in the 1900s. She loved her job covering the social news, but Parsons hated small-town life and keeping house. Almost from the beginning, she regretted her marriage to John Parsons and later said the only good thing to come from the union was her daughter, Harriet. She obtained a divorce, which she would always hide, after about two years of marriage. She would rack up another failed marriage and another secret divorce, along with a serious affair with a married man, all before arriving in Hollywood.

Parsons moved to Chicago after her first marriage ended and began writing "scenarios" for a studio called Essanay, which made silent films with Charlie Chaplin and a very young Gloria Swanson. It was at Essanay that Parsons developed her love of the movies—and of rubbing elbows with stars. She left the studio in 1914 to write "Seen on the Screen," one of the first-ever movie gossip columns for the *Chicago Record-Herald.* She moved to New York and a spot on the *New York Morning Telegraph* four years later.

In perhaps her canniest career maneuver, Louella Parsons began to promote quite strenuously a young actress named Marion Davies. Parsons knew Davies was the mistress of newspaper tycoon William Randolph Hearst, and shrewdly she criticized him in print for devoting too much ink to the budget of his company's *When Knighthood Was in Flower* (1922) rather than the superb acting of Davies. Bemused, Hearst offered Louella a job at the *New York Journal American.* By 1929 Louella Parsons presided over all Hearst entertainment pages, including those of the *Los Angeles Examiner* and the *Indianapolis Star.*

Still holding on to her girlish dreams of love and romance, Louella married again in January 1930. Harry Watson Martin, a urologist nicknamed "Docky," was a notorious partier who once jumped into an empty swimming pool on a bender and broke his neck. He held the bones together himself until they could be set. Martin also gained a reputation as a "clap doctor" around Hollywood and supposedly served as the unofficial house doctor for Lee Frances, a madam.

His friendliness with local medical labs gave Louella more than one scoop on who was pregnant or ailing in Hollywood, but she was genuinely devoted to Docky. After honeymooning at Hearst's San Simeon estate, they settled into their apartment at the Villa Carlotta hotel, where they rented a separate place just for the wedding gifts. Docky escorted her around town and the two could often be found necking in a corner—if he wasn't already unconscious. One popular story about Docky told how he once fell down drunk on the floor and stayed there. When someone moved to help him up, Louella cried, "Oh, don't touch him, please. He has to operate at eight o'clock in the morning."

By the 1950s, Louella was a veteran. She had survived the humiliation of her own sorry performance in a Busby Berkeley movie based on her radio show. And she had survived "boy wonder" Orson Welles. His *Citizen Kane,* which took its inspiration from her legendary boss Hearst, had nearly cost Parsons her job. As a Hollywood insider, she should have known about the film long before its release, should have found a way to shut down the production. But while the 1950s also offered unexpected challenges to "Lolly," she faced them with her usual pluck and persistence.

The advent of television made some of Parsons's scoops obsolete, since news was reported as it happened. The studio system was dying. Soon signing a seven-year contract to one company would be unheard of. The studios themselves were changing, in the wake of Red scares, the court-ordered separation of movie theaters and studios on grounds of monopolistic practices, and the rise of television. By the end of the decade, most of the people Louella Parsons knew were gone. Dore Schary and Nicholas Schenck had left MGM; Darryl Zanuck had left Twentieth Century Fox. Former MGM chief Louis B. Mayer, Harry Warner, and Columbia's Harry Cohn had died. She suffered two personal losses within months of each other in the summer of 1951—her husband Docky Martin and Hearst.

Martin's funeral garnered almost as much press coverage as Hearst's, with photos of his grave site and pallbearers and, of course, the stars who turned out to honor him (and Louella). Among the mourners were Marion Davies, Mr. and Mrs. Darryl Zanuck, Tyrone Power, and Dorothy Lamour. But while the *Los Angles Examiner* reported that seventy-year-old Louella had been "prostrated with grief" at the hospital when she learned of Docky's death, she was back on the job within weeks.

Without Hearst's protection, though, Louella was treated differently by the newspaper syndicate he had built. The prose that *Time* magazine once described as "chatty, intimate, informal, verbose and, on the whole, knowledgeable hodgepodge" was flattened into newspaper boilerplate. Columns once marked "MG" for "must go as is" were now edited like every other writer's. Only occasionally would Louella call the *Los Angeles Examiner* to complain that something had been changed.

A different kind of star began to emerge in Hollywood in the 1950s as well, at the same time that the old guard retreated. By 1954 stars Louella had promoted like Clark Gable, a box office draw for fifteen years, were leaving MGM. Louella had a harder time recognizing the newer crop of celebrities, and when she did, many remained indifferent to her. Marilyn Monroe never needed Louella's help, although it didn't stop the columnist from bashing her in print. "All of us were sorry to see her do all that posing for newsreels after her separation from Joe DiMaggio," Parsons wrote in January 1955. ". . . She didn't seem sincere."

Marlon Brando was another star who wouldn't play nice with the gossip columnists. He adamantly demanded privacy, a foreign concept in Hollywood. Louella told the young actor to consider a new profession. "We Americans don't even permit our Presidents the luxury of a private life," she said. She continued to needle Brando in her column as well. When he announced in early 1955 that he would marry Josane Mariani-Berenger, he said, "[But] I don't put much stock in engagements," which prompted Louella to write, "This takes the prize as the year's low in taste, sir."

Although she may have been diminished a bit, Louella and her column still retained power and cachet in the 1950s. Celebrity weddings, and divorces, continued to be the mainstays of her coverage. Parsons even seemed to take pride in breaking such personal news before the stars were ready to release it. An item from May 1950 describes Liz Taylor's disappointment when the press reported her engagement to Nicky Hilton before she could announce it to friends at a special party. But to Louella, getting the scoop was too important. "I was one of the first to tip the [wedding] date on my radio show, and the word spread like wildfire—so Elizabeth's pretty announcement party was definitely on the anticlimax side," Louella wrote proudly.

Parsons had long been known as "love's undertaker" for her reports on celebrity breakups and her preachy disapproval of divorce, despite two divorces of her own, continued through the decade. In January 1950, she lamented the breakup of Shirley Temple and John Agar's "perfect" marriage, detailing the shock and disappointment "fans" of the young star felt. ". . . It was as if a beloved child had met with disaster." Marital discord often warranted a mention as well, such as an item from June 1950 that detailed a fight at a party between Bette Davis and her husband, William Grant Sherry. "One minute they were dancing lovey-dovey and the next you could hear Bette all over the place telling Sherry off in no uncertain terms," she wrote. But Louella could defend a celebrity couple as well, such as in June 1955 when rumors were circulating that Debbie Reynolds and Eddie Fisher had manufactured their relationship for publicity purposes. "If Debbie and Eddie aren't sincerely in love, neither were Romeo and Juliet," Parsons said.

Her column, which ran in the *Examiner* and under the banner of "Louella Parsons' Good News" in *Modern Screen*, was not without its upbeat tidbits. She wrote of the 1,821 requests from fans to adopt the puppies of Gregory Peck's Alsatian dog. She mocked herself in a report on her first appearance at the popular "Charleston Night" at the Mocambo club in Hollywood. "It was a fatal error! Now I'm a Charleston addict and don't care who knows it," she wrote. When fans supposedly wanted to know what it was like for Louella to interview Katharine Hepburn, she responded, "Well, let me say she was swell!" Louella saved her most maudlin and gushing praise, though, for the moments when celebrities became parents. When June Allyson announced her pregnancy in August 1950, Louella wrote, "Happy? Both June and Dick are just walking on clouds. They believe a miracle has happened and all Hollywood is delighted with them!"

Louella Parsons, shown here with Clark Gable during her radio show, virtually invented the genre of the gossip column. Favorite topics in the 1950s included Liberace and Marlon Brando. *Bettmann/Corbis.*

But Louella was at her bitchy best when she was pointing the bony finger of indignation. She took Rita Hayworth to task for letting Dick Haymes dominate her career. When Dean Martin and Jerry Lewis were quarreling in the fall of 1955, she wrote that she'd "like to spank" them. When Bing Crosby was dating Kathryn Grant, the actress gave an interview to a small-town newspaper in which she said that Hollywood gossip columnists "make up a lot of stuff" and that Louella Parsons was the worst offender, reporting on intimate details of Grant's life without ever having met her. Parsons, who found out about the comments, warned her in print that it wasn't a good idea for a struggling starlet to take on the press and that columnists do a great deal to promote young actors. "Suppose no columnist had printed that Bing Crosby took Kathryn to the Academy Awards," Parsons wrote. "Half the publicity she received since then has been hinged on that date!"

Louella was also quite cruel to Joan Crawford in August 1955, when she wrote that the actress was washed up and likely would make "one, maybe two" more movies. For someone who wasn't far from her own retirement, Louella took too much delight in writing that despite the recent revival of Crawford's career, ". . . I think our girl has had it!"

Parsons delighted in rebuking stars for presenting a less than perfect public image. She criticized Betty Hutton for dressing up as a dusty ranch hand for a party: "I know she meant to be funny . . . but I still don't think that the way to fans' hearts is through looking ugly." She called Montgomery Clift on the carpet for his careless dressing habits: "I'm personally bored with that rumpled-shirt, unmade-bed routine," she wrote. Even a celebrity's coiffure could became a target for Louella, as when she wrote that Gloria Swanson's hair was so short "that Mary Martin will have to look out for her 'most shorn' honors."

In the mid-1950s, Louella discovered the pianist and entertainer Liberace. Her catty remarks are funny today, revealing how oblivious she was to the real meaning of his flamboyance. "I wish Liberace wouldn't wear red ruffled shirts, fancy shoes and black and gold brocaded evening clothes," she wrote in January 1955. "He's too talented and too nice a person to go in for such extremes in clothes." A photo with the column shows Liberace snuggling awkwardly with a woman named Joanne Rio, and the caption notes how they are always together but not engaged. A month later, Louella detailed the breakup of Liberace and Rio, after the woman spoke too candidly with the press. "Girls, if you have any hope of becoming Mrs. Liberace (and apparently a lot of women would like to) don't ever write a series of articles about the piano-player idol," Parsons wrote. Apparently, when Rio spoke to reporters about what it was like to date and kiss Liberace, "Wowie! That did it!" and the pianist broke off the relationship. Parsons claimed that when she ran into him later, Liberace explained himself: "Before I get married, I want to be the aggressor and do the courting myself—in private!"

By April 1955, though, Louella was reporting that Liberace was squiring a starlet named Wendi Bartlett and looking "more handsome than ever, having lost fifteen pounds." Indeed, weight was always an obsession with Louella. Although she would cry if anyone hinted at her own weight problem, Louella had no qualms about calling a star like Mae West "fat." And in one schizophrenic column from July 1955, Louella wrote that Jennifer Jones was nearly unrecognizable because "she is much plumper than I remembered" but that Janet Leigh is "too painfully thin."

The rivalry between Louella and Hedda Hopper raged through the 1950s. When Charles Brackett and Billy Wilder wanted the pair to play themselves in a late scene of *Sunset Boulevard*, Hedda thought it would be a hoot. She imagined a scene in which the columnists would both rush for the telephone at the same time. Hedda would then trip and say, "After you, Louella." But when Louella learned that Hedda had been asked to do the film first, she balked. "Get her off," Parsons said. "I won't be in it if she is." Indeed, only Hedda got the cameo. In 1955 *Life* magazine wanted to do a story about the columnists, with a photo of the two together on its cover. Hedda agreed. Louella did not. The magazine never got its photograph.

The 1950s also saw Louella honored with more and more testimonial dinners and tributes by a Hollywood that was perhaps sentimental about her and the old ways of doing business. She'd win the California Women's Press Club's Golden Flame Award and go on to become the first woman to receive the Mount Sinai Men's Club's "Heart of Gold" award. Louella's thirtieth anniversary as a columnist was marked by a Masquers Club event in April 1953 at which Eddie Cantor candidly admitted, "I am here for the same reason everybody else is—we were afraid not to come."

In 1959 the Screen Directors Guild wanted to give a new award for "outstanding critical appraisal" of films to a *Los Angeles Times* reviewer named Philip K. Scheur. The guild knew Louella would be miffed to see someone else recognized. So they made up a "special citation" for her to acknowledge her "loyalty, devotion, and many valued contributions to the motion picture industry." The outpouring of affection for Louella in the 1950s prompted Hedda Hopper to say her rival had accepted "every conceivable and inconceivable degree, doctorate, scroll, and plaque held out by college or corporation."

Parsons also experienced a renaissance of sorts in 1956 when CBS devoted a sixty-minute drama to her life entitled *Climax*. Louella's only concern was that actress Teresa Wright not make her "too sweet." Wright heeded her advice, it seems, as *New York Times* critic Jack Gould thought her portrayal of Louella "fairly dripped with lilac-scented acid." *New York Post* critic Jay Nelson Tuck meanwhile quipped that it should have been called "Auntie Climax."

In the mid-1950s, Louella began following the stars to Las Vegas, watching singers like Frank Sinatra and Dean Martin perform. Since Docky's death, Louella's swain had been songwriter Jimmy McHugh, famous for such hits as "I'm in the Mood for Love" and "On the Sunny Side of the Street." When she was in a Las Vegas audience, press agents and managers implored their singers to include a McHugh medley and dedicate it to Louella to get a favorable mention in her column.

Rumors swirled that McHugh was only using Louella for the press coverage. If mentions of his name in her column dropped off, the rumor went, so did the frequency of his phone calls. It's true that in 1951 her column mentioned McHugh only two or three times. In 1952 she put his name in her column twenty times, and by 1953 a film of his life story was reported to be in production. Sarcastic Hedda Hopper opined that their romance "may hit rock bottom before the script hits the soundstage." But the bond between the two went beyond mere commerce. And perhaps Hedda was only jealous, as McHugh had dated her briefly in the early 1940s.

Despite her hearty public image, though, health problems began to plague Louella in the early 1950s. A column from December 1952 details a get-well party Jimmy McHugh hosted for her, complete with flowers floating in the swimming pool. She doesn't mention her ailment, although other reports said she had suffered a seizure. She later had a serious heart attack. As the decade waned, she took comfort in prayer, kneeling on her back lawn by a ten-foot statue of the Virgin Mary. At dusk, this gift from McHugh that she cherished would automatically be bathed in light. Her column began to fill with ludicrous items such as one in which she called Nancy Sinatra and her future husband Tommy Sands "two of my best friends."

She retired in November 1964. Even as the official announcement ran that Dorothy Manners would take her place, Louella Parsons was moving to a nursing home. Despite comebacks from various ailments before, she could not recover from what would now be called Alzheimer's disease. Friends and relatives visited but she no longer recognized them and would weep. Once while he visited, she asked Jimmy McHugh if he had heard the sad news. He said he had not. "Jimmy McHugh passed away," she told him.

Hollywood soon forgot Louella and her reign as queen of the gossip columnists. Less than three years after her retirement, two magazines had to run apologies and corrections for referring to her as "the late Louella Parsons." She remained in a nursing home until her death in 1972.

HEDDA HOPPER was more flamboyant—and edgier—than the daffy Louella. She had come to column-writing toward the end of a frustrated movie career in which she played everything from a female sea captain to the title role in a silent film called *Mona Lisa*. Wielding her pen like a weapon, then, was perhaps an act of revenge on Hollywood. "What inspired you to write such nasty things about me?" actress Merle Oberon once asked. Hedda responded, "Bitchery, dear. Sheer bitchery."

Born Elda Furry in Altoona, Pennsylvania, she left school after eighth grade, and at twenty-two ran away to become a chorus girl, alternately changing her name to Elda Curry and Elda Millar. It wasn't until she became the fifth wife of Broadway stage actor DeWolf Hopper that she paid ten dollars to a Mrs. Cochrane, a combination astrologer, numerologist, and psychoanalyst, to change her first name. The resulting "Hedda" won only scorn from her husband. "Hedda lettuce, Hedda cheese," he griped, but stopped confusing her with his previous wives, who had oddly similar-sounding names: Edna, Ida, Ella, and Nella.

At fifty-five, DeWolf Hopper was older than Hedda's father when she married him in a ninety-second ceremony. He was famous for his recitations of the poem "Casey at the Bat" and infamous for being a roué. DeWolf was not much to look at, either. His skin had a bluish tint caused by swallowing too much silver nitrate, which he gargled for a throat condition. Severe typhoid had left him hairless as well. Still, Hedda described "Wolfie" as a "six-foot-three riot."

Hedda soon eclipsed her husband with a successful film career. Although she wanted starring rather than supporting roles, Hedda admitted to enjoying playing "bad women" because "good women are so deadly dull." She earned a reputation as "the worst cat on the screen" for constantly trying to upstage the stars of her films. Once, for a film called *Virtuous Wives* (1918), Hedda spent her entire $5,000 salary on clothes. She wanted to be so chic she'd steal the picture from its star, Anita Stewart, and it worked.

She would make nineteen pictures in four years, eventually earning $1,000 a week. The figure bothered her husband, who after decades on the stage had only begun to earn the same salary. Wolfie's unrepentant philandering also did not help the strained marriage. Hedda caught him with another woman and sued him for divorce in 1922.

A year later, Hedda and her young son moved to Hollywood. Shrewdly, she wrote long, gossipy letters to none other than Louella Parsons, who rewarded her with brief mentions in the column. Hopper knew the roles in productions like *Diamond Handcuffs* and *Venus of Venice* were ridiculous but stayed for the money. "I wasn't a star," she later wrote. ". . . I was the mean woman who made the stars look good. I've slapped more children, tumbled down more houses of cards, kicked over more building blocks and rapped more innocent knuckles than any female fiend in an old-time orphanage."

More and more, though, her scenes ended up on the cutting-room floor. She signed with a new agent named Dema Harshbarger, who tried to break her of bad habits like accepting a Mixmaster instead of a paycheck for doing a commercial. With her help, Hedda began to land better roles, including parts in *Midnight* with Claudette Colbert and *The Women* (1939), directed by George Cukor. She could also be heard on the radio in a dramatic serial called *Brenthouse*.

Hopper's renewed exposure led to an offer from the Esquire Feature Syndicate to write a Hollywood column. She agreed and her byline began appearing in thirteen newspapers in the late 1930s. Studio chiefs like Louis B. Mayer took delight in seeing the development of a potential rival to Louella Parsons, who had worn out her welcome with demands about exclusives and sniping criticisms. When the *Los Angeles Times* picked up Hedda's column in February 1938, the real battle began. Every producer in town read it.

According to Hedda, she started off by writing only "nice" items of gossip. "Hollywood," she said, "laughed smack in my face." So she decided to make a name for herself by letting the fur fly. She took David O. Selznick to task for casting the British Vivien Leigh as Scarlett O'Hara in *Gone With the Wind,* thus insulting every American actress. At a time when reporting on plastic surgery was still relatively taboo, Hedda wrote that Mary Livingston (Mrs. Jack Benny) had a nose job, which had made her self-conscious. "But her new nose is—to say the least—classy," she wrote. Meow.

Hedda switched to the *Register-Tribune* syndicate in 1940. When the *Chicago Tribune* and the *New York Daily News* picked up the column, her circulation soared to more than 17.5 million readers. The column appeared in eighty-five metropolitan papers, three thousand small dailies, and two thousand weeklies. Her salary grew to $110,000 a year and she bought a home in Beverly Hills.

She worked slavishly, often racking up as many as 130 hours a week on the job. And she didn't do it alone. Her staff included two "leg men," a rewrite woman, two secretaries, two girls to answer mail, and an agent/manager, not to mention the legion of dentists, beauticians, nurses, salesmen, and servants who offered tips.

Hedda gained a reputation as an anti-Semite for her column comments. Really, though, she was an isolationist. Her son Bill had reached draft age and she didn't want him going off to war. She couldn't resist a wisecrack, either, even if it were inappropriate. Once when someone suggested she visit Israel, for instance, she retorted, "Why do I need to? I live in Beverly Hills."

Her coverage of World War II at times seemed truly bizarre. At one point she praised Joseph Stalin, whom she referred to quite familiarly as "Joe," for ordering movie theaters to remain open during the sieges of Stalingrad and Leningrad. "There's a man who recognizes the value of pictures and makes the most of it," she wrote.

Not every actor accepted Hedda's printed abuse. Joseph Cotten warned her to stop printing items about him and actress Deanna Durbin. When she didn't and he ran into her at a party, Cotten kicked her in the backside. Joan Bennett sent Hedda a skunk on Valentine's Day, 1950. The note attached read, "I stink and so do you." With a newspaper column at her disposal, though, Hedda always had the last word. She said the skunk was "beautifully behaved. I christened it Joan." (Hedda later gave the skunk to James Mason and his wife.)

But the ultimate insult to Hedda was when anyone confused her with the competition. Hedda's leg man Jaik Rosenstein remembered the day Hedda thought studio executive Sam Goldwyn had given a story about a new Ingrid Bergman movie to another reporter. Rosenstein offered, "Maybe he couldn't help it." "Oh, I wasn't giving him hell about that," she laughed. "I was screaming at him because he got mixed up and called me 'Louella' twice. I don't mind losing the story, but nobody can call me that!"

Hedda did have a soft spot for the common man, though. Leg man Rosenstein recalled her sudden generosity to the beleaguered support staffs of Hollywood. One night in the early 1950s, restaurateur Mike Romanoff gave a huge tent party that went on until five in the morning. The waiters and other kitchen workers worked thirteen-hour shifts. Hedda asked for a list of their names. She wrote each a personal thank-you note and attached a five-dollar bill.

But after World War II, Hedda Hopper became as famous for rabid anti-Communism as for her temper and wacky, tacky hats. She grew increasingly political, making friends with Joseph McCarthy and conservative Barry Goldwater. She once referred to MGM Studios as "Metro Goldwyn Moscow." She used her column to bash those who had joined organizations she considered "hostile" to American interests. Among her targets: screenwriter Clifford Odets, Lauren Bacall, Shelley Winters, playwright Arthur Miller, and Fredric March. Perhaps the only beneficiary of her boosterism was war hero turned actor Audie Murphy. Without her lobbying, he might not have won the starring role in John Huston's epic *The Red Badge of Courage* (1951).

Her efforts to ferret out Communism went too far for the chairman of the House Un-American Activities Committee, who in 1951 asked her to tone down her prose. She couldn't censor herself, though, and earned a public reprimand from the editor of the *New York Daily News* in 1953. He chided her for "trying to settle international affairs." He said her call to boycott Judy Holliday and José Ferrer was ridiculous. George E. Sokolsky, a virulent anti-Communist and newspaper columnist, criticized her "bloodbath attitude" and said she gave his cause a bad name. Even Gypsy Rose Lee, who considered Hopper a friend and refused to talk politics with her, thought that Hedda had become "rather ridiculously conservative."

Hedda seemed indestructible in the 1950s, though. Her autobiography *From Under My Hat* became a best-seller just seven days after its September 1952 release. Director Cecil B. DeMille even wrote a rather fawning "review" of it in the *Los Angeles Times*, praising Hopper's bravery. She appeared in an episode of *I Love Lucy*, playing a press agent Ricky meets on a visit to Hollywood. She performed well and became friends with Lucille Ball. Even the feared and hated *Confidential* could not besmirch her. The magazine hired private investigators to delve into her background but called them off after six months of work produced exactly nothing that would make hot copy.

She did get into one dustup in 1959 with fellow columnist and television personality Ed Sullivan. Sullivan accused Hopper of offering guests on her own short-lived television show free publicity in her column, rather than paying them for their appearances. She called him "a liar." Sullivan, whose column appeared in the *New York Daily News* along with Hopper's, shot back. He said Hedda "used to hang around the fringes of show business. She's no actress. She's certainly no newspaperwoman. She's downright illiterate. She can't even spell. . . . [A]nd yet she's established a reign of terror out there in Hollywood."

Ed Sullivan was peeved that he had just paid Charlton Heston $10,000 to read from the Bible on his show while Hedda had offered the minimum union wage of $210 for Heston's upcoming appearance on her show. Heston, sensing he had opened a can of worms, then backed out of his agreement with Hopper, citing further commitments to Sullivan's show. He added that he thought her program was only a local presentation. "What would I be doing on a local show?" Hopper fumed. If it had been anyone else but Sullivan, someone without a column of his own, Hedda surely would have declared all-out war on him. But she chose, judiciously, to let the disagreement pass.

Hedda seemed to specialize in longer articles that pointed up the fallible nature of celebrities. One piece in a January 1950 *Modern Screen* magazine was entitled "Mistakes They Never Confess." She said Orson Welles "could have rivalled the brilliant record of the Barrymores if he hadn't tried to make like a screwy one-man band." And Charlie Chaplin would have found renewed success if "he hadn't made the mistake of angling his art toward Moscow." Under a subhead that read "Error, Error, Everywhere," Hopper asked plaintively, "How can stars go so wrong, act so blandly and blindly stupid?"

Hopper wrote another long feature for *Modern Screen* in May 1950 entitled "Hollywood Takes Its Medicine." It explored the growing popularity of psychoanalysis among celebrities and noted that stars such as Victor Mature, Robert Mitchum, George Sanders, Ava Gardner, Susan Hayward, and Vincent Price had sought therapy. While Hedda endorsed the idea, she wondered idly if it wasn't "just another Movietown vogue, a fad of fakery." Her blunt prose style was rather insensitive by today's standards, such as when she wrote, "Tackling the job of ironing out a sick mind is no picnic," and "Judy Garland's crack-up was cured in part by probings into her confused nerves—and she'll need more to stay steady."

The real "waxworks": an aging Hedda Hopper poses with wax figures from *Sunset Boulevard*, an ersatz Erich von Stroheim, Gloria Swanson, and William Holden. The acid-tongued columnist had a circulation of more than 17.5 million at her peak. *Courtesy of the Academy of Motion Picture Arts and Sciences.*

But like Louella, Hedda found the 1950s more than a little baffling. She was horrified by the Kinsey Report that detailed American sexual behavior, and horrified further by the Supreme Court decision that abolished some censorship laws. Obscene films, she said, surely would flood the U.S. market. She thought the film version of Tennessee Williams's *A Streetcar Named Desire* was offensive as well. In a June 1951 column, she described the scene in which Marlon Brando says to Vivien Leigh, "I wonder what it would be like to have an affair with you." Hedda wrote, "I wonder how that bit of dialogue got by the censor. I thought the play was sordid. I think the picture is more sordid." She hated another film version of a Williams play, 1959's *Suddenly Last Summer*, because it was "all about homosexuals and cannibalism." She asked Tennessee Williams why he always went "to the sewer" for inspiration. He responded that he had had a difficult childhood, to which Hedda replied, "But you've grown up now, haven't you?"

Hedda Hopper disliked Marlon Brando and Montgomery Clift, the new brand of star. Give her a Clark Gable or a Jimmy Cagney, not a youngster wearing blue jeans or a skimpy undershirt. Oddly enough, though, Hedda Hopper became an early booster of James Dean, who was also a student of Method acting.

After watching *Rebel Without a Cause*, she described Dean as one of the most talented actors she had seen in many years. She felt so devoted to him that she attacked other reporters when they wrote of conflict between Dean and director George Stevens on the set of *Giant*. She had a long conversation with Dean about Stevens which she inexplicably never printed. He was overworked, not having had the vacation after *Rebel* that the studio had promised, and frustrated by Stevens's techniques, such as having Dean wait on the set all day even if he had only a small scene to perform. Dean poured his heart out to Hedda Hopper, telling her that he knew he was only "a small cog in a big organization like Warner's but I'm an individual." He said, "I think I have talent and I don't take this kind of bullshit from anybody." Stevens, according to Dean, was "insecure." "When a man doesn't know the personal boundary of his art, then he shouldn't put boundaries around others," Dean said.

When he died in October of 1955, Hedda's emotions overflowed. "He was a tragic figure. So few understood him. He was reaching out for love and understanding, but got so little. . . . He was like the parched earth longing for the rain," she wrote in her column. ". . . It will be a long time before we see his like again. I loved that boy and I always will." She chastised the Academy when it failed to award Dean a posthumous Oscar, and became a one-woman clearinghouse for grieving Dean fans. Hundreds of them wrote to Hedda, on lined white paper torn from notebooks and on scented pink stationery. They told her she was the only columnist who really "got" him. They shared poems and drawings, even photographs of their James Dean scrapbooks. They sent checks to her, too, donations for a Dean memorial Hedda wanted to erect somewhere in Hollywood. She had to return the money when her efforts stalled, but she signed each letter personally.

Hopper also liked another Hollywood rebel, Steve McQueen. She spotted him first in 1959 in television's *Wanted—Dead or Alive*. "I like that feisty little bastard," she told her assistant. "Get him in here for an interview." The pair had a kind of playful relationship, McQueen calling Hedda "Slim" and showing up for their meetings in a strange cap. "I want you to know I wore my crazy hat for you," he'd say.

In a May 1959 interview, Hedda asked McQueen if he'd ever been in jail. He answered reluctantly. "I got into situations I wasn't bright about. I didn't have any conception of what I was like . . . so I got into trouble," he said. "You been in jail?"

"Certainly," Hedda answered.

"I'm going right over to Louella Parsons and plant this—it would make headlines," McQueen said.

"I can tell you a story about her that's worse than that," Hedda deadpanned.

After reports of a wild weekend with Sinatra's Rat Pack in New York during which McQueen threw cherry bombs from the window of his hotel room, Hopper took him aside. She urged him not to choose a role in Sinatra's entourage over his own acting career. He decided he wouldn't and Hedda backed him enthusiastically.

In the early 1960s, Hedda Hopper asserted her influence more than ever. With Louella on the way out, she felt her power growing. She enjoyed promoting politicians like Barry Goldwater and Richard Nixon, bashing the Beatles, and railing against the new sexual candor in film. Aside from the occasional skunk, she had faced few challenges, until she decided to write another book.

McCall's magazine excerpted *The Whole Truth and Nothing But* in October and November of 1962. The first shipment of the magazine sold out in twelve hours, and upon its release the book sat on the bestseller list from February through June 1963. Hopper was thrilled, crowing that all the lawyers in town were scouring the spicy book.

Indeed they were. Michael Wilding, Elizabeth Taylor's fourth husband, sued for $3 million when he read about his alleged homosexual affair and the fictitious meeting Hedda had had with him and Liz to discourage their marriage. He later settled for $100,000, half of which would be paid by Hedda herself. She also admitted to a "reckless and wanton disregard" of Wilding's rights in printing the item "with intent to injure his feelings."

Publicly, Hedda Hopper refused to comment on the case and tried to maintain her dignity. Her son believed she was deeply humiliated, though, and never recovered from the lawsuit. A host of health problems began to plague her as well. She needed amplifiers on her phones to compensate for hearing loss and began to have heart trouble. She died quite suddenly from complications related to pneumonia in 1966.

OF THE DOMINANT gossip columnists, Sheilah Graham was by the far the most glamorous. Younger and prettier than Parsons and Hopper, she looked more like the actresses she followed than the dowdy scribes. Her personal story was something out of a movie, too. In fact, a film version of her life would reach the screen in the 1950s.

Graham had a tough, Dickensian childhood. She grew up in the East London Home for Orphans, where she suffered such cruelties as having her hair shorn and being denied sweets. She always thought the latter had saved her career, though. A job demonstrating toothbrushes on her pearly whites at a London department store led to a stint as a showgirl.

Graham literally reinvented herself, transforming "Lily Shiel" into "Sheilah Graham," a glamour girl who traveled in the smartest British sets. The former orphan scraped her way to the top of British society, answering any questions about her background by saying her long-dead parents had owned a great deal of property in London and schooled her with tutors at home. She married a British army major, decorated for his service in World War I. It was on his arm that Graham was presented to Queen Mary and King George V at Buckingham Palace. But her marriage to the much older man was short-lived and she came to New York in 1933, quickly establishing herself as a "do anything for a story" kind of journalist. She got an exclusive by sneaking into Al Capone's house in Florida, describing it for *New York Evening Journal* readers.

On Christmas Eve, 1935, she decided to take a pay cut and become a Hollywood columnist. By August of 1936, she was the subject, instead of the purveyor, of gossip. An item in *Daily Variety* reported, "Studio publicity heads may take action to ban girl correspondent for big newspaper feature syndicate. Gal has been sniping at Hollywood pictures. . . . Has had several brushes with studios. . . . There is now talk of getting [the Hays Office] to call in hatchet men."

Graham met F. Scott Fitzgerald at a party in the summer of 1937. She remembered staring at him as blue-gray smoke from his cigarette swirled around his melancholic face. Although it is hard to believe today, when works such as *The Great Gatsby* and *This Side of Paradise* are staples of high school and college reading lists, Fitzgerald had fallen out of favor in the 1930s. His books were out of print and he struggled to publish the occasional short story in a magazine, while he watched contemporaries such as Hemingway and Steinbeck flourish. He was considered so passé that in her column Graham sometimes described actresses as "old-fashioned F. Scott Fitzgerald types" when she wanted to paint them as silly has-beens. And she hadn't read any of his books.

Fitzgerald had moved to California to find work as a screenwriter. He was plagued by alcoholism and anxiety, worrying about how to pay for his wife Zelda's care at a North Carolina sanitarium and his daughter's private school tuition. But he was buoyed by Graham's optimism and joie de vivre. She described their affair, which would last until his death in 1940, as both passionate and tender, a sanctuary from the cruel vagaries of Hollywood. Although briefly under contract to MGM, Fitzgerald never had a major movie success. His work on such films as *A Yank at Oxford*, *Honeymoon in Bali*, and *The Women* went uncredited. His only screenwriting credit was *Three Comrades*, a 1938 picture starring Robert Young and Margaret Sullavan, which told the story of three German soldiers in love with the same woman after the end of World War I.

Graham meanwhile was finding that her hard-nosed reporting methods didn't play as well in the movie town as they had in New York. She admitted she was "too outspoken" and respected "no sacred cows." In short, Graham was too honest. Her first few months on the job included a string of gems including the revelation that Clark Gable was getting a double chin and that actress Kay Francis painted on her famous widow's peak.

Graham burned many a bridge. She zinged the brainless MGM production *Suzy*, starring Jean Harlow: "I can't understand why a company with the best producers, the best writers, the best actors, the best cameraman, should make a picture like *Suzy* which has the worst acting, the worst photography, the worst direction."

Studio bigwigs and self-important restaurateurs weren't safe either. Of the famed Trocadero, Graham wrote, "Not even the doubtful pleasure of rubbing elbows with Louis B. Mayer can compensate for the high prices charged for rather inferior food." She offended more than Mayer with that line. She didn't know that the Troc's owner, Billy Wilkerson, also published the *Hollywood Reporter*. Graham's editor at the North American Newspaper Association, her syndicate, chastised her. "You are not Walter Winchell," he telegrammed.

Graham survived a mild scare in the early 1950s, at the height of the Communist inquisition under way in Hollywood. Just after becoming an American citizen, she joined the Committee for the First Amendment, a group of actors and other Hollywood types who opposed blacklisting. A newspaper ad for the group included her name. An anonymous citizen then began writing weekly letters to the editor accusing her of being a Communist. She began to think her job might be in jeopardy, until the citizen revealed himself or herself to be a quack. The letter writer cited such evidence as how Graham, in one column, had referred to Peter Lawford's red socks and Elizabeth Taylor's "flaming red sweater," concluding innocuously that "red is obviously the color to wear this summer."

Graham tried to tame her "Hollywood Today" column but still

enjoyed the occasional outburst, such as when she visited actress Constance Bennett on a movie set. The actress didn't like some bad press Graham had written. Surrounded by a coterie of girlfriends, she looked the columnist up and down and said, "It's hard to believe that a girl as pretty as you can be the biggest bitch in Hollywood." Graham deadpanned, "Not the biggest, Connie, the second biggest."

Bennett fumed but Graham got the last laugh, with a little help from Scott Fitzgerald. He had known Bennett years before as a "party girl," always making the rounds at Princeton University functions, and he gave Graham the put-down she needed. In her column the next day she wrote, "It's lucky no children happened to be on Constance Bennett's set yesterday. Her language was absolutely shocking. Poor Connie. Faded flapper of 1919 and now, symbolically cast as a ghost in her latest production."

Savvy and sarcastic, Graham sounded less preachy than the other columnists even when she took a shot at everyone's favorite target: Lana Turner. When the actress announced the breakup of her third marriage, to alleged millionaire Bob Topping, Graham wrote, "Lana Turner is saying that Bob Topping owes her $82,000. Moral—never marry a trust fund."

Graham vowed she would earn as much with her writing as the most popular studio stars—$5,000 a week. She came closest in 1954, when the *Sheilah Graham Television Show* debuted with a $5,000-a-week budget.

At her peak in the mid-1950s, twenty million people read her syndicated column. She wrote a monthly article for *Photoplay*, a twice-a-month *TV Guide* column, and various articles in fan magazines like *Silver Screen*. She also edited occasional specials for Dell, such as *Sheilah Graham's Hollywood Yearbook* and *Sheilah Graham's Hollywood Romances*.

She later took her name off these "Sheilah Graham" magazines, complaining that the publishers had made them too salacious. She didn't give details but blamed the change of tone on *Confidential* magazine's success. ". . . While correcting a *Sheilah Graham's Hollywood Yearbook*, I realized that the editor had made every actor a queer and every woman a degenerate," she said.

Sheilah Graham often scooped Hopper and Parsons but didn't

always print what she knew. She claimed she heard about Ingrid Bergman and Roberto Rossellini's extramarital baby scandal weeks before the others but declined to print it. She also took the rivalry between the columnists quite personally.

Louella Parsons lived only a few doors down from Graham on Maple Drive in Beverly Hills. Once, in the early 1950s, as a publicity stunt, Parsons hosted a holiday party for celebrity children. Hopalong Cassidy, TV cowboy, would make an appearance. Graham hinted that her children wanted to meet him. Parsons failed to pick up on the obvious prompt. Irritated by the slight, Graham persuaded Hopalong to make a stop at the Graham household before going on to the party. She had a photographer on hand and the pictures of young Wendy and Bobby with Hoppy made the papers long before shots of Louella's event.

Graham's orphan past made her especially sensitive to any kind of exclusion. Wendy Fairey, Graham's daughter, remembered Liza Minnelli's third birthday party. Judy Garland had rented a donkey to give rides to all the children. But the press photographers kept letting more important stars' children climb aboard. Graham "seized the pony," placed her daughter on it, walked around the corral, did the same for young son Robert, and then left.

Graham did not mind writing about herself in her column, either, especially if it gave her an exclusive. A June 1953 edition of "Sheilah Graham's Personal Report on the Stars" in *Silver Screen* magazine carried a feature on her wedding (her third) to Stanley Wojtkiewicz, a former football coach at a California prison. Her new husband, who went by the nickname "Bow Wow," hardly warranted a mention, but Graham gleefully reported that two hundred guests were invited "and four hundred showed." Among the stars in attendance were Rock Hudson (who came stag), Stewart Granger, Jeanne Crain, and Dean Martin. Marilyn Monroe also came to the reception and got into a bit of a tiff with Joan Crawford. Crawford reportedly told Monroe that she was "disgusting," which prompted Marilyn to whisper in Graham's ear, "She was pretty disgusting herself when she started."

When Sheilah began divorce proceedings against "Bow Wow" three years later, the news never reached her own column, although the legal machinations were covered by other local papers. The *Los*

Angeles Times reported that Sheilah, fifty-one, had been ordered to pay her ex-husband, then thirty-nine, $250 a month for three months and turn over to him Graham's $42,000 Malibu beach house. The divorce became final on January 10, 1957. Graham had told the court that Bow Wow was "always calling me stupid and shouting at me" and "made me absolutely a nervous wreck."

LIKE HER rivals, Sheilah Graham in the 1950s was still dishing out harsh judgments of celebrities. Next to a slick photo of herself with a glamorous, neat blonde hairdo, she opined in April 1953, "I wish I had the nerve to suggest Greer Garson cut her hair: She'd be prettier." She called up-and-coming actress Terry Moore an "insistent sexpot" and chided her for dating a British actor known for performing Shakespeare. "Methinks the lady doth date too much," Graham wrote. She showed no mercy to Bette Davis, either, and ridiculed her effort to return to the stage, saying that "even her best friends admit her singing and dancing are in the amateur class."

Although she dwelled on the same obsessions as her fellow columnists, Graham could be especially cutting. She loved to lampoon Marilyn Monroe, whom she called "the Doctrine." She thought it ironic that *Gentlemen Prefer Blondes* (1953), with buxom stars Monroe and Jane Russell, had been shot in two dimensions "when it needed three or four." In July 1953, when Tony Curtis was filming *All American*, Graham reported he was having a hard time working with the real football players hired for the film and that the athletes called him "the girl." Young Robert Wagner was also a favorite target of Graham's. After he dyed his hair black for a role in *Prince Valiant* (1954), she reported he did it to look more mature for his new girlfriend Barbara Stanwyck, who was much older than he. Graham said he might as well "change it to gray to match hers." Months later, seeing him on the set of the film, she said his legs looked "spindly" under his "leather skirt."

Graham liked to blast Zsa Zsa Gabor, too. A December 1953 column called Gabor's first revue in Las Vegas "a big floperoo." Graham's June 1954 column suggested someone retire Zsa Zsa, since she was "pretty, but no longer in the first flush of youth," and "so far has given no evidence of acting ability." A month later, Graham tattled that Zsa

Gossip columnist Sheilah Graham chronicled her affair with novelist F. Scott Fitzgerald in her memoir, *Beloved Infidel*. A film version, starring Gregory Peck and Deborah Kerr, reached the screen in 1959. *Bettmann/Corbis.*

Zsa talked about her sister behind her back, quoting her as saying that Eva Gabor took acting too seriously. "Who does she think she is, Helen Hayes?" said Zsa Zsa.

Sheilah Graham became famous for more than her gossip column and catty ways, though. The fact that she had been novelist F. Scott Fitzgerald's lover soon piqued the interest of Hollywood producer Jerry Wald, who had read Fitzgerald's books and asked novelist John O'Hara to write a screenplay for a biographical film. When O'Hara told him that the character of Kathleen in *The Last Tycoon* was modeled after Sheilah Graham, the producer went straight to the source.

Graham should have known better. As a Hollywood columnist, she knew the inside dish, knew Wald's reputation for ruining works of inspired writing when he brought them to the screen. Graham was a single mom with two children to feed, though, and maybe she was drawn to the cash Wald was flashing. Initially, she offered to sell Fitzgerald's letters to Wald for $7,000. But he talked her into writing a book, entitled *Beloved Infidel* after a poem Fitzgerald wrote about Graham.

Wald consulted with a book editor, who suggested Graham get a collaborator after the first 100,000 words she had penned proved disappointing. The editor recommended Gerold Frank, the coauthor of two best-sellers, Lillian Roth's *I'll Cry Tomorrow* and Diana Barrymore's *Too Much, Too Soon*. Both had been bought for films.

Sheilah Graham described Frank as "cool" when she approached him about the project. He was reluctant to take on another collaboration, "to do another woman." Graham remembered how he showed her copies of two recent pieces he had published, waving them and saying, "You know, I write for *The New Yorker*."

Indirectly, Jerry Wald persuaded Frank to take the job. Wald "could never wait for anything, especially for a contract to be signed," Graham recalled. Hoping to create a buzz about *Beloved Infidel*, the film, he leaked information to any newspaper that would listen. The *New York Times* was one of them. When Frank picked up his paper one morning to read of the hot new movie deal, he quickly called Graham. The writer who had once seemed condescending to the gossip columnist experienced a sudden change of heart. He was dying to help write her book.

Wald's sly maneuverings backfired on him, though. Other studios heard about the project and knew Sheilah Graham hadn't signed a contract yet. Warner's offered $60,000 for the unwritten book. Metro anted up with $70,000. Graham had the producer right where she wanted him, and was able to increase her price to $100,000, along with a sweet little 5 percent profit share. Years later, she mused, "I wonder at what moment the money becomes interesting and you want to make a profit on what began as a noble idea."

Gerold Frank soon moved into Graham's Beverly Hills house for weeks at a time, recording her stories on reels of tape. Graham did not particularly like her coauthor. She wrote in *The Rest of the Story* that Frank had "little personality of his own" and speculated that this very quality enabled him to write good biographies, since he could escape into the lives of other people.

As she often did in her column, Graham seemed to take a perverse delight in pointing up his faults in her later books. She described him as "pompous" and "in love with his prose," adopting a "hushed-cathedral attitude toward his writing." She even poked fun at his physical appearance, claiming that his "baldness somehow [gave] him an air of stern solidity." "The wart on his nose hypnotized me," she said. "Soon after commencing his later, unsuccessful book with Zsa Zsa Gabor, he had the wart removed, and I rather resented it."

Graham sounds more than a little insecure about her first real book project. Frank had a reputation as a respected hard news journalist. He began his career with the Hearst's *Journal American* in New York and then worked as a war correspondent for various news agencies. Perhaps Graham thought he had more of a pedigree than she did. In fact, Frank did lend the book a certain weight. Together they produced what *The New Yorker* called "the very best portrait of F. Scott Fitzgerald that has yet been put into print." Critic Edmund Wilson praised the intimacy of the work, noting that there was "too much dignity at the core" of Graham and Fitzgerald for the book to be something sordid.

Frank had good writing skills but even better researching methods. He did the bulk of the interviews with sources such as Arnold Gingrich, the editor of *Esquire* who bought some of Fitzgerald's last stories, and Dr. Clarence Nelson, who had tended the failing Fitzgerald in his last alcoholic year of life. Frank unearthed telling and important anecdotes. He learned of a feverish night in which Fitzgerald had become entangled in his pajamas and imagined that he was paralyzed. From a psychiatrist in New York, he also learned that Fitzgerald had suffered from a sugar deficiency in his blood that caused a physical craving for liquor and sweets.

Graham took Frank to all her old haunts. She showed him the Malibu beach house, where she had installed Fitzgerald in hopes that the change of scene would improve his mood, help him write, and keep him from turning to alcohol. She showed her coauthor her old apartment where Fitzgerald had conducted his "college of one," a series of lessons designed to make the uneducated Sheilah well read, and where he later died. A freeway had swallowed another house that they sometimes shared in Encino. "And where the pomegranate hedges and the two magnolia trees . . . ? The small roses no longer bloomed everywhere as in Scott's day," Graham wrote of revisiting the estate.

Although he had originally wanted a film only about Fitzgerald's life, Wald soon expressed interest in Graham's own personal story as well. He praised the first half of *Beloved Infidel*, which has nothing to do with Fitzgerald and chronicles her travails as an orphan turned showgirl in England. Indeed Fitzgerald does not make an appearance until part three.

The story would offer a substantial, meaty role for an actress. Deborah Kerr said she read the book "in one sitting" and especially enjoyed the first part about Sheilah Graham's childhood. When she heard it would be a film, she cabled her agent from her home in Switzerland: "DON'T DELAY. GET ME THE PART OF SHEILAH IN BELOVED INFIDEL." Graham thought her "too controlled, too thin and too ladylike." She believed Marilyn Monroe or Jean Simmons would have suited the screen Sheilah better, but did not care much as long as her story remained intact.

Graham had thought she was lucky when Jerry Wald bought the film rights to *Beloved Infidel*. After the screenplay of the film was finished, Wald sent her a copy as a courtesy. "We both knew he did not have to do that, but I was an important columnist and it was safer not to upset me," Sheilah Graham wrote nearly thirty years later. "However, I was upset."

The whole first act of the story had disappeared. Ever the diplomat, Wald put Graham on the payroll for a week to rewrite parts of the script. "It was impossible to dent this man," she recalled. Graham spent a week in a two-room suite at Fox, twice reducing her secretary to tears because she felt so overworked and producing more than 150 pages of new script, but none of her changes were realized.

Some of the blame belongs to Gregory Peck, who played the part of prima donna better than that of the tortured Scott Fitzgerald. Peck, by contractual agreement with the studio, brought his own writer to the picture. The fact that he also brought his uninspired acting is Wald's fault, though. Sheilah Graham had suggested Richard Basehart from *La Strada* for the role of Fitzgerald—"even Bing Crosby would have been better" than Peck, she said—but Wald insisted "on having much more important stars." The producer had first envisioned Paul Newman or Montgomery Clift for the part of the novelist, but gave in to studio suggestions that he take Peck. The result is numbingly dull.

Peck admitted later to Graham that he "hadn't wanted to do the film at all." He thought the love story angle needed strengthening, and "also I knew I was nothing like Scott Fitzgerald, so I decided to play it as any American writer. It could have been John Steinbeck or William Faulkner or Hemingway."

Peck's generic portrayal robs the film of intensity. He plods through every scene, refusing to acknowledge the pain Fitzgerald felt toward the end of his life, both personally and professionally. His failures at screenwriting were mounting and his luminous early works seemed forgotten. Graham details this in *Beloved Infidel* in one particularly heartbreaking scene. When Fitzgerald sees that his play *A Diamond as Big as the Ritz* is being staged at the Pasadena Playhouse, he decides to attend the opening-night performance. He and Sheilah don their best evening clothes and travel to the theater in a rented limousine.

When they arrive at the playhouse, the beautiful, terra-cotta-colored Spanish mission style building is half dark. Fitzgerald at first thinks he may have the wrong date. "With a sinking feeling, I waited in the deserted lobby while he went off to find someone," Graham wrote. "When he returned, his walk wasn't quite as jaunty. 'It's the students—they're giving the play in the upstairs hall.' "

Some moments of the film did move Graham, though. She said she swooned when Peck delivered the line "I love you, Sheilo." But she must have been remembering her real-life affair with Fitzgerald because there is little chemistry between Peck and Kerr onscreen. Even when a drunken and growling Fitzgerald fights with Graham, the scenes seem subdued.

In the book version of *Beloved Infidel*, the battles climax in "the great drinking binge of 1939." Fitzgerald gets drunk one night and grabs a gun, threatening to commit suicide. Graham grapples with him for the weapon until he screams out all her humble beginnings, including the thing she hated most, that she had started life as a Jew. "Take it and shoot yourself, you son of a bitch," Graham replies, furious and hurt. "I didn't pull myself out of the gutter to waste my life on a drunk like you." The screen version lacks this anger or passion, although the gun goes off as it did not in reality.

When Wald asked Sheilah Graham what she thought of the film after its preview, she complained only that it was too long. She remembered that a strange feeling of disconnection came over her. "This was my life—actual names, actual events—and I felt absolutely nothing," she said. Neither did anybody else. In fact, the whole thing is a yawn.

Rival gossip Louella Parsons had included a complimentary item in her column when *Beloved Infidel* was bought by Twentieth Century Fox, calling Graham "brave and courageous" for telling her story. "I know I would not have been as generous to her," Graham said. Indeed Hedda Hopper now took the opportunity to spread a mean-spirited and false rumor, claiming that Gregory Peck " would not allow her on set."

Graham could take the nasty dig from Hedda, but the movie was a major disappointment to her. By the 1960s, she was calling it "a complete disaster." She may have started the project with dollar signs in her eyes, but as it progressed she saw the book as a tribute to Scott Fitzgerald. *Beloved Infidel* was her own powerful story as well, and it hurt to see herself reduced in the film to nothing more than a mistress and nurse to a famous author. "I had but one life to give to my producer, and Jerry Wald ruined it," she said.

Graham learned what *Peyton Place* author Grace Metalious had just a year before. "When you have sold your story to a motion picture company, you have sold your soul to the devil," Graham wrote later. "They can change your name, the title, the story, they can make you fictitious, they can make you real, they can cut anything they like, add anything they like, they can sell you to television, they can sell you down the river. All they cannot do, according to the contract, is hold you up to public ridicule and scorn."

Graham hated the publicity for *Beloved Infidel* more than the movie. Print ads in *Life* magazine showed Gregory Peck and Deborah Kerr kneeling on the sands of Malibu with a banner above: "The Unsweetened Sins of Scott Fitzgerald and Sheilah Graham." Another featured a line from "Beloved Infidel," the poem Fitzgerald had written for Graham. Below the words "Let Every Lover Be the Last . . . ," Deborah Kerr cried in Peck's arms. Kerr wears a bathing suit, a not so subtle allusion to the movie that made her a star, *From Here to Eternity*.

Graham was furious, knowing the sensational ads were an attempt to compensate for the lackluster quality of the film. She thought they gave a wrong impression of the movie—and of her. It is a testament to her power as a columnist, and maybe to the power of a threatened lawsuit, that Fox stopped running the ads.

Perhaps Graham felt so disillusioned because she wrote about the movie industry and thought she understood it. As a columnist, she often wielded more influence than the average contract actor. She had grown accustomed to independence and control, too, and didn't expect to be shut out of the movie's creation. After all, Graham was a woman who had always shaped her own destiny.

Although she had adapted better to the 1950s than her elder compatriots in deep-dish gossip, Graham still could sense that the party was drawing to a close, for her and the rest of old Hollywood. She was prescient about the end of the studio system and the rise of television. As early as November 1953, she predicted in her column that "within five years most of the top movie stars will be freelancing." She cataloged the stars who planned to retire completely or leave the studio that year, including Deborah Kerr, Van Johnson, and Betty Grable. She blamed television for the "bloodless revolution." A month later, she observed another "sign of the times," that people hawking guides to the stars' homes on Sunset Boulevard had changed their strategy. They now offered "guides to your favorite movie *and TV* stars' homes."

By 1959 Graham had been in Hollywood for more than twenty years. *Beloved Infidel* had proved to be a bitter disappointment. It had not improved her image or career. It had not restored the literary reputation of F. Scott Fitzgerald either.

In the fall of that year, his alma mater Princeton University cruelly caricatured him. During the halftime show of the football game with Yale, the Princeton marching band played "Roll Out the Barrel" and danced about in mock drunkenness as a tribute to "Princeton's gift to literature, F. Scott Fitzgerald." The alumni weekly was one of the few voices of indignation, writing, "The mind boggles at the inane spectacle of publicly vilifying the memory of a Princeton alumnus—almost literally dancing on his grave—and especially of one so pathetically devoted to Princeton." But the damage was done. Sheilah Graham had been in the stands that afternoon. She had just presented the president with a parcel of Fitzgerald manuscripts that morning.

Graham had grown tired of Hollywood, tired of the endless charades and the phony fishbowl way of life. "Hollywood is no longer a place, it's a condition," she said. With the profits from *Beloved Infidel*, she moved back east to be closer to her children, who were in school there. She would write her column from New York with the help of a "leg man" in Los Angeles.

She would find her way west again, eventually. She had tapped into a growing feeling about Hollywood, though. It was not what it used to be. The film industry had changed. Movies often were made not in Hollywood but in exotic locations around the world. Sheilah Graham would follow the movies to London, Rome, Paris, Athens, and Madrid. Many stars had already moved to Switzerland or other European countries. She began to notice more stars on the Via Veneto in Rome than on Hollywood Boulevard, and she observed that London's soundstages were so full of American productions that the British had to make their films in the south of France and Yugoslavia. "Hollywood was no longer the movie capital of the world," Graham wrote. "With a hundred series grinding out in every studio and at NBC, CBS and ABC, it was now the television center of the world."

CHAPTER 15

THE DARK AT THE TOP OF THE STAIRS: WILLIAM INGE'S AMERICAN DREAMS

PLAYWRIGHT WILLIAM INGE was hiding out in a hotel room in Wilmington, Delaware, on January 26, 1950. His first production, *Come Back, Little Sheba*, was set to open there that night. He was anxious and agitated. Part of the play's budget had been spent on a private psychiatric clinic where Inge had sought treatment for alcoholism, and he was still taking Antabuse, a drug that would make him violently sick if he touched a drop of liquor. The Theatre Guild had backed the play and one of its assistants was keeping a close eye on Inge, knowing the stress could be too much for him. The assistant took all of Inge's clothes to the dry cleaner's, forcing him to stay in his room wearing a robe and slippers. The hotel was instructed not to send up anything from room service, no matter how often he called.

The plan worked. Inge stayed sober and attended the opening of his play, witnessed the audience's warm response. It was a hit in Wilmington and then in Boston. When it opened on Broadway on February 15, 1950, it quickly became "the play to see." It ran for 190 performances. The stars of the show, Shirley Booth and Sidney Blackmer, would win Tony Awards. The movie rights to *Come Back, Little Sheba* would net $150,000 for Inge. The play was his last shot at a different kind of life, and unbelievably, it succeeded. The former drama teacher and newspaper writer from Kansas was seeing his dreams realized. He moved to Manhattan's Central Park West, taking an apartment on a low floor of the famous Dakota because he feared heights.

That night in Wilmington ushered in a decade of success for Inge. Today, inexplicably, he is nearly forgotten. But by the end of the 1950s three of his long-running Broadway plays—*Come Back, Little Sheba*, *Bus Stop*, and *Picnic*—were made into profitable and interesting movies. *Picnic* won the 1953 Pulitzer Prize. Critics compared his work to that of other great American artists such as Walt Whitman, Sherwood Anderson, Theodore Dreiser, and Edward Hopper. In less than ten years, his plays and sales to the movies would earn him more than $1 million, enough to start a modern art collection of de Koonings, Pollocks, and Modiglianis.

But as Inge said later, "I think a lot of writers are depressed with success." In Inge's case, it would be more accurate to say that he was depressed with everything. "People with emotional problems are just as unable to cope with good news as with bad," he said. "It's not the nature of the experience—it's that they can't handle any emotional experience, good or bad."

It is ironic that the creator of such tender and poignant works as *Come Back, Little Sheba* and later *Splendor in the Grass* could not bear his own emotions. Yet perhaps this is why each story is so suffused with longing. Inge's characters often have a keen and schizophrenic yearning both to escape the confines of their small-town existence and to be accepted and loved within the confining bonds of marriage and family. Sex, and its accompanying trauma, is also a major motif in his work. America in the 1950s thus could not have been a more perfect arena for his tales of the tug-of-war between expression and repression, between sex and chastity.

Like all great artists, William Motter Inge came by his themes, and his neuroses, naturally. He was born in Independence, Kansas, the youngest of Luther and Maude Inge's four children. Luther was a traveling dry-goods salesman, leaving his wife behind to serve as the sole parent for long stretches at a time. In his autobiographical novel *My Son Is a Splendid Driver*, Inge described his household as a kind of "nervous matriarchy," a situation that worsened when his older brother died. "I felt guilty if I had a cold—because it upset her," Inge said later, after years of psychoanalysis. ". . . She [his mother] sapped my physical adventurousness and I felt held down."

Before he even understood it, sex was also a thorny issue for Inge. He could sense the tension between his parents but didn't know the cause. He would later learn that his father occasionally strayed while on the road and that his mother came to resent her husband's advances. When he was an adult, Inge's mother told him about her wedding night. She had been so frightened and disgusted by what happened that she fled to her parents' house the next day, begging to come home.

Sex became a greater source of confusion and anxiety when "Billy" Inge went off to college at Kansas University in the fall of 1930. *My Son Is a Splendid Driver*, considered to be mostly accurate about his formative years, details one of his first sexual experiences, a crude "gang bang" in the basement of the Sigma Nu fraternity house. He feared that his masculinity would be questioned if he did not participate but was repulsed by the spectacle and his role in it. Inge's novel described his first vague homosexual experience as well. As a freshman, he had to share a bed with his roommate in the fraternity house. On more than one occasion, he woke up in the arms of this boy, who pretended he was just "dreaming." The incidents, though, confirmed what Inge had always suspected.

College also gave Inge his first opportunity to act. He studied the plays of Shakespeare, Molière, O'Casey, and Shaw, a background that informed Inge's own work, although critics would later argue it contributed to his "mastery of convention." He wanted to pursue a career in acting, but doubted his ability. He chose instead to seek a master's degree in English and become a teacher, first at a high school and then at an exclusive women's college in Columbia, Missouri. But he regretted his decision almost immediately. Frustrated teachers would later populate his plays, like Rosemary in *Picnic*, who begs Howard to marry her. "Each year, I keep tellin' myself, is the last. Something'll happen. Then nothing ever does—except I get a little crazier all the time," she says.

Dissatisfied with his job, Inge suffered from restlessness and depression, along with worsening insomnia. A doctor suggested Inge try having a cocktail before dinner and a beer before bed. It was a prescription all too easy for him to follow, and he drank alone more and more often in the late 1930s and early 1940s. Inge also started taking the bus into Kansas City on the weekends. He'd make the 150-mile trip to see his psychiatrist, and the long bus rides gave his imagination room to roam. He had begun to write tentatively around this time, and his observations would later lead to the plot for his play *Bus Stop*.

Kansas City also offered Inge anonymity. He could visit gay bars or have brief affairs without anyone at his college discovering his secret. Inge was no libertine, though. For the whole of his life, he remained tormented by his homosexuality. And while his work was often critical of the way relationships can breed dependency, his plays also glorify the "normalcy" of the heterosexual couple and often seem like valentines to a way of life he himself could not have.

Despite his personal demons, Inge moved slowly but steadily toward his dream of writing professionally, finally leaving his professorship in the spring of 1943 to become a drama critic at the *St. Louis Star-Times*. It was writing criticism that ultimately emboldened Inge to craft his own plays. As he watched some mediocre new stage production, he began to think he could do better.

A meeting with playwright Tennessee Williams inspired him further. In November of 1944, Inge interviewed Williams about his new play *The Glass Menagerie*, which was about to begin a pre-Broadway run in Chicago. The two felt an immediate connection, and some Williams biographers have said the two later had a brief sexual affair, although Inge never confirmed this.

That New Year's Eve, Inge traveled to Chicago to see the premier of *Menagerie*. Seeing Williams's drama, rife with family issues and sexual tensions, spurred Inge to write about his own life. He saw how Williams had taken the raw material of his youth and family and turned it into drama. "I always tried to write like Noël Coward, with each attempt an embarrassing failure. Now I knew where to look for a play—inside myself," Inge later wrote in his journal.

Inge wrote his first real play in three months in 1945. He called it *Farther Off from Heaven*, but would later change it to *The Dark at the Top of the Stairs*. The play told the story of an overbearing mother, an absent salesman father, and their children, a shy daughter and an

Playwright William Inge's *Come Back, Little Sheba, Picnic,* and *Bus Stop* were all made into successful movies in the 1950s. But his dramas about small-town America fell out of favor in the late 1960s. *Photofest.*

effeminate son. Inge's new friend Tennessee Williams liked *Farther Off from Heaven* and sent it to his agent, Audrey Wood, who promptly rejected it.

But the genie was out of the bottle. Inge wanted desperately to be a playwright. He was encouraged when a regional theater producer in Texas, a friend of Tennessee Williams, wanted to stage *Farther Off from Heaven*. Months later, in February 1948, his new play *Front Porch*, later titled *Picnic*, was produced in St. Louis. It filled all one hundred seats of the Toy Theatre each night of its two-week run.

Success seemed to draw close and then recede. One moment Inge would feel buoyed by the local enthusiasm for his work, and then the next he would feel depressed by Audrey Wood's rejection of him. He had lost his job as a theater critic and was miserable teaching college again. He often drank a fifth of whiskey in one day. By Easter of 1948, Inge realized he had a drinking problem and began attending Alcoholics Anonymous meetings.

Inge's struggle with alcoholism would inform the play he wrote that summer. Inspired by his eccentric aunt, *Come Back, Little Sheba* tells the story of Lola and Doc, a childless middle-aged couple who take in a boarder, just as Inge's parents did when he was growing up. At first, the presence of the young female college student brings a new energy to the house, but soon it stirs up all the old hurts of Lola and Doc's marriage. Marie is the age of the daughter they might have had, the child Lola was carrying when she "had to" marry Doc, the child she later lost in a miscarriage. The girl is also a college student, reminding Doc of how he had to drop out of school to support Lola, becoming a chiropractor instead of "a real M.D."

And as in most Inge plays, there is the undercurrent of sex and its sorrows. Doc becomes increasingly disturbed when he catches Marie making out with her boyfriends in his living room. A queer mix of jealousy and fatherly concern threatens his newfound sobriety. One night he discovers that Marie and her boyfriend have been alone in her bedroom. Tormented, he takes the lone bottle of whiskey kept "for company" out of the house, smuggled in his coat. He comes home raving drunk, sparking a violent battle with his wife in which he threatens Lola with an ax (a knife in the movie). The bender lands Doc in the city hospital to dry out. Long-suffering Lola takes him back, Marie moves out to get married, and peace is restored.

"I was kind of spellbound while I wrote this play. I couldn't believe I'd done it. Here I'd written a really good play," Inge said. "And it moved me deeply." He told a friend, "I have written my heart out." Tennessee Williams loved the play, and so did Williams's agent, Audrey Wood, who took Inge on as a client.

Come Back, Little Sheba reached the screen in 1952 with Daniel Mann from the Broadway production directing and Shirley Booth as Lola. Burt Lancaster plays the brooding, taciturn Doc, struggling to "work the twelve steps" to sobriety. Chosen purely for box office appeal, he seems a bit too young for the part. (He was thirty-eight.) One reviewer complained that "in the simple matter of age he is quite wrong, and the heavy lines of make-up and the whitened hair do not convince." But Lancaster does give a convincing portrayal of sexual confusion. One scene has Doc, alone in the bathroom, smelling Marie's lilac bath salts. He closes his eyes and nearly swoons.

Lancaster uses his big, athletic body to dramatic effect as well. Usually the star of films that called for him to flex his muscles more than to demonstrate emotional sensitivity, Lancaster had urged director Daniel Mann to cast him for his very strength. Doc, to Lancaster, was not essentially weak, but instead smothered by Lola's neediness. Lancaster literally towered over Booth, and when he explodes during his violent scene with Lola, he is so physically threatening that he becomes believably murderous. His clenched jaw makes his words into body blows. "You fat slut," he shouts at Lola, coming at her with a knife and then strangling her. ". . . I'm gonna fix you."

Variety praised Lancaster's performance, saying he did a "fine job" and that he had an "unsuspected talent." The *New York Times* also saw a new and surprising seriousness in him. "The excellence of Mr. Lancaster as the frustrated inarticulate spouse, weak-willed and sweetly passive, should not be overlooked," Bosley Crowther wrote.

Shirley Booth is clearly the film's star, though. Best known for her later role as TV's "Hazel," she was described by one movie magazine as "probably the most unactressy actress who ever lived." Booth was forty-five when she made her film debut in *Sheba*. Although she had brought many characters to life in Broadway plays such as *The Philadelphia Story*, she was usually passed over when those plays reached the screen because of her plain looks. "I became convinced pictures would never play any part in my career. Hollywood obviously wasn't interested in me," Booth said. "I decided to face that fact, and dismiss any hopes I had ever had along those lines."

Producer Hal Wallis offered her a screen test for the role, and it soon became clear that no one but Booth could play the lonely housewife who pines for her lost dog, Sheba. With every gesture and intonation, she gets the nervous, disheveled, lonely Lola exactly right. Her nasally voice is appropriately childlike and grating when she calls her husband "Daddy." She is a woman caught between hope and dread, between a vision of her life she desperately needs to believe and the reality she faces every day. "You didn't know I was gonna get old and fat and sloppy. . . . I didn't know it either, Doc," she says, her eyes wide, as if she knows she's pathetic but can't stop herself from saying the words. "Are you sorry you had to marry me?"

Director of photography James Wong Howe skillfully shot one scene as if from inside the darkened kitchen cabinet where the whiskey is kept. The door swings out, opened by Lola, and we see her staring up at the emptiness where the bottle should be. Her lips start to tremble slightly as she realizes that Doc has taken it. The look of pure panic on her face wordlessly tells the audience that a terrible crisis is coming.

In a Paramount press release promoting *Sheba,* Shirley Booth candidly described the difference between stage acting and film work:

> The camera, I've found, is no respecter of footlights or privacy. It goes anywhere. And where it goes, it tattles. I can't hide a thing from it. It's frightening. It's ghastly. It's awful in its privacy-destroying prying. It's the most shattering experience of my life. I hope I live through it.

Booth not only survived the role, she shone. After the film performance that the *New York Times* called "skillful and knowing," she was nominated for an Academy Award. William Inge himself loved Booth's performance in *Sheba.* He told the *Hollywood Citizen-News* that he thought she had the "the most expressive and sensitive camera face since Garbo." He was especially moved by the scene in which Lola and Doc are talking about their lost dog as they lie beside each other, in separate twin beds. Doc says of Sheba, "Some things should never grow old," and then the camera captures a close-up of Booth. "We see the wistful expression of melancholy and immediately we have a feeling for Lola's unrealized youth and her present emotional immaturity," Inge said. ". . . The close-up was a little shocking to me, the author of the play, for I saw an insight which I had worked industriously to develop gotten very easily in another way."

Like Lola herself, though, Booth would not experience an unadulterated moment of happiness at what was the pinnacle of her career. When her name was called during the Oscar telecast, Booth started up the stairway to the stage. Her bluish-pink Valentina dress had been cut especially so she wouldn't stumble. But she tripped on the full skirt anyway and fell. To her credit, she quickly gathered herself and accepted the statuette for best actress. *Time* magazine, which put Shirley Booth on its cover on August 10, 1953, couldn't help noting the Oscar incident and the similarity between Booth's own life and Lola's. ". . . Childless in two marriages, Shirley has filled her life with pets, naming most of them after roles and phrases from her plays."

In addition to providing Booth with her Academy Award, *Sheba* won best picture honors at the Cannes Film Festival. The film had been profitable for Inge as well. After his initial fee, he also earned a share of the profits, which must have been sizable since it brought in a reported $3.5 million at the box office.

Sheba's success sparked a flood of interest in Inge's work and in the playwright himself. He found the attention difficult to bear, afraid that the secret of his homosexuality would be revealed. Inge carefully chose which invitations to parties or other gatherings he would accept, and when he did attend, he often left after a few minutes. The strain of meeting social obligations also made it harder for Inge to maintain his sobriety, as it was embarrassing to explain why he wanted ginger ale rather than a martini, or why he did not drink wine with dinner. On occasion, he still sought treatment from the private sanitarium in Greenwich, Connecticut, that had enabled him to stay sober enough to witness *Sheba*'s first stage performances.

Inge was surprised and confused by how little fulfillment his new success brought him. No one understood the odd disappointment of his answered prayers. When he mentioned he was still undergoing psychoanalysis, his friends were baffled. They wondered why he needed it now that he had finally reached his goals. Inge felt as if even old acquaintances from Kansas, who began to pepper him with requests for complimentary show tickets, were more thrilled to know a real Broadway playwright than he was to be one. For Inge, already shy and withdrawn, success only isolated him further.

He felt immediate pressure to top himself as well, and set about crafting a new play. While *Sheba* was dark and disturbing, a look into "a gloomy household," Inge wanted next to write "a play that took place in the sunshine." The result was *Front Porch*. Revised from an earlier Inge work, it tells the story of a drifter and the agitation he causes among a group of small-town women.

Lawrence Langner of the Theatre Guild, who had helped stage *Sheba*, read Inge's new work and liked the idea of it, but felt the play was too sprawling, too long, and too complicated. He felt, in essence, that Inge was trying too hard for a sophomore success. Still, he thought that in the right hands, the new work could sing, so he suggested Josh Logan, who had directed such Broadway hits as *South Pacific* and *Annie Get Your Gun*, as the director. Inge approached Logan, telling him that there was something "sunny" about his work and that Inge wanted "some sun" on the new play.

Logan thought *Front Porch* had moments of tenderness and beauty, but that it lacked structure and needed a more upbeat conclusion. He wanted a new title, too, since his suggestions for changes eliminated the setting that gave the play its name. Inge agreed to retitle the play *Picnic*, but he fought Logan on drastically changing the ending. Inge had the drifter Hal leave town after seducing Madge, the local beauty queen. Logan knew the audience wanted a happy ending and urged him to write one, but Inge didn't want to be "corny." He insisted that having Madge live on in her small town after being "besmirched" was more realistic. Each time Inge would bring a new ending to the director, Logan recalled, it was "the same one, only drearier." "He was afraid of being slick, of pandering to the public with a 'happy ending,' so he kept writing this endlessly slow dimout," Logan said.

Inge finally yielded when audiences at out-of-town previews didn't respond to what Logan called the negative ending's "Chekhovian inconclusiveness." The director finally persuaded Inge to have Madge run away with Hal. "She'd obviously end up where her mother is, deserted by her man, saddled with brats and destitute," Logan said. "Is that happy? Is that corny?"

Picnic debuted on Broadway in February of 1953. It would run for 477 performances with enthusiastic praise from critics like Brooks Atkinson of the *New York Times*. Inge had "a knowledge of people and an instinct for the truth of the world they live in," Atkinson wrote. "The promise of *Come Back, Little Sheba* is abundantly fulfilled." Hollywood came calling after *Picnic* won the Pulitzer that year, and he sold it to Columbia Pictures for a reported $350,000.

Inge was still plagued by depression, though. It stung that his most successful play resulted from changes he had made only reluctantly. He struggled with phobias, too, fearing high places, crowded subways, and eating in public at restaurants. He couldn't write if anyone else were in his Dakota apartment. He also had unresolved issues with his parents, who were too old and ill to see any of his New York plays. In three years, he tried to visit his parents three times. Twice he turned back when the train reached Chicago. He made it the third time, but could bear to stay only twenty-four hours. When his father died in 1954, Inge did not attend the funeral.

He had misgivings about Columbia's 1955 film production of *Picnic* as well, especially since Josh Logan would again direct. And despite its filming at several locations in Kansas, using local residents as extras, Inge would not visit the set. But he should not have fretted so about the fate of his work. Even though every scene from the first drafts of *Front Porch* did not survive, the resulting film version of *Picnic* still has all of Inge's essential themes, the nostalgia and yearning that make his work so powerful. The film won two Academy Awards, for color art direction and set decoration, and garnered several more Oscar nominations, including one for best picture and one for best director.

Picnic also made Kim Novak, the former "Miss Deep Freeze" appliance model, a star. Rumors have long circulated that Columbia chief Cohn forced Logan to accept Novak in the role of Madge. But Logan only objected to Novak's close-cropped, lavender-tinged hair, preferring instead that she wear a long auburn wig. Cohn did fight Logan on this briefly, saying her hairdo would allow the studio to market her to the audience as the new "It" girl, the "lavender blonde." Logan argued not only that William Inge would have a heart attack if his character had purplish hair, but that with the wig, Novak looked closer to "the girl on the cover of a candy box" that Madge should be.

Logan sensed that Kim Novak understood Madge, too. Like the two sisters in *Picnic*, Kim had been known as "the pretty one" in her family, while her sister was known as "the smart one." Logan had a feeling that "Kim had actually been living inside Madge all her life." Indeed Novak radiates a kind of melancholic ambivalence in *Picnic*, and it is this and not her comely face alone that lends authenticity to her portrayal of Madge. Bored by her small town and her reign as its beauty queen, Madge is full of longing and loneliness, in spite of all the attention from the richest boys in town.

But Novak could also smolder onscreen. The sultry slow dance between Madge and Hal at the Labor Day picnic is still one of the sexiest film moments ever. Inge wrote the scene to be taut with anticipation, since the characters never touch each other until the first bars of "Moonglow" begin to play. William Holden seems a bit too old for the part in most of the film, but in this scene his sinewy body and slightly weathered face complement most pleasingly the young and dewy Kim Novak.

Rosalind Russell gives a wonderful performance as the boozy, pent-up old maid desperate to hook a husband. Not only is the story of her search for love a moving subplot of the film, but the role was a godsend to Russell, who by 1955 was struggling to find good parts. She was so eager to play Rosemary that she told director Josh Logan not to soften her wrinkles with makeup or camera tricks. "I want to look like a real leathery Kansas dame," she said.

Susan Strasberg is also charming and real as the nosy little sister, half in awe of and half appalled by the beautiful and distant Madge. The daughter of famed acting coaches Lee and Paula Strasberg, she was just sixteen years old when she played Millie.

Beyond its bittersweet story, though, *Picnic* is a beautifully photographed film. James Wong Howe, who also shot *Come Back, Little Sheba,* lovingly records in color the lonely grain elevators and waving wheat of the flat Middle West. The actual Labor Day picnic scenes are also lushly filmed, with red-faced crying babies and people eating watermelon. The nighttime scenes are particularly ethereal. Tiny lights twinkle on the water as a swan boat carries Madge, the newly crowned Queen of Neewollah, to her crowd of admirers. (Neewollah is Halloween spelled backward, and refers to a local Kansas ceremony Bill Inge remembered from childhood.) Hal and Madge's dance scene is also lovely, with pastel Japanese lanterns glowing above their slowly swaying forms.

But the happy ending still bothered Inge, and would haunt him for years. He changed the final scenes of *Picnic* hundreds of times, eventually bringing a rewritten, retitled version to the stage in the 1970s. As Josh Logan had predicted, though, no one liked the decidedly unhappy denouement and *Summer Brave* was a failure on Broadway. In Logan's memoirs, published three years after Inge's death, he still sounded bitter about the wrangling over *Picnic*. "[Inge] accepted graciously as sole author the Critic's Award and the Pulitzer Prize, the huge movie sale and the worldwide success of the movie itself, and yet he would not give up until he had announced—with his finger pointed at me—how foolish the world was to like this golden play," Logan wrote.

In 1955, as *Picnic* was being released in movie theaters, Inge brought his new play *Bus Stop* to the stage. A romantic comedy, it tells the story of a no-talent, down-on-her-luck nightclub singer and a cowboy who falls in love with her at first sight. Again, audiences and critics loved it. It ran on Broadway for 478 performances. Writing in the *New York Herald-Tribune*, Walter Kerr said Inge had written "the best play we've had all season." And Brooks Atkinson of the *New York Times* said, "Having written a wonderful play two years ago, William Inge has written a better one. The performance is glorious." Twentieth Century Fox bought the screen rights and turned it into a smash hit, with Marilyn Monroe as the nightclub singer Cherie and a newcomer named Don Murray as "Beau" Decker, the cowboy.

Monroe had just renegotiated her contract with Fox for more money and more control over her projects. She reduced the number of films she had to make for the company from fourteen in seven years to just four. She earned the right to approve the director for her films as well, along with a cameraman. The new contract also allowed her to work on films outside of Fox, making it possible for her to establish her own company, Marilyn Monroe Productions.

Bus Stop was the first film Monroe made under the new contract. While excited to be taking on a role from a well-received Broadway play, she felt immense pressure to live up to the new terms she had negotiated and prove her worth. She had just taken up Method acting as well, studying at the Actors Studio. The media had jeered her decision with headlines around Hollywood asking "Will Acting Spoil Marilyn Monroe?" She was anxious to show what a serious actress she was.

But *Bus Stop* may not have offered her the best vehicle. Released in August 1956, the film was not as critically acclaimed as *Picnic*, despite direction from Josh Logan and a script by George Axelrod. Unlike

Marilyn Monroe offers a twangy version of "That Old Black Magic" in *Bus Stop*. She was thrilled to be in a film based on a serious play by William Inge, with whom she struck up a warm friendship. *Courtesy of the authors.*

Come Back, Little Sheba and other early Inge works, it has no deeper, universal themes to save it. It is not funny or moving. Marilyn Monroe has a ridiculously bad southern accent as Cherie. She spends most of the movie in a hideous teal green costume that looks like a cross between a mermaid and a peacock. While the costume helped illustrate Cherie's threadbare existence, Monroe is still showing more skin than substance.

And the one scene Monroe was truly proud of was cut from the film. In it, everyone but Cherie and another woman has fallen asleep on the bus late at night. Cherie confides in the woman about her past, her dreams for the future, what she wants in a man. Monroe had always struggled to memorize long passages of dialogue, and it took two days of intense shooting, with Logan coaxing all the way, to complete the scene. When she finished, though, Monroe felt she had finally performed well in a long, serious soliloquy. Logan, too, was thrilled. He fought to keep the speech in the film but executives at Fox overruled him, saying it didn't advance the plot. Monroe was furious and hurt when she learned *Bus Stop* would be released without the scene. She never forgave Logan, who she believed had betrayed her, and had never really believed in her talent.

Bus Stop also lacks any real chemistry between Monroe and her costar Don Murray. She reportedly was miffed that he paid more attention to supporting actress Hope Lange than her. (He'd later marry Lange.) But Murray's onscreen performance didn't inspire anyone, either. He talks in an unbelievable hayseed drawl and he can't seem to say a line—he must shout it. Oddly, Logan wanted Murray to yell because he thought it helped characterize Beau as wild and untamed. But the effect is less cowboy than rodeo clown, so exaggerated are his mannerisms.

Still, Murray must be given some credit. *Bus Stop* was his first film and he eagerly accepted the role, even if it meant risking humiliation. He was tall and lean, appearing too skinny on film to be a strapping cowboy, so the wardrobe department outfitted him with extra sweatshirts under his oversize shirts to add bulk to his frame. And Murray gamely offered to ride a horse in a real parade on only ten minutes' notice (and with some goading from Marilyn Monroe). He had never sat on a horse before, but he had the presence of mind to wave to Marilyn and the camera captured the whole thing in one take.

Edward G. Robinson Jr. also had a cameo in *Bus Stop*. His father asked director Josh Logan to consider his son Manny for the film. Logan had directed Robinson in the play *Middle of the Night* and had learned of Manny's troubled adolescence and young adulthood. Manny, then twenty-three, had always wanted to act. Although he was only in one brief scene at the café where Cherie sings, he took it seriously. "I think I had exactly one line in the finished film. But I got $750—my top movie price—for one week's work," Manny remembered. "Just the idea of getting up early in the morning, slapping the make-up on, and getting to the set on time for all that make-believe made me feel alive."

Like *Picnic*, *Bus Stop* has some interesting crowd scenes. Logan, it seems, enjoyed the "cast of thousands" shot. In *Bus Stop*, he used the real parades and hoopla staged for the annual Junior Chamber of Commerce Rodeo in Phoenix, Arizona. One scene has Cherie becoming confused and running right through the arena while Beau wrestles a steer to the ground. Filmed during the ten-minute intermission in the rodeo, the stands are full of genuine fans with sun-seared faces and cowboy hats who whoop and shout in character.

But the story of *Bus Stop* has not aged well and now seems quite dated and sexist. Heading for the rodeo, Beau the cowboy says he's going to "find me an angel" and when he does he'll get those "little ol' wings pinned right to the ground." When he spots his "angel" in line to board a bus, he literally lassoes her with his rope and puts her over his shoulder. He essentially kidnaps her, carrying her onto the bus he's taking back to Montana.

Later he apologizes, explaining that he's never had a girlfriend and doesn't know how to treat one. She, in turn, pours out her heart to him, explaining that she's had boyfriends in the past, "quite a few." He tells her that doesn't matter, he likes her just the same.

This scene may be the only redeeming thing about *Bus Stop*, if only for the wonderful close-up of Marilyn and her pale, tear-stained face. Logan remembered the difficulty of capturing the moment on film. Because it was shot in Cinemascope, the gimmicky, wide-screen technique created to demonstrate the superiority of movies over television, getting a close-up was difficult. Actors' faces could become distorted on film if they were less than five feet away from the camera lens. The director talked the camera crew into using several "diminishing" lenses so they could get closer to Marilyn without marring the image. And her pallor, while enhanced with make-up, comes across as convincingly as her emotions because she was fighting bronchitis during two weeks of shooting.

Although Inge did not write the screenplay of *Bus Stop*, he did help with some advance publicity for the film. He also struck up a friendship with Marilyn Monroe, who was drawn to Inge's intelligence and creativity. The fact that he was not interested in her sexually also seemed to give their relationship a kind of tenderness it might have lacked otherwise. Inge and Monroe would occasionally be linked in the media during the mid-1950s, but their interest in each other was purely platonic.

THE BACK-TO-BACK film successes of *Picnic* and *Bus Stop* made any William Inge work a coveted commodity in Hollywood and on Broadway. Again, he felt increased pressure to top himself. But, miraculously, he managed to do it with a rewritten version of his very first play, *Farther Off from Heaven*. Now titled *The Dark at the Top of the Stairs*, the play, directed by Elia Kazan, debuted on December 5, 1957.

New York Times critic Brooks Atkinson called it Inge's finest play, while Walter Kerr of the *New York Herald Tribune* described it as "wonderfully evocative." But the praise was not as universal as it had been for his earlier works. Wolcott Gibbs of *The New Yorker* disliked the episodic nature of the play and thought there were "too many abrupt shiftings from folk comedy to quite another mood," while Patrick Dennis of the *New Republic* thought it a "literate soap opera." Audiences didn't seem to mind, though.

"The play was a hit and I sold the screen rights to Warner Brothers for a film," Inge's agent Audrey Wood recalled. "But after that, Bill's career began to move in another direction, steadily away from success."

His friendship with Tennessee Williams also came to an end around this time. The professional rivalry between them had grown too great to sustain a relationship. The huge success of the play *Picnic* had come just before Williams's failed *Camino Real*. The final breach came in 1957 when Williams's *Orpheus Descending* opened in March and ran for eight weeks, while Inge's *The Dark at the Top of the Stairs* ran for 468 performances.

Another personal blow to Inge was the professional criticism he got in a *Harper's* article by critic Robert Brustein entitled "The Men-Taming Women of William Inge." The article, which appeared in August 1958, was harsh. "Considering the modesty—one is tempted to say the mediocrity—of his work, it is clear that the excitement over

Inge has been inspired by something other than the intrinsic value of his plays," Brustein wrote. He suggested that the plays succeeded because they glorified the noble blandness of Midwesterners and "endowed the commonplace with some depth."

Brustein went on to say that Inge's plays had "practically no action" and were "preachy" endorsements of a family life in which females ultimately dominated their once threatening men. The critic called *Bus Stop* "a vulgar folk vaudeville" (which is rather accurate) and thoroughly trashed *The Dark at the Top of the Stairs*, especially Kazan's direction:

> What with all the nut-cracking, chicken-eating, behind-patting, jewelry-fingering, and yawning that went on, [Inge's] characters were rarely empty-handed or empty-mouthed—and in a play almost devoid of climaxes we were served a climax every five minutes. . . . *Dark* drones on like a Midwestern cricket, making no powerful statement, displaying no moving action, uttering no memorable dialogue.

The *Harper's* cover story was far from adulatory, but Inge overreacted. He called Brustein and cried. Inge's assistant said the story marked "the beginning of the end" for the playwright, who ventured out less and less from his new Sutton Place apartment. Self-doubt corroded his creativity just as he set about writing a new play, *A Loss of Roses*, and an original screenplay that would become *Splendor in the Grass*.

A Loss of Roses essentially is two stories. One involves the tension in the Oedipal relationship between a widow and her twenty-one-year-old son. The other story involves the emotional downfall of an aging actress named Lila Green who comes to stay with the widow and her son. While Inge had always successfully woven various thematic threads together before, the new play seemed to lack focus.

Audrey Wood recognized the play's problems and urged him to kill the production before it debuted in the fall of 1959. But Inge insisted. It played for only twenty-five performances. The *Times*'s Brooks Atkinson, who had always lavished praise on Inge, called *Roses* "dull." A few months later, *Theatre Arts* magazine would run a long story about it entitled "Anatomy of a Failure."

Inge fled for the West Coast in the early 1960s. In New York, he was the author of a recent Broadway flop, but in Hollywood, he was a genius whose plays had spawned three major hit films. His adapted screen version of *The Dark at the Top of the Stairs* was a success in 1960, and he followed it with *Splendor in the Grass* in 1961. Written for producer/director Elia Kazan, *Splendor in the Grass* gave Warren Beatty his film debut and offered Natalie Wood one of her favorite, serious roles. She even named her yacht, from which she later slipped and drowned, the *Splendour*. The film won an Academy Award as well, bolstering Inge's self-esteem when he desperately needed it.

He returned immediately to the theater with a play called *Natural Affection*, but the 1950s were over and so was his long run of dramatic success. Critics savaged the play, including Edith Oliver of *The New Yorker*, who called Inge "a junior-varsity Tennessee Williams." When the play closed after just thirty-six performances, Inge decided to leave New York for good. He sold his apartment on Sutton Place and bought a house in the Hollywood Hills on Oriole Drive, in the "bird streets" over Sunset Boulevard that were so popular with stars like Rock Hudson.

He taught intermittently at the University of California's Irvine campus and wrote a few screenplays for lackluster films. But by 1970 he was spending whole days alone in his bedroom. Audrey Wood remembered a visit to see him. "I was shocked at what I saw," she said. "Bill had fallen off the wagon again and the alcohol had caused him to become grossly fat."

His autobiographical novel *My Son Is a Splendid Driver* was published in 1971. It sold 7,792 copies. Inge's despair worsened and his sister Helene became like a nurse to him. It all reached a sad conclusion on June 10, 1973, when William Inge went out to the garage of his house. He did not open the door. He sat in his Mercedes-Benz and turned on the engine. His sister found him dead in the morning.

On the day of his death, the manuscript of a new novel he had finished, *The Boy from the Circus*, was found in the living room of his house. It had just been rejected by a New York publisher.

CHAPTER 16

THE WAXWORKS: MAE WEST, GLORIA SWANSON, AND *SUNSET BOULEVARD*

HOLLYWOOD HAS never been kind to older actresses. They often found themselves pushed to the edges of the frame, playing the matron long before retirement age—if they worked at all. No longer starlets but not ready for the rest home, veteran actresses had to tread carefully. New ventures—in Las Vegas, on Broadway, even an unusual role in a film—could backfire. And, like Mae West and Gloria Swanson in the 1950s, they could find themselves not only fighting age discrimination but stereotypes they themselves helped to create, personas that had become frozen in time.

By the 1950s, Mae West had shimmied and swayed her way through five decades, scandalizing America with her double entendres and racy plays. She wasn't about to stop, either, even if she wasn't in the movies anymore. The aged Mae could be a somewhat disturbing sight. One writer recalled how Madame Tussaud's immortalized her in wax after the 1950 revival of her play *Diamond Lil*. "By the mid-1950s, however, Mae began to seem something of a wax figurine herself—to everyone but Mae," he wrote.

Mae West, in essence, simply refused to accept the fact that she was aging, that she might not be able to pull off the sex goddess shtick anymore. She would just go on wearing her tight gowns and telling her slightly naughty jokes, wearing ever more makeup in hopes that no one would notice how old she really was. It seemed that she might get away with it, at first. The 1950s, in fact, offered Mae a kind of renaissance. Ultimately, though, it was more like a metamorphosis. By the end of the decade, Mae West would be transformed from a playful but genuine sex symbol to a high-camp curiosity. And she hadn't changed a thing.

The year 1950 began promisingly for West with the revival of *Diamond Lil*. Originally staged in 1928, it was the baroque period piece about the Gay Nineties that made West famous for her costumes and quips. Inspired by her mother's nickname "Champagne Til," the show was peppered with one-liners, including her trademark "Come up 'n' see me sometime." West had written the play as well and the novel of *Diamond Lil* had sold over 95,000 copies, so its return to the stage was especially triumphant for her. West toured the country, bringing Lil back to Broadway four separate times, the last in 1952.

Critics, but not Mae, seemed surprised by *Diamond Lil*'s success.

"I feel like a million tonight. . . . But one at a time," quipped Mae West during her Las Vegas act. Then in her sixties, West performed with fifteen muscle men in the Sahara Hotel from July 1954 intermittently through 1959. *Bettmann/Corbis.*

Wolcott Gibbs of *The New Yorker* wrote, "I guess that Miss West's charm both as a playwright and as an actress is unique and perennial." Critic George Jean Nathan said that "Mae West is not much of an actress by tony critical standards and *Diamond Lil* by any such standard is trash. But—let the tumbril come if it must—they are disgracefully good sport." *Life*'s critic explained West's appeal this way: "Mae is not exactly a Love Goddess. She is a razzle dazzle priestess of sexy, barroom humor whose sayings have become a part of the nation's folklore."

Back in the spotlight, Mae immediately resumed her role as diva. Miriam Goldina, an actress who played the part of Russian Rita in the *Lil* revival, remembered how Mae didn't like to be even slightly upstaged. The actress was slender, a sylph beside Mae's voluptuous figure. So Mae had her maid come by Goldina's dressing room to make sure the actress wrapped a blanket around her waist and wore it under her costume. Goldina also had been a protégée of Stanislavski, so she used his techniques to add depth to a scene she had with Mae. "Oooh, what're ya gettin' yourself so worked up for? Why ya gettin' all excited?" Mae asked the actress. "They didn't come tuh see you. They're here tuh see me, see? And don't you forget it!"

Goldina was stunned. "The first time she did that with her back to the audience, talking to me, I almost forgot my lines," the actress said. She soon left the production. When the director tried to woo her back, Goldina told him no, "not even for $1,000 a week." "It's that bad?" he asked. "Worse," said the actress. "When you work for Mae West, it is not for art but from hunger."

Spurred on by the success of *Lil*'s revival, West launched *Come on Up—Ring Twice* in 1952. Although basically a rehashing of her other plays, it still did relatively well and Mae earned $3,500 a week plus a share of the profits. The *Toronto Star Weekly* declared that only West could have made the play a success. "Its dialogue is corny and its situations are far-fetched. With anybody else as its star, it could easily be a tedious bore."

West had always created her own opportunities when others didn't present themselves. Early in her career, when she couldn't get a part on Broadway, she wrote her own plays. And in the 1950s, after the *Lil* revivals ended and she couldn't find a film role she liked, she pioneered a new kind of entertainment—the Las Vegas lounge act.

Then in her sixties, Mae performed the show at the Sahara, surrounded by fifteen muscle men in tiger-striped G-strings, from July 1954 intermittently through 1959. Teetering on her high heels, she hardly moved at all, letting her bevy of beefy boys do all the heavy lifting. They were mere props, there to prompt Mae's signature lines like "It's not the men in your life, it's the life in your men" and serve as a handsome backdrop to songs such as "I Like to Do All Day What I Do All Night" and "Take It Easy, Boys, and Last a Long, Long Time."

Variety covered Mae's Vegas premiere on July 27, 1954. "Sex is the point in this gambling town this week. And it's being made the easy way by Mae West, who made her nitery debut tonight at the Sahara Hotel." *Variety* predicted that Mae would set attendance records with quips like "I feel like a million tonight. . . . But one at a time."

James Bacon, writing in the *Los Angeles Herald and Express*, observed that Mae's Vegas show was drawing more women than men. "Mae is the greatest ego booster to mature women since the invention of the girdle," he said. West sat down for an interview with Bacon in her bedroom so that he could tell his grandchildren "how you spent an hour in Mae West's boudoir, taking notes." Interestingly, she revealed that she had turned down the role of the "matron" in *Pal Joey* because "Joey makes a sucker out of this dame and that's against my whole concept of handling men. The girls over 21 always came to my shows because I boosted their ego the way I loved 'em and left 'em."

Despite the supposed pseudofeminism of her lounge act, it bordered on bad taste—and made West seem ridiculous. One night in her Las Vegas show, Mae reportedly had the men wear nothing but capes. With their backs to the audience, they paraded past West so that she could appraise and comment on their anatomy. Producer Charles O'Curran choreographed the routines for the show, substituting exercise for dance. He explained its crude appeal.

"I'd underscore muscle movements with music and have one guy keep looking down at his crotch as if that was supposed to move, too," O'Curran said. ". . . This one fellow was always a little late on everything. The psychology behind it was to get the audience to think, 'Why does she keep that rotten dancer?' Then they came to the conclusion, 'Oh, he must have a big prick.' The audience always howled."

A twenty-one-year-old Mr. America named Richard DuBois had

inspired the Vegas act, but another one of Mae's muscle men would become a longtime lover. Ex-wrestler Chester Ribonsky, who later changed his name to Chuck Krauser and then Paul Novak, lived with Mae West for more than twenty-five years. He had proven his devotion to Mae during what she perceived as a time of crisis.

Another man in her act, former Mr. Universe Mickey Hargitay, had begun a very public affair with blonde bombshell Jayne Mansfield. This hurt West's pride, as she loathed the much younger Mansfield. She could not have missed the similarities between herself and the young actress, either. Both had made a living by re-creating themselves as parodies of sex. Mansfield even seemed to borrow some of West's old vaudeville tricks, such as pretending that her dress strap had "broken" and exposing her breast.

West reportedly wanted to boot Hargitay from the Vegas act in May 1956. He barged into West's dressing room to confront her, and Chuck Krauser punched him, earning Mae's affection forever. Finally, in her sixties, Mae had the kind of press she had dreamed of, two younger men fighting over her.

Hargitay filed charges against Krauser, prompting more media reports of how Krauser "planted a tremendous haymaker on Mickey's head because he is in love with Miss West and was defending her against abusive language by Hargitay." Hargitay came to court sporting a black eye and a limp. Mae herself had to take the stand. According to the *Los Angeles Mirror*, Mae testified that " '[Hargitay] was standing at the doorway and when he went like that'—she threw up a diamond-laden hand—'Chuck hit him.' " Hargitay denied that he threatened West or Krauser. "It was like a dream," he said. "If I had raised my hand it was only a gesture."

Mae was no stranger to controversy. Indeed, her early career had thrived on it. She had spent eight days in jail for "lewd acts" in 1926. She had been convicted of lewd behavior for belly dancing in the play she had written called *Sex*. Thanks in part to the provocative title, it ran for 375 performances. Eighty percent of the audiences had been men. Headlines also rang out in October of 1928, "Mae West in Paddy Wagon Again." Police had closed another play she had authored, *The Pleasure Man*, because it featured "female impersonators." Mae won a court injunction to prevent further interference and the show went on.

But the Krauser/Hargitay dustup was different. While it became a cause célèbre, it had little to do with free speech or Mae's sexy act. It seemed to alter her image further, shifting it away from Mae West as character to Mae West as caricature.

Although she occasionally fanned the flames of controversy when it came to her professional life, she fought hard to keep her personal life private. When *Confidential* magazine ran a story in November 1955 entitled "Mae West's Open Door Policy," she found herself the subject of the wrong kind of media attention. The story enraged her because it hinted she'd had an affair with black boxer Albert "Chalky" Wright. "To get the lowdown this reporter made the rounds of California's boxing arenas where the name West is as well known as Spalding," wrote *Confidential*. The story alleged that West had dropped by the boxer's dressing room after a fight, "cased his brawn," and then asked him to "come on up"—and to be her chauffeur.

Confidential tattled that Chalky Wright found another "jalopy jockey" ensconced at her Ravenswood home, but that he soon had the job. The article detailed how Mae gave him $1,000 to get a divorce, gifted him with a sporty Duesenberg, and bought a new home for his mother.

But the Duesenberg was the car Chalky drove Mae in and he denied their affair in signed affidavits. *Confidential* was forced to print a retraction. Twenty-four hours before he was to testify against *Confidential* in the criminal libel suit against the magazine, the chauffeur was found dead in his bathtub. The weird coincidence made many suspicious, although no link between the two events was ever confirmed. Publisher Robert Harrison later pulled the plug on the magazine in November of 1957.

IN 1959 Mae West released her autobiography *Goodness Had Nothing to Do with It*. The book sold well and got good reviews, although it was strangely unrevealing. The identities of most of her lovers remained protected, and the steamiest love affair detailed in the book is Mae's passionate pursuit of her own career. As she later told *Playboy* magazine, "I concentrate on myself most of the time; that's the only way a person can become a star in the true sense. I never wanted a love that meant the surrender of my self-possession. . . . [My career] was first and it still is. I do nothin' but look after myself and my work. Good reviews is my favorite reading matter."

Mae's autobiography does give the reader a few glimpses into her true self, such as the frustration she sometimes felt at being an icon. ". . . Few people knew that I didn't always walk around with a hand on one hip, pushing my hairdress and talking low and husky," she wrote. "I had created a kind of Twentieth Century Sex Goddess that mocked and delighted all victims and soldiers of the great war between men and women."

In October of 1959 the publishers of *Goodness Had Nothing to Do with It* threw a party for Mae at the Beverly Hilton. She came in character, as the *Los Angeles Mirror News* described:

> She stood at the entrance awhile, carefully checking the audience. Then she undulated across the room, a tiny, plump figure in skin-tight white satin, trailing a white fox and expensive perfume. Her jewels were unbelievable. . . .

West then ensconced herself in a corner of the room where she could hold court from her "famous, old, bosom-out, bent-knee position."

Weeks after the October 1959 release of her autobiography, Charles Collingwood taped a segment with Mae West for the CBS interview show *Person to Person*. Censors squelched the piece before it aired, though, saying that "certain portions of the interview with Mae West might be misconstrued." An entertainment reporter with the *Los Angeles Times* watched the offending interview and found her double entendres mild, such as when Collingwood asked if she followed foreign affairs. "I've always had a weakness for foreign affairs," West answered. She also repeated many of her favorite, and increasingly tired, stories, giving, for example, the reason for the mirrors on her bedroom ceiling, "I like to see how I'm doing."

West was surprised when CBS decided not to run the interview, but said she wasn't hurt by it at all. "If that's what they call suggestive, then we have different standards," she said. "I just didn't think there was anything wrong with it and the crew taping the show shared my opinion."

Indeed her comments were not really objectionable. But the sight of a woman nearing seventy still clinging to a sex goddess image essentially unchanged from her first vaudeville act must have seemed strange.

SHE HAD cultivated adoration from her fans, but West had never become part of the social scene in Hollywood. She coveted her privacy and rarely left her apartment at the Ravenswood, decorated with Louis XIV furniture from a Paramount movie. One writer described the style of the pale rooms with their mirrors and nude paintings and sculptures of Mae as "superb late wedding cake."

She would often invite reporters to this pearly lair in the 1950s. On her own turf, she could set the ground rules. She could control the environment. With lighting, with makeup, with the movie-star accouterments around her, she could cast her spell, flirting with the usually male journalists. West would forbid any tape recordings or photographs of her, thus enabling her to maintain an almost "Wizard of Oz" facade. She was still trotting out the old gems: "When I'm good, I'm good, but when I'm bad, I'm better," and "Between two evils, I always pick the one I never tried before." Without the proof of an unretouched photo or recording, she hoped the public wouldn't realize how old she was getting. It was ingenious, really. She could keep her name in the papers without her image losing too much luster.

By the late 1950s, Mae had emerged as "the queen of camp." Mae West film festivals became popular. One weekend Universal ran a double bill of her films *I'm No Angel* and *She Done Him Wrong*. The box office pull was greater than that of any other Universal picture in current release. Mae West jokes were in vogue again, too, such as:

> Mae West calls a Chinese laundry and says, "Where the hell is my laundry? Get it over here right away."
>
> When the Chinese delivery boy shows up at her door he says, "I come lickety-split, Miss West."
>
> "Never mind that," she says. "Just gimme the laundry."

West simply kept reprising a role she'd played for fifty years. But she did feel compelled to keep up with popular culture. This led to slightly pathetic, but funny, forays into television and music. She appeared on an episode of *Mister Ed* in March 1964, with the horse making a play on her famous line. "Maybe she can come up and *shoe* me sometime," he said. Sillier still were the records she cut in the 1960s and 1970s. Asked why she would venture into rock and roll, West responded it was because of "popular demand by my fans." Her album *Way Out West* featured her singing the Beatles' "Day Tripper" and Bob Dylan's "If You Gotta Go." Other hits included "Shakin' All Over," "Treat Him Right," and "You Turn Me On." Her Christmas album was equally ludicrous, with Mae crooning such hits as "Put the Loot in the Boot, Santa" and "Santa, Come Up and See Me."

Mae claimed that whole football teams were showing up at her apartment, that a whole new generation of young men was being turned on to her in the 1960s. According to Mae, parties of up to fifty college boys would get together to watch her old movies on TV. At one college, the house mother didn't want them staying up late, so they rented a room just to watch the movies there. But when a reporter pressed her on this, asking which college it was, Mae conveniently couldn't remember.

Mae continued to act through the 1970s, appearing in *Myra Breckinridge* (1970), based on Gore Vidal's novel, and *Sextette* (1978), a film version of a play West had written years before. The Edith Head costumes couldn't hide West's girth. The camera cruelly recorded her ravaged face (she was in her mid-eighties), one shot capturing her left eye floating out of control. A bad wig and too much pancake makeup did nothing to improve the situation.

Costar Tony Curtis called it "the most bizarre project of my life." He described the lengthy rituals it took to get her ready for a day's work. "Mae's bodyguard would drive her in at eleven, and at ten after they'd start on her hair. Then they would take her into a kind of bathroom/dressing room for her daily enema which took another half hour," Curtis said. "Then they put wardrobe on her, and maybe by one-fifteen they'd wheel her onto the set. So I left for work when she started her enema." (Mae had always sworn by colonics, claiming she picked up the habit because the rest rooms on the vaudeville circuit were so filthy she wouldn't use them. She said daily enemas left her smelling "just as sweet at either end.")

Curtis recalled that she was quite deaf and a little blind and had difficulty moving, especially in the high platform shoes she needed to bolster her diminutive stature. She covered the shoes with long dresses. "She was always encased. When they wanted her to turn around in the scene, since she couldn't hear, a prop man would lie flat on the floor with his arms stretched out around her feet, and turn her around, literally," he said. "She was like the battleship *Potemkin*."

The film is full of unintentionally funny song-and-dance routines, including a West duet with young Timothy Dalton in which they sing "Love Will Keep Us Together." Audiences were cool toward the film and critics were brutal. Although the *Village Voice* described it as "one of the most innocently perverse star vehicles ever made," Vincent Canby described West as "a plump sheep that's been stood on its hind legs, dressed in a drag-queen's idea of chic, bewigged and then smeared with pink plaster." Rex Reed wrote that Mae West's voice sounded like "an old cat having a bad dream."

The film had proved costly to more than her ego, though. The strain had weakened her and in August 1980 she suffered a stroke that left her tongue paralyzed. She died soon after. Following a service at Forest Lawn in Los Angeles, Mae's body was laid to rest at Cypress Hill Cemetery in Brooklyn.

Mae West remains a pop culture icon, though. She's still on Broadway, too, in a sense. Claudia Shear's *Dirty Blonde*, a play about West and her legacy, found surprise success in 2000. But Mae would have expected nothing less. "I see myself as a classic," she said in 1971. "I never loved another person the way I loved myself. I've had an easy life and no guilts about it. I'm in a class by myself. I have no regrets."

DIRECTOR BILLY WILDER originally wanted Mae West to play the role of Norma Desmond in *Sunset Boulevard*. She declined, of course. The story was too dark. And West would never have wanted to be the star of a film in which the relationship between a young man and a much older woman turns ugly.

But even without Mae West, *Sunset Boulevard* makes its point about old Hollywood. There's a short scene in the film, easily upstaged by the midnight monkey burial or Norma's final descent into madness, in which three old actors have joined the fading silent film star in the parlor of her crumbling mansion for a night of bridge. "The waxworks," quips struggling screenwriter Joe Gillis, and, in fact, there is something ghastly about the figures gathered around the table. But the scene lingers in the imagination when one realizes that the actors are all playing themselves. Anna Q. Nilsson had been a star in the 1920s. H. B. Warner had played Christ in Cecil B. DeMille's 1927 picture *The King of Kings*. The legendary Buster Keaton also appears, his features ravaged by alcohol abuse. Even Gloria Swanson as Norma Desmond is, to an extent, playing herself. The scene "came closest to giving us all the creeps," Swanson recalled.

Billy Wilder, director and cowriter of *Sunset Boulevard*, intended to evoke that response. With its tale of an aging star and the young writer who becomes her kept man, the film is provocative enough. By emphasizing its verisimilitude, though, Wilder reveals the hidden truths of the world's cruelest company town—from the isolation of forgotten celebrities to the crass efficiency of producers. Not only a thrilling and strange piece of entertainment, the film also is an indictment of Hollywood.

From its inception, *Sunset Boulevard* was art meant to imitate life. For the role of faded silent-screen star Norma Desmond, Wilder chose Gloria Swanson, who first found success long before the "talkies." Many of the film's props came from Swanson's home and scrapbooks. One shot pans across a table covered with Swanson's film stills, the photographs in old frames capturing her young face and heavily painted eyes. The portrait in Norma's living room was painted by Geza Kende at the request of Swanson's then lover, Joseph P. Kennedy. Wilder also borrowed a film clip of "Norma" in her prime from a failed Swanson film Kennedy had produced, *Queen Kelly* (1929). Designer Edith Head created exotic, exaggerated, slightly outdated costumes, which also borrowed from Swanson's past. She wears a hat with a peacock feather in her scene with Cecil B. DeMille, a visual allusion to a headdress she wore in a film he directed called *Male and Female* (1919).

Wilder's casting choices more obviously referred to his star's Hollywood past. Like the bridge players, DeMille plays himself, with his scenes shot on the real set of 1949's *Samson and Delilah*, the film he was making at the time. "Hello, young fellow," DeMille says, greeting "Norma" the same way he once did a young Gloria Swanson.

Erich von Stroheim, who directed Swanson in the silent film *Queen Kelly*, plays Norma's ex-husband and butler, Max. It was Max, in his former life as a director, who made Norma a star. When he mourns his failed career, the scenes are particularly poignant. Wilder knew that von Stroheim, too, had never lived up to his early promise and eventually was ruined as a director because of continual cost over-runs and box-office flops. Hedda Hopper also has a cameo late in the film, playing herself. Wearing a giant hat, she calls her newspaper's copy desk from Norma's bedside phone. "As day breaks in the murder house . . ." she begins.

Swanson's dialogue plays on the fact that she was an aging silent film star. Watching the clip of a real movie she had made, Gloria/Norma says, "Still wonderful, isn't it? And no dialogue. We didn't need dialogue. We had faces. There just aren't any faces like that anymore. . . ." Another line has Norma saying, "Without me there wouldn't *be* any Paramount studios." Indeed Swanson's six-year stint at the studio strengthened Paramount. The night Norma throws her New Year's party, for Joe alone, she tells him about the polished tile floor and how Valentino recommended it for dancing the tango. Swanson actually had tangoed with the heartthrob in a film and later struck up a tender friendship with him.

Another scene has Norma trying to entertain a bored Joe Gillis with impersonations. She dresses up as a Mack Sennett bathing beauty, twirling parasol and all. It was Sennett who gave Swanson her start when she first came to Hollywood. The same scene shows her doing a very good imitation of Charlie Chaplin with a mustache drawn on with an extinguished match. Swanson, in fact, had appeared with Chaplin in a film when she was still a teenager in Chicago.

Even the film's decrepit mansion recalls Gloria Swanson's former home. She actually had lived on Sunset Boulevard, in a twenty-two-room Italian palazzo surrounded by palm trees near the Beverly Hills Hotel. Swanson moved to the house, originally built by King Gillette, at the tender age of twenty-three and promptly added a golden tub to the black marble bathroom. The movie mansion, meanwhile, was at 3810 Wilshire Boulevard, at the corner of Crenshaw and Irving. Built in 1924, it eventually belonged to the second Mrs. J. Paul Getty as part of her divorce settlement. Nothing was added to the house's structure, although set designers did add a pool, with noncirculating water, for the key opening scene. Nicholas Ray would use the emptied pool in his 1955 film *Rebel Without a Cause*. Two years later, the house was destroyed and a twenty-two-story office building of the Getty Oil Company was erected. It still stands.

Facts weren't just borrowed from Gloria Swanson's life, though. In the character of Joe Gillis, Wilder evokes his own shaky start in Hollywood. Born near Vienna, Austria, Wilder as a young man moved to Berlin to seek his fortune as a writer. He wrote witty profiles and articles on sports. On one assignment, he met legendary psychoanalyst Sigmund Freud. He moonlighted as a "taxi dancer," dancing with any unattached, usually older woman who was willing to pay for his services. It was a lucrative way to supplement his spotty income from journalism, but he soon lost the extra cash when he wrote a story about his experiences.

He began writing scripts early on, and when he moved to America after Hitler's rise to power, Wilder pursued his goal in earnest. He faced constant rejection in those early years. Not unlike Joe in his tiny place at the Alto-Nido Apartments, Wilder slept on a Murphy bed in his $75-a-month room at the Chateau Marmont hotel. He, too, had a hard time paying his bills until the success of such classics as *Double Indemnity* (1944) and *The Lost Weekend* (1945).

Just as Norma dreams of making *Salomé*, Gloria Swanson was also looking for a comeback. By 1950 she'd been gone from films for fifteen years, except for an appearance in a 1941 movie called *Father Takes a Wife*. Swanson thought the role of Norma Desmond was the "bigger than life" role she needed to stage a triumphant return. Indeed she received her third Academy Award nomination for her performance.

Swanson didn't win the Oscar, though; the award went instead to Judy Holliday for *Born Yesterday*. And *Sunset Boulevard* would not renew her career as she hoped. It was as if she had performed too well. To 1950 audiences, she *was* Norma Desmond. They had forgotten the actress behind the painted eyebrows, behind the turban and the witchy pronouncements. Scripts came to her after the film, but all the parts resembled Norma Desmond. "It was Hollywood's old trick: repeat a successful formula until it dies," Swanson said. ". . . I could go on playing [the part] in its many variations for decades to come, until at last I became some sort of creepy parody of myself, or rather of Norma Desmond—a shadow of a shadow."

Norma Desmond was a film character, though, an exaggeration of reality. Swanson was only fifty when she played her. After Mae West declined Wilder's offer, he tried to remember silent film stars. Pola Negri came to mind, but he thought her accent too thick. In "another bout of insanity," he approached Mary Pickford for the part. She was confused at first and then appalled. Wilder and coauthor Charles Brackett realized they had made a terrible mistake and slunk away, asking for her forgiveness. Finally, fellow director George Cukor suggested Gloria Swanson. She seemed instantly right to him, although Wilder was surprised he had almost forgotten her.

Wilder also didn't get his first choice for Joe Gillis. Originally, he wanted Montgomery Clift to play the writer. Clift declined the role because of the relationship between a younger man and an older woman. Clift had allegedly had an affair with Libby Holman, a popular singer from the 1920s. Her career evaporated after a scandal in which she shot her husband. Although the death was later ruled an accident, Holman was ruined and became an alcoholic. Clift lived with her for months at a time at Holman's sprawling New England mansion. The parallels between *Sunset Boulevard* and his own life would prove too uncomfortable, and too dangerous, for Clift.

With just two weeks to go before shooting was to start, Wilder selected William Holden for the role of Gillis. Although Holden had become an actor just after graduating from Pasadena Junior College, he had not had any major success. *Sunset Boulevard* would make his career. He would earn an Oscar nomination for his role and finally won an Academy Award in another Wilder picture, 1953's *Stalag 17*. Initially, though, the director worried that the age difference between Swanson and Holden, who was thirty-one, did not appear great enough.

Wilder tried to keep the details of his new film a secret, taking steps not unlike those taken by Orson Welles during *Citizen Kane*'s production. He used the title *A Can of Beans* as an innocuous cover title. He stamped an early draft of the script with "This is the First Act of Sunset Boulevard. Due to the peculiar nature of the project, we ask all of our co-workers to regard it as top secret —Brackett and Wilder."

Wilder purposely offered his actors minimal, vague direction, trying to provoke some instinctual responses from them. Holden complained that he felt frustrated as an actor, that he needed to know more about Gillis's character. "How much do you know about Holden?" Wilder countered.

The intensity of *Sunset Boulevard* took its toll on Swanson as well. The famous final scene where she descends the staircase proved especially difficult. Wilder wanted her to come down via the inside of the staircase, where the winding steps were narrowest. Terrified of falling in high heels, Swanson opted to go barefoot. She completed the scene as if in a trance, exactly what it called for. "Print it!" Wilder shouted, and she burst into tears.

It was the climax of a career that began in silent films when Swanson was just fifteen. She costarred opposite Charlie Chaplin in films for Essanay Studios in Chicago before moving to Hollywood, where she landed a $100-a-week contract from the Mack Sennett Studio. When that studio began offering her roles only in slapstick films, she went to Famous Players–Lasky, where her long professional relationship with Cecil B. DeMille would begin.

Her first picture for DeMille was *Don't Change Your Husband* (1919), a comedy about the dangers of a wife thinking that the "grass is greener" with someone else. Soon he put her in lavish dramas with stories drawn from history and the Bible. Swanson adored DeMille and his fatherly ways, even how he "wore his baldness like an expensive hat." She was always surprised at what he brought out in her, such as the courage to let a lion put his paw on her bare back for a scene in *Male and Female*. Starring in DeMille's blockbusters made Gloria Swanson a star, and by 1921 she was earning $2,500 a week.

Swanson's star continued to rise through the 1920s. She sold a house in upstate New York in order to finance her first film production, an unheard-of maneuver for a woman then. And her performance in *Sadie Thompson* garnered a best actress nomination for the first Academy Awards in 1928.

But an ill-fated love (and business) affair with bootlegger and politico Joseph P. Kennedy left Swanson smarting and struggling to find film roles in the 1930s. She left Hollywood in 1938, almost forty and with most of her money gone.

She drifted through another marriage, her fifth. She had a brief stint on television in the late 1940s with an early version of the afternoon talk show, complete with fashion and cooking segments. Swanson had never seen the new medium, though, and when she finally watched television, she was so horrified she quit.

When director Billy Wilder asked to screen-test her in January 1949, Swanson almost said no. She felt she never performed well in tests and didn't want to do it, even though she had worked with Wilder before in *Music in the Air.* Her agent encouraged her to take the part. Hollywood was thrilled by her performance. Louis B. Mayer hosted a dinner for her and twenty guests before they made their way to a private screening at Paramount, which ended in a long standing ovation for Swanson. Actress Barbara Stanwyck was so moved by the performance, she kissed the hem of Swanson's gown.

Swanson went on a three-month publicity tour for *Sunset Boulevard,* even appearing on the TV panel show *Twenty Questions.* Then she finally made it to Broadway, at fifty-one, in a play called *Twentieth Century* written by Ben Hecht and Charles MacArthur. She and her costar José Ferrer were in the middle of the play's run the night of the Academy Awards in 1951. Ferrer was nominated for best actor for his performance in *Cyrano de Bergerac.* The two met later at a restaurant called La Zambra, where they listened to the radio broadcast of the Hollywood ceremony. Also in New York that night were Celeste Holm, a nominee for best supporting actress for her role in *All About Eve,* and Judy Holliday, best actress nominee for *Born Yesterday.*

William Holden had also garnered a best actor nomination for *Sunset Boulevard* but Ferrer won. The award was a surprise, most of all to Ferrer. No one had expected him to win because the House Un-American Activities Committee had subpoenaed him to appear the following month and various media (including columnist Hedda Hopper) had been harassing him. Gloria Swanson remembered hearing Ferrer's voice coming over the radio and from across the room at the same time as reporters got his reaction.

Thrilled, Ferrer said the award signified an act of faith, a vote of confidence on his behalf. When a dense reporter asked if he was making a political statement, Ferrer said, "You're goddamned right I am! I meant it as a rebuke to all the people who tried to affect the voting by referring to things that are (a) beside the point and (b) untrue."

Judy Holliday beat out Swanson, Bette Davis, Anne Baxter, and Eleanor Parker for the Oscar. Swanson remembered the way she moved to embrace her, "Judy, darling." But the actress didn't hear her. She seemed to be laughing and crying at the same time, as her father and husband, along with her director George Cukor, congratulated her. The third nomination had not proven to be the charm Swanson needed.

No film script appealed to her. She didn't want to play Norma Desmond again and again. So she stayed in New York, appearing on Broadway in *Nina*, costarring David Niven. She knew the play had problems and tried to have some of her lines rewritten. When writer Samuel Taylor, who adapted the script from the French version by André Roussin, declined to make the changes, Swanson went to the press. She made it clear to the *Los Angeles Herald-Examiner* in November 1951 that, although unhappy with the play, she would go through with it because she was a professional under contract and because "people have bought tickets for the show and I don't want to disappoint them." *Nina* flopped and she wouldn't return to the stage for another twenty years.

Columnist Hedda Hopper, who considered herself an authority on almost everything related to Hollywood, advised Swanson to take advantage of the interest in her generated by *Sunset* and star in a film version of *Dinner at Antoine's* by Frances Parkinson Keyes. According to Hopper, Swanson was irked by the suggestion. "I couldn't possibly play the mother of an eighteen-year-old daughter," Swanson reportedly said. "The part's too old for me." Swanson was the mother of two daughters and a son at the time, as well as the grandmother of three.

While Swanson insisted that she was still a versatile actress, the media was obsessed with her age, never letting anyone forget that she wasn't twenty-one anymore. An advertisement for Jergens face cream asked, "Will you be as fascinating as Gloria Swanson at 52?" A *Saturday Evening Post* article just after the release of *Sunset* hailed the comeback of "Grandma Gloria Swanson." An August 1950 article in *Cue* magazine was kinder, calling her "the most glamorous grandmother in America." Swanson herself began to internalize the coverage, telling *Cue* that the teenagers who turned out to see her on the *Sunset* publicity tour "must have been told about me by their mothers or grandmothers. I must seem like Charlie Chaplin or Bon Ami or a tin lizzie or something."

Swanson did play a mother in her next film, *Three for Bedroom C* (1952), although her character's daughter was not a teenager. The light comedy told the story of a movie actress hurrying back from New York to Hollywood in order to turn down a new role. Without a train reservation, she tries to commandeer the compartment assigned to a professor. They "meet cute" and fall in love, despite various plot complications.

Swanson in later years said she didn't know where the studio found the actor who played the professor, James Warren, but her autobiography says she discovered him herself. He was selling paintings in a Los Angeles gallery when Swanson demanded that director Milton Bren cast him opposite her. But the film did little for the handsome Warren or Bren, who had also written the script. It didn't help Swanson's efforts to maintain her career's momentum, either.

Three for Bedroom C seemed like an odd choice to follow her performance in the fine and serious *Sunset Boulevard*. It's true that Swanson wanted to play a character completely different from Norma Desmond (although in both roles, Swanson plays an actress). But in some scenes, *Three for Bedroom C* bordered on slapstick, which Swanson had always hated. And there is something pathetic about seeing her crawling around on the floor of the train compartment, a literal comedown from the power and drama of *Sunset Boulevard*.

Critics were harsh. "Efforts at Comedy Defeated By Story" read the headline over the *Hollywood Reporter*'s review of *Three for Bedroom C*. "Gloria Swanson is lovely to look at but she, to put it mildly, is somewhat miscast in a cloyingly kittenish role," the *Reporter* opined. "And James Warren seems too accurately cast in a part that calls for nothing but looking befuddled." *Variety* called it a "trite romantic comedy, poorly done," while *Cue* called it "dull and bumbling." Tom Coffey, writing in the *Los Angeles Mirror*, tried to show restraint: "I won't go into all the asininity these characters perpetrate. For Mr. Bren's sake I'll just stop here."

The *Motion Picture Herald* noted that the movie featured Swanson in "numerous gowns of her own creation which should appeal to the ladies." But most had more pointed observations. "*Three for Bedroom*

After *Sunset Boulevard,* Gloria Swanson found herself typecast as Norma Desmond. She tried romantic comedy in the film *Three for Bedroom C* in 1952 (costarring James Warren, left), but it flopped. *Courtesy of the authors.*

C is Gloria Swanson's second comeback film and it is no *Sunset Boulevard,*" wrote *Time* magazine. Swanson had chosen the movie exactly because it wasn't like her last one. She only wanted a chance to do comedy, to "get away from the *Sunset Boulevard* image." Alas, it proved hard to shake, and her effort to go in a completely different direction failed.

In 1953 she seemed to give up on hopes of a sustained return to the screen. She signed with television's Crown Theatre to introduce all twenty-six dramas and appear in four of them. She candidly told *Los Angeles Daily News* columnist Erskine Johnson, "I doubt if I'll ever do another movie. . . . I'll never top *Sunset Boulevard.*"

She wouldn't act again in a big-screen production until 1956, in a film alternately called *Nero's Mistress, Nero's Big Weekend,* and *My Son Nero.* Swanson shot the film during a long trip to Europe, where she also dabbled as a reporter for the wire service United Press International. Supposedly a satiric look at Roman life, the film was difficult to follow.

Swanson plays scary, intimidating Agrippina, mother of the emperor Nero. Not only is her son afraid of her, so, it seems, is her very young costar Brigitte Bardot. Indeed Swanson dominates her scenes, including one of a silly orgy in which she steps regally over prone revelers. Again critics thought the material was beneath her talents and that the film in general was "a big nothing." It wasn't released widely in America until 1962, and then it passed into oblivion with little notice. The *Los Angeles Herald-Examiner* said it was "so ludicrous that viewers will laugh in spite of themselves."

Swanson decided that if she couldn't shrug off the ghost of Norma Desmond, then she would embrace it. Long before inspiration struck Andrew Lloyd Webber, Gloria Swanson wanted to make *Sunset Boulevard* into a stage musical. Paramount owned the rights and did not discourage her from embarking on the project. She spent her own money to pay for the British team of Dickson Hughes and Richard Stapley to complete the score and lyrics for *Boulevard*. In her retooled version, Norma would allow Joe to leave and find a happy ending with Betty.

Although it lacked the dramatic punch of the movie, Swanson's idea was not far-fetched. She could even sing. But on February 20, 1957, Paramount inexplicably withdrew its support for the project. After putting so much energy and money into it, Swanson was stunned to read the letter from Russell Holman, a Paramount executive. "It would be damaging for the property to be offered to the entertainment public in another form as a stage musical," he wrote weakly. Recordings of the entire completed score can still be found in the Gloria Swanson archives at the University of Texas.

The late 1950s and 1960s found Swanson appearing on an episode of *This Is Your Life*, along with guest appearances on shows such as *Straightaway*, *Dr. Kildare*, *Burke's Law*, and *The Beverly Hillbillies*. She told the *Los Angeles Mirror News* in October 1958 that she would love to act again in movies, "But what can I do—hit the producers over the head and tell them they should hire me?" She blamed her predicament, and that of other older actresses, on the male producers of movies. "It's all wrong," she said of films that had "sixty-year-old actors in love scenes with twenty-year-old girls." Swanson mused that the producers wanted to see such films because they were all old men themselves, many of whom had married much younger women. "They think that is a normal way of life." Swanson chastised the moviemakers, saying that they were ignoring a large market for their products by alienating older women. It was the women of America, she said, who had made the movie industry successful in the first place. No one, then or now, seemed to hear her.

In 1976 Swanson would marry the New York writer William Dufty. The author of Billie Holiday's biography *Lady Sings the Blues* and coauthor of Manny Robinson's autobiography, *My Father, My Son*, Dufty became Swanson's sixth husband. An early enthusiast of health food and vegetarianism like Swanson herself, Dufty would later remark that the only thing he had in common with the screen legend was their "mutual hatred of refined sugar." In fact, when he wrote a book on the evils of sweets in 1975 entitled *Sugar Blues*, Swanson went on a tour of thirty cities to promote it. After her death in 1983, Swanson's personal library was sold to the Gotham Book Mart in New York. Despite a lifetime in the movies and her love of art, Swanson had only books on health, diet, and well-being.

Swanson loved Carol Burnett's spoof of *Sunset Boulevard* so much that she went on the comedienne's show in 1973, singing and doing a Charlie Chaplin imitation she'd perfected as a girl extra at Essanay. She'd have a role playing herself in the disaster movie *Airport 1975* as well. In the end, though, it wasn't Sadie Thompson or DeMille's biblical heroine that Gloria Swanson would be remembered for. It would always be Norma Desmond. As she lamented in her autobiography, "I may not have got an Academy Award for it but I had somehow convinced the world once again of that corniest of all theatrical clichés—that on very rare artistic occasions the actor actually becomes the part."

CODA

IN THE SUMMER of 1960, John F. Kennedy came to Los Angeles to receive his party's nomination for president. Kennedy spent the days leading up to the nomination at the spacious beachfront home of Peter Lawford and Kennedy's sister, Pat, where he swam and greeted small crowds that had gathered on the Santa Monica beach to watch him coming out of the sea like a god. His white teeth shone from fifty yards away, brilliant against his tan face. It wasn't the California sun that gave Kennedy his permanent glow, however, it was his high intake of cortisone, which he used to treat his Addison's disease and painful back.

"Jack resembled not so much a politician," wrote Richard Mahoney in *Sons & Brothers*, "as a Hollywood leading man."

Norman Mailer, sent to cover the convention for *Esquire* magazine, even compared Kennedy to Marlon Brando. He noted that Kennedy, like the actor, "had the remote and private air of a man who had traversed some lonely terrain of experience, of loss and gain, of nearness to death, which leaves him isolated. . . ."

Mailer, from his perch at the Biltmore Hotel, "the ugliest hotel in the world," was among the first journalists to recognize how, with Kennedy's nomination in Los Angeles, politics and Hollywood glamour had become fused. "America's politics would now be also America's favorite movie . . . ," Mailer wrote.

Kennedy's youth was still somewhat of a political liability that convention week, but it attracted young writers like Mailer, confident enough to speak to power. "Here is a man," Mailer wrote, "who announces a week prior to the convention that the young are better fitted to direct history than the old."

So perhaps it is more than just symbolic that during that summer in Los Angeles the vast Kennedy family, with its countless cousins and children, were sprawled out in Louis B. Mayer's old house on the beach at Santa Monica, sitting around the former MGM chief's exalted dining room in their bathing suits.

Kennedy's nomination was also offering the country something that until now was exclusively a Hollywood creation—the hero. But this wasn't Washington, Lincoln, or Roosevelt. Kennedy was part of a different lineage—Barrymore, Cagney, Flynn, Bogart, Brando, and Sinatra. Free to write thirty years later about all that he saw during that week at the Democratic convention in his novel *Harlot's Ghost*, Mailer, in the guise of his character Modene, reports that "the parties went on forever. Toward the end, Jack took a group to a friend's suite at the Beverly Hilton. . . . I drifted into the bedroom. . . . [H]e was in bed, and I couldn't believe it—there was also another woman, one of the ones I had seen in the convention box. She was just about out of her clothes."

Mailer's *bête noir* at the time was Gore Vidal. Vidal, too, was in Los Angeles that summer, not so much as a journalist but as an alternate delegate to the convention from New York. Vidal was the last screenwriter under contract to MGM before the studio system collapsed, where he worked on the screenplay for *Ben Hur*. He was also a candidate for Congress and a relative of Jacqueline Bouvier Kennedy. And he was the author of *The Best Man*, then a hit on Broadway.

Vidal was at home in both worlds—the world of Hollywood movie stars and the world of New York socialites and politicians. On the night of July 12, 1960, the writer took over Mike Romanoff's restaurant, bringing the New York delegation together with Vidal's old Hollywood friends. Vidal's biographer described it as one of "the early synergistic mixtures of Hollywood and politics." It was a strange affair. Norman Mailer sat at the bar, lugubriously nursing a drink. "What's wrong?" Vidal asked. "You're too successful," Mailer answered.

Movie stars mingled with politicians that night. "Gary Cooper," wrote Gore Vidal in his memoir, "wanted to meet Tammany Hall." The future president of the National Rifle Association, Charlton Heston, gave his host a fulsome greeting. Bing Crosby was also in attendance. Lyndon Johnson was there, too, telling anybody who would listen why he was the only one who could defeat Nixon in the fall.

But the guest of honor, John Kennedy, was nowhere to be found, just as on the following night, when Tony Curtis and his wife Janet Leigh gave a star-studded party for Kennedy. Gore Vidal was there, in spite of being ill with pneumonia. He remembered, "There were a lot of round tables and about 200 or 300 movie stars, and I was waiting there where Janet Leigh presided with Frank Sinatra and some bimbo and me. They waited for Jack and they waited for Jack." Eunice Kennedy, John's sister, left the room to make a phone call. "He's gone to the movies," she returned to tell the assembled guests. Which meant, Vidal recalled, "that Jack was off fucking." "I looked at Sinatra and it was Attila the Hun," Vidal said. "If he could have killed Jack and half the earth he would have."

On the night of Kennedy's nomination, Vidal took historian Arthur Schlesinger Jr. and the Harvard economist Kenneth Galbraith to a late dinner at the Luau, a Polynesian restaurant in Beverly Hills. Part of its campy decor included a giant ship's wheel in front of the restaurant. Galbraith seized it, shouting, "This is the ship of state." But the wheel was mounted permanently in place and Galbraith succeeded only in ripping off some spokes. Later, after much rum, and exhausted after the week's events, the three men playfully argued about which one of them would have to tell the future president "to stop saying 'between you and I.' " But instead of preparing Kennedy's acceptance speech, Gore Vidal took his pneumonia "home to the Hudson Valley, where I had a lot of explaining to do about the immoral Hollywood party that I had given."

THE KENNEDYS were not strangers to Hollywood. Jack's father Joe Kennedy was the financial pirate who had owned a couple of movie studios and taken a mistress from its earliest nobility—Gloria Swanson.

In the 1940s, Jack was quick to pounce on the Hollywood beauties his father cast off. But as a senator in the 1950s, he began what Gore Vidal described in his memoir as "a collection of beddable stars that would, in time, outdo that of his father." Kennedy's conquests included Gene Tierney, Angie Dickinson, and even Marlene Dietrich, who had a tryst with Kennedy in the White House just hours before she was to receive an award for aiding Jewish refugees. Now, with the campaign winding down and Kennedy about to be crowned by the Democrats in Los Angeles, he was in his element. And it was his early rivals for the nomination, Johnson of Texas and Humphrey of Minnesota, who felt out of place among the imported palm trees, private pools, wraparound sunglasses, and all that glamorous pulchritude.

Jack had always been interested in Hollywood gossip. Truman Capote remembered one evening when Kennedy seemed positively bored with affairs of state but became transfixed by the talk at the table about certain Hollywood leading men and their sexual prowess.

But now Frank Sinatra was in charge as Jack Kennedy's social director in Los Angeles, as he would be for Kennedy's inaugural six months later (before being, in Sinatra's view, unceremoniously dumped by the Kennedys for his mob affiliations).

The Lawfords' house had originally been built by Louis B. Mayer in 1926. Its ceilings were fifteen feet high. There was even a complete stage under the floorboards that rose on hydraulic lifts at the press of a button. Twenty years earlier, filled with Mayer's cigar smoke, it was perhaps the most important home in Hollywood. After Peter Lawford married into the Kennedy family, he purchased the house with its five bedrooms. Sinatra had the run of it the week before Kennedy accepted the nomination. It was Sinatra who was really Kennedy's sponsor in Hollywood, as well as one of his greatest fund-raisers. It impressed Kennedy when he emerged from his brother-in-law's pool to hear Sinatra, with a single phone call, wheedle a $10,000 contribution out of some schnook back east. "Frank," Kennedy said. "I'm going to tell my father that you're better at raising money than he is."

Sinatra even told Lawford, his host, how to dress, admonishing him for wearing a silk shirt and a cherry-red bow tie while Sinatra was showing his respect for the Kennedys by wearing a dark suit and a skinny black tie. He ordered Lawford to change his clothes. Lawford resisted and Sinatra exploded. Only the shoeless entry of Jack Kennedy, who emerged from his nap around five in the afternoon, calmed matters. "I like the way Peter dresses, Frank," Kennedy said. "Even though my life's ambition is to be like you." Sinatra explained to Kennedy that among the guests might be "some friends from Chicago," typical Sinatra euphemisms for organized crime figures. "Well, Frank," Kennedy told his friend. "Just make sure they leave their shades in the car."

Kennedy admired Sinatra's sense of style—his soft suits, his Italian loafers, the way men seemed to fall in love with him, and the women. Sinatra had brought many young women into Kennedy's tent that year, particularly before a big battle. The future president confessed to Sinatra that his satyrism was medicinal: "If I don't have a woman and it goes on for as long as three days, I get a terrible headache. I'm totally useless." Kennedy told him that should he win the election over that stiff Nixon, he wanted Frank to organize the inaugural gala. He wanted it to be "like *Ed Sullivan*," like "that show you do in Vegas"—that very show at which Kennedy, as a senator, had once been introduced at ringside.

ONE EVENING, shortly before Kennedy's acceptance speech in front of eighty thousand people at the Los Angeles Coliseum, Sinatra arranged to bring two generations of Hollywood royalty together to meet the candidate. There were about fifty guests at the Lawfords' house that night, standing in the garden near the children's playground. The ascendant and the soon-to-be-retired were in attendance. As the sun set over the Pacific, Pat O'Brien, Milton Berle, and Darryl Zanuck rubbed elbows with Tony Curtis, Angie Dickinson, studio head Arthur Krim, and Janet Leigh. Sinatra encouraged Kennedy to ask some of the stars at the party, including Juliet Prowse and Judy Garland, to participate in a barnstorming tour for him during the fall campaign. Kennedy agreed, thinking it was a great idea.

Despite Sinatra's invitation, no mafia chief attended the Lawfords' party that night. The mob was leaving nothing to chance, though. Fred Otash, who had cut his teeth as an investigator for *Confidential* magazine, was hired to place listening devices in the Lawford home. Sam Giancana and the Chicago Syndicate were listening.

But the evening that Sinatra had fretted over soon deteriorated into a kind of Friars Club roast of Sinatra as Milton Berle and others heckled him for putting on airs in the rarefied atmosphere of the Kennedy circle. Berle and others thought this skinny kid from Hoboken was overreaching and seemed at best silly and at worst pretentious.

At a private party for Kennedy at Chasen's given by Averell Harriman, Oscar Levant made one of his rare public appearances, accompanied by his long-suffering wife June. Shelley Winters was there, and Gore Vidal. Edie Adams, the wife of the great, anarchic actor and comedian Ernie Kovacs, was at the party, as were actresses such as Angie Dickinson and Shirley MacLaine. Levant was enchanted by the young, articulate candidate with the ready wit. He approached the forty-two-year-old Kennedy. "Your father said I was the only Jew he could stand," Levant boasted to Kennedy. "I don't want to hear another word," Kennedy responded, trying to embrace an early form of political correctness. He tried to put as much distance as possible between Levant and himself.

Kennedy's association with Hollywood wouldn't end at his election. Soon after his inauguration, Warner Brothers began production on a film version of *PT 109*, the Robert J. Donovan book that told of Kennedy's heroics in the South Pacific during World War II. A national search to find the perfect actor to portray the young naval war hero followed. Cliff Robertson, who had a small part in the film adaptation of William Inge's *Picnic*, won the starring role.

HOLLYWOOD WAS now a different place. The studio system was in collapse. One studio, RKO, would become a purveyor of television, the sworn enemy of everything Hollywood stood for in the 1950s. "Hollywood is through," Howard Hughes remarked when his company was finally sold. Movies were now made on location. The warehouses full of lavish sets and costumes were no longer needed and Hollywood auctioned off its wares, with Clark Gable's swim trunks and Judy Garland's shoes going to the highest bidder. Kenneth Anger wondered what became of all those glittery souvenirs, such as Greta Garbo's ski suit from *Two-Faced Woman*. "What freak fan or fanatic is wearing you at this moment, parading up and down in front of what broken mirror of the mind?" he asked.

The decade that began with Gloria Swanson as Norma Desmond ended with Jack Kennedy, the son of her former lover, in the White House, with Frank Sinatra in charge of entertainment. The 1950s were definitely over.

ACKNOWLEDGMENTS

A GREAT MANY people contributed to this work. First, to the eyewitnesses, those who shared with us their thoughts and recollections of Hollywood in the 1950s. Some have since died, but we appreciated their generosity and, in many cases, their hospitality and their tolerance: Steve Allen, Lauren Bacall, Don Bachardy, Henny Backus, James Bacon, Peter Basch, Burt Boyar, Amanda Levant Carmel, Leslie Caron, Betty Comden, Tony Curtis, Brad Dexter, David Diamond, Clifton Fadiman, Wendy Fairey, Adolph Green, James Hill, Jean Howard, Joe Hyams, Quincy Jones, Gene Kelly, Murray Kempton, John Kerr, Werner Klemperer, Irv Kupcinet, Gavin Lambert, Marguerite Lamkin, Speed Lamkin, Ring Lardner Jr., Jack Larson, Ernest Lehman, June Levant, Hilary Mackendrick, Rosemary Mankiewicz, Roddy McDowall, Ivan Moffat, Walt Whitman Odets, Jack Paar, David Raksin, Shirley Rhodes, Cliff Robertson, Lillian Ross, George Sidney, Arthur Silber Jr., George Stevens Jr., Al Vanderbilt, Connie Wald, Loray White, and Elaine Young.

To Graydon Carter, the brilliant visionary of *Vanity Fair* whose love of the movies launched two of the pieces that appear in this book, our deepest gratitude, and to Doug Stumpf at *VF*—as Noël Coward once said, "Affection is a beautiful thing"—thank you for your artistry and your insight. And to *Vanity Fair's* Stephen Levey, the best and the brightest.

We are also grateful to Art Cooper, the editor in chief of GQ, and managing editor Martin Beiser for their appreciation of *Confidential* and the Howard Rushmore story, which appeared in a somewhat different form in their magazine.

This book began as an answer to a question posed by the novelist James Ellroy, "Where is the *City of Nets* for the 1950s?" While this isn't quite what James had in mind—it's not exhaustive in the way that Otto Friedrich's classic is—it is our subjective, aerial view of a time and place. Perhaps this is the right moment, then, to thank James Ellroy and his wife, the film critic and novelist Helen Knode, for their encouragement and support and, dare we say it, their enthusiasm for Hollywood in the 1950s.

To Gerald Howard, who saw the promise of a good story, and who gave us the chance to write this book. And to our editors—Neil Giordano, who brought a novelist's keen eye and sure hand to the prose of not one but two unruly scriveners. To Alane Mason, who put her elegant imprimatur on the final manuscript. We are deeply grateful for her editorial precision, her unerring ear, and her staggering intelligence. And to Stefanie Diaz, whose many gifts made our job so much easier.

To Joy Harris and Leslie Daniels, our agents for *The Bad and the Beautiful*, who saw the light at the end of the tunnel. Especially to Leslie, a wonderful actress herself, for her exceptional patience. And for her warmth and wit, which sustained us on this long road.

We'd like to thank the Academy (the Academy of Motion Picture Arts and Sciences Library, that is), especially Barbara Hall and Faye Thompson, Special Collections archivists there. We'd also like to thank the Library of Congress and the District of Columbia Public Library for their services.

Finally, to our spouses, Nancy Schoenberger and Lee Banville, with love and appreciation for many hours of unpaid tech support, endless encouragement, and the good humor to endure yet another screening of *Imitation of Life* (sorry).

A deep bow to you all.

BIBLIOGRAPHY

Andreychuk, Ed. *Burt Lancaster: A Filmography and Biography*. Jefferson, N.C.: McFarland and Company, 2000.

Anger, Kenneth. *Hollywood Babylon*. San Francisco: Straight Arrow Books, 1975.

——. *Hollywood Babylon II*. New York: Dutton, 1984.

Bacon, James. *Made in Hollywood*. Chicago: Contemporary Books, 1977.

Bertin, Celia. *Jean Renoir, A Life in Pictures*. Translated by Mareille Muellner and Leonard Muellner. Baltimore and London: The Johns Hopkins University Press, 1991.

Bessie, Alvah. *Inquisition in Eden*. Berlin: Seven Seas Publishers, 1967.

Biskind, Peter. *Seeing Is Believing: How Hollywood Taught Us to Stop Worrying and Love the Fifties*. New York: Pantheon Books, 1983.

Blesh, Rudi. *Keaton*. New York: Macmillan, 1966.

Bosworth, Patricia. *Montgomery Clift*. New York: Harcourt, Brace, Jovanovich, 1978.

Bragg, Melvyn. *Richard Burton: A Life*. Boston: Little, Brown and Company, 1988.

Brown, Peter H. *Reluctant Goddess*. New York: St. Martin's Press, 1986.

Callow, Simon. *Charles Laughton: A Difficult Actor*. New York: Grove Press, 1987.

Capote, Truman. *Answered Prayers: The Unfinished Novel*. New York: Random House, 1987.

Chaplin, Charles. *My Autobiography*. New York: Simon and Schuster, 1964.

Chaplin, Charles, Jr., with N. M. Rau. *My Father, Charlie Chaplin*. New York: Random House, 1960.

Clinch, Minty. *Burt Lancaster*. New York: Stein and Day, 1985.

Cottrell, John, and Fergus Cashin. *Richard Burton, Very Close Up*. Englewood Cliffs, N.J.: Prentice-Hall, 1971.

Crane, Cheryl, and Cliff Jahr. *Detour*. New York: Avon Books, 1988.

Curtis, Tony, and Barry Paris. *Tony Curtis: The Autobiography*. New York: William Morrow and Company, 1993.

Dalton, David. *James Dean: The Mutant King*. New York: St. Martin's, 1974.

Dardis, Tom. *Keaton: The Man Who Wouldn't Lie Down*. New York: Scribner, 1979.

Darin, Dodd, with Maxine Paetro. *Dream Lovers: The Magnificent Shattered Lives of Bobby Darin and Sandra Dee*. New York: Warner Books, 1994.

Davis, Sammy, Jane Boyar, and Burt Boyar. *Yes I Can: The Story of Sammy Davis, Jr.* New York: Farrar, Straus and Giroux, 1965.

Deford, Frank. *Big Bill Tilden: The Triumphs and the Tragedy*. New York: Simon and Schuster, 1975.

Dick, Bernard. *City of Dreams: The Making and Remaking of Universal Pictures*. Lexington, Ky.: University Press of Kentucky, 1997.

Donaldson, Scott. *Fool for Love: F. Scott Fitzgerald*. New York: Congdon and Weed, 1983.

Durgnat, Raymon. *Jean Renoir*. Berkeley, Calif.: University of California Press, 1974.

Eells, George. *Hedda and Louella: A Dual Biography of Hedda Hopper and Louella Parsons*. New York: G. P. Putnam and Sons, 1972.

Eells, George, and Stanley Musgrove. *Mae West: A Biography*. New York: William Morrow and Company, 1982.

Eisenschitz, Bernard. *Nicholas Ray: An American Journey*. New York: Faber & Faber, 1993.

Fairey, Wendy W. *One of the Family*. New York: W. W. Norton and Company, 1992.

Ferris, Paul. *Richard Burton: The Actor, the Lover, the Star*. New York: Berkley Books, 1982.

Fischer, Lucy, ed. *Imitation of Life*. New Brunswick, N.J.: Rutgers University Press, 1991.

Fishgall, Gary. *Against Type: The Biography of Burt Lancaster*. New York: Scribner, 1995.

Forshey, Gerald E. *American Religious and Biblical Spectaculars*. Westport, Conn.: Praeger Publishers, 1992.

Friedrich, Otto. *City of Nets*. Berkeley and Los Angeles: University of California Press, 1986.

Gabler, Neal. *An Empire of Their Own: How the Jews Invented Hollywood*. New York: Crown Publishers, 1980.

——. *Winchell: Gossip, Power, and the Culture of Celebrity*. New York: Alfred A. Knopf, 1994.

Gates, Phyllis, and Bob Thomas. *My Husband, Rock Hudson: The Real Story of Rock Hudson's Marriage to Phyllis Gates*. Garden City, N.Y.: Doubleday and Company, 1987.

Geist, Kenneth L. *Pictures Will Talk: The Life and Films of Joseph L. Mankiewicz*. New York: Scribner, 1978.

Goodman, Ezra. *The Fifty-Year Decline and Fall of Hollywood*. New York: MacFadden Books, 1961.

Graham, Billy. *Just as I Am*. New York: HarperCollins, 1997.

Graham, Sheilah. *The Rest of the Story*. New York: Coward-McCann, 1964.

——. *Confessions of a Hollywood Columnist*. New York: William Morrow and Company, 1969.

——. *Hollywood Revisited*. New York: St. Martin's Press, 1985.

Graham, Sheilah, and Gerold Frank. *Beloved Infidel: The Education of a Woman*. New York: Henry Holt and Company, 1958.

Guiles, Fred Lawrence. *Hanging on in Paradise: Selected Filmographies by John E. Schultheiss*. New York: McGraw-Hill, 1975.

Halliday, Jon. *Sirk on Sirk: Conversations with Jon Halliday*. London: Faber & Faber, 1997.

Havoc, June. *More Havoc*. New York: Harper and Row, 1980.

Hermann, Dorothy. *S. J. Perelman: A Life*. New York: Putnam, 1986.

Hillier, Jim, ed. *Cahiers du Cinéma: The 1950s; Neo-Realism, Hollywood, New Wave*. Cambridge, Mass.: Harvard University Press, 1985.

Hopper, Hedda. *From Under My Hat*. Garden City, N.Y.: Doubleday and Company, 1952.

———. *The Whole Truth and Nothing But*. Garden City, N.Y.: Doubleday and Company, 1963.

Houseman, John. *Front & Center*. New York: Simon & Schuster, 1979.

Hudson, Rock, and Sara Davidson. *Rock Hudson: His Story*. New York: William Morrow and Company, 1986.

Hyams, Joe, with Jay Hyams. *James Dean, Little Boy Lost: An Intimate Biography*. New York: HarperCollins, 1996.

Isherwood, Christopher. *Diaries*. Edited and introduced by Katherine Bucknell. New York: HarperCollins, 1997.

Jeffers, H. Paul. *Sal Mineo: His Life, Murder, and Mystery*. New York: Caroll and Graf Publishers, Inc., 2000.

Kaplan, Fred. *Gore Vidal: A Biography*. Garden City, N.Y.: Doubleday and Company, 1999.

Kelley, Kitty. *Elizabeth Taylor: The Last Star*. Boston: G. K. Hall, 1981.

———. *His Way: The Unauthorized Biography of Frank Sinatra*. New York: Bantam Books, 1986.

Kerouac, Jack. *Selected Letters, 1957–1969*. Edited by Ann Charters. New York: Viking, 1999.

Kleno, Larry. *Kim Novak on Camera*. San Diego, Calif.: A. S. Barnes, Publishers, 1980.

Klinger, Barbara. *Melodrama and Meaning: History, Culture, and the Films of Douglas Sirk*. Bloomington, Ind.: Indiana University Press, 1994.

Kotsilibas-Davis, James. *The Barrymores: The Royal Family in Hollywood*. New York: Crown Publishers, 1981.

Leaming, Barbara. *Marilyn Monroe*. New York: Crown Publishers, 1998.

Leonard, Maurice. *Mae West: Empress of Sex*. Secaucus, N.J.: Carol Publishing Group, 1991.

Levant, Oscar. *The Unimportance of Being Oscar*. New York: G. P. Putnam's Sons, 1968.

Logan, Joshua. *Josh: My Up and Down, In and Out Life*. New York: Delacorte Press, 1976.

———. *Movie Stars, Real People, and Me*. New York: Delacorte Press, 1978.

MacLaine, Shirley. *My Lucky Stars: A Hollywood Memoir*. New York: Bantam Books, 1995.

MacShane, Frank. *The Life of John O'Hara*. New York: Dutton, 1980.

Madsen, Axel. *John Huston*. Garden City, N.Y.: Doubleday and Company, 1978.

Mailer, Norman. *Conversations with Norman Mailer.* Edited by J. Michael Lennon. Jackson, Miss.: University Press of Mississippi, 1988.

——. *The Time of Our Time*. New York: Random House, 1998.

Martin, William. *A Prophet with Honor: The Billy Graham Story*. New York: William Morrow and Company, 1991.

Marx, Arthur. *Everybody Loves Somebody Sometime (Especially Himself): The Story of Dean Martin and Jerry Lewis*. New York: Hawthorn Books, 1974.

McNally, Dennis. *Desolate Angel: Jack Kerouac, the Beat Generation, and America*. New York: Random House, 1979.

Metalious, Grace. *Peyton Place*. New York: Julian Messner, 1956.

Miller, Arthur. *Conversations with Arthur Miller.* Edited by Matthew C. Roudané. Jackson, Miss.: University Press of Mississippi, 1987.

Miller, Gabriel. *Clifford Odets*. New York: Continuum, 1989.

Mills, Hilary. *Mailer: A Biography*. New York: Empire Books, 1982.

Morella, Joe, and Edward Z. Epstein. *Jane Wyman: A Biography*. New York: Delacorte Press, 1985.

Morley, Sheridan. *A Talent to Amuse: A Biography of Noël Coward*. Garden City, N.Y.: Doubleday and Company. 1969.

O'Hara, Frank. *Meditations in an Emergency*. New York: Grove Press, 1967.

O'Hara, John. *Selected Letters of John O'Hara*. New York: Random House, 1978.

Parsons, Louella. *The Gay Illiterate*. Garden City, N.Y.: Doubleday and Company, 1944.

Perry, George. *Sunset Boulevard: From Movie to Musical*. New York: Henry Holt and Company, 1993.

Peters, Margot. *The House of Barrymore*. New York: Alfred A. Knopf, 1990.

Quirk, Lawrence J. *The Films of Gloria Swanson*. Secaucus, N.J.: Citadel Press, 1984.

Ray, Nicholas. *I Was Interrupted: Nicholas Ray on Making Movies*. Edited and introduced by Susan Ray. Berkeley, Calif.: University of California Press, 1993.

Renoir, Jean. *My Life and My Films*. Translated by Norman Denny. New York: Atheneum, 1974.

Robinson, David. *Chaplin: His Life and Art*. New York: McGraw-Hill. 1985.

Robinson, Edward G., Jr., with William Dufty. *My Father, My Son*. New York: Frederick Fell, 1958.

Rosenstein, Jaik. *Hollywood Leg Man*. Los Angeles: Madison Press, 1950.

Ross, Lillian. *Moments with Chaplin*. New York: Dodd, Mead and Company, 1978.

Ross, Lillian, and Helen Ross. *The Player: A Profile of an Art*. New York: Simon and Schuster, 1962.

Saxton, Martha. *Jayne Mansfield and the American Fifties*. Boston: Houghton Mifflin, 1975.

Selznick, Irene Mayer. *A Private View*. New York: Alfred A. Knopf, 1983.

Shuman, R. Baird. *William Inge*. Boston: G. K. Hall and Company, 1989.

Spoto, Donald. *Rebel: The Life and Legend of James Dean*. New York: HarperCollins, 1996.

Strasberg, Lee, and Robert H. Hethmon. *Strasberg at the Actors Studio*. New York: Viking Press, 1965.

Swanson, Gloria. *Swanson on Swanson*. New York: Random House, 1980.

Thomas, Bob. *King Cohn: The Life and Times of Harry Cohn*. New York: Putnam, 1967.

Thomson, David. *A Biographical Dictionary of Film*. Third edition. New York: Alfred A. Knopf, 1994.

Tilden, Bill. *My Story: A Champion's Memoirs*. New York: Hellman, Williams, 1948.

Tomkies, Mike. *The Robert Mitchum Story: "It Sure Beats Working."* Chicago: Regnery, 1972.

Toth, Emily. *Inside Peyton Place: The Life of Grace Metalious*. Garden City, N.Y.: Doubleday and Company, 1981.

Turner, Lana. *Lana: The Lady, the Legend, the Truth*. New York: Eltee Productions and Hollis Alpert, 1982.

Vidal, Gore. *Palimpsest: A Memoir*. New York: Random House, 1995.

Viertel, Salka. *The Kindness of Strangers*. New York: Holt, Rinehart and Winston, 1969.

Voss, Ralph F. A *Life of William Inge: The Strains of Triumph*. Lawrence, Kans.: University Press of Kansas, 1989.

Walls, Jeannette. *Dish: The Inside Story on the World of Gossip*. New York: Spike/Avon Books, 2000.

Ward, Carol M. *Mae West: A Bio-bibliography*. New York: Greenwood Press, 1989.

Weales, Gerald Clifford. *Odets, the Playwright*. New York: Methuen, 1985.

Winters, Shelley. *Shelley, Also Known as Shirley*. New York: William Morrow and Company, 1981.

——. *Shelley II: The Middle of My Century*. New York: Shelley Winters Productions, 1989.

Wolfe, Tom. *The Purple Decades*. London: Pan Macmillan Publishers, 1993.

Wood, Audrey, and Max Wilk. *Represented by Audrey Wood*. Garden City, N.Y.: Doubleday and Company, 1981.

Zolotow, Maurice. *Billy Wilder in Hollywood*. New York: Putnam, 1977.

INDEX

Page numbers in *italics* refer to illustrations.

Abbott, Bud, 184
Abbott and Costello Meet Captain Kidd, 184
Academy Awards, 259–60, 342–43
Actors Lab, 176, 178, 180, 183
Actors Studio, 109, 177, 320
Adams, Edie, 354
Adler, Stella, 232, 241
African Queen, The, 185
Agar, John, 281
Agee, James, 184–85, 192
AIDS, 144, 154
Alda, Robert, 267
All American, 299
Allen, Corey, 111–12
All I Desire, 142
All My Sons (Miller), 87, 90
All That Heaven Allows, 13, *146*, 151–52
Allyson, June, 205, 281
Ambler, Eric, 166
American in Paris, An, 163–65, *164*, 167–73, *171*, 173, *179*
American Tragedy, An, 156, 178, 182
  see also Place in the Sun, A
Anderson, Lindsay, 101
Anderson, Paul Thomas, 238
Anger, Kenneth, 354
Arnaz, Desi, 41
Arnow, Max, 200, 209
Astaire, Fred, 168
Atkinson, Brooks, 317, 320, 324, 325
Atomic City, The, 64
Axelrod, George, 320

Bacall, Lauren, 63, 137, 152, 289
Backus, Jim, 81, 114, 116, 117
Bacon, James, 207, 330
Bad and the Beautiful, The, 255
Baker, Carroll, 109
Baker, Josephine, 22
Balcon, Michael, 228
Ball, Lucille, 14, 290
Bankhead, Tallulah, 50
Bardot, Brigitte, 346
Barker, Lex, 255, 256, 259, 263
Barrymore, Diana, 47–48
Barrymore, Drew, 96
Barrymore, Ethel, 95
Barrymore, John, 47, 95, 96, 301
Barrymore, John, Jr. (John Drew Barrymore), 83, 95–97, *96*
Barth, Marty, 89–90
Basch, Peter, 236, 237
Basehart, Richard, 304
Baxter, Anne, 343
Beatty, Warren, 326
beauty standards, 18, 19
Beebe, Lucius, 219
Belafonte, Harry, 212

Bell, Book, and Candle, 212, 214
Beloved Infidel, *300*, 301–7
Bendix, William, 159
Benedek, László, 121
Ben Hur, 133
Bennett, Constance, 51, 297
Bennett, Joan, 288–89
Benny, Jack, 288
Bergen, Candice, 174
Bergman, Ingmar, 158
Bergman, Ingrid, 289, 298
Berkeley, Busby, 279
Berle, Milton, 13, 14, 353
Bernstein, Elmer, 234
Bessie, Alvah, 65–71, *66*, *70*, 76, 80
Bessie, Clare, 67, 71, 76
Bessie, Dan, 80
Biberman, Herbert, *70*, 71
biblical epics, 14, 127–30, *128*
Big Fisherman, The, 132
Bigger Than Life, 101, 119
Bitter Victory, 119
blacklisting, 67–68, 80, *89*, 296
Blackmer, Sidney, 308
Bogart, Humphrey, 18, 30, 63, 137, 204
Boone, Pat, 249, 251
Booth, Shirley, 308, 313, 314–16
Boroff, George, 92–93
Boyar, Burt, 204, 205, 206, 208, 212, 213, 216
Boyar, Jane, 204
Brackett, Charles, 12, 284, 340
Bragg, Melvyn, 135
Brando, Marlon:
  brooding film persona of, 103, 144, 145, 349
  film roles of, 78, 104, 121, 292
  gossip columnists' criticisms of, 280, 282, 292
  Los Angeles homes of, 133–34
  as Method actor, 177, 181
Brecht, Bertolt, 139, 161
Breen, Jay, 22–23, 48
Breen, Joseph, 192–93
Bren, Milton, 344
Brennan, Walter, 14
Brinken, Lydia, 140
British Academy of Film and Television Arts, 240
Britt, May, 215
Broken Blossoms, 191–92
Brown, David, 220, 228–29, 240, 242–43
Brown, Edmund G. "Pat," 41
Bruce, Nigel, 133
Brustein, Robert, 324–25
Brynner, Yul, 252
Burnett, Carol, 347
Burr, Raymond, 14
Burton, Dan, 33
Burton, Richard, 133–38
  film career of, 119, 129, 135–36, 137–38
  on Method acting, 181–82
  in religious epic, 129, 130, 131, 133, *134*, 135
  theater background of, 130, 133, *134*, 135
  Thomas's poetry recited by, 137, 156, 157
  Zanuck's contract rejected by, 135–36
Bus Stop (film), 89, 309, *312*, 320–24, *321*
Bus Stop (Inge), 309, 311, 320, 325

Cabot, Bruce, 37
Cagney, James, 71, 292
Cahn, William, 219
Cain, James M., 254
Calhoun, Rory, 31, 39, 149
California Institute for the Arts, 239
Calvet, Corinne, 32, 41
Canby, Vincent, 336
Cannon, Jimmy, 40
Cantor, Eddie, 284
Capone, Al, 295
Capote, Truman, 220, 352
Capra, Frank, 76, 199
Carnelia, Craig, 242
Caron, Leslie, 163–65, *164*, 168, 172, 173, 174–75
Cassavetes, John, 109
Cassidy, Hopalong, 298
censorship, 103, 105, 252, 292
Chambrun, Jacques, 245–46
Chandler, Raymond, 183
Channing, Stockard, 274
Chaplin, Charlie:
  Bessie's script suggestion for, 68
  early career of, 278, 338, 341
  fatherhood of, 92, 97–98
  in Hollywood social circles, 50, 159
  marriages of, 92, 93, 98
  politics of, 290–91
  sons directed by, 93–95, 97

Swanson's imitation of, 338, 347
Tilden's friendship with, 47, 50, 53–54, 55, 56
Chaplin, Charlie, Jr., 83, 89, 91–92, 95, 96, 97–98, 157
Chaplin, Lolita McMurray (Lita Grey), 92
Chaplin, Oona O'Neill, 93, 98, 159
Chaplin, Saul, 92, 170, 171, 173
Chaplin, Sydney, 83, 91–95, 97, 98
Chateau Marmont, 102, 112–13
Chayefsky, Paddy, 225
Chicago Seven, 120–21
child actors, 110–11, 140, 268
Chrétien, Henri, 128
Christianity:
in film themes, 123–26, 128–33, 192–93
of Hollywood personalities, 125–27
Christopher Movement, 126
Cinemascope, 14–15, 118, 127–28, *128*, 129, 132, 323
Circle, 92–93, 94
Ciro's, 203–4, *203*, 204, 205
Citizen Kane, 279, 340
civil rights, 13, 17
Cleopatra, 135, 137
Clift, Montgomery, 133–34, 174
brooding film persona of, 144, 145, 181–82
film roles of, 156, 178–83, *179*, 304, 340
gossip columnists' criticism of, 283, 292
as Method actor, 177, 179, 181
Winters's performance critiqued by, 180–81, 188
Climax, 285
Clinton, Bill, 29, 33
Clurman, Harold, 77, 177, 230, 232, 241
Coates, Paul, 87
Cobb, Lee J., 68–69, 76–78, 79–80, 87, 178
Cocks, Jay, 121
Coe, Barry, 252
Coen brothers, 238
Coffey, Tom, 344
Cohen, Mickey, 259, 262
Cohn, Harry, 140, 141, 192–93
background of, 199
Davis-Novak involvement opposed by, 196, 209–10, 211–12, 213
death of, 197, 213–14, 279
dictatorial manner of, 196, 197, 199–200, 207, 251
killing of *Confidential* story on, 39
Novak's career controlled by, *198*, 199, 200–202, 206, 207, 214, 318
Cohn, Jack, 200, 209, 213
Cohn, Roy, 26, 29, 30, 31
Colbert, Claudette, 287
Cole, Lester, *70*
Cole, Nat King, 216
Collingwood, Charles, 333
Collins, Joan, 166, 167
Colman, Ronald, 133
Columbia Studios, 39, 140, 200, 209, 211, 251, 279
Come Back, Little Sheba (film), 313–16, 319, 321
Come Back, Little Sheba (Inge), 308–9, *312*, 313, 317
Committee for the First Amendment, 296
Communism, 296
Confidential Red-bashing and, 24, 26, 64–65
directory of film-industry connections to, 65, 72
Hollywood Ten prosecutions and, 65–71, *66*, *70*, 77, 80
Hopper's war against, 275, 289–90, 291, 342
HUAC and, 73–74, 76–77, 78, 80, 182, 222, 229, 342
Rushmore as turncoat against, 24, 25–30, 31, 33, 64–65
Confidential, 13, 17–46
advertisements in, 18–19
anti-Communist material in, 24, 26, 64–65
circulation levels of, *18*, 21, 23, 31, 34, 37
Hollywood scandals researched for, 37–39
homophobic articles in, 17–18, 47–49, 56, 57–62, 63, 103, 149–50
lawsuits against, 25, 40–42, 187, 332
pictorial style of, 21
publicity hoax of, 33–36
public-service exposés in, 19, 39
racial concerns in, 17, 22, 210–11
Rushmore as editor of, 12, 30–40, 57
on sons of film stars, 85–86, 88
Conger, Darva, *236*
Connery, Sean, 259
Connors, Chuck, 14
Conroy, Jack, 25–26

Conte, Ruth, 93, 94
Coogan, Jackie, 96–97
Cooper, Gary, 350–51
Cooper, Merian C., 14
Coppola, Francis Ford, 120
Corso, Gregory, 175
Cortez, Stanley, 184, 192
Costello, Lou, 184
Cotten, Joseph, 51, 57, 288
Coward, Noël, 62–63, 311
Crain, Jeanne, 298
Crane, Cheryl, 255, 257–59, 260, 261–63, 265–66, 268, *271*
Crane, Steve, 256, 257, 262
Crawford, Cheryl, 177
Crawford, Christina, 262
Crawford, Joan, 257, 283, 298
Crews, Laura Hope, 261
crime, organized, 21, 39, 353
Crosby, Bing, 126, 282–83, 351
Crosby, Kathryn Grant, 282–83
Crosland, Alan, 234
Crowther, Bosley, 194, 253, 314
Cukor, George, 287, 340, 343
Curtis, Tony, 144, 237
  background of, 225, 226
  film roles of, 112, 219, 225–26, *226*, 230–31, 238, 239, 299
  on Lehman, 227
  on Mackendrick as director, 234
  on Mae West, 335–36
  1960 Kennedy campaign and, 351, 353
  on Novak-Davis relationship, 207
  on Odets, 229, 230, 233

Dailey, Dan, 60
Dalton, Timothy, 336
Dandridge, Dorothy, 40, 187
Daniel and the Women of Babylon, 133
Dante, Michael, 257
Darin, Bobby, 273
Darin, Dodd, 273
Dark at the Top of the Stairs, The (Inge), 311–12, 324, 325, 326
David and Bathsheba, 14, 127, 132
Davies, Marion, 278, 280
Davis, Bette, 281, 299, 343
Davis, Sam, Sr., 202
Davis, Sammy, Jr., 137
  career of, 202–206, *203*, 215, 216
  death of, 216
  marriages of, 196, 212, 213, 215
  in romances with white actresses, 13, 17, 39, 196–97, *203*, 206–13, 215, 216
Day, Doris, 144, 154, 166, 265
Dean, James, *101*, 102, 118
  acting style of, 109, 112, 117, *118*, 177, 292
  early death of, 100–101, 116, 167, 292–93
  emotional persona of, 81, 103, 117, 144, 146
  family background of, 113
  N. Ray as director of, 99, *106*, 107–9, 114, 116, 120
  on Stevens as director, 181, 182, 292
  as teen idol, 166
Dee, Sandra, 266, 268–74, *271*
Defiant Ones, The, 13
de Havilland, Olivia, 50, 183, 256
Demetrius and the Gladiators, 130, 132
DeMille, Cecil B., 50, 75–76, 123, 129, 133, 290, 337, 341, 347
Demme, Jonathan, 155
Dempsey, Jack, 125
Derek, John, 102
De Scaffa, Francesca, 37, 224
Devil's Disciple, The, 228, 239
Diamond Lil (West), 327, 328–29
Dickinson, Angie, 352, 353, 354
Dietrich, Marlene, 62, 158, 352
DiMaggio, Joe, 166, 280
Dmytryk, Edward, *66*, *70*, 71
Donahue, Troy, 149, 272–73
Donen, Stanley, 163
Donovan, Robert J., 354
Douglas, Kirk, 155, 255, 259
Douglas, Lloyd C., 128, 130, 142
Dreiser, Theodore, 156, 178, 179, 182, 183
Dreyfuss, Richard, 138
DuBois, Richard, 330–31
Dufty, William, 347
Dufy, Raoul, 171
Duggan, Tom, 33, 34
Dunne, Philip, 130, 132
Durbin, Deanna, 288
Dyer, Richard, 267

Ealing Studios, 228, 239
East of Eden, 107, 109, 115, 167
eating disorders, 269–70, 273
Egan, Rex, 88

Egyptian, The, 14
Eisenstein, Sergei, 100
Ekberg, Anita, 18, 38
El Morocco, 206
Epstein, Jerry, 93
Epstein, Julius, 222
Equus, 138
Essanay Studios, 278, 341, 347
Evans, Colleen Townsend, 125, 126–27

Fairbanks, Douglas, 50
Fairey, Wendy, 298
Fassbinder, Rainer Werner, 155
Faulkner, William, 251–52
Federal Bureau of Investigation (FBI), 26–29, 31, 36, 67
Feeney, F. X., 234, 235, 236, 239
Feldman, Charles, 137
Ferrer, José, 289, 342
Figgis, Mike, 214
Fine, Benjamin, 81
Fisher, Eddie, 167, 281
Fisher, M. F. K., 161
Fitzgerald, F. Scott, 276, 295–96, 297, 300–301, *300*, 302–7
Fitzgerald, Zelda, 295
Flynn, Errol, 49, 50, 52, 66, 204
Foch, Nina, 169, 172
Fonda, Jane, 121, 237
Fontaine, Joan, 63
Ford, John, 126
Forman, Milos, 121
Forrestal, James, 33, 35, 36
Foster, Vincent, 33
Fox, Mardou, 174–75
Frances, Lee, 279
Francis, Kay, 296
Frank, Gerold, 301–2
Frankenheimer, John, 241
Freed, Arthur, 163, 165, 167, 168, 169–71, 173
French cinema, 158
French Line, The, 199
From Here to Eternity, 145, 200, 306
From Under My Hat (Hopper), 290

Gable, Clark, 41, 204, 280, 282, 292, 296, 354
Gabor, Eva, 300
Gabor, Zsa Zsa, 32, 63, 166, 299–300, 302
Galbraith, John Kenneth, 351
Garbo, Greta, 49, 50, 51, 62, 158, 181, 315, 354
Gardner, Ava, 17, 39, 160, 207, 260, 291
Garfield, John, 77, 178, 255
Garfield, Sidney, 221
Garland, Judy, 63, 291, 298, 353, 354
Garroway, Dave, 125
Garson, Greer, 125, 299
Garvin, Ruth, 32, 45–46
Gates, Phyllis, 149–50, 151, 152–54, 155
Gentlemen Prefer Blondes, 299
George V, King of Great Britain, 295
Gershwin, George, 163, 165, 169–70, 173, 267
Gershwin, Ira, 163, 169
Gershwin, Lee, 163
Giancana, Sam, 211, 353
Giant, 153, 166, 181, 292
Gibbs, Wolcott, 324, 329
Gidget, 272
Gielgud, John, 135
Giesler, Jerry, 40, 53, 88, 149
Gilbert, George, 205
Gingrich, Arnold, 302
Ginsberg, Henry, 166
Gish, Lillian, 191–92, 193, 195
Glass Menagerie, The (film), 251
Glass Menagerie, The (Williams), 311
Godard, Jean-Luc, 100, 158, 194–95
Golden Boy (Odets), 177
Goldwater, Barry, 289, 293
Goldwyn, Samuel, 277, 289
Gone With the Wind, 26, 261, 288
Goodman, Ezra, 30, 38, 39, 238
Goodness Had Nothing to Do with It (West), 332, 333
Gore, Altovise, 215
Gould, Jack, 285
Grable, Betty, 51, 306
Graham, Billy, 123–26, 127
Graham, Martha, 222
Graham, Sheilah, 294–307
  background of, 275–76, 294–95, 298, 303, 304–5
  candor of, 296
  celebrity friendships with, 277
  film based on love affair of, *300*, 301, 303–7
  Fitzgerald's relationship with, 276, 295, 297, 300–307, *300*
  gifts received by, 276–77

Graham, Sheilah *(continued)*
as Hollywood columnist, 126, 132, 295, 296–300, 306
marriages of, 295, 298–99
motherhood of, 298, 307
physical appearance of, 294, 297, 299
on religious figures, 126
on television vs. film industry, 306, 307
Grahame, Gloria, 100
Grand Illusion, 160
Granger, Farley, 49, 50, 102
Granger, Stewart, 298
Grant, Cary, 249, 270
Grant, Kathryn, 282–83
Grease, 273–74
Greatest Story Ever Told, The, 133
Green, Johnny, 170, 173
Green, Lila, 325
Gregory, Paul, 185, 187, 188, 189, 192–93
Grey, Lita (Lolita McMurray Chaplin), 92
Griffith, D. W., 100, 159, 191
Group Theatre, 76–77, 176, 177, 230, 232
Grubb, Davis, 184–85, *186*, 189–91
Guare, John, 242
Guétary, Georges, 169
Guinness, Alec, 228, 239
Guthrie, A. B., 229

Hamlisch, Marvin, 242
Hargitay, Mickey, 331, 332
Harlot's Ghost (Mailer), 350
Harlow, Jean, 296
Harriman, Averell, 354
Harrison, Robert, 19–24, 31, 56, 86, 206
background of, 20, 21, 30
Confidential dissolved by, 332
Confidential started by, 21–23, 30
Hollywood scandals researched for, 37–38
homophobic articles published by, 56, 57, 58, 59, 60
libel suit against, 40–42
personal style of, 23–24, 30
on public-service journalism, 19–20, 39
Rushmore's death and, 45, 46
Rushmore's disappearance and, 33–35
Harrison, Stephen, 33, 35
Harrison, Susan, 218, 235–37, *236*, 240
Hayden, Tom, 121
Hayes, Helen, 111, 300
Hayes, John Michael, 250, 252
Haymes, Dick, 199, 282
Hays Office, 103, 252, 295
Hayward, Susan, 291
Hayworth, Rita, *198*, 199, 200, 201, 223, 260, 282
Head, Edith, 337
Hearst, William Randolph, 278, 279, 280
Hearst newspapers, 26, 278, 302
Hecht, Ben, 342
Hecht, Harold, 222, 223–27, 229, 234, 236, 238, 239, 240, 242
Hecht-Hill-Lancaster, 222–25, 228, 229, 230, 235, 238, 240, 242
Heiress, The, 183
Hellman, Lillian, 52
Hemingway, Ernest, 39, 295
Henie, Sonja, 125
Hepburn, Katharine, 51, 281
Heston, Charlton, 290, 351
Heydrich, Reinhard, 140
High School Confidential!, 82, 96–97, 98
Hill, James, 222–23, 225, 227, 232, 233, 235, 238, 242
Hilton, Nicky, 277, 281
Hitchcock, Alfred, 34, 186, 197, 241, 250
Hitler, Adolf, 139, 140, 339
Hitler's Madman, 140–41
Hockney, David, 162
Hoffman, Abbie, 120–21
Hoffman, Irving, 220–21, 237–38
Hogan's Heroes, 158
Holden, William, 16, 116–17, *198*, *291*, 319, 340, 341, 342
Holliday, Judy, 289, 339, 342, 343
Hollywood:
aging studio heads in, 15–16, 279
British actors in, 133–36, 137–38
censorship concerns in, 103, 105, 252, 292
children of movie stars in, 82–98, 257–59, 260, 261–63
European directors in, 140–42, 158–63
gossip-columnists' power in, 13, 276–77
location shooting vs., 307, 354
older actresses of, 327–47
political activities linked with, 349–54
public-relations control in, 38, 39
religious subjects in, 125–33, *128*, 193
studio system eroded in, 13, 213, 276, 279, 306, 350, 354

Sunset Boulevard as indictment of, 11–12, 15–16, 336–37
television industry centered in, 307
Hollywood Research, Inc., 37–38, 42
Hollywood (Unfriendly) Ten, 67, 69–71, *70*, 77, 80
Holm, Celeste, 342
Holman, Libby, 340
homosexuality, 47–63
film portrayals of, 102–3
of Hollywood stars, 57–63, 144, 145, 148–49
of Hollywood tennis pro, 47, 48–57
tabloid press on, 17–18, 47–49, 56, 57–62, 63, 103, 149–50
Hoover, J. Edgar, 24, 27, 28, 31, 36, 43, 213, 220
Hope, Bob, 126, 276
Hopper, Dennis, 111, 113–14, 121
Hopper, DeWolf, 286–87
Hopper, Hedda, 13, 252–53, 286–94, 343
abusive style of, 286, 288–89, 305
anti-Communism of, 275, 289–90, 291, 342
background of, 286
best-selling books written by, 290, 294
failed film career of, 275, 286, 287
gossip column written by, 213, 287–89, *291*, 292–93
lawsuit against, 294
marriage of, 275, 286–87
motherhood of, 114, 287, 288
Parson's rivalry with, 277, 284, 285, 287, 289, 293
power wielded by, 277, 293
sexual candor in films criticized by, 292, 293–94
Hopper, William, 114, 288
Hour of Decision, 125
Houseman, John, 100, 101, 117, 227
House Un-American Activities Committee (HUAC), 182, 289, 342
actors appearing before, 73–74, 76–77, 342
film as veiled defense of, 78
friendly witnesses of, 76–77, 78, 80, 222, 229
screenwriters summoned before, 66–67, 69
Howard, Jean, 137, 157
Howard, John, 47–48
Howe, James Wong, 217, 231–32, 315, 319
Hudson, Rock, 39, 139, 259–60, 269, 298, 326
birth name of, 144
celebrity of, 148, 153
death of, 144, 154–55
first starring role of, 144, *145*, 146–47, *146*, 148, 265
homosexuality of, 144, 145, 148–49, 153, 154
marriage of, 149–51, 152–54
wholesome film image of, 144–47, 151, 152
Hughes, Dickson, 346
Hughes, Howard, 354
Humphrey, Hubert, 352
Hunter, Ross:
acting background of, 139, 264
Dee discovered by, 268, 269, 270, 272, 273
glamour stressed by, 264–65
Sirk's collaborations with, 141–42, *143*, 148, 151, 154, 266, 267
Hunter, Tab, 60–62, 149
Hurst, Fannie, 265
Huston, John, 107, 153, 289
Hutton, Betty, 283
Huxley, Aldous, 159, 166
Hyams, Joe, 113, 166
Hytner, Nicholas, 242

I Love Lucy, 290
Imitation of Life, 13, 142, 264–68, *271*, 273
Inge, William:
alcoholism of, 308, 310–11, 313, 316, 326
childhood of, 309–10, 319
films based on plays of, 12, 89, *198*, 309, *312*, 313–16, 318–24, *321*, 326, 354
homosexuality of, 310, 311, 316
screenplays written by, 326
Isherwood, Christopher, 156, 157, 159, 166
Ives, Burl, 29

Jackson, Mahalia, 266
Jaffe, Sam, 77
Jarmusch, Jim, 100
Jary, Hilde, 140
Jessel, George, 173, 174
Johnson, Erskine, 345
Johnson, Lyndon, 351, 352

Johnson, Van, 62, 306
Jolson, Al, 173–74
Jones, Jennifer, 284
Joseph and His Brethren, 132–33
juvenile delinquency, 81–82, 96–97, 99, 104, 105, 106, 109, 111

Kael, Pauline, 191
Kaper, Bronislau, 158
Kaye, Danny, 214
Kazan, Elia:
 on Dean, 107, 108, 115
 with Group Theatre, 77, 177
 as HUAC witness, 78, 80
 Inge's dramas directed by, 324, 325, 326
 on N. Ray's films, 115, 116, 122
 on Odets, 241
 on parental figures in film, 115
Keaton, Buster, 51, 337
Kefauver, Estes, 21, 30, 81
Kellaway, Cecil, 255
Kelly, Gene, 163–65, *164,* 168, 170, *171,* 172, 173
Kelly, Grace, 15
Kempton, Murray, 40
Kende, Geza, 337
Kennedy, Arthur, 254
Kennedy, Jacqueline Bouvier, 350
Kennedy, John F., 215, 349–50, 351–54
Kennedy, Joseph P., 126, 337, 341, 351
Kenny, Nick, 219
Kentuckian, The, 227
Kerouac, Jack, 174–75
Kerr, Deborah, *300,* 303, 304, 305, 306
Kerr, Walter, 320, 324
Kibbee, Roland, 222
Kilgallen, Dorothy, 125, 210, 211, 219
King Kong, 14
Kinsella, James, 154
Kinsey Report, 292
Klee, Paul, 161
Klemperer, Otto, 158
Klemperer, Werner, 158
Klinger, Barbara, 144
Kohner, Paul, 266
Kohner, Susan, 266–67
Korda, Alexander, 186
Krauser, Chuck (Chester Ribonsky; Paul Novak), 331, 332
Krim, Arthur, 353
Kupcinet, Irv, 210

Ladd, Alan, 102
Lamas, Fernando, 256
Lambert, Gavin, 101
Lamour, Dorothy, 280
Lancaster, Burt:
 at Academy Awards, 259
 death of, 242
 film roles of, 218, 313–14
 gossip columnist portrayed by, 218, 219, 220, 221, 226, *226,* 231, 238
 production company of, 222–25, 226–27, 228, 233–35, 238, 239, 240
 as womanizer, 224
Lanchester, Elsa, 187
Land of the Pharaohs, 14
Landon, Michael, 96
Lane, Anthony, 239
Lang, Fritz, 95, 158
Lange, Hope, 252, 254, 322
Langner, Lawrence, 317
Lardner, Ring, Jr., 66, *70*
Larson, Jack, 174
Last Tycoon, The (Fitzgerald), 300
Laughton, Charles, 183–86, *186,* 187–92, *194,* 195
Lawford, Pat Kennedy, 349, 353
Lawford, Peter, 296, 349, 352, 353
Lawrence, D. H., 251
Lawrence, Gertrude, 251
Lawson, John Howard, 69, 70, *70,* 71, 77
Lazarovich, William (Bill Lawrence), 33, 35
Lee, Gypsy Rose, 289–90
Lehman, Ernest:
 background of, 219
 on Curtis, 231
 on Hecht-Lancaster production company, 223–25, 238–39
 on Hoffman, 220, 221
 later years of, 241, 242–43
 press-agent experience of, 219–20, 221–22, 227
 screenplays written by, 217–18, 226–27, 228–29, 230, 231, 235, 238–39, 241, 243
 on Winchell, 218, 219, 220, 240
Leigh, Janet, 207, 284, 351, 353
Leigh, Vivien, 288, 292
Lemmon, Jack, 197

Lerner, Alan Jay, 167, 169, 173
Levant, Oscar, 137, 163, 165–72, *171*, 173–74, 241, 354
Levinson, Barry, 238
Lewin, Albert, 159–61
Lewis, Jerry, 204, 282
Lewis, Robert, 177
Liberace, 14, 42, 63, 187, *282*, 283–84
Life of Emile Zola, The, 71
Lightning Over Water, 122
Lindner, Robert M., 103, 104
Linn, Clarence A., 42
Little Caesar, 86
Livingston, Mary, 288
Loeb, Phil, 77
Loew, Arthur, Jr., 166
Logan, Joshua, 89, *198*, 201, 317, 318, 319–20, 322, 323
Lollobrigida, Gina, 225
Lomax, Alan, 100
Lombard, Carole, 51
Loren, Sophia, 260, 270
Los Angeles County Museum, 73
Loss of Roses, A (Inge), 325
Louis, Jean, 201, 265, 268, 273
Lubitsch, Ernst, 159
Luddy, Tom, 120
Lytess, Natasha, 94

Macao, 158–59
MacArthur, Charles, 342
McCarten, John, 132
McCarthy, Joseph, 12, 24, 26, 27, 28–29, 31, 229, 289
MacDonald, Jeanette, 149
McDowall, Roddy, 175
McHugh, Jimmy, 285, 286
Mackendrick, Alexander "Sandy," 218, 227–28, 229, 231, 232–35, 236, 239–40, 242
Mackendrick, Hilary, 228, 239–40, 242
MacLaine, Shirley, 354
MacMurray, Fred, 201
McMurray, Lolita (Lita Grey Chaplin), 92
McQueen, Steve, 293
McWhorter, Richard, 233
Madonna, 154
Magnificent Obsession, 142–44, *143*, *145*, 146–47, 148, 151, 265
Magritte, René, 165
Mailer, Norman, 349, 350
Maltz, Albert, *70*
Mangold, James, 234
Mankiewicz, Joseph, 75
Mann, Daniel, 313, 314
Mann, Thomas, 159
Manners, Dorothy, 286
Mansfield, Jayne, 18, 110, 249, 331
March, Fredric, 289
Marsh, Sy, 216
Martin, Dean, 282, 285, 298
Martin, Harry Watson "Docky," 275, 278–79, 280, 285
Martin, Mary, 283
Marty, 225
Marx, Groucho, 121
masculinity, Hollywood portrayals of, 103, 144–46
Mason, James, 119, 133, 289
Massey, Raymond, 115
Mastin, Will, 202, 205
Mature, Victor, 129–30, 132, 291
Matusow, Harvey, 29
Maugham, W. Somerset, 246
Maupin, Armistead, 150
Maxwell, Elsa, 62
Mayer, Louis B., 213, 256, 279, 287, 296, 342
  Hollywood home of, 350, 352
  Sunset Boulevard resented by, 15–16
Mayer, Peter, 242
Mayes, Herbert, 220
Mazzola, Frank, 111
MCA, 227
Messner, Kitty, 246–47
Metalious, Grace, 244–51
  best-selling novel written by, 244–49, *246*, 250, 252
  death of, 254
  family life of, 245, 247, 248, 249
  Peyton Place film and, 12–13, 249, 250–51, 253, 305
Method acting, 88, 109, 176–77, 179, 180, 181–82, 183, 292, 320
Meyer, Emile, 235
MGM Studios, 140, 168, 175, 279, 280, 289, 350
Miglietta, Ethel, 95
Mildred Pierce, 257
Milland, Ray, 133
Miller, Arthur, 77, 87, 229–30, 289
Milner, Martin, 218, 234

Mineo, Sal, *101*, 122, 272
background of, 112
death of, 101, 119–20
film acting of, 102, 112, 116–17, 119, 267
N. Ray's relationship with, 100, 102, 114
Minnelli, Liza, 298
Minnelli, Vincente, 163, *164*, 165, 167–71, 172, 173, 255
Mitchum, Robert, 159, 185–89, 193–94, 291
background of, 186, 187
gossip magazine sued by, 40, 41, 187
Laughton as director of, 185–86, *186*, 187–89, 191, 195
Moffat, Ivan, 156, 157, 159, 182
Monroe, Marilyn, 80, 155, 197, 200
acting ability of, 320–22, 323
acting studied by, 94, 176, 183, 184, 320
femme-fatale persona of, 18, 256
film career of, 250, 303, 320, *321*
gossip columnists and, 280, 298, 299
husbands of, 166, 230, 280
Inge's friendship with, *321*, 324
self-destructiveness of, 230
Moore, Juanita, 266, 267
Moore, Terry, 252, 299
Moorehead, Agnes, *146*
Mr. Texas, 123–24, 125
Mr. Wonderful (Styne and Gilbert), 205–6
Murnau, F. W., 100
Murphy, Audie, 267, 289
Murray, Don, 320, 322
Murrow, Edward R., 60
Mussolini, Benito, 200
My Son Is a Splendid Driver (Inge), 309–10, 326
My Son Nero (*Nero's Mistress*; *Nero's Big Weekend*), 345–46
My Story (Tilden), 54–55

Nader, George, 148, 149
Nathan, George Jean, 329
Natural Affection (Inge), 326
Navaar, Jack, 148–49, 153–54
Navasky, Victor, 222
Nazism, 139–40
Negri, Pola, 340
Nero's Mistress (*Nero's Big Weekend*; *My Son Nero*), 345–46
Newlin, Dika, 157
Newman, Paul, 109, 269, 304
New York Daily Graphic, 20–21
Niarchos, Stavros, 73, 74–75
Night of the Hunter, The, 184–95, *186*
casting of, 185–89, 191–92
censorship concerns on, 192–93
critical responses to, 191, 193–95, *194*
story of, 184–85, 189–91, 192–93
Nilsson, Anna Q., 337
Nina (Taylor), 343
Niven, David, 63, 133, 343
Nixon, Pat, 215
Nixon, Richard, 215, 293, 351, 353
Nolan, Jack Edmund, 253
nouvelle vague, 100, 120, 158, 194–95
Novak, Kim, 270
background of, 197–99, 200, 202, 208
career of, 196, 197–202, *198*, 209, 214, 215, 260, 318–19
physical appearance of, 197, 198, 201
Sammy Davis Jr.'s relationship with, 13, 196–97, *203*, 206–13, 214, 216
in tabloid press, 39
Novak, Paul (Chester Ribonsky; Chuck Krauser), 331, 332

Oberon, Merle, 286
O'Brien, Margaret, 110
O'Brien, Pat, 353
obscenity laws, 292
Ocean's 11, 206
O'Curran, Charles, 330
Odets, Clifford, 68, 161, 289
as consultant on *Rebel Without a Cause*, 105
death of, 241
HUAC and, 229–30
physical appearance of, 229, 230
screenplays written by, 218, 229–30, 232–33, 234, 239, 240–41
theater background of, 76, 177, 229, 230, 232
O'Hara, Frank, 15
O'Hara, John, 300
O'Hara, Maureen, 41, 187
Oiltown U.S.A., 124–25, 127
Oliver, Edith, 326
Olivier, Laurence, 129, 135, 239
Onassis, Aristotle, 73
On the Waterfront, 78, 79, 145, 249
Oppenheimer, J. Robert, 64–65

Ornitz, Samuel, *70*
Orr, William, 103
Otash, Fred, 154, 353

Page, Norman, 254
Paige, Janis, 204
Palimpsest (Vidal), 102
Pal Joey, 201, 330
Pandora and the Flying Dutchman, 160, 161
Paramount Studios, 338, 346
Parker, Eleanor, 343
Parks, Larry, 76
Parsons, Louella, 278–86
  awards received by, 284
  background of, 278
  celebrity journalism developed by, 278, 282
  gossip column of, 126, 269, 279–84, 285, 305
  Graham's scoop of, 298
  H. Hopper's rivalry with, 277, 284, 285, 287, 289, 293
  power wielded by, 276, 277, 280
  radio show of, 282
  retirement of, 285–86, 293
  romantic involvements of, 275, 278–80, 285
Pasadena Playhouse, 304
Pearlman, Edward, 43, 45
Peck, Gregory, 281, *300*, 303–4, 305, 306
Peppard, George, 174, 175
Perkins, Tony, 39
Perona, John, 206
Petit, Roland, 163
Peyton Place (film), 249–60
  mother-daughter relationship in, 257, 258, 260
  novel's characters changed in, 252, 253, 305
  performers in, 244, 251, 252–53, 254, 255, 256–57, 262
  producer of, *246*, 249, 250, 251–52
  screenplay of, 200, 250, 252
  success of, 254, 259, 260
Peyton Place (Metalious), 12–13, 244–49, *246*, 250
Philips, Lee, 253
Pickford, Mary, 50, 340
Picnic (film), *198*, 201, 318–20, 323, 324, 354
Picnic (Inge), 309, 310, 312, *312*, 316–17
Pillow Talk, 265
Pine, David A., 70–71
Place in the Sun, A (*An American Tragedy*), 109, 156, 165, 178–83, *179*, 182, 188
Platt, Ed, *118*
Porter, Cole, 62
Portrait in Black, 273
Postman Always Rings Twice, The, 254–55
Powell, Dick, 41, 281
Power, Tyrone, 41, 129, 256, 280
Presley, Elvis, 59, 240, 250
Price, Vincent, 15, 291
Princeton University, 306–7
Production Code, 103, 105, 192, 252
Protestant Film Commission, 127
Protestant Motion Picture Council, 193
Proust, Marcel, 189
Prowse, Juliet, 353
PT 109, 354
Pulp Fiction, 155

Queen Kelly, 337, 338
Quigley, Martin, 21

racial issues, 13
  of biracial offspring, 266
  film boycott and, 26
  in hotels and nightclubs, 204, 205–6
  of interracial romance, 197–98, 206–13, 215
  in military, 202–3
  in tabloid press, 17, 22
Raft, George, 51, 75
Rainer, Louise, 229
Rank, J. Arthur, 124
Rathbone, Basil, 133
Rat Pack, 202, 293
Ray, Man, 159–63, 165
Ray, Nicholas, 99–122, 159, 167
  actors' relationships with, 100–102, *106*, 107–9, 112, 113–14, 116, 120
  background of, 99–100, 104
  casting decisions of, *101*, 107–9, 110
  later career of, 119, 120–21, 122
  male sensitivity portrayed by, 103
  in scriptwriting process, 104–7, 109, 119
  Sunset Boulevard mansion used by, 102, *106*, 116–17, 339
  visual style of, 117–19
Ray, Susan Schwartz, 108, 121–22

Reagan, Ronald, 13, 154
Rear Window, 250
Rebel Without a Cause, 100–20, *118*, 121, 292
actors' freedom in, 99
casting of, *101*, 103, 107, 109, 110–12
cinematography of, 117–19
director-actor relationships in, 100–101, *106*, 107–9, 112, 113–14, 116
homoerotic relationship in, 102–3
N. Ray's cameo appearance in, 122
parental authority portrayed in, 81, 114–15, 116
script written for, 102, 103, 104–7, 109–10, 119
Sunset Boulevard location used in, 102, *106*, 116–17, 339
teenage rebelliousness in, 81, 82, 99, 104
Red Channels, 65, 72
Reed, Rex, 336
Reeves, George, 14
Reinhardt, Max, 158
religious belief:
censorship and, 193
epic films with themes of, 127–33, *128*
of Hollywood personalities, 125–27
Reluctant Debutante, The, 272
Remick, Lee, 109
Renoir, Jean, 100, 158, 159, 160, 161
Restless Years, The, 270
Revere, Anne, 182, 183
Reynolds, Debbie, 62, 110, 281
Rhapsody in Blue, 169, 267
Ribonsky, Chester (Chuck Krauser; Paul Novak), 331, 332
Richardson, Ralph, 183
Richmond, Martin, 42, 43
RKO, 129, 354
Robe, The, 14, 128–32, *128*, 133, *134*, 135, 137
Robertson, Cliff, 354
Robinson, Edward G., 72–76, 125
anti-Communist investigations and, 72–74, 76, 89
art collection of, 72–73, 74–75, 89, 91,
fatherhood of, *83*, 84, 85–86, 87–88, 89, 90–91, 322
marriage of, 72–73, 89, 91
Robinson, Edward G., Jr. "Manny," 72, 74, 83–91, *83*, *89*, 95, 322–23, 347
Robinson, Gladys Lloyd, 72–73, 74, 75, 88, 91
Robinson, Jay, 130
Robson, Mark, 257
Rockwell, Rick, 236
Rogers, Roy, 249
Romanoff, Mike, 289, 350
Romeo and Juliet (Shakespeare), 105, 210
Rooney, Mickey, 256
Roosevelt, Eleanor, 26
Roosevelt, Franklin D., 26
Rosenbaum, Jonathan, 120, 121
Rosenman, Leonard, 107, 108, 109, 113
Rosenstein, Jaik, 289
Ross, Dick, 123
Ross, Frank, 129
Ross, George, 219
Ross, Lillian, 93
Rossellini, Roberto, 100, 158, 298
Rostova, Mira, 177, 181
Roth, Lillian, 301
Rubin, Jerry, 120
Rushmore, Frances McCoy, 32–33, 36–37, 42–45, *44*
Rushmore, Howard, 24–46, *25*, *44*
as anti-Communist, 24, 26–30, 31, 39–40, 64–65, 66
background of, 24–27, 30
as *Confidential* editor, 30–40, 57
death of, 43–45, *44*
marriages of, 32–33, 36–37, 42–43, *44*, 45–46
pseudonyms used by, 32, 35, 58
publicity-hoax disappearance of, 33–36
as witness in libel trials, 25, 40, 41, 42
Russell, Jane, 159, 299
Russell, Rosalind, 319
Ryan, Robert, 184

"Samson" ads, 18–19
Sanders, George, 291
Sands, Tommy, 285
Sands Hotel, 207, 209, 211, 212
Sarris, Andrew, 163, 168, 172
Saxon, John, 82, 272
Schary, Dore, 279
Schenck, Nicholas, 279
Scheur, Philip K., 284
Scheyer, Galka, 161
Schildkraut, Joseph, 71
Schine, G. David, 26, 29

Schlesinger, Arthur, Jr., 351
Schoenberg, Arnold, 157, 158, 162, 166, 167
Schulberg, Budd, 78, 251
Scofield, Paul, 135
Scorsese, Martin, 189, 238
Scott, Adrian, 69
Scott, Lizabeth, 58–60
Scott, Robert, *70*
Screen Directors Guild, 284
screenwriters, blacklisting of, 67–68, 80
Sellers, Peter, 239, 276
Selznick, David O., 51, 149, 228, 288
Sennett, Mack, 338
Sex (West), 331
Sextette, 335–36
Shakespeare, William, 105, 184, 299
Shaw, Artie, 221, 256, 257
Shaw, George Bernard, 139, 228
Shear, Claudia, 336
Sheridan, Ann, 142
Sherry, William Grant, 281
Shulman, Irving, 106–7
Shurlock, Geoffrey, 103
Sidney, George, 200, 201, 202
Sidney, Steffi, 113
Silber, Arthur, Jr., 204, 207, 208, 212, 215–16
Simmons, Jean, 129, *134*, 269, 303
Sinatra, Frank, 63, 85, 135, 204, 206, 208, 249, 285
  film career of, 76, 78–79, 201
  generosity of, 79
  in Kennedy political milieu, 215, 351, 352–53, 354
  on Novak-Davis liaison, 211
  Rat Pack entourage of, 293
Sinatra, Nancy, 285
Sirk, Douglas, 97, 139–44, 266, 273
  blindness in films of, 142, *146*, 147, 155
  film-directing career of, 140, 141, 155
  German background of, 139–40, 141
  on Hudson, 145, 148
  Hunter's collaborations with, 141–42, *143*, 151, 154, 265, 267
  ironic symbolism used by, 147, 151–52
  later years of, 155
  on trash vs. high art, 142, 144
Skelton, Red, 214
Skolsky, Sidney, 176, 219
Smell-O-Vision, 15
Smith, Liz, 175
Sobol, Louis, 219, 221, 238
Sokolsky, George, 26, 289
Sons and Lovers, 251
Sothern, Ann, 149
Sound and the Fury, The, 251–52
Spiegel, Sam, 78
Splendor in the Grass, 309, 325, 326
Stack, Robert, 147, 152, 256
Stalag 17, 158, 340
Stalin, Joseph, 288
Stanislavski, Konstantin, 77, 88, 177, 179, 329
Stanwyck, Barbara, 142, 299, 342
Stapley, Richard, 346
Starr, Kenneth, 29
Steinbeck, John, 295
Stern, Stewart, 102, 109
Sterner, James, 24–25, 26
Stevens, George, 107, 156, 178–80, 181, 182, 183, 292
Stewart, Anita, 287
Stewart, James, 197, 212
Stompanato, Johnny, 12, 259–63, 264, 265, 266, *271*
Strasberg, Lee, 77, 109, 177, 241, 319
Strasberg, Paula, 177, 319
Strasberg, Susan, 319
Stravinsky, Igor, 161
Streetcar Named Desire, A, 78, 166, 292
Strindberg, August, 139
Styne, Jule, 205
Subterraneans, The, 174–75
Suddenly Last Summer, 292
Sullavan, Margaret, 296
Sullivan, Ed, 125, 219, 221, 290
Summer Place, A, 13, 272–73
Sundowners, The, 95
Sunset Boulevard, 126, 336–44, 347
  Academy Award nominations for, 342, 343
  casting of, 336, 340, 342
  celebrity cameos in, 284, 337–38
  corpses in original opening of, 11–12
  critical success of, 15, 342
  as cultural commentary, 11–12, 13, 15–16, 336–37
  mansion set of, 102, *106*, 116–17, 338–39
  Mayer's loathing of, 15–16
  as stage musical, 346

Sunset Boulevard (continued)
Swanson typecast in, 337, 338, 339–40, 344, 345, *345*, 347
von Stroheim's appearance in, 158, 160, *291*, 338
wax figures of performers in, *291*
Sunset Towers, 133–34
Supreme Court, U.S., 292
Suzy, 296
Swanson, Gloria:
age discrimination and, 327, 343–44, 346–47
career renewal sought by, 339–40, 343–47, *345*
physical appearance of, 273, 283, 343
romantic involvements of, 125–26, 338, 341, 347, 351
in silent films, 126, 278, 337, 338, 341
in *Sunset Boulevard*, 16, 126, 160, 273, *291*, 337, 338, 339–40, 341, 342, 344, 347, 354
television appearances of, 342, 345, 346, 347
Sweet Smell of Success, 13, 217–43
as Broadway musical, 242–43
casting of, 218, 219, 225–26, 230–31, 235, *236*
cinematography of, 217, 231–32
critical reactions to, 237, 238, 239–40
director of, 218, 227–28, 233–35
production company of, 222–25
script of, 217–18, 228–30, 232–33
story of, 217, 218–19, 234–35
Winchell as basis for character in, 218, 219, *226*, 237–38, 240

tabloid culture, 13
see also Confidential
Take Me to Town, 142
Tamblyn, Russ, 96, 97, 254
Tarantino, Quentin, 155
Tarkington, Booth, 52
Tate, Sharon, 239
Tati, Jacques, 108
Tatlock, Jean, 65
Taylor, Elizabeth:
beauty of, 137, 167, 182
on Burton's acting, 135
in films, 179, *179*, 180, 182, 183
gossip columnists and, 276, 277, 281, 296
husbands of, 137, 138, 166, 167, 277, 281, 294
Taylor, Samuel, 343
television, 21, 152, 157
development of, 13–14, 127
film actor separation from, 14
film studio decline linked to, 279, 306
gossip columnist programs on, 290, 297
Hollywood cinema rivalry with, 14, 15, 127, 279, 354
Temple, Shirley, 269, 281
Ten Commandments, The, 14, 75–76, 133
tennis celebrities, sex scandals on, 47–57, *49*
Theatre Guild, 308, 317
This Is Cinerama, 14
Thomas, Danny, 126, 276
Thomas, Dylan, 137, 156–57
Thomas, Lowell, 14
Thomson, David, 100, 241
Thoreau, Henry David, 151
Three Comrades, 296
3-D movies, 15
Three Faces of Eve, The, 260
Three for Bedroom C, 344–45, *345*
Tierney, Gene, 125, 352
Tilden, "Big Bill," 47, 48–57, *49*, *53*
Tiomkin, Dimitri, 158
Todd, Michael, 39, 167
Topping, Bob, 256, 297
Torn, Rip, 149
"To the Film Industry" (O'Hara), 15
Touch of Evil, 97
Tovar, Lupita, 266
Townsend, Colleen, 125, 126–27
Trapeze, 225, 238
Travolta, John, 155
Tree, Iris, 159
Trocadero, 296
Truffaut, François, 158, 194–95
Trumbo, Dalton, 69, 70, *70*, 71, 72, 74
Tuck, Jay Nelson, 285
Turner, Lana, 62
film career of, 13, 254–55, 256, 260, 262, 264, 267, 273
marriages of, 255, 256, 257, 263, 297
as mother, 257–59, 260, 261, 262, 264, 265–66, 268
in *Peyton Place*, 13, 244, 253, 254, 255–58, 260
on power of gossip columnists, 276

Stompanato death and, 12, 259–63, 264, *271*
Twelve Angry Men, 69
Twentieth Century Fox, 279

Unfriendly (Hollywood) Ten, 67, 69–71, *70*, 77, 80
United Artists, 227
Universal Studios, 39, 139, 144, 225–26, 267, 270
Until They Sail, 269, 270
Uris, Leon, 61, 105–6

Valentino, Rudolph, 338
Van Doren, Mamie, 96, 97
Varsi, Diane, 252–53, 254
Vertigo, 197, 208, 214
Vidal, Gore, 102, 335, 350–51, 354
Vidor, King, 141
Viertel, Berthold, 158
Viertel, Salka, 158, 159
Virtuous Wives, 287
von Sternberg, Josef, 158–59
von Stroheim, Erich, 158, 160, *291*, 338

Wagner, Robert, 299
Wald, Jerry, 173
Academy Awards show produced by, 259
background of, 251
casting decisions of, 250, 251–52, 255, 256–57, 303–4
film rights acquired by, 103, *246*, 249, 251, 300–301, 303
on Novak's career potential, 200
script development and, 250, 251, 303, 305
Walden (Thoreau), 151
Walker, Herbert V., 41
Walker, Robert, 60
Waller, Fred, 14
Wallis, Hal, 314
Walsh, Raoul, 61
Wanger, Walter, 123
Warner, Harry, 83–84, 279
Warner, H. B., 337
Warner, Jack L., 103, 105, 117–18
Warren, James, 344, *345*
Washington, Fredi, 266
Wasserman, Lew, 227
Waters, John, 15
Wayne, John, 103, 125
Webb, Clifton, 51
Webb, Jack, 249
Weisbart, David, 110
Weld, Tuesday, 237
Welles, Orson, 97, 226, 227, 231, 279, 290, 340
Wenders, Wim, 121, 122
West, Mae, 41, 259–60, 327–36
in Broadway revival, 327, 328–29
egocentricity of, 239, 332–33, 336
Las Vegas nightclub act of, *328*, 329–31
love affairs of, 331, 332
physical appearance of, 284, 333, 335–36
television appearances of, 333–34, 335
What Makes Sammy Run? (Schulberg), 251
While the City Sleeps, 95
White, Loray, 212, 213
Whole Truth and Nothing But, The (Hopper), 294
wide-screen technology, 14–15, 118, 127–28, *128*, 323
Wiegand, William, 185
Wilde, Cornel, 165
Wilde, Oscar, 139
Wilder, Billy, *106*, 158, 227, 241, 284
background of, 11, 339
casting choices of, 336, 337–38, 340, 342
directorial style of, 340–41
Hollywood critique in work of, 11–12, 16, 336–37
Mayer's attack on, 15–16
Wilder, John, 269, 272
Wilding, Michael, 166, 167, 294
Wild in the Country, 240–41
Wild One, The, 82, 104, 121
Wilhelm II, Emperor of Germany, 182
Wilkerson, Billy, 256, 296
Williams, Esther, 82
Williams, Tennessee, 241, 254
film versions of plays of, 78, 251, 292
Inge's literary career and, 311, 312, 313, 324, 326
Williams, William Carlos, 16
Will Mastin Trio, 202, 203–4, 205
Willner, George, 221
Willson, Henry, 61, 146, 149–50, 153, 154
Wilson, Earl, 21, 221
Wilson, Edmund, 302

Winchell, Walter, 13, 21, 125, 296
decline of, 240
as model for *Sweet Smell of Success* character, 218, 219, 220, 221, 226, 237–38, 240
in mutual admiration with *Confidential,* 20, 22, 30, 31
Winters, Shelley, 49, 50, 92–93, 94, 109, 156–57, 289, 354
acting career of, 176, 178–79, 183, 193
on Chaplin as director, 94
film performances of, 178–81, *179,* 182, 188
Method acting studied by, 176–77, 178, 179, 180
in Shakespeare class, 183–84
Wolfe, Ian, 109
Wolfe, Tom, 17, 20, 24, 43
Women, The, 287, 295–96
women's pictures, 251, 267
Wood, Audrey, 312, 313, 324, 325, 326
Wood, Grant, 72
Wood, Michael, 14
Wood, Natalie, 237
career of, 110–11, 120, 149
death of, 100–101, 120
family background of, 111, 113
film roles of, *101,* 102, 111, 117, 122, 326
romantic affairs of, *106,* 113–14, 121
Woodward, Joanne, 260
Woollcott, Alexander, 63
Wright, Albert "Chalky," 332
Wright, Frank Lloyd, 99–100, 101
Wright, Teresa, 285
Written on the Wind, 97, 147, 152, 154
Wyler, William, 107
Wylie, Philip, 115
Wyman, Jane, 142, 144, *145, 146,* 147, 148, 151, 152, 154, 257

Yes I Can (Davis), 204
Young, Robert, 14, 296
youth culture, 82, 120

Zanuck, Darryl, 127, 129, 135–36, 159, 279, 280, 353
Zinnemann, Fred, 109
Zoetrope Studios, 120
Zugsmith, Albert, 97, 147